Iraq in the Twenty-First Century

Much has been written about the events surrounding the 2003 Anglo-American invasion of Iraq and its aftermath, especially about the intentions, principles, plans and course of action of US policy, but much less attention has been given to the consequences of US policy on Iraqi political and social development. This book provides an in-depth analysis of the impact of US policy on the social and political development of Iraq in the twenty-first century. It shows how not just the institutions of the state were destroyed in 2003, leaving the way open for sectarianism, but also the country's cultural integrity, political coherence and national-oriented economy. It outlines how Iraq has been economically impoverished, assessing the appalling situation which ordinary people, including women and children, have endured, not just as a result of the 2003 war, but also as a consequence of the 1991 war and the sanctions imposed in the following years. The book argues that the social, political and cultural ruin that accompanied the Iraq war was an absolute catastrophe, that the policies which had such adverse effects were the foreseeable consequences of deliberate policy choices, and that those responsible continue to evade being made accountable.

Tareq Y. Ismael is a Professor in the Department of Political Science at the University of Calgary, Canada.

Jacqueline S. Ismael is a Professor in the Faculty of Social Work at the University of Calgary, Canada.

Durham Modern Middle East and Islamic World Series

Series Editor: Anoushiravan Ehteshami, University of Durham

1. Economic Development in Saudi Arabia
Rodney Wilson, with Abdullah Al-Salamah, Monica Malik and Ahmed Al-Rajhi

2. Islam Encountering Globalisation
Edited by Ali Mohammadi

3. China's Relations with Arabia and the Gulf, 1949–1999
Mohamed Bin Huwaidin

4. Good Governance in the Middle East Oil Monarchies
Edited by Tom Pierre Najem and Martin Hetherington

5. The Middle East's Relations with Asia and Russia
Edited by Hannah Carter and Anoushiravan Ehteshami

6. Israeli Politics and the Middle East Peace Process, 1988–2002
Hassan A. Barari

7. The Communist Movement in the Arab World
Tareq Y. Ismael

8. Oman: The Islamic Democratic Tradition
Hussein Ghubash

9. The Secret Israeli–Palestinian Negotiations in Oslo
Their success and why the process ultimately failed
Sven Behrendt

10. Globalization and Geopolitics in the Middle East
Old games, new rules
Anoushiravan Ehteshami

11. Iran–Europe Relations
Challenges and opportunities
Seyyed Hossein Mousavian

12. Islands and International Politics in the Persian Gulf
The Abu Musa and Tunbs in strategic perspective
Kourosh Ahmadi

13. Monetary Union in the Gulf
Prospects for a single currency in the Arabian Peninsula
Emilie Rutledge

14. Contested Sudan
The political economy of war and reconstruction
Ibrahim Elnur

15. Palestinian Politics and the Middle East Peace Process
Consensus and competition in the Palestinian negotiation team
Ghassan Khatib

16. Islam in the Eyes of the West
Images and realities in an age of terror
Edited by Tareq Y. Ismael and Andrew Rippin

17. Islamic Extremism in Kuwait
From the Muslim Brotherhood to Al-Qaeda and other Islamic political groups
Falah Abdullah al-Mdaires

18. Iraq, Democracy and the Future of the Muslim World
Edited by Ali Paya and John Esposito

19. Islamic Entrepreneurship
Rasem N. Kayed and M. Kabir Hassan

20. Iran and the International System
Edited by Anoushiravan Ehteshami and Reza Molavi

21. The International Politics of the Red Sea
Anoushiravan Ehteshami and Emma C. Murphy

22. Palestinian Christians in Israel
State attitudes towards non-Muslims in a Jewish state
Una McGahern

23. Iran–Turkey Relations, 1979–2011
Conceptualising the dynamics of politics, religion and security in middle-power states
Suleyman Elik

24. The Sudanese Communist Party
Ideology and party politics
Tareq Y. Ismael

25. The Muslim Brotherhood in Contemporary Egypt
Democracy defined or confined?
Mariz Tadros

26. Social and Gender Inequality in Oman
The power of religious and political tradition
Khalid M. Al-Azri

27. American Democracy Promotion in the Changing Middle East
From Bush to Obama
Edited by Shahram Akbarzadeh, James Piscatori, Benjamin MacQueen and Amin Saikal

28. China–Saudi Arabia Relations, 1990–2012
Marriage of convenience or strategic alliance?
Naser M. Al-Tamimi

29. Adjudicating Family Law in Muslim Courts
Cases from the contemporary Muslim world
Edited by Elisa Giunchi

30. Muslim Family Law in Western Courts
Edited by Elisa Giunchi

31. Anti-Veiling Campaigns in the Muslim World
Gender, modernism and the politics of dress
Edited by Stephanie Cronin

32. Russia–Iran Relations Since the End of the Cold War
Eric D. Moore

33. Islam and Pakistan's Political Culture
Farhan Mujahid Chak

34. Iraq in the Twenty-First Century
Regime change and the making of a failed state
Tareq Y. Ismael and Jacqueline S. Ismael

35. Islamism and Cultural Expression in the Arab World
Abir Hamdar and Lindsey Moore

36. The Emerging Middle East: East Asia Nexus
Edited by Anoushiravan Ehteshami and Yukiko Miyagi

Iraq in the Twenty-First Century

Regime change and the making of a failed state

Tareq Y. Ismael and
Jacqueline S. Ismael

LONDON AND NEW YORK

First published 2015
by Routledge
2 Park Square, Milton Park, Abingdon, Oxon OX14 4RN

and by Routledge
711 Third Avenue, New York, NY 10017

Routledge is an imprint of the Taylor & Francis Group, an informa business

© 2015 Tareq Y. Ismael and Jacqueline S. Ismael

The right of Tareq Y. Ismael and Jacqueline S. Ismael to be identified as authors of this work has been asserted by them in accordance with the Copyright, Designs and Patents Act 1988.

All rights reserved. No part of this book may be reprinted or reproduced or utilised in any form or by any electronic, mechanical, or other means, now known or hereafter invented, including photocopying and recording, or in any information storage or retrieval system, without permission in writing from the publishers.

Trademark notice: Product or corporate names may be trademarks or registered trademarks, and are used only for identification and explanation without intent to infringe.

British Library Cataloguing in Publication Data
A catalogue record for this book is available from the British Library

Library of Congress Cataloging in Publication Data
Ismael, Tareq Y.
Iraq in the twenty-first century : regime change and the making of a failed state /
Tareq Y. Ismael and Jacqueline S. Ismael.
pages cm. -- (Durham modern Middle East and Islamic world series ; 34)
Includes bibliographical references and index.
ISBN 978-1-138-83133-9 (hardback) -- ISBN 978-1-315-73663-1 (ebook) 1. Iraq-
-Politics and government--2003- 2. Iraq--Social conditions--21st century. 3. Iraq
War, 2003-2011--Influence. 4. Failed states--Iraq. 5. Postwar reconstruction--Iraq.
6. Political culture--Iraq. I. Ismael, Jacqueline S. II. Title.
DS79.769.I76 2015
956.7044'3--dc23
2014025516

ISBN: 978-1-138-83133-9 (hbk)
ISBN: 978-1-315-73663-1 (ebk)

Typeset in Times New Roman
by GreenGate Publishing Services, Tonbridge, Kent

In memory of 'Ali al-Wardi (1913–1995) on his centennial, a professor and mentor to generations of Iraqis

Contents

List of illustrations	xii
Notes on authors	xiii
Preface	xiv
List of abbreviations	xvi

1 Introduction: Iraqi ruination—the humanitarian costs of an imposed state — 1

From "debating" the war to seeing its reality 4
An outline of what follows 8

PART I

Deconstruction and reconstruction of the state — 11

2 Whither Iraq? Beyond Saddam, sanctions and the occupation — 13

Civilizational foundations and imperial imposition 13
The impact of Saddam Hussein's dictatorship (1968–1990) 15
"Shock and awe" and the humanitarian catastrophe of
*   sanctions (1990–2003) 17*
The 2003 invasion and occupation of Iraq 20
Regime change, reconstruction and the resistance to
*   external impositions 21*
State building versus nation building 25
The Kurdish question 27
Foraging for legitimacy: the occupation's Interim
*   Governing Council 31*
Conclusion 34

x   *Contents*

3   Killing the state and undermining the nation   40

American militarism and the neoconservatives 42
Regime change, Iraq and the politics of hegemony in
the Bush Administration 46
The Anglo-American orchestration for war on Iraq 50
Controlling the narrative in the absence of WMDs and the
proliferation of chaos 54
The combined roles of the INC and OSP 57
American credibility: occupation versus liberation 59
The American neoliberalization of Iraq 60
2005 Iraqi elections and the draft constitution 65

4   The sectarian state in Iraq and the new political class   77

The social setting of pre-invasion Iraq 78
Modern Iraqi politics and the development of Iraq's
political diaspora 84
The occupation of Iraq and the engineering of political sectarianism 89
Sectarianism and the patrimony of Iraq's oil 96
Iranian strategic depth and Shia political forces 98
Conclusion 102

5   The hallmark of the new state: political corruption   110

Replacing tyranny with anarchy and claiming it was order 115
A spoils system? 135
Conclusion 136

PART II
People in the quagmire   147

6   Children of the occupation: a decade after the invasion   149

Approach to topic 149
Sanctions context (1990–2003) 151
Invasion context 157
The post-invasion military occupation context 159
Discourse versus policy 162
Conclusion 164

Contents xi

7 Iraqi women under occupation: from tribalism to neo-feudalism 170

Emergence of women onto the stage of modern Iraqi history 170
Qâsim and the revolution of 1958 176
Women under the Ba'th regime 179
Under the sanctions regime 182
US occupation and neo-feudal bondage 184
Conclusion 190

8 Iraq in the twenty-first century: retrospect and prospect 198

Resisting an untenable future 205

Epilogue: blowback from regime change 216

The emergence of ISIS 222
Tri-partition of Iraq and the expansion of chaos 227

Appendix 1. Declaration of the Shia of Iraq (2002) 232
Appendix 2. Law of Administration for the State of Iraq for
    the Transitional Period [TAL], March 8, 2004 245
Appendix 3. Iraqi Constitution (2005) 266

Index 302

Illustrations

Figure

6.1   Iraq: under-five mortality rate disparities   163

Tables

2.1   Iraq's public expenditures as a percentage of GNP in 1960, 1987
      and 1990   16
6.1   UN and civil society discourse on the children of Iraq   150
6.2   Infant and child mortality: impact of the sanctions regime   151
6.3   Malnutrition and deaths in Iraqi children under five years of age   157

Notes on authors

Tareq Y. Ismael is Professor of Political Science at the University of Calgary, Canada. He also serves as president of the International Centre for Contemporary Middle Eastern Studies and is author/co-author and editor of numerous works on Iraq and the Middle East, including *Iraq: The Human Cost of History* (2003), *The Iraqi Predicament: People in the Quagmire of Power Politics* (2004), *The Rise and Fall of the Communist Party in Iraq* (2008), *Cultural Cleansing: Why Museums were Looted, Libraries Burned and Academics Murdered* (2010), *The Sudanese Communist Party: Ideology and Party Politics* (2013), *International Relations of the Contemporary Middle East* (2014) and *Government and Politics of the Contemporary Middle East: Continuity and Change* (2nd ed. 2015).

Jacqueline S. Ismael is Professor of Social Work at the University of Calgary, Canada, and is co-editor of the *International Journal of Contemporary Iraqi Studies*. She has published extensively on Canadian social policy and international social welfare, and has also co-authored a number of works with Tareq Y. Ismael, including *The Communist Movement in Syria and Lebanon* (1998), *The Iraqi Predicament: People in the Quagmire of Power Politics* (2004) and *Government and Politics of the Contemporary Middle East: Continuity and Change* (2nd ed. 2015). Her latest work is with William Haddad, entitled *Barriers to Reconciliation: Case Studies on Iraq and the Palestine–Israel Conflict* (2006).

Preface

Over the past decade we have been following the events surrounding the 2003 Anglo-American invasion of Iraq and its aftermath. While many books on the topic of US policy in Iraq—focusing on various dimensions of the principles, plans and course of action of US policy—have been published since the invasion,[1] there has been woefully limited attention to the consequences of policy on Iraqi political and social development. We hope the imbalance will be addressed by this book's focus on the impact of US policy on the social and political development of Iraq in the twenty-first century. Part I, "Deconstruction and Reconstruction of the State," examines US policy in Iraq and its impact on Iraq's political development. Part II, "People in the Quagmire," assesses the social and cultural fallout from US policy.

The nucleus of this book comes from a series of articles published earlier in the *International Journal of Contemporary Iraqi Studies*, which have been reassessed, revised, recast and updated for this work, bringing the articles' treatment of the subject up to date and informed by recent developments. This has been a very rewarding, yet complicated, endeavor that required support from too many people to list here fully. Each had a role that made this effort possible. Our research assistant and former graduate student, Chris Langille, certainly is at the top of the list. He has not only raised issues but also challenged some of our more contentious claims, reminding us often that the argument will be undermined where not strongly substantiated. Another research assistant and graduate student, Ali Al-Radhi, often argued for a more comprehensive and focused approach to avoid overwhelming the reader. At the same time our other research assistant, Eric Jensen, who came in late to this project, has devoted his time to make sure this book is technically and stylistically rigorous. We are also under deep obligation and gratitude to our friend, Les MacDonald, whose critical eye and astute recommendations during his final review and editing of the manuscript took this work to another level. Three dear friends, Ahmed Mousa Jiyad, Walid Khadduri and Greg Muttitt, were so kind as to review the facts presented in the section on oil and helpful in finalizing and ensuring the accuracy of the section, helping us to avoid speculation. Aisha Biberdorf must be thanked as well for her hard and imaginative work on the book's cover. Also, we have so many friends who have commented on so many different drafts and versions of this work to whom we both owe a great deal. Of course, it must also be said that while so many people have helped us, and we are grateful to each of them, we take responsibility for the claims and opinions presented in this book.

The system of transliteration adopted in this study generally follows the format used by the *International Journal of Middle Eastern Studies*; however, the names of political figures and places will follow the common spelling.

Tareq Y. Ismael and Jacqueline S. Ismael
Calgary, Alberta

Note

1 AAUP. (2014). *Books for Understanding*. Retrieved March 17, 2014, from Books for Understanding: www.booksforunderstanding.org/iraq/list.html

Abbreviations

AEI	American Enterprise Institute
CIA	Central Intelligence Agency
CPA	Coalition Provisional Authority
CPI	Commission on Public Integrity
DIA	Defense Intelligence Agency
DPG	Defense Planning Guidance
DU	depleted uranium
GAO	Government Accountability Office
GFIW	General Federation of Iraqi Women
IGC	Iraqi Governing Council
INA	Iraqi National Alliance
INC	Iraqi National Congress
ISCI	Islamic Supreme Council of Iraq
ISIS	Islamic State of Iraq and the Levant
JAC	Joint Action Committee
KDP	Kurdistan Democratic Party
NED	National Endowment for Democracy
OSP	Office of Special Plans
PNAC	Project for a New American Century
PUK	Patriotic Union of Kurdistan
QRF	quick reaction force
RTI	Research Triangle Institute
SCIRI	Supreme Council for Islamic Revolution in Iraq
SIGIR	Special Inspector General for Iraq Reconstruction
TAL	Transitional Administrative Law
UN	United Nations
UNAMI	United Nations Assistance Mission for Iraq
UNDP	United Nations Development Programme
UNESCO	United Nations Educational, Scientific and Cultural Organization
UNICEF	United Nations Children's Fund
UNIFEM	United Nations Development Fund for Women
UNMOVIC	United Nations Monitoring, Verification and Inspection Commission

UNSC	United Nations Security Council
USAID	United States Agency for International Development
WMD	weapon of mass destruction
WTC	World Trade Center

1 Introduction

Iraqi ruination—the humanitarian costs of an imposed state

Over ten years have passed since the 2003 Anglo-American invasion of Iraq, and this solemn anniversary prompted little assessment of the consequences that were visited on the Iraqi people. Nor has there been any serious official consideration of responsibility for the fallout that continues to spread from the decision, exemplified by the spree of violence that caused thousands of deaths over the first half of 2014 (Griffis, 2014a, 2014b, 2014c; UNAMI, 2014). At most, the violence and devastation that was visited upon Iraq following the Anglo-American invasion has been considered collateral damage—unintended consequences purportedly balanced by the "good intentions" that liberated Iraqis from the dictatorial regime of Saddam Hussein. Any causal connection between the invasion and occupation of Iraq, and the violence that has ensued, has been dismissed. Coverage of Iraq in English-language media declined markedly prior to the US withdrawal (Ricchiardi, 2008), and coverage of the humanitarian impact of escalating violence on Iraqis following 2011 has been scant. To the extent that the costs of the Iraq war are assessed, they are examined in terms of American "sacrifice," albeit cloaked in terms of "blood and money" and of the perceived impact to American credibility. This absence of an Iraqi perspective or recognition of Iraqi suffering was embodied in the discourse used to debate the Iraq war during the 2008 presidential election, surrounded that engaging the Obama Administration's commitment to end the war, and, more recently, became evident when the Islamic State of Iraq and the Levant (ISIS) captured Mosul in June 2014. In 2008, Presidential candidate Barack Obama, a critic of the Iraq war, argued:

> [I]t is important for us not to be held hostage by the Iraqi government in a policy that has not made us more safe [...] and is costing us dearly not only and most importantly in the lost lives of our troops, but also the amount of money that we are spending that is unsustainable and will prevent us from engaging in the kinds of investments in America that will make us more competitive and more safe.
>
> (*New York Times*, 2008)

Nevertheless, by 2014, with American troops no longer stationed in Iraq and the war now a silent memory in the American public consciousness, President

2 *Introduction*

Obama did revisit the Iraq war and American responsibility therein. Prompted by Russian military intervention in the Ukraine which saw the "annexation" of the Crimea, Obama dismissed the notion that America's lawless invasion of Iraq set a precedent for Russian irredentism (or, in any case, weakened America's moral credibility in criticizing the Russian action), claiming that:

> Russia has pointed to America's decision to go into Iraq as an example of Western hypocrisy. Now, it is true that the Iraq War was a subject of vigorous debate not just around the world, but in the United States as well. I participated in that debate and I opposed our military intervention there. But even in Iraq, America sought to work within the international system. We did not claim or annex Iraq's territory. We did not grab its resources for our own gain. Instead, we ended our war and left Iraq to its people and a fully sovereign Iraqi state that could make decisions about its own future.
>
> (Obama, 2014a)

Indeed, President Obama did oppose military intervention in Iraq—as a Presidential candidate he proposed the withdrawal of US military forces, a policy he would bring to fruition in 2011. Iraqis, however, were not afforded such a respite from the violence and deprivation unleashed by Anglo-American policy. Nor did the retreat of US military forces signal the end of US influence over Iraq, as tens of thousands of private contractors remained behind as well as the largest US embassy in the world. As for the remainder of President Obama's claims in this 2014 address—the purportedly "vigorous debate" surrounding the invasion, America's willingness to "work within the international system," and Iraq purportedly being a "fully sovereign state that could make decisions about its own future"—these, and many other claims, are the subject of critical review in this book. A less sanguine view of the Iraq war would be that the Anglo-American invasion of Iraq represented "the single worst foreign policy decision in American history"—in the view of former State Department Foreign Service Officer Peter Van Buren, who spent a year in Iraq as a Team Leader for two Provincial Reconstruction Teams (Van Buren, 2013). While sympathetic to US war aims, Peter Monsoor, a retired US Army officer who served as executive officer to General David Petreaus, was nonetheless critical of the early years of the Anglo-American occupation. In explicating and critiquing US occupation efforts, he identifies the sources of failure in: (1) de-Ba'thification, which heavily targeted Sunnis, "causing some to fear the loss of Sunni power and ultimately create[d] a political base for insurgency"; (2) disbanding the Iraqi Army, which left many of the soldiers "without jobs," leaving many ostracized and driving them into the arms of the insurgency; and (3) empowering sectarian politics. Monsoor argued that the combination of these three factors intensified the detrimental effects on the future of Iraq and the region:

> Rather than creating a governing body from the ground up, the Iraq Governing Council was filled with ex-patriots that had been out of the country during

Saddam Hussein's rule. The effect was to create a non-representative governing body that began replacing long term government administrators with their own political followers.

(Schuldt, 2014)

Indeed, the Iraq war was a disaster for the US in terms of blood and treasure, as well as loss of credibility. Former Central Intelligence Agency (CIA) officer Paul Pillar has argued that to this day the US "continue[s] to suffer from the domestic as well as the regional consequences of that misadventure" (Pillar, 2014). Yet, those who crafted and implemented this grand misadventure, as well as those who promoted and enabled it, have retained their audience and continue to advocate further aggressive interventions around the world. While widely acknowledged to have been a failure, advocates of US military intervention have not been chastened, as evidenced by NATO actions in Libya as well as expansion of the covert actions in Pakistan, Yemen, Somalia and across the Sahel. Calls for a similar robust military response to the conflict in Syria, the breakdown of order in Ukraine following the overthrow of Viktor Yanukovych, as well as the kidnapping of several hundred young women in Congo, all exhibited little humility or nuance regarding the application of military force for political ends. Moreover, that the same voices suffered little loss of prestige over US policy in the Middle East broadly, and Iraq in particular, raises questions over responsibility within US political culture and public discourse, leaving a global audience to question whether Iraqi deaths and suffering fail to register. In President Obama's 2014 speech to the US military academy at West Point, Iraq would emerge as little more than an afterthought, with Obama mentioning the matter in passing only by way of his praising US soldiers for their military service as well as using the speech as a way of contrasting his foreign policy to that of his predecessor George W. Bush (Obama, 2014b). Hillary Clinton, the former US Senator, Secretary of State and much-speculated Presidential favorite for the 2016 election, would—in her 2014 memoir *Hard Choices*—similarly evade any moral responsibility towards the Iraq question. Clinton, as a US Senator, voted in favor of the 2002 Iraq war resolution, and continued to defend her vote during the 2008 Democratic Party Presidential primary when running against Obama. By 2014, however, she would disavow her vote, writing, "I thought I had acted in good faith and made the best decision I could with the information I had. And I wasn't alone in getting it wrong. But I still got it wrong. Plain and simple" (Rucker, 2014). Failing to take note of the consequences of US policy, the entrenchment and institutionalization of sectarianism, a return to authoritarian rule under Nûrî al-Mâlikî's regime, the rise of competing authoritarian centers of power across the Iraqi landscape, the loss of state authority over large swaths of territory and the attendant decline in personal security, with militias consolidating urban spaces from 2013, revealed a lack of concern for Iraq in Washington. Outside US policy circles, discussion remained untethered, with English-language media attention sparse and analysis tying this perilous state of affairs to the US project of post-2003 state building unacknowledged. While this crescendo of appalling indicators was evident, if ignored, the

4　*Introduction*

takeover of Mosul by ISIS in June 2014 unleashed newfound vitality to a needed public debate. However, the framing of ISIS's rise would be explained almost entirely as being in reaction to any and all factors aside from the Anglo-American construct. Moreover, in English-language media, Iraqi voices remained silent and the humanitarian impact neglected to a secondary concern behind the "threat" ISIS posed to Western "interests." As a signal slander to Iraqis' suffering over the last two decades, the voices of those responsible were afforded pride of place in media coverage. Former Coalition Provisional Authority (CPA) head L. Paul Bremer (Bremer, 2014) former UK Prime Minister Tony Blair (Blair, 2014) and the neoconservative and liberal internationalist coterie all pointed to the seeming ISIS-led destruction of a fictive US-crafted Iraqi state. That al-Mâlikî's pernicious sectarianism, the failures of the broader Iraqi political class empowered through US occupation to manage the affairs of state or that regional disruptions all played a role is clear. However, the Iraqi state left behind following Anglo-American withdrawal was already imploding through the centrifugal forces empowered by the occupation. As this book makes plain, those forces were evident to observers, especially Iraqis, and signaled the outcome of the Anglo-American policy of unilateral war, regime change and the imposition of a new political order.

From "debating" the war to seeing its reality

Unlike the war's planners and propagandists, for Iraqis, the legacy of the war is far more than an afterthought. For them, the war was a historical period that approached an extermination event: deaths in the hundreds of thousands, the displaced in the millions, and the specter of a decline into long-lasting "war of all against all" that threatens the existence of Iraqi nationhood itself. Such a lack of self-reflection for the consequences of US action does not augur well for the future direction of US policy across an increasingly strife-ridden *mashriq*. Moreover, it fails to acknowledge the calamitous humanitarian aftermath to the Anglo-American occupation that Iraqis are necessarily required to attend to every day. In spite of enormous petroleum wealth, Iraq's development following the degradation of Ba'thist rule and depredation of the neoliberal policies of Anglo-American occupation belies the challenges left silent in public discourse. This is not a product of a lack of appropriate data and analysis. Surveying reports by international organizations such as the World Bank and the United Nations Assistance Mission for Iraq (UNAMI), international NGOs such as Transparency International and Amnesty International, and indeed US and UK government agencies such as the US State Department, the now shuttered Special Inspector General for Iraq Reconstruction (SIGIR) or the UK Foreign and Commonwealth Office provides sober reading. The World Bank ranks post-occupation Iraq as second-to-bottom only to Yemen within the region in its human development index and as the third-most corrupt nation in the region (ahead of Libya and Yemen), while Transparency International places it second behind only post-Gaddafi Libya. Metrics of government effectiveness, political stability and violence, rule of law, and non-public sector employment and economic development all appear dismal, with the al-Mâlikî government's performance placing Iraq at or near the bottom of the global table. This is with a key distinction being made by the World Bank, that such measures see Iraq today as worse off than under the regime of Saddam Hussein. Further, the US State Department and Amnesty International identify Iraq's state security forces as being habitual abusers of human rights, a point augmented with their expanded operations in Anbar across 2014, as noted by the UK Foreign and Commonwealth Office (Cordesman, 2014).

Not all US policymakers have avoided reflecting on their government's policies vis-à-vis Iraq; Richard N. Haass (2009, p. 6)—now serving as the President of the Council on Foreign Relations, and at the time the director of the State Department's Policy Planning Staff—suggested that "had I known then what I know now, namely, that there were no weapons of mass destruction (WMDs) and that the intervention would be carried out with a marked absence of good judgment and competence, I would have been unalterably opposed." While stripped of triumphalism, such a trivial expression of regret remains beholden to American exceptionalism, and continues to mute Iraqi narratives of the US–Iraqi experience. This is especially critical when recalling that US policy with regards Iraq did not begin with the horrendous 9/11 attacks on America. Iraqis had suffered through US support for the Ba'thist regime and its war against the Islamic Republic of Iran in the 1980s, and especially during the "sanctions decade" that followed the 1991 Gulf War. Without apology or accountability from those who led the war effort, Iraqi losses are assumed, to borrow an odious and infamous phrase from earlier tolls levied on the Iraqi populace, to be "a price" that was "worth it" (Pilger, 2000). The mundane treatment of the Iraqi catastrophe and the crafting of a political narrative that absolves the US of responsibility must be contested. One of the few voices questioning the Western narrative, Hans von Sponeck, UN Humanitarian Coordinator for Iraq (1998–2000), who resigned in protest at the impact of such policies on Iraqis, has succinctly summed up the Iraq tragedy in a *cri de coeur*:

> What we have done to you in the name of freedom and democracy has no parallel in history. We have trampled the truth concerning your suffering, we endeavoured to solicit allies through bribery and ruthlessly marginalized those who objected to our imperial intentions. Brute force became the substitute for the promise of 1945 "to save future generations from the scourge of war." It was you who paid the price [...] There was indeed an axis of evil, an alliance of governments, think-tanks, media and corporations erecting a massive wall of disinformation. Iraq and Al Qaeda, weapons of mass destruction and terrorism, we told the world, were a lethal combination [...] Where were those weapons of mass destruction we assuredly would find? We suffered no guilt and made no apologies. Unfortunately for you, no plan was made for starting the healing. Victors are victors. Chaos suited us well [...] but we made certain that the oil administration was safe. Our concerns were not yours, quite to the contrary. We watched and encouraged your anger and hate. Yes, your dictator deserved it. However, the greed, yours and ours,

6   *Introduction*

raped our common heritage. Your museums are empty, your libraries burnt, your universities destroyed. Only your pride is still there [...] and our guilt. *Will you ever forgive us?*

(Sponeck, 2003)

Pulitzer-prize-winning journalist Thomas Ricks (2006, p. 4) persuasively argues that we cannot view the wars against Iraq in 1991 and 2003 as isolated events. Rather, a distinction is helpful in contextualizing violence against Iraq, which is that between physical violence and psychological violence. In applying this distinction to Iraq, we should view warfare against Iraq in 1991 and 2003 as two physical wars that bookended 12 years of relentless psychological warfare. The engagement of foreign power and policies directed against Iraq over the past two decades was ostensibly directed solely at the Ba'thist regime. In effect, these policies led to regime decapitation, state termination and social dissolution.

At multiple levels, the war has changed the trajectory of human history. At the international level, ever since the Peace of Westphalia in 1648, the concept of territorially sovereign nation-states has been the crux of the international system and the study of international relations (IR). States have violated, indirectly, the sovereignty of other states in what Richard Cottam (1967) calls "competitive interference" in which one state seeks to subvert the internal environment of another state for foreign policy reasons. Competitive interference provides a way for states to avoid open violation of sovereignty, and it became a frequently used, though controversial, tool of foreign policy during the twentieth century, especially during the Cold War. Iraq has been the target of competitive interference from the US many times, the most glaring example being the sponsorship, planning and execution of the 1963 Ba'thist coup. In this case the US Consulate in Basra made it abundantly clear that they were aware of human rights violations and of the bloodbath that followed the coup, as evidenced by their direct communication with National Guard leadership and Iraqi Ba'th regional command (Matthews, 2011, pp. 641–643). This application of competitive interference avoided allegations of US violation of Iraqi sovereignty, although in reality it occurred, as US officials interfered with and reshaped the internal politics and institutions of Iraq.

At the twilight of the Cold War, the notion of a "rogue state" emerged as a classification for a state that was a threat to world peace through its flagrant disregard of international norms and human rights. Although not existing in international law and closely hewing to Anglo-American global interests, the application of "rogue state" status provided for public censure of designated opponents within an increasingly unipolar global order. Moreover, such designation often signaled increasing levels of economic sanction from the US government and its monopoly of international financial mechanisms. Examination of the US-led invasion of Iraq in 2003 and its consequences reveals the beginnings of the open disregard and violation of the notion of Westphalian sovereignty, displaying the foundations of a new world order in which state sovereignty is no longer a basis of the international system. This provides evidence to support Noam Chomsky's (2013) recent charge of "the quiet acceptance at home of the doctrine that the US has every right to act as a rogue state [...] More accurately to be the one rogue state that is powerful enough to act with impunity: in recent years, to carry out aggression at will, to terrorize large regions of the world with drone attacks and much else." Further, then UN Secretary General Kofi Annan declared in 2004 that "I have indicated it [the invasion of Iraq] was not in conformity with the UN charter. From our point of view and from the charter point of view it was illegal." Annan added that the invasion "was not sanctioned by the UN Security Council or in accordance with the UN's founding charter." In the same vein, the UK's Chilcot Inquiry was undertaken to determine just how the Blair government was able to go to war given that it was "advised before the war by all 27 attorneys in their Foreign Affairs Office that war on Iraq [would be] unlawful" (Herman, 2013). A similar investigation conducted by the US Senate and House Committee "has shown through all disclosed evidence that all of the justifications for the war with Iraq were known to be lies at the time they were presented to the public" (Herman, 2013). However, despite these conclusions from government sources in the UK and the US, the American mass media are reluctant to give them coverage and both governments actively delay the publication of their respective reports (Cusick, 2013; Herman, 2013).

At the national level, the war changed the course of Iraqi development. Modern conceptions of the state—particular pluralistic models and Weberian rational-legal models—view society as a collection of competing individuals and communities whereby the state, justifying its authority on legal/rational grounds, serves to adjudicate competing claims within society on behalf of a common good. In the case of Iraq, as with postcolonial states generally, the Iraqi state pursued, from the monarchical period onward, a strategy of nation building—literally, in terms of infrastructure and social welfare; and conceptually, in terms of instilling a cross-cutting notion of Iraqi nationhood—and national independence. This project aimed at supplanting traditional categories of identity (religious sect, ethnicity, tribal) in service of a broader and inclusive "Iraq." And while the boundaries of the modern Iraqi state are historically contiguous with a long-understood community, tribal-feudal social structures, folk sectarianism and ethnic division were forces that the Iraqi state sought to subdue in service of national unity. From its inception as a modern state in 1920, the course of national development was along the path of pluralism and the amelioration of sectarian division. Always a struggle in a pluralist society like Iraq, the state project was the primary instrument for abating sectarian divisions, whether through military conscription, public education or the development of a social welfare structure funded by a state-centered oil sector. This project, although it degenerated through war and crushing economic sanctions (1990–2003), nevertheless saw achievements in shaping Iraqi identity and restraining the chauvinism rooted in identities of the pre-state era.

The obliteration of the Iraqi state following the Anglo-American invasion ended this integrative process. Under the tutelage of Anglo-American occupation authorities, the Iraqi state that had been fashioned following World War I was deconstructed; in its stead a weak and decentralized state, organized on ethnosectarian division and

8   *Introduction*

infused with neoliberal doctrine, was constructed. This process not only exposed Iraqis to predation, manifested through worsening social and economic conditions across all relevant metrics, but also released the demon of sectarianism to decimate the social fabric of Iraqi society. US attempts to reconstruct the state in the aftermath of invasion and under the umbrella of occupation, efforts made with minimal Iraqi input or support, denied popular sovereignty and violated the norms of international law. The postwar period witnessed the end of the postcolonial state-building project, and marked the deconstruction of Iraqi nationhood.

An outline of what follows

Surveying the ruins of Iraqi society, precipitated by the events from 1991 onward (the first Gulf War, the UN sanctions and finally the Anglo-American invasion and occupation), it is not sufficient to regret these developments as merely the spillover of war, a relic of authoritarianism, or a social/cultural form of "collateral damage." The consequences of the invasion of Iraq and decapitation of the Iraqi state in cultural, political and human terms are rooted in explicit policy choices taken over the last two decades. The consequences that followed from these policy choices require close scrutiny. Thus, this work is a survey of the social, political and cultural ruin that accompanied the Iraq war, identifying the great power policy choices that precipitated this ruin. The perspective of deliberate policy choice is presented throughout the book—which is to say, the fact that the events in occupied Iraq did not simply "happen," but were foreseeable consequences of a set of policy choices taken by occupation authorities, whether embodied by the US Coalition Provincial Authority, the chimera of indigenous Iraqi rule embodied in the Interim Governing Council, or in the ethnosectarian political arrangement engineered once "sovereignty" was returned to Iraq. As a result of these drastic conditions, subnational allegiances have eclipsed national loyalty as ethnosectarian differences—previously relegated to Iraq's social substrata—have been institutionalized within Iraq's body politic. These cleavages have been embodied by Iraq's new political class, which serves as an indigenous face to a project of state deconstruction, cultural erasure and humanitarian catastrophe.

The pauperization and destruction of Iraq, through economic sanctions and war, destroyed the country's cultural integrity, political coherence and nationalist-oriented economy. Moreover it served to eliminate Iraq as a regional power and plausible secular nationalist challenger in the region. Paradoxically, the collapse of the Iraqi state and society has benefited a regional challenger, in this case Iran, which was better positioned than the US to deploy its proxies within Iraq. This development has intensified the regional sectarian struggle, with first Iraq, and then Syria, as battlegrounds for a sectarian proxy war between Iran and the representatives of Sunni traditionalism (led by Saudi Arabia and the Arab Gulf states). Post-war Iraq, in any case, has lost the capacity to direct its own affairs and assert an Iraqi national identity, having been deconstructed, fragmented and marginalized.

Chapter 2, "Whither Iraq?," establishes the theoretical and historical base for the book as a whole, providing a sketch of the effects of dictatorship, sanctions and war on Iraqi society, while posing the question of whether Iraq can survive the calamities it has endured. Chapter 3, "Killing the State and Undermining the Nation," considers one of the prime features of the Anglo-American war, the deconstruction of the Iraqi state and the attempt to reconstruct an Iraqi society that is weak and pliant, without substantive sovereignty or independence in charting its own course. Chapter 4, "The Sectarian State in Iraq and the New Political Class," interrogates a key political and social phenomenon of post-war Iraq, the rise of a virulent and politicized sectarianism that destroyed the social basis of Iraq, and investigates Anglo-American responsibility for this development. Chapter 5, "The Hallmark of the New State: Political Corruption," surveys and analyzes the wearying prevalence of corruption that has marked post-war Iraqi society, illustrating the double-dealing and self-serving maneuvering of the new political class that was engineered into power by occupation authorities. Finally, Chapters 6 and 7, respectively, consider the fate of Iraq's most vulnerable, children and women, who have been forced to bear the harshest burden of the great power politics witnessed in Iraq over the last two decades.

References

Blair, T. (2014). *Iraq, Syria and the Middle East—An essay by Tony Blair*. Retrieved June 15, 2014, from Office of Tony Blair: www.tonyblairoffice.org/news/entry/iraq-syria-and-the-middle-east-an-essay-by-tony-blair/

Bremer, L. P. (2014). *Only America Can Prevent a Disaster in Iraq—Without U.S. help, the civil war may spiral into a regional conflict as other countries, including Iran, intervene*. Retrieved June 16, 2014, from *The Wall Street Journal*: http://online.wsj.com/news/article_email/l-paul-bremer-only-america-can-prevent-a-disaster-in-iraq-1402869886-lMyQjAxMTA0MDEwNTExNDUyWj

Chomsky, N. (2013, November 5). *Why the Rest of the World no Longer Wants to be Like U.S.* Retrieved January 16, 2014, from AlterNet: www.alternet.org/world/chomsky-who-wants-be-us?paging=off&current_page=1#bookmark

Cordesman, Anthony H. (2014, May 1). *Hitting Bottom: The Maliki scorecard in Iraq*. Retrieved May 15, 2014, from CSIS: http://csis.org/publication/hitting-bottom-maliki-scorecard-iraq

Cottam, R. W. (1967). *Competitive Interference and Twentieth Century Diplomacy*. Pittsburgh: University of Pittsburgh Press.

Cusick, J. (2013, November 14). *Exclusive: US blocks publications of Chilcot's report on how Britain went to war with Iraq*. Retrieved January 9, 2014, from *The Independent*: www.independent.co.uk/news/uk/politics/exclusive-us-blocks-publication-of-chilcots-report-on-how-britain-went-to-war-with-iraq-8937772.html

Griffis, M. (2014a, January 11). *Iraq Clashes, Attacks Leave 48 Dead, 37 Wounded*. Retrieved January 16, 2014, from Antiwar.com: http://original.antiwar.com/updates/2014/01/11/iraq-clashes-attacks-leave-48-dead-37-wounded/

10 Introduction

Griffis, M. (2014b, January 12). *More Bombs for Baghdad, Clashes in Anbar*. Retrieved January 16, 2014, from Antiwar.com: http://original.antiwar.com/updates/2014/01/12/more-bombs-for-baghdad-clashes-in-anbar-59-killed-119-wounded/

Griffis, M. (2014c, January 15). *Iraq's Bloody Day*. Retrieved January 16, 2014, from Antiwar. com: http://original.antiwar.com/updates/2014/01/15/iraqs-bloody-day-115-killed-145-wounded/

Haass, R. (2009). *War of Necessity, War of Choice: A memoir of two Iraq wars*. New York: Simon and Schuster.

Herman, C. (2013, January 4). *UK Chilcot Inquiry: "The Iraq war was unlawful."* Retrieved January 16, 2014, from Global Research: www.globalresearch.ca/uk-chilcot-inquiry-the-iraq-war-was-an-unlawful-unanimous-legal-opinion-of-foreign-office-lawyers/5317696

Matthews, W. C. (2011). The Kennedy Administration, Counterinsurgency, and Iraq's First Ba'thist Regime. *International Journal of Middle East Studies, 43*(4), 635–653.

New York Times. (2008, February 26). *The Democratic Debate in Cleveland*. Retrieved January 16, 2014, from *The New York Times*: www.nytimes.com/2008/02/26/us/politics/26text-debate.html?pagewanted=12;ref=politics;_r=1amp&_r=0

Obama, B. (2014a, March 26). *Remarks by the President in Address to European Youth*, Speech in Brussels, Belgium. Retrieved April 2, 2014, from the White House: www.whitehouse.gov/the-press-office/2014/03/26/remarks-president-address-european-youth

Obama, B. (2014b, May 28). *Transcript of President Obama's Commencement Address at West Point*. Retrieved June 7, 2014, from *The New York Times*: www.nytimes.com/2014/05/29/us/politics/transcript-of-president-obamas-commencement-address-at-west-point.html

Pilger, J. (2000, March 4). *Squeezed to Death*. Retrieved January 9, 2014, from *The Guardian*: www.theguardian.com/theguardian/2000/mar/04/weekend7.weekend9

Pillar, P. (2014, May 5). *The President Strikes a Nerve*. Retrieved May 6, 2014, from National Interest: http://nationalinterest.org/blog/paul-pillar/the-president-strikes-nerve-10355

Ricchiardi, S. (2008, June/July). *Whatever Happened to Iraq?* Retrieved June 16, 2014, from *American Journalism Review*: http://ajrarchive.org/article.asp?id=4515

Ricks, T. (2006). *Fiasco: The American military adventure in Iraq*. New York: Penguin Press.

Rucker, P. (2014, June 5). *Hillary Clinton on Iraq Vote: "I still got it wrong. Plain and simple."* Retrieved June 7, 2014, from *The Washington Post*: www.washingtonpost.com/blogs/post-politics/wp/2014/06/05/hillary-clinton-on-iraq-vote-i-still-got-it-wrong-plain-and-simple/

Schuldt, C. (2014). *Mansoor Presents Expert's View on Iraq*. Retrieved June 7, 2014, from *The Journal*: www.nujournal.com/page/content.detail/id/549962/Mansoor-presents-expert-s-view-on-Iraq.html?nav=5009

Sponeck, H. C. (2003, June 1). *To an Unknown Iraqi*. Retrieved November 10, 2013, from The Translators Network for Linguistic Diversity: www.tlaxcala.es/pp.asp?reference=10257&lg=en

UNAMI. (2014). *Civilian Casualties*. Retrieved June 15, 2014, from UNAMI: www.uniraq.org/index.php?option=com_k2&view=itemlist&layout=category&task=category&id=159&Itemid=633&lang=en

Van Buren, P. (2013, March 7). *Why the Invasion of Iraq Was the Single Worst Foreign Policy Decision in American History*. Retrieved May 2, 2014, from *The Guardian*: www.thenation.com/article/173246/why-invasion-iraq-was-single-worst-foreign-policy-decision-american-history#

Part I

Deconstruction and reconstruction of the state

2   Whither Iraq?

Beyond Saddam, sanctions and the occupation

Civilizational foundations and imperial imposition

The territory of today's Iraq is relatively geographically consistent with the ancient land of Mesopotamia. The bulk of the Iraqi population still lives in the fertile alluvial plain, which is situated between the Tigris and Euphrates rivers. This geographic region is often referred to as the cradle of civilization as it was the birthplace of writing, which was accompanied by advances in the arts and sciences and the emergence of complex social, political and economic institutions. Ancient Mesopotamia introduced the world to a plethora of "firsts": the first recorded epic poem, the first stringed musical instrument, the first written code of law, the Prophet Abraham, the first city-state, and so forth (Teresi, 2002). If the history of the Near and Middle East (circa 3100 BCE to 500 CE) could be condensed by time-lapse cinematography into a 24-hour documentary, for the first three hours we would be watching Ancient Mesopotamian states (prominently Neo-Assyria and Neo-Babylonia), and for 90 percent of the remaining 21 hours, Mesopotamia and Ancient Egypt would dominate the picture. The territory of Iraq, in other words, has been a cohesive historical unit and a catalyst to civilization since the dawn of recorded history, with a myriad of patterns of interaction interconnecting the diverse peoples of the area through space and time.

In the medieval period (circa 500 to 1500 CE), Iraq played a central role in the rise of Islamic civilization. The golden age of classical Islamic civilization was initiated under the Abbasid Caliphate (Dynasty), which was founded in Baghdad in 750. From the ninth to the thirteenth centuries, Baghdad was the center of extraordinary cultural and intellectual development and the cultural bridge between ancient and modern civilization. Under the tutelage of the Abbasid Dynasty, Baghdad became a center of learning and the pursuit of knowledge was championed. In 1184 there were 30 independent schools in Baghdad, in addition to an engineering school and three medical schools. Private and public libraries were established and contained tens of thousands of books and manuscripts. From this wellspring bloomed the multicultural, multi-ethnic mosaic of Islamic civilization fostered from intellectual diversity and cross-cultural synergy (Ismael et al., 2004, pp. 55–56).

Following the Mongol destruction of Baghdad in the thirteenth century, Iraq moved to the sidelines of world history, first as a backwater of the Ottoman Empire,

14 *Deconstruction and reconstruction of the state*

until it became a backwater of the British Empire in the twentieth century. On the eve of British occupation in 1917 the territory of present-day Iraq consisted of three independently administrated provinces under the Ottoman Empire: Mosul, Baghdad and Basra. Because it had been a nominal part of the Ottoman Empire, Iraqi elements did not play a central role in the machinations of Ottoman politics. Rather, Iraq was politically, socially and economically localized. Congruent with provincialism was the social structure, which was derived from segmented agrarian communities. The communities were differentiated by tribal, ethnic and/or religious affiliation, and held together by the interlocking patterns of exchange, co-operation and conflict that had evolved through socioeconomic and cultural interaction over millennia (Jabar, 1995, pp. 52–53).

With the collapse of the Ottoman Empire following World War I and the carving up of the Arab world into British and French mandates, Britain occupied Iraq and merged the three provinces into the new state of Iraq under its colonial administration. Direct British rule, the presence of the British military, the British failure to honor their promise to end the occupation and the exorbitant taxes that were at a much higher level than those of the Ottomans (Liu, 2004) provided the catalyst for the emergence of an Iraqi resistance movement, and precipitated the Revolt of 1920 that cost the British Exchequer up to £56 million (Jabar, 1995, p. 194).[1] In response to the revolt, Winston Churchill, then the British Secretary of State for War, introduced the military tactic of carpet bombing whole villages with explosives and tear gas[2]—an earlier manifestation of the "shock and awe" doctrine adopted by the US military eight decades later (Ullman & Wade, 1996). Men, women and children fleeing from gassed villages in panic were then machine-gunned by low-flying British planes. The British Royal Air Force routinely bombed and used gas against the Kurd, Sunni and Shi'ite tribes in an effort to quell the resistance (Liu, 2004). To justify this, Churchill said, "I do not understand the squeamishness about the use of gas. I am strongly in favour of using poison gas against uncivilised tribes" (Liu, 2004). The tenacity of Iraqi resistance, however, demonstrated to Britain the impossibility of ruling Iraq by military might, and Britain nominally transferred sovereignty to a puppet regime and withdrew to military bases.

Britain was the architect of the modern Iraqi state and organized an elected parliamentary system and constitutional monarchy modeled on its own Westminster system. However, the system was in reality a façade for a puppet administration that had little room for maneuvering outside British interests. A descendant of the Prophet from the Hashemite line, Faisal, was brought in as the first king. He represented the continuation of Muslim unity which the Ottoman Caliphate had symbolized, and thus enjoyed a modicum of political legitimacy for an otherwise alien political ruler. The various local power groups—the notables, cultural elite, merchants and land owners, and the Iraqi officers who had served in the Ottoman army—were integrated into the modern bureaucratic machinery of the state, and the elected parliament was designed to place minimal constraints on the Iraqi monarchy. After more than three decades of British suzerainty over the modern Iraqi state, local power groups grew increasingly restive with British limitations on Iraqi sovereignty as well as the plundering of Iraq's oil wealth, while Arab nationalist ideology grew increasingly popular among the disenfranchised majority. In 1958 a military coup led by General 'Abd-ul-Karîm Qâsim put an end to the royal regime and declared Iraq a republic. The emergence of Iraq as a republic, ruled by a nationalist military regime, placed the country in the fulcrum of regional and international political dynamics and Iraq became a contested zone for Arab nationalist and Cold War politics (Jabar, 1995, pp. 54–59). In this context, outside influences from regional and international actors began to sponsor factions within Iraq in a bid to gain a controlling interest in Iraq's future. A coup led by Iraqi-based Arab nationalists adhering to Ba'thist ideology brought down the Qâsim regime in 1963, before it too was in turn brought down eight months later by a military coup. It is no longer a secret that the Ba'th coup d'état of 1963 was facilitated by the covert efforts of the Kennedy Administration and the CIA. According to Weldon Matthews (2011),

> [the Kennedy Administration] cultivated supportive relationships with Ba'thist officials, police commanders, and members of the party's militia, despite the regime's wide-scale human rights violations. The American relationship with militia members began before the coup that brought the Ba'thists to power, and Ba'thist police commanders involved in the coup were trained in the United States.
>
> (p. 635)

'Alî Sâlih al-Sa'dî, a Ba'th leader of the 1963 coup, confirmed this by openly stating, "we came to power on the CIA train" (Sa'id, 1999, p. 291). While in a matter of months a military coup returned a Republican government to power, Iraq thereafter remained an important focus of US foreign policy as it vied with the Soviet Union for global hegemony.

The impact of Saddam Hussein's dictatorship (1968–1990)

With further help from the US the Ba'th returned to power in 1968 (Rashid, 2002, pp. 164–166). By the time Saddam Hussein assumed the presidency in 1979, the Ba'th, awash with oil wealth, had already established a totalitarian regime in Iraq through control of a command economy, the subordination of the army and other sources of state coercion, including total control of the media and other vehicles of communication. What gave the totalitarian Ba'th state its pervasive and oppressive power was not the fact that it was the largest employer by virtue of ownership of the public sector, it was rather the fact that the state was the owner of the oil sector and sole producer therein. The phenomenal oil price increases which began in 1974 rendered the state economically independent from the production capacity of Iraqi society (the primary, secondary and tertiary sectors combined) and hence made the state unaccountable. Oil revenue helped the Ba'th regime create a political economy of patron–client relations where personal relationships and crony capitalism were the driving forces, thus recasting the business class to

16 Deconstruction and reconstruction of the state

mirror the class of the ruling clan, and distorting state–society relations as a result (Jabar, 2004). Unchecked by financial constraints and inflamed by a toxic combination of geopolitics internationally, heady nationalism regionally and neo-tribal parochialism nationally, the Ba'th, and Saddam Hussein in particular, sought for the self-aggrandisement of the state through extravagant military expenditures (Table 2.1).

Nationally, Saddam's regime achieved virtually total control, first of the Ba'th Party apparatus, then of Iraqi society, through a combination of ruthless coercion, financial co-optation and a complex web of security agencies spying on the population and on each other. Subordination to the state of civil society and culture sapped them of their vitality and ultimately their viability. Saddam's regime sought leadership of the Arab world by championing Arab issues, especially the Arab–Israeli question. By invading Iran, Saddam sought to fill the geopolitical vacuum created by the collapse of the Shah's regime and the emergence of the Islamic state in Iran by conquering the last political center of the Shia. This ignited an eight-year war that not only exposed the superficial vanity and strategic naiveté of the Iraqi military establishment (for all its armaments and manpower), but it also exhausted the state financially and left it ideologically bankrupt. This embroilment of Iraq in a lengthy war with Iran (1980–1988) seems to have been a successful application of the US strategy of "dual containment" (Hadar, 1998). Both Iraq and Iran posed a potential threat to Israel for various reasons, and Iran represented a direct ideological challenge to US interests by offering a "third way" out of the Cold War's global competition between the US and the USSR for world hegemony. The economies of both Iraq and Iran were severely damaged during the war with US and other Western states sponsoring and supplying both sides in the war.

What further aggravated each country's economic problems was a 7 percent decline in the value of petroleum revenue by 1986. The war's economic damage to Iraq was at least US$120 billion in lost oil exports, which amounted to more than the total Iraqi oil exports since 1973. In 1988 Iraq incurred a debt of $90 billion, with about $40 billion owed just to Saudi Arabia and Kuwait. The Iraqi oil revenue for the same year was $13–15 billion; but civilian imports were $12 billion, debt service $5 billion, and another $1 billion was spent on salaries for guest workers (T. Y. Ismael, 2001, pp. 216–217). The economic loss

Table 2.1 Iraq's public expenditures as a percentage of GNP in 1960, 1987 and 1990

	1960	1987	1990
Health	1	0.8	0.8
Education	5.8	4.6	5.1
Military	7.3	30.2	27.4

Source: Sivard, 1993.

was profound: Iraq's GDP per capita declined from $6,052 in 1977 to $2,944 in 1988. Iran suffered even greater economic setbacks than Iraq because it financed its war effort internally but, unlike Iraq, Iran emerged without having developed untenable financial obligations to other states in the region. Drawn into the vortex by the toxic combination (geopolitics internationally, nationalism regionally and parochialism nationally), the Saddam regime hurled the Iraqi state further down the path of military adventurism, culminating in the invasion of Kuwait in 1990.

"Shock and awe" and the humanitarian catastrophe of sanctions (1990–2003)

The Iraqi invasion of Kuwait in August 1990 resulted in the United Nations Security Council's (UNSC) imposition of the severest international sanctions regime ever imposed. The stated intent of the sanctions regime was to force an Iraqi withdrawal from Kuwait. However, Resolution 687 (UNSC, 1991) gave no clear conditions for the conclusion of the sanctions regime, merely stating in paragraph 24 that "until a further decision is taken by the Security Council" the sanctions would remain in place. Taking advantage of the lack of a concluding condition, US President George H. W. Bush rejected the primary purport of Resolution 687 and barred even the relaxation of the sanctions as long as Saddam remained in power. President Clinton later concurred, and Secretary of State Warren Christopher announced in 1994 that Iraqi compliance was not enough to lift the embargo, thus changing the substance of the Security Council ruling unilaterally (Chomsky, 2003, p. 30).

While the 1991 US-led military campaign, dubbed "Operation Desert Storm," completely destroyed Iraq's civil infrastructure, it left Saddam Hussein's regime intact. In the immediate aftermath of the war, these appeared as unintended consequences. However, the resolute maintenance of the rigid sanctions regime over the next 13 years supports the contention widely accepted in the Arab world that these were covert objectives, not unintended consequences (Ismael & Ismael, 1999). Denis Halliday and Hans Von Sponeck have argued that, if the sanctions had been directed against preventing a WMD program rather than targeting the Iraqi population (because of the way they were administered by the UK and US), the Iraqis might have been able to send Saddam to the fate of other Cold War-era tyrants, such as Suharto, Marcos, Ceausescu, Mobutu and Duvalier (Chomsky, 2003, p. 249).

Following the conclusion of the war in 1991, Iraqi per capita income fell from $2,279 in 1984 to $627 in 1991 and decreased to as low as $450 in 1995. Numerous surveys and reports conducted by the government of Iraq and UN agencies over the decade following the Gulf war detailed the deepening of the complex humanitarian crisis precipitated by the war and exacerbated by the continuing sanctions regime (Ismael & Ismael, 2004, pp. 126–165). The 1999–2000 Report of the United Nations Development Programme (UNDP) Iraq Country Office summarized the situation as follows:

18 *Deconstruction and reconstruction of the state*

Iraq's economy has been in crisis since the imposition of economic sanctions in 1990. Despite the Oil-for-Food program, the country continued its decline into poverty, particularly in the south. Food supplies continue to be inadequate in the centre and south of the country; the prevalence of general malnutrition in the centre and south has hardly changed. Although the rates have stabilised, this happened at "an unacceptably high level." In the area of child and maternal health, in August 1999, UNICEF and the Government of Iraq released the results of the first survey on child mortality in Iraq since 1991. The survey showed that under-five child mortality had more than doubled from 56 deaths per 1000 live births in 1984 to 131 deaths in the period 1994–1999. At least 50% of the labour force is unemployed or underemployed; a shortage of basic goods, compounded by a drought, has resulted in high prices and an estimated inflation rate of 135% and 120% in 1999 and 2000 respectively [...] Most of the country's civil infrastructure remains in serious disrepair. GDP per capita dropped to an estimated US$715 [from US$3,508 before the Gulf war], which is a figure comparable with such countries as Madagascar and Rwanda.

(2000, p. 6)

Food production and availability were major factors exacerbating the problem of increasing morbidity and mortality in Iraq under the sanctions regime. Fueled by lavish oil income in the 1970s and 1980s, the Ba'th had substituted domestic agricultural development with the importation of foodstuffs from the international market. As a result, agricultural and domestic industrial sectors were not only undeveloped but languished as the market was deluged with imported goods. Under the embargo imposed by the sanctions regime, oil revenue precipitously declined and food importation was seriously curtailed. By 2000, with rising food prices and declining per capita income, the UNDP estimated that the average family spent as much as 75 percent of their income on food. As a result, dietary energy supply had fallen from 3,120 to 1,093 kilocalories per capita/per day by 1994–1995, with women and children singled out as the most vulnerable members of Iraqi society. Despite a UN target of 2,463 kilocalories and 63.6 grams of protein per person per day, the nutritional value of the distributed food basket did not exceed 1,993 kilocalories and 43 grams of protein. In addition, replacement parts for repairs to civil infrastructure destroyed by the 1991 aerial bombardment as well as components essential to increase agricultural production were embargoed. Reflecting the economic impact of war and sanctions on Iraq's economy, the rate of inflation after the imposition of the sanctions regime increased from 18 percent in 1975 to 2,000 percent in 1992, and the exchange rate of the Iraqi dinar to the US dollar dropped from 1:3 in 1972 to 180:1 in 1993; in other words, the dinar was equivalent to less than 1 US cent (Jabar, 1995, pp. 168–169).

A variation of the forthcoming "oil for food program" was proposed in August 1991 under UNSC Resolution 706, which was designed to allow Iraq to export up to $1.6 billion worth of oil to fund the importation of essential humanitarian needs such as food and medicine. The envoy of the Secretary General, however, argued Iraq would need three times as much to simply meet the basic needs to sustain human life. As Iraq rejected this initial proposal, the country was allowed to purchase humanitarian goods via a different route, on a case-by-case basis, under the watch of the 661 Committee, or better known as the "Iraq Sanctions Committee" (Gordon, 2010). The 661 Committee was comprised of 15 members, representing each of the member states of the Security Council, who were given complete authority over the implementation of the sanctions regime. Joy Gordon (2010) describes that much of the 661 Committee's time

> was occupied with determining the parameters of the humanitarian exemptions and reviewing individual applications for exemptions. For the 661 Committee this mandate was shaped by two competing mandates: it was charged with enforcing the sanctions regime imposed on Iraq, and also with granting exemptions to it. The committee operated by consensus, and when any member of the committee objected to any purchase, the committee's default position was denial. There was no transparency and little consistency on the part of the committee. The large majority of requests were denied without explanation. From 1990 to 1995 this procedure of the 661 Committee was the sole legal means for Iraq to import any goods.
>
> (pp. 23–24)

During the time of the 661 Committee through to 1996, the government of Iraq had been distributing food baskets of 1,200 kilocalories per day (UN Office of the Iraq Program, 2003). The prevalence of malnutrition in Iraqi children under five almost doubled from 1991 to 1996 (from 12 to 23 percent). Acute malnutrition in the center and southern regions rose from 3 to 11 percent for the same age bracket. Indeed, the World Food Programme (WFP) indicated that, by July 1995, average shop prices for essential commodities stood at 850 times the July 1990 level. While the humanitarian aid program in Iraq, initiated in 1996 with the oil-for-food program, successfully staved off mass starvation, the level of malnutrition within Iraq remained high and directly contributed to the morbidity and mortality rates (UN Office of the Iraq Programme, 2003). Commenting on the findings of the United Nations Children's Fund's (UNICEF) 1999 Iraq Child and Maternal Mortality Surveys, then UNICEF Executive Director Carol Bellamy noted that sanctions had caused the deaths of half a million Iraqi children under five (UNICEF, 1999).[3] The 2003 State of the World's Children report, which UNICEF issued, stated: "Iraq's regression over the past decade is by far the most severe of the 193 countries surveyed" (Chomsky, 2003, p. 126). Furthermore, Saddam's ability to skim off his share of profits during the oil-for-food program did not go unnoticed. Much of the money was used to fund the construction of 50 new presidential palaces, in what General Tommy Franks rightly described as the "Oil for Palaces Program" (Bremer & McConnell, 2006, p. 29). The impact of the sanctions regime on Iraq was overwhelming and multifarious. While it pauperized the Iraqi people, it also strengthened the grip of Saddam's regime while simultaneously weakening opposition groups.

20 *Deconstruction and reconstruction of the state*

Under the suzerainty of the Security Council the Iraqi state lost control of its air space in the north and south; nonetheless, it maintained territorial jurisdiction in the center and the south, and nominal power in the north, where a pseudo-state led by Kurdish parties enjoyed de facto autonomy under US protection. In this aberrant context the Iraqi people, excluding the Kurds, suffered a cynical game of brinksmanship between Saddam's regime and the US–UK-led Security Council, nominally with regard to WMDs. Bombed back to a pre-industrial stage of development by 1991's Operation Desert Storm, the people reverted to pre-industrial social patterns for survival in the aberrant socio-political and economic situation shaped by the sanctions regime. Tribal, religious and ethnic bonds of community reciprocity and exchange re-emerged as central institutions bridging personal and social security.

At the regional and international levels, sanctions served to isolate Iraq both politically and economically. Iraq's invasion of Kuwait in 1990 not only exacerbated ideological tensions in the Arab world between the conservative Gulf states, led by Saudi Arabia, and nationalist groups, but also dealt a terminal blow to Arab nationalism as an ideological force in regional politics. The invasion precipitated the collapse of organized Arab opposition to Israel and the acceptance by Arab regimes of US military bases on Arab territory. Until the Gulf war in 1991 the Ba'th had championed the cause of Arab unity and the Palestinian question, and had kept in the forefront of Arab politics the relationship between the Palestine question and imperialism. In the face of this collapse, Israel's right wing became more politically strident, as reflected in Ariel Sharon's provocative walk to the al-Aqsa mosque in Jerusalem on September 28, 2000, igniting the second Intifada. The second US military defeat of the Iraqi state (April 9, 2003) within 21 days of the initiation of the war[4] was traumatic for all Arabs, who perceived it as a reflection of the bankruptcy of Arab regimes after three generations of nation building. The toll of sanctions on the Iraqi people, and the perceived collusion of Arab regimes in the destruction of Iraq, fueled the rise of anti-Western sentiment throughout the Arab world, and inflamed the increasing schism between Arab governments and their populations (Ismael & Ismael, 2004, pp. 9–38).

The 2003 invasion and occupation of Iraq

The most immediate impact of the invasion was the systematic destruction of a large portion of Iraq's cultural heritage and infrastructure. While represented in the US media as an unintended consequence of freedom expressed by a formerly oppressed people, it was portrayed differently in the Islamic world. Rather, the free rampage of organized looting of cultural, educational and health facilities and the wholesale burning of historical records symbolized an intentional policy of cultural cleansing. This perception was even more prevalent in Iraq than throughout the rest of the Islamic and Arab world, as many Iraqis took great pride in their unique history, where the cultural connection to their locale extended far beyond the Baghdadi Caliphate into the very origins of civilization itself. The significance of the looting and destruction of Iraq's cultural symbols cannot be overstated. The

American forces, while guarding only the Ministry of Oil, watched the burning and the looting of Baghdad indifferently, and even refused to intervene when people requested their help. Attention in Washington was focused on tearing asunder the assumed cultural basis of an irrational opposition to explicitly "Western" values and mores. Iraq, it was argued, was the initial salvo in a process to bring about changes irrevocably altering the region and its peoples. As George W. Bush (2003) said in his speech at the United States Chamber of Commerce:

> Iraqi democracy will succeed—and that success will send forth the news, from Damascus to Teheran—that freedom can be the future of every nation. The establishment of a free Iraq at the heart of the Middle East will be a watershed event in the global democratic revolution.

"Operation Iraqi Freedom" also reduced the public infrastructure to rubble (Watenpaugh et al., 2003).[5] The quality of life in Iraq, already seriously compromised by almost 15 years of international sanctions, deteriorated even further under the occupation. Reflecting this, a report conducted by the Fafo Institute for Applied International Studies found that acute malnutrition among Iraqi children between the ages of six months and five years had increased from 4 percent before the US invasion to 8 percent after a year of occupation (Fafo, 2005, p. 63). The death toll of the US occupation on Iraqi civilians has been estimated at over 100,000 (and has been estimated to be as high as 1.12 million by Opinion Research Business Poll [Reuters, 2008]) by a study undertaken by Johns Hopkins and Columbia universities in collaboration with al-Mustansriyah University (Roberts et al., 2004). In the most recent report, which was conducted by four institutions including the University of Washington, researchers went to 2,000 randomly selected houses in 100 clusters throughout the country. Following their exhaustive research, they put the number of deaths at 461,000 from 2003 to 2011 (Hagopian et al., 2013, p. 10). Of course, that doesn't include sectarian violence following the US withdrawal, which has only intensified through the period following the 2014 parliamentary elections. Most individuals reportedly killed by coalition forces were women and children. The risk of death from violence in the period after the invasion was 58 times higher than in the period before the war (Roberts et al., 2004, p. 1857).[6]

Regime change, reconstruction and the resistance to external impositions

The United States Agency for International Development (USAID) appointed the Research Triangle Institute (RTI) as one member of a battalion of private contractors attempting to fashion Iraq's legal, economic, political and social institutions in a manner conducive to US interests. Most of the contracts were funded by USAID and structured as foreign aid. RTI recruited and mobilized expatriate and indigenous Iraqis to reconstruct the institutions of state and civil society (Docena,

22 *Deconstruction and reconstruction of the state*

2004). In accordance with their contract with USAID, RTI sought to staff its reconstruction planning venture with "the most appropriate 'legitimate' and functional leaders"—that is, educated Iraqis, particularly expatriate Iraqis who were residents of the US (Docena, 2004, p. 15). The definition of "legitimate," according to Fritz Weden of the USAID Office of Transition Initiatives, is "those groups, those leaders that you can work with" (Docena, 2004, p. 15). The task of the RTI was to ensure that only the "legitimate" leaders—those not opposed to US occupation and Iraq's westernisation—prevailed, in order to create a base that would support the reconstruction of Iraq according to the neoliberal model. Thomas Carothers, director of the Democracy Project at the Carnegie Endowment for International Peace, said: "Beneath the new interest of the United States in bringing democracy to the Middle East is the central dilemma that the most powerful, popular movements in Iraq are the ones that we are deeply uncomfortable with" (Docena, 2004, p. 16).

While the RTI acted as a public recruiting office, the National Endowment for Democracy (NED) and its affiliates were developing the machinery for scores of political formations expected to contest the national elections planned for January 30, 2005, allowing these sanctioned parties an inside track through being selected to serve on the Constitutional Assembly. Various US-sponsored contractors held workshops for teaching a US government-approved perspective on democracy. Larry Diamond, a senior adviser to the CPA and former co-director of NED, offered a preview of this project in a lecture at Hilla University in January 2004. Diamond told his audience that a basic element of "democracy" is a "market economy," and among the most fundamental rights is the right to own property—a view affirmed by USAID. This, in turn, called for a kind of democracy in which social equality is not a necessary aim and in which inequalities may in fact be necessary (Docena, 2004, p. 17). In Latin America USAID has a long history of coercing governments to agree with policy "suggestions." However, in Iraq, NED and USAID attempted institutional reconstruction, not reform. Their point of entry into Iraq was the US occupation, not diplomacy. In this case, "legitimate leaders" are not to be identified and co-opted, as in Latin America, but to be groomed and primed. While there was a so-called "transfer of sovereignty" on June 28, 2004 following increasing domestic Iraqi opposition, the US continued to exercise power over the interim government. Considering the appointed Prime Minister (2003–2005) Iyâd 'Allâwî's negligible power base in Iraq and his dependence on US protection, such US influence was assured.[7] US administrators evidenced little respect in their Iraqi protégés, with CPA head L. Paul Bremer exclaiming that "[t]hose people couldn't organize a parade, let alone run the country" (Bremer & McConnell, 2006, p. 171). Moreover, such attitudes about the Iraqis placed in authority over such a momentous task as constructing the post-2003 state-building project did not emerge following their appointment, but rather prior to their deployment to Iraq. In the estimation of Zaid Al-Ali, a legal adviser to the UN focusing on constitutional, parliamentary and judicial reform in Iraq from 2005 to 2010, "The CPA and its allies were [...] faced with a choice: to emphasize unity over division [...] or to treat Iraqis as incapable of governing themselves democratically and to reinforce the divisions within the system of government. Sadly, the second option had been selected well before the 2003 invasion" (Al-Ali, 2014, p. 65). Thus, it was deemed that there was no need to reform Iraq's laws, or to include Iraqis in the drafting process, because Iraqis who had not found themselves in the exiled opposition were deemed suspicious. The first elected government would be starting fresh, without the bureaucratic legacy of the Ba'thist regime, barring great swaths of Iraqis from participating in the reconstruction. All of this was possible through the opportunities presented by the occupation because the first step towards policy change in Iraq had been dropping bombs, rather than legitimation and constituency building (Docena, 2004, p. 20). John Agresto, senior adviser to the Iraqi Ministry of Higher Education and Scientific Research's focus on the rebuilding of Iraq's education system, noted his fellow American's incongruous attitude to Iraqi engagement in the process. In contrast to what America's own founding constitutional principles implied, Agresto noted that rather than selecting talented Iraqis representative of the entire community to populate a new regime, US designs had alternative criteria:

> We're more than happy to do exactly the opposite of what [our Constitution tried to do]—we seek out the loudest and most virulent factions and empower them [...] [W]e gather together the representatives of the most antagonistic factions and think that's good democracy. We've done nothing to blur the lines separating people and everything to sharpen them. We will not see moderate and thoughtful people representing the wider interests of Iraq; rather we'll see ideologues chosen for the very reason that they were not mild, moderate or thoughtful but because they were ideologues.
>
> (Agresto, 2007, p. 107)

Agresto saw such efforts as corrupting governance through the promotion of narrow interest, fashioning representation to represent sectarian or other artificial constructs, rather than allowing Iraqi leaders to reflect the desires of the broader society. This elite and foreign-driven effort faced immense popular opposition outside the narrow confines of the cubicles manned by contractors. Despite the appearance of unfettered latitude for action, events outside the safety of the "Green Zone," however, exposed the intensity of the Iraqi resistance and the unpopularity of the USAID and NED project to remodel Iraqi society. Reflecting that this popular reaction to Anglo-American designs was anticipated, in an exclusive interview with *Asia Times* in June 2004, two elite members of the Iraqi resistance declared that their plan had been organized months in advance of the US invasion in March 2003 not to fight the invasion, but to expel the occupation that was sure to follow (Grange, 2004).

An increasing number of popular protests across central and southern Iraq reflected the growing hostility to the occupation. To pacify the growing resistance, in April 2004 the US military besieged Fallujah, a small city in the so-called Sunni triangle about 60 kilometers northwest of Baghdad. On April 6, 2004, the first siege of Fallujah was initiated with intense air and ground assaults. For

24   Deconstruction and reconstruction of the state

almost a month a virulent campaign of urban warfare was undertaken, but failed to pacify the city. In the face of intense international pressure and signs of increasing co-operation among Sunni and Shi'ite groups, the US military was forced to pull back and withdraw from Fallujah. However, the interruption of the occupation's reliance on a military strategy of pacification was only temporary, and attention turned to Shi'ite opposition groups. Al-Ṣadr's rejectionist movement had become a lightning rod for armed resistance to the US occupation in the Shi'ite south, and increasing confrontations between US and al-Ṣadr forces culminated in a three-week siege of Najaf in August 2004 (Weinstein, 2004). This siege also failed to produce a military victory because Ayatollah al-Sistânî, the highest religious Shi'ite authority, brokered an agreement between al-Sadr and US forces. As the dust settled, three parties stood on the ruins of the holy city—Muqtaḍâ al-Ṣadr, the government and the Hawza (the Shi'ite religious elite led by Ayatollah al-Sistânî):

> Al-Sadr movement did not accomplish a military victory; and it was not destined to do so, given the balance of power. But they did not lose either. They melted away with a large portion of their weapons and they were not forced to comply with demands to disband [...] and they are invited, indeed encouraged, to participate in the political process.
>
> (Kadhim, 2013)

Following the resolution of the Najaf siege the US military turned its full attention once again to the resistance in the Sunni triangle, and in November 2004 the second siege of Fallujah was initiated. This time the US forces planned the complete elimination of independent news coverage or of any means of communication, going so far as to block cell phones (Klein, 2004), in order to reduce the city to rubble, thus attempting to quell the spirit of the resistance in preparation for the January election. An estimated 300,000 of Fallujah's 350,000 inhabitants fled as more than 12,000 ground forces sealed off the city, but an estimated 50,000 civilians remained—the elderly, the sick, the young and those with nowhere else to go.[8] In addition, it was estimated that roughly 3,000 insurgents remained in the city, although some had fled prior to the attack (Filkins & Glanz, 2004). The assault on the city began on November 7, 2004, and by November 18 the insurgency was declared "broken" by the senior US marine commander in Iraq (US Claims Success in Fallujah Offensive, 2004). However, the fighting continued, and despite efforts by the US to cut off communication from the city, reports emerged that the US was using napalm and poison gas (Kay, 2004).[9] As one commentator noted, "[t]he Falluja police-state strategy represents a sign of weakness, not strength" (Schwartz, 2004).

Immediately following the "successful" siege of Fallujah, which the US had claimed was the heart of the resistance, and from which fighting immediately flared up again following the lifting of aerial bombardments (Daragahi, 2004), major attacks were carried out on a Baghdadi checkpoint on December 13 and 14, 2004 (McCarthy & Mansour, 2004) and on a US military base near Mosul on

December 22, killing over 20 people, including at least 18 US military personnel (US Army Base Hit in Mosul, 2004). In a message to Asia Times Online from the Netherlands, Nadâ al-Rubaiʻî, a member of the Central Committee of the Iraqi Patriotic Alliance, a group that was part of the Iraqi national resistance movement both inside and outside Iraq, said:

> Everything in the resistance movement is clear [...] There is agreement on one issue; that is, getting freedom from foreign occupying forces and their handymen. It is agreed that only Iraqi people would decide the course of government in the post-liberation era.
>
> (Shahzad, 2004)

The growing guerrilla warfare and the increasing sophistication of the attacks disrupted US supply lines to the point that the US military had to resort to air-dropping equipment and supplies into US bases, an incredibly costly venture, in order to reduce the risks incurred by land transport (Schmit, 2004).

The destruction of Najaf and Fallujah provided the people of Iraq with graphic lessons on the occupation's use of collective punishment. Even as the Fallujah siege eased, the US strategy of military pacification expanded throughout the Sunni triangle, and small-scale assaults were initiated on targeted areas in Mosul, Ramadi, Samarra and other towns that manifested any signs of organized resistance. In spite of the occupations, assaults by the Iraqi resistance continued to escalate in frequency, boldness and ferocity. By mid-January 2005 it was clear that the Anglo-American occupation could not pacify the Sunni triangle sufficiently to allow for any opportunity for democratic elections scheduled for January 30 of that year. Reflecting the growing discomfort about the elections in the US establishment, on January 12, 2005, the *New York Times* called for their postponement. As expected, low voter participation in largely Sunni areas reflected the hostility toward the continued US attacks on predominantly Sunni areas. In al-Anbar Province, for example, voter turnout was a meager 2 percent, while it was over 70 percent in Shiʻite-dominated areas such as Najaf and Karbala (Dulami et al., 2005).

State building versus nation building

With the consummation of decolonization in the 1950s, the term "nation building" became prominent in liberal discourse to rationalize a Western-sponsored process of decolonization that favored the integration of disparate groups and communities of people into facsimiles of liberal democracies. In effect, nation building represented a liberal development strategy in the economic and political context of decolonization, with nation-states promoted as the agents for transforming pre-modern communities into economically liberal and politically stable entities.[10] While the concept of nation building focused on political process, the corollary concept of state building focused on the structure and functions of government. Similarly, Eurocentric state-building theory has its roots in classical liberal

26 *Deconstruction and reconstruction of the state*

theory.[11] Ill-equipped for both nation building (inclusion of disparate social groups in the political process) and state building (the development of a political system of governance), and unabashedly seeking to usurp Iraq's economic assets, US policy in Iraq created a wellspring of antipathy regarding any form of collaboration with US agents, as well as massive support for the growing resistance movement. Iraq's experiences with the two models of political construction (nation and state building) in its modern history provide insight into the challenge of political reconstruction. The first model was undertaken by Britain in the aftermath of its occupation, and therefore presents a relevant comparison with the US effort. The monarchical system of governance established by Britain incorporated an important symbol of cultural legitimacy—Hashemite authority; and embraced all national power groups, not only in the political process but in the political economy of the state, through the creation of a landlord class that cut across traditional tribal and ethnic groupings. This allowed the effective management of the countryside and, through education, the civil service and the military created systems for the national integration of the middle classes. However, it marginalized the dispossessed and impoverished the peasantry. Moreover, the urban/rural contradiction manifested in the state's political economy progressively destabilized the state. Like the Anglo-American project almost a century later, when facing the seeming contradictions of Iraqi social organization, elite opinion grew frustrated with indigenous diversity and efforts to centralize authority. In his diary King Faisal I questioned the existence of an "Iraqi" people as well as their strong opposition to central authority. This viewpoint has been highlighted in many histories of Iraq written in English-language scholarship, giving it a power to frame understandings around a sectarian and identity scaffolding that ignores Iraqi experience. As Ziad Al-Ali notes, "[n]ot only was Faisal [I]'s statement one of the first instances of senior government officials (in this case, the head of state) politicizing sectarianism to obfuscate the state's failures, but [the statement] also did enormous damage to international perceptions of Iraq's people" (Al-Ali, 2014, p. 21).

In contrast to the British model, the Ba'th model based its political system on nationalist symbols of legitimacy, and the party apparatus initially provided the mechanism for inclusion of all social groups in the political process, particularly the urban and rural poor. While the nation-building process was thus more inclusive of social groups than the monarchical system, it attempted to co-opt the already active nationalist groups, or to marginalize them in the event of their opposition or rejection of Ba'thist rule. Opposition movements proliferated, as was the case with the communists, the National Democratic Party and even some factions within the Ba'th Party itself. Through the Ba'th socialist program many social entitlements, such as healthcare, education, housing and electrification, provided significant improvements to the poor. The party apparatus replaced education, the civil service and the military as the system of national integration. However, under Saddam the command economy was quickly transformed into a type of crony capitalism, and the party apparatus into a personality cult. Thus, a complex web of national security agencies emerged to enforce the new cult of personality based on the paternalistic visage of "Papa Saddam." A combination of totalitarianism and kinship resulted in vibrant networks of nepotism and the creation of a "thick" ruling clan-based class deeply embedded in the social structure (Jabar, 2004). As Faleh Jabar (2004), the Director for the Iraq Institute for Strategic Studies, puts it, "[This was] not just a small elite group, but rather an entire social layer united by blood, as well as by economic and financial ties," which led to the marginalization of the old social classes and the middle classes of the monarchy (Batatu, 1978). The crony-based economics of Saddam's regime, intensifying under the imposed austerity of UN sanctions, initiated a process of socioeconomic polarization of society where the wealthy few contrasted with the pauperized mass of the population. These two examples serve to illustrate the significance of nation building for political stability. While both models had inherent fault lines, the British model provided relative political stability for almost four decades (1921–1958), and the Ba'th model for more than a decade (1968 to about the mid-point of the Iraq–Iran war, we would estimate). How did the US effort compare? After an occupation lasting more than eight years, political stability is not a phrase that comes to mind when describing Iraq. More than a decade after Iraq's transition to a democratic system, sectarian and criminal violence remain resilient. The current sectarian conflict, noticeably absent under the previous two models, is the defining political structure of post-war Iraq. The fragility of the Iraqi state is undeniable, which is further being tested by the Syrian civil war. While the al-Mâlikî-led government continues to consolidate its power and impose its narrative of Iraqi nationalism, Sunni and Kurdish leaders mobilize their populations on explicitly ethnic and sectarian lines, making the prospects of a future nation that transcends ethnic and communal boundaries difficult to envision.

The Kurdish question

State building and nation building within Iraq has long been complicated by the question of Kurdistan, the Kurdish-majority provinces in Iraq's north. Contrary to contemporary narratives that sectarianism in Iraq has been embedded in the social fabric since before the "artificial" formation of Iraq and its three main ethnosectarian identities, Kurdish, Sunni and Shia, the idea of a geographical "Iraq" was common in the late Ottoman Empire and followed closely to the modern borders of Iraq (Visser, 2010a, p. 296). That is to say that there was some local consensus that a centralized state of Iraq was desirable prior to the British Mandatory period. Yet, while Iraqi Kurdistan has long been conceived as part of a contiguous territory we now recognize as Iraq, Kurds—who constitute roughly 20 percent of Iraq's population—are a non-Arab community with a distinct cultural identity and their own language. Through the modern era of the Iraqi state, Kurdish ethnic identity would frequently clash with the ideological prerogatives of the centralizing Iraq state who would, at points, pursue an Arab nationalist ideology that contained elements of racial particularism at odds with a multiethnic Iraq.

Under the monarchy there had been limited revolts in the 1920s followed by periods of open rebellion. By the 1930s, in response to military incursions and

28   Deconstruction and reconstruction of the state

the settling of Assyrians near Barzânî tribal territory under Anglo-Iraqi direction, the Barzânî Rebellion—led by Sheikh Ahmad of Barzan—emerged, lasting from the summer of 1931 to the fall of 1932. In 1943, Mulla Mustafa Barzânî, the younger brother of Sheikh Ahmad and future leader of the Kurdistan Democratic Party (KDP), began to build alliances with other Kurdish tribes in a bid to build a sufficiently formidable bloc to demand autonomy from the central government. However, after such demands were refused, the bloc collapsed around tribal fault lines, and Barzânî fled to the Republic of Mahabad (a separatist Kurdish enclave in Iran) in 1946, prior to moving on to the Soviet Union prior to the collapse of that Kurdish republic (Ismael & Ismael, 2011, p. 192). Thus, early Kurdish political movements in Iraq were oriented around Barzânî tribal affinities rather than Kurdish nationalism qua Kurdish nationalism.

The ideas of Kurdish autonomy, Kurdistan, gained currency in Iraq in the 1960s (Visser, 2010b, p. 78). The emergence of the idea of an autonomous Kurdistan was not the product of an "endless story of confrontation between the Kurds and other Iraqis"—as "there is not much material to support this information as far as the late Ottoman (1831–1914) and the monarchy (1921–1958) periods are concerned"—but rather because of the relatively permissive environment provided for the Kurds following the inauguration of the republican regime in Iraq (Visser, 2010b, p. 78). General Karîm Qâsim, the first republican leader of Iraq, had recognized the Kurds as partners in Iraq with Arabs. The ascent of Kurdish nationalism in Iraq has been described by Visser as:

> [The] Kurdish autonomy movement [...] would often adopt tough bargaining positions, but [...] nevertheless tended to ultimately stay loyal to the framework of a unified Iraqi state. Negotiations [with the Ba'th] in the 1970s broke down not over the idea of Kurdish autonomy as such, but rather as the result of the oil-rich city of Kurkuk having been added to the Kurdish list of desiderata in a rather abrupt manner during the course of the negotiations.
>
> (Visser, 2010b, p. 78)

However, the autonomy movement, still led by Mulla Mustafa Barzânî, had become more assertive by the 1960s when "[f]riction between Qasim and Barzânî, initially of a personal nature, spilled over into a political confrontation over local autonomy within Iraq"; Qâsim attempted to supress the Kurdish aspirations for autonomy and Barzânî responded with armed resistance beginning in September 1961 (Ismael & Ismael, 2011, p. 222).

Under the Ba'th regime, an "Autonomy Accord" agreement was negotiated in 1970 that would grant the Kurds autonomy and their own executive and legislative institutions to be developed over a four-year transitional period. This four-year respite from open conflict gave the Ba'th regime time to consolidate its power, but also isolated Kurdistan from national integration. The Kurds distrusted the pan-Arab ideology of the Ba'th, who in turn rejected Kurdish autonomy, and such mistrust and mutual acrimony would lead to bloody conflict returning in 1974. Baghdad was confident it could reassert itself in Kurdistan without loosening its grip elsewhere, while Barzânî was under the impression he could negotiate from a position of strength with the backing of his foreign allies, Iran and the US. The two sides' divergent interpretations of the Autonomy Accord, along with their mutual over-confidence, created tensions that again erupted into violence in 1974 after the Ba'th stacked the Kurdish executive and legislature with people who supported closer ties with Baghdad. In 1975, Saddam Hussein (then the Iraqi vice-president) and the Shah of Iran signed the Algiers Agreement, effectively cutting off the Kurds from the material and financial support of both Iran and the US, leaving Kurdish fighters unable to sustain warfare against the central government. Barzânî fled to the US, where he would pass away in 1979 (Ismael & Ismael, 2011, pp. 222–223). With its leadership in disarray and without foreign support, Kurdish territory became subject to a Ba'thist "Arabization" project. Entire Kurdish villages, with tens of thousands of people, were relocated southwards, their homes destroyed. In their place, Arabs were settled across the Kurdish region. In 1976 the KDP fractured into what would become a second dominant movement of Kurdish nationalism, the Patriotic Union of Kurdistan (PUK), which was led by Jalâl Ṭâlabânî ("an old friend of the United States with many admirers in Washington" [Bremer & McConnell, 2006, p. 214]). Both the KDP and PUK were able to regroup their peshmergas (militias) and party structures. When the Iran–Iraq war broke out, the KDP and PUK were able to once again fight, alternating support for Iran and Iraq, while frequently fighting each other as well. For Iraq's part in the war, Saddam launched the Anfal campaign on the Kurdish territory that, from 1987 to 1988, killed between 100,000 and 200,000 people (from bombings, mustard gas and ground engagements) while destroying over 4,000 villages. The atrocities committed by the central state in the 1970s and 1980s truly radicalized the Kurdish autonomy movement and instilled a strong separatist current that would inform the formation of the Kurdistan Regional Government (KRG) from 1991.

In May 1988, following the Anfal campaign and the conclusion of the Iran–Iraq war, Mas'ûd Barzânî (who assumed control of the KDP following the death of his Father, Mulla Mustafa Barzânî) and Jalâl Ṭâlabânî formed the Iraqi Kurdistan Front, a KDP and PUK-dominated coalition with five other minor Kurdish. This unified body consolidated the control of the nationalist movement into the hands of the KDP and PUK. Thus, the Barzânî and Ṭâlabânî clans have remained dominant in Kurdish national affairs in Iraqi Kurdistan ever since. The US and UK created and enforced a no-fly zone in northern Iraq beginning in 1992, which gave the Kurds space and protection from Saddam's regime. Elections were held for the first time for the KRG in 1992, with the outcome of a virtual tie between the KDP and PUK leading to the creation of a coalition government that has remained largely unopposed. With the 2005 Iraqi elections, Barzânî became President of Iraqi Kurdistan and Ṭâlabânî became the first post-Ba'th President of Iraq. Both parties have remained in power, though the PUK suffered the loss of many seats in the 2013 KRG election when it was displaced from its position as the second-largest party by Goran (the Movement for Change). The PUK has been further challenged by the ill health of Jalâl Ṭâlabânî, who suffered a stroke in 2012.

30 *Deconstruction and reconstruction of the state*

The KRG came to receive 13 percent of Iraq's oil income under the oil-for-food program, establishing a precedent by which the KRG would be provided a set allotment of the Iraqi federal budget post-2003. This income, in conjunction with "customs fees" from exports through the border with Turkey, enabled it to finance a variety of projects, providing economic development and social services to the region, as well as lobbying efforts in Washington DC and European capitals. These efforts built upon earlier efforts by the Kurdish parties to develop support for the national cause, especially following 1992, as well as hosting a conference of the US-sponsored Iraqi National Congress (INC) in 1992.[12] Despite a civil war between the KDP and PUK from 1994 to 1998, Kurdistan still managed to create a robust public infrastructure in the period before the 2003 invasion of Iraq, as well as dominate the INC and the rest of the anti-Saddam Hussein movement patronized by the US. Barzânî and Țâlabânî were able to win the confidence of the US and European authorities, particularly after the ascension of the Bush Administration, and especially at the London conference of December 2002.[13]

Kurdish efforts to improve relations with the US would pay off, particularly their positive relations with Paul Bremer, allowing them to select members for the Governing Council (GC) in occupied Iraq. Barzânî and Țâlabânî were able to pressure for the inclusion of both the Al-Da'wa party as well as Ibrâhîm al-Ja'farî to be included within the Governing Council. Claiming that there could be "no political process in Iraq without this 'historical' party" (Voice of Kurdistan, 2012), the Kurdish representatives were able to promote Arab Shi'a parties amenable to their interests. Thus, they were able to directly affect the direction post-Saddam Iraq and its future constitution would take by positioning the Da'wa party in a place of influence. It was also during this period that the autonomy movement, with its goal now achieved, looked for ways to protect its gains in a future post-Saddam Iraq by exploring federalism. Beginning in the 1990s, the KRG began to promote Iraqi federalism as a constitutional proposal (Visser, 2010b, p. 79). The proposal envisaged a Kurdish–Arab partnership of two equal federations in Iraq, with Kurdish influence entrenched through quota arrangements in the central government and international guarantees provided via UN recognition of a federation of Iraqi Kurdistan (Visser, 2010b, pp. 79–80). By the time of the invasion, the KRG was among the supporters of a united, albeit binational, post-Saddam Iraq in which Kurdistan remained an autonomous region, though not making sovereign claims over control of the local oil industry or the need for a private military (Visser, 2010b, pp. 79–80). However, during the Anglo-American occupation and particularly under the administration of Paul Bremer (2003–2004), the US managed to alienate the Kurds in the negotiations surrounding the drafting of the Transitional Administrative Law (TAL). Bremer's ideal was a federation based on the pre-existing 18 governorates of Iraq, which necessarily would cause the division of the KRG and its local institutions (Visser, 2010b, p. 80). This proposal to establish legislative divisions within the KRG was seen as unacceptable and alienated the KDP and PUK who had worked so long for autonomy and who agreed on the need for a unified Kurdish front vis-à-vis the federal state. The CPA's stance under Bremer left Kurdish authorities open to the influence of Peter

Galbraith, a former US diplomat who became a formal adviser to, and lobby-ist for, the KRG in 2003. Galbraith and the KRG leaders devised a negotiating strategy that had the KRG demand control of natural resources, exclusive control of security and judicial supremacy within its territory, thereafter lobbying the CPA and US government to this end as well.[14] According to Galbraith (2006, p. 161), these demands were essentially rejected in the final formulation of the TAL, which led the Kurds to adopt a harder line when negotiating the draft of the permanent constitution in 2005. However, the TAL established Iraq as a federal state in which Kurdistan retained its autonomy:

> The Kurdistan Regional Government is recognized as the official govern-ment of the territories that were administered by that government on 19 March 2003 in the governorates of Dohuk, Arbil, Sulaimaniya, Kirkuk, Diyala and Neneveh. The term "Kurdistan Regional Government" shall refer to the Kurdistan National Assembly, the Kurdistan Council of Ministers, and the regional judicial authority in the Kurdistan region.
>
> (Appendix 2)

Thus, Kurdistan developed a separate economic, political, judicial and interna-tional infrastructure, all built within the Iraqi federal system. The KRG negotiates its own contracts with foreign companies in spite of the al-Mâlikî government's insistence that such acts are unconstitutional; it holds its own elections for its executive and legislative bodies; it maintains its own set of laws and courts; it hosts over 30 consulates and trade missions (Department of Foreign Relations, KRG, n.d. a); and it has representation in 14 countries (Department of Foreign Relations, KRG, n.d. b). Moreover, the KRG has established itself as a highly influential political force within the central Iraqi government and a united, cohe-sive bloc in the Iraqi parliament, as a needed component in coalitions and as an arbiter (for example, the Arbil agreement in 2010) (Visser, 2012, p. 238), despite a blatant interest in weakening the power of the central government of Iraq and pilfering it.[15] Iraq's Kurds, long culturally distinct within Iraq, have increasingly, particularly in the post-1991 era, developed degrees of political and economic autonomy. This historical trajectory of Iraqi Kurdistan has placed it in the unu-sual position of being *in* Iraq while not necessarily being *of* Iraq. Any discussion of Kurdish affairs within Iraq, hence, needs to be considered from a position of distinction; while Kurdistan remains legally within Iraq, its development has increasingly rendered it a matter to be discussed separately from Iraq generally.

Foraging for legitimacy: the occupation's Interim Governing Council

In an effort to gloss an acceptable Iraqi cover for the occupation effort, the CPA established the Interim Governing Council to serve as a legitimating authority. In search of its component leadership, Ayad 'Allâwî was allowed to initiate the INC. While 'Allâwî suffered from a lack of popular support and legitimacy,

32 Deconstruction and reconstruction of the state

he had decades of experience marshaling anti-regime efforts from abroad and maintained close ties to US and Arab Gulf leaders. On August 18, 2004, the INC was heralded as an effort to bestow legitimacy on the interim regime by allowing broader representation in state institutions. Instead it widened and deepened political fractures in Iraqi society. In order to enhance the legitimacy of the interim government, the INC would have had to elect a Council more representative of significant segments of Iraq's national political forces in place of such popular support or in recognition of the various strands of political opposition found within Iraq. While it incorporated the two main Kurdish political forces of northern Iraq, the KDP and PUK, it nonetheless marginalized many Arab political forces, incorporating in their place the expatriate Iraqis who returned on the heels of the US occupation. National political forces in Iraq's central and southern regions were largely composed of Sunni and Shi'ite Arab rejectionists who opposed the occupation. Within the Arab rejectionist camp, up to August 2004, the Hawza had represented the main Shi'ite body, and the Sunni Muslim Clerics' [Scholars'] Association the main Sunni body. In addition to the rejectionist camp, indigenous political forces included a number of smaller civil society groups organized around the interests of ethnic and religious minorities, tribal leaders who all sought a greater role in the transition, as well as a small but sophisticated number of political parties of a secular nationalist orientation. Thus, rather than opting for a policy of inclusion of national forces, the parties that have controlled the transition (the US and expatriate Iraqis) created the Iraqi Governing Council (IGC) in their image to work with the US occupation forces through 'Allâwî's regime. This exclusion of significant national political forces from the nation-building process alienated many of the social groupings that would have liked to have been a part of the discussion on the future of Iraq, which in turn increased the legitimacy of the rejectionist camp amongst all Iraqis. Moreover, in protest of the Fallujah siege, the Islamic Party, Iraq's most influential Sunni political group, withdrew from the government, and the Sunni Muslim Clerics' Association urged Iraqis to boycott the planned January 2005 elections. Leaders of the Iraqi Islamic Party also cited security as a reason for withdrawing the Sunni Party's slate of 275 candidates. Insurgents carried out around 260 attacks on election locations, including nine suicide bombings, ultimately resulting in more than 40 deaths (Carroll & Howard, 2005). By mid-November 2004, 47 political parties and groups had already declared their boycott of the elections, citing that the election plans "[do] not speak for the Iraqi people as long as [they are] 'imposed' by the US-backed interim government and rejected by a clear majority" (Cole, 2004). Even in the Kurdish region, support for an early election was modified to assume a middle course between the Sunni demand for delaying the election and the urging of Shi'ites (under Ayatollah al-Sistânî's guidance) for no delays in the expression of democratic rights. Mas'ûd Barzânî, leader of the KDP, informed the UN envoy that, "while we are ready for the election on January 30, we will not oppose its delay [...] if that will ensure a more comprehensive and inclusive election" (Azzaman (Baghdad), 2004). In response, 42 political parties connected to al-Hawza and Ayatollah al-Sistânî rejected any delay (Sly & al-Jarrah, 2004). In effect, the occupation's ill-conceived sequencing following the emergence of a predictable opposition to Anglo-American rule thereby came to reflect an emerging split along sectarian lines. According to a Knight Ridder report on December 27, 2004, even the Shi'ite bloc was divided as to the form of government. A secular democracy was championed by al-Ṣadr and Aḥmad Chalabî, but a more focused religious-oriented government was advocated by the Da'wa Party and the Supreme Council for Islamic Revolution in Iraq (SCIRI) (Allam, 2004). As violence continued to escalate in the Sunni triangle and the north, in November and December 2004, 17 major political parties called for the elections to be delayed, including the acting Prime Minister's Al-Wifâq al-Waṭanî Party and the Iraqi Islamic Party. Mohsen Abdul Hamid, head of the Iraqi Islamic Party, told reporters in Baghdad:

> We asked to postpone the election long ago because we believe the security situation in the country is not suitable to hold elections, and the Iraqis don't understand the elections yet. We need enough time, at least six months, to prepare ourselves because the security issue is very complicated.
>
> (Vick, 2004)

Further, the Sunni Muslim Clerics' Association urged Iraqis to boycott the planned January elections.

With the escalating insurgency, US military tactics were increasingly meeting vociferous opposition around the globe. The cumulative impact of the Najaf and Fallujah campaigns indicated that the US was losing the war in Iraq politically. Reflecting the increasing international opposition to the US occupation of Iraq, on September 16, 2004, UN Secretary General Kofi Annan told the BBC that the US-led invasion of Iraq had been illegal, and warned that "[there could not be] credible elections if the security conditions continue as they are" (Excerpts: Annan interview, 2004). And on November 17 the UN High Commissioner for Human Rights, Louise Arbour, called for an investigation into the allegedly disproportionate use of force and strikes against civilians in Fallujah (UN Seeks Probe into Fallujah War Crimes, 2004). Additionally, in the Arab world, US policy in Iraq was increasingly being compared to Israeli policy in the West Bank and Gaza. Two 2004 opinion polls, one commissioned by the Arab American Institute and the other by the University of Maryland and Zogby International, reported an increasing anti-American sentiment among all ages across the Arab world as a response to US foreign policy and the occupation of Iraq under the leadership of President Bush (Dawoud, 2004). According to the Arab American Institute (2004, p. 5) poll, the first thought "America" brought to mind for the majority of those polled was overwhelmingly "unfair foreign policy." Such pressures required that both Iraqi sovereignty was warranted and US timeframes for engagement in the reconstruction needed to be shortened; this at a time when insurgency actions were rapidly increasing and the Bush Administration blurred the "Global War on Terror" with the violence in Iraq. As we shall see, such entanglements were the outcome of poor planning as well as more than a decade of US policy, which

34 *Deconstruction and reconstruction of the state*

devastated the Iraqi populace prior to the 2003 regime change, and culminated in the destruction of the Iraqi state by Anglo-American military force and its expansive occupation under the CPA.

Conclusion

During the era of Cold War politics, economic sanctions had a lesser effect on countries than in the years following. When one side imposed economic sanctions, the other side undermined them (e.g. the US embargo on Cuba was mitigated by the Soviet Union). With the collapse of the Soviet Union, however, sanctions became an increasingly effective tool with regards to achieving political objectives. In the post-Cold War era, the suspension of state sovereignty has become commonplace as a means of "promoting democracy" by the remaining hegemonic state actor, namely the US. Iraq can be considered a prime case study of this strategy.

In the "post-Camp David" Middle East, Iraq represented a rejectionist Arab nationalist regime that—alongside neighboring Iran—formed a (nominal) threat to Israel and, moreover, a roadblock to American/Israeli hegemony over the region. In this sense, the US wars against Iraq in 1991 and 2003 were not separate events, but two violent bookends to the same conflict. The American intervention in Baghdad aspired to remove the hostile Ba'thist regime, ideally to replace it with a regime that would: (a) be amenable to America's regional interests related to oil production; (b) orient itself towards the "post-Camp David" accommodationist line vis-à-vis Israel; and (c) represent a check on Iranian regional power, as part of the US's "dual containment" strategy. Judged on those strategic goals, the US intervention in Iraq has been a failure, having produced a regime that, while more compliant than the preceding Ba'th regime, is deeply tied to its Iranian neighbor, who exert far more influence on the Iraqi government than at any point in modern history.

Nevertheless, the effect of this extended, multi-phased US war on Iraq has been devastating, particularly when mind is paid to the UN sanctions of the 1990s that served as a prelude to the 2003 war.[16] The overwhelming and far-reaching measures undertaken by the US under the auspices of the UN precipitated a downward spiral from which Iraq would not recover. According to Gordon (2010):

> The comprehensive nature of the embargo resulted in complex problems, in which one emergency situation triggered others, and there were no means to intervene in a way that could stop the chain of events. In response to the food shortages, for example, Iraq increased rice production. However, the conditions for the production of rice resulted in water stagnation; this in turn generated mosquitoes and malaria; but there was neither insecticide available to control the mosquitoes nor drugs available for the treatment of the malaria. There were complex ongoing crises in Iraq throughout the entire sanctions period.
>
> (p. 35)

The state of Iraq has yet to recover from the systematic destruction of its society and institutions. Despite near-record oil production and GDP estimated to be $360 billion by 2015 (Kami & Bayoumy, 2012), Iraq remains a country divided by sectarian and ethnic cleavages, paralyzed by the disconnect between elected officials and ordinary citizens, fearful of an all but certain future. The future prospects of the country are grim. Iraq's youth component is the fastest growing in the country, with 16.6 million, over 50 percent of Iraq's total population, under the age of 18. Of these 16.6 million, 1 in 6 are orphans, and not a single one has experienced life in the absence of sanctions, war or both.

Notes

1 Equivalent to nearly £2.2 billion in 2012 (Browning, n.d.).
2 Earlier formulations of tear gas more commonly caused permanent blindness or even death than those of today.
3 See Ali et al. (2003) and Jones (1999) for more analysis of the survey's findings.
4 The war began on March 20, 2003 and Baghdad was captured by the coalition on April 10, 2003, 21 days later.
5 See Fattah (2004) for an account of the destruction and pillaging of academic institutions in Iraq.
6 For more on the human costs of the Gulf war, the sanctions period and the Iraq war see Chapter 6.
7 In Iraq, 'Allâwî is jokingly referred to as "the Mayor of Baghdad" as a result of his political impotence.
8 The size of the population varies from 250,000 to 350,000, depending upon the source; and the size of the population remaining in Fallujah when the ground assault was initiated also varies. The figure cited here is the most conservative estimate. According to an article by James Cogan (2004) the US military estimated that between 100,000 and 150,000 civilians were still in Fallujah when the ground assault was initiated.
9 See also Mike Whitney's *Firebombing Fallujah* (2004).
10 For further details on nation-building theories, see Geuss (2001), Hippler (2002) and Sørensen (2001, pp. 19–20, 75–80).
11 On state-building theory, see Fukuyama (2004) and Geert (1963).
12 See Chapter 4 for more on the 1992 conference of the INC.
13 See Chapter 4 for more on the London conference.
14 It is also worth noting that these new negating points would serve the personal and business interests of Galbraith, who came to work as a Mediator for DNO, a Norwegian oil company, and won a contract for them from the KRG in the spring of 2004 (Glanz, 2009).
15 The Kurdistan Alliance voted unanimously in favor of the retirement law (Going Global, 2014), which provides MPs with incredibly lavish retirement benefits. See Chapter 5.
16 See Ricks (2006) for more on US foreign policy vis-à-vis Iraq.

References

Agresto, J. (2007). *Mugged by Reality: The liberation of Iraq and the failure of good intentions*. Jackson, TN: Encounter Books.

36 Deconstruction and reconstruction of the state

Al-Ali, Z. (2014). *The Struggle for Iraq's Future: How corruption, incompetence, and sectarianism have undermined democracy.* New Haven: Yale University Press.

Ali, M. M., Blacker, J., & Jones, G. (2003). Annual Mortality Rates and Excess Deaths of Children Under Five in Iraq, 1991–98. *Population Studies, 57*(2), 217–226.

Allam, H. (2004, December 27). *Iraq's Shiite Leaders Disagree on Whether New Government Should be Religious or Secular.* Retrieved December 28, 2004, from Knight Ridder: www.kansas.com/mld/kansas/news/special-packages/iraq/10508314.htm.

Arab American Institute. (2004). *Impressions of America.* Retrieved January 27, 2014, from Arab American Institute: www.aaiusa.org/page/-/Polls/ArabOpinion/ImpressionsOfAmerica_2004.pdf

Azzaman (Baghdad) (2004, November 30).

Batatu, H. (1978). *The Old Social Classes and the Revolutionary Movements in Iraq.* Princeton, NJ: Princeton University Press.

Bremer, L. P., & McConnell, M. (2006). *My Year in Iraq: The struggle to build a future of hope.* New York: Simon and Schuster.

Browning, R. (n.d.). *Historic Inflation Calculator.* Retrieved January 14, 2014, from This is Money: www.thisismoney.co.uk/money/bills/article-1633409/Historic-inflation-calculator-value-money-changed-1900.html

Bush, G. W. (2003, November 6). *President Bush Discusses Freedom in Iraq and the Middle East.* Retrieved January 27, 2014, from The White House: http://georgewbush-whitehouse.archives.gov/news/releases/2003/11/20031106-2.html

Carroll, R., & Howard, M. (2005, January 31). *Allawi Woos Minorities With Call for Unity.* Retrieved July 2, 2013, from *The Guardian*: www.theguardian.com/world/2005/feb/01/iraq.rorycarroll?INTCMP=SRCH

Chomsky, N. (2003). *Hegemony or Survival: America's quest for global dominance.* New York: Henry Holt.

Cogan, J. (2004, November 11). *US Assault Leaves Fallujah in Ruins and Unknown Numbers Dead.* Retrieved January 6, 2014, from World Wide Socialist Web Site: www.wsws.org/en/articles/2004/11/fall-n11.html

Cole, J. (2004, November 18). *Election Boycott Announced Forty Seven.* Retrieved from Informed Comment: www.juancole.com/2004/11/election-boycott-announced-forty-seven.html

Daragahi, B. (2004, December). *US Bombing Marks Return of Fallujah's Displaced People.* Retrieved January 6, 2014, from Cambridge Solidarity With Iraq (CASI): www.casi.org.uk/analysis/2004/msg00532.html

Dawoud, K. (2004, August). *Arab Opinions.* Retrieved June 19, 2013, from *Al-Ahram Weekly*: http://weekly.ahram.org.eg/2004/701/in2.htm

Department of Foreign Relations, KRG. (n.d. a). *Current International Offices in the Kurdistan Region.* Retrieved February 15, 2014, from Kurdistan Regional Government: http://dfr.krg.org/p/p.aspx?p=37&l=12&s=020100&r=363

Department of Foreign Relations, KRG. (n.d. b). *KRG Offices Abroad.* Retrieved February 15, 2014, from Kurdistan Regional Government: http://dfr.krg.org/p/p.aspx?p=40&l=12&s=020100&r=364

Docena, H. (2004). Silent Battalions of "Democracy." *Middle East Report, 232,* 14–21.

Dulami, E., Faraj, C., & Tawfeeq, M. (2005, February 14). *Shiite Alliance Wins Plurality in Iraq.* Retrieved July 2, 2013, from CNN: www.cnn.com/2005/WORLD/meast/02/13/iraq.main/

Excerpts: Annan interview. (2004, September 16). Retrieved January 6, 2014, from BBC News: http://news.bbc.co.uk/2/hi/middle_east/3661640.stm

Fafo. (2005). *Iraqi Living Conditions Survey 2004*. Baghdad: Central Organization for Statistics and Information Technology. Retrieved January 6, 2014, from www.fafo.no/ais/middeast/iraq/imira/Tabulation%20reports/eng%20analytical%20report.pdf

Fattah, H. (2004). Iraqi Universities and Libraries: One year after the occupation. *Middle East Studies Association Bulletin, 38*(1), 24–27.

Filkins, D., & Glanz, J. (2004, November 8). *With Airpower and Armor, Troops Enter Rebel-Held City*. Retrieved June 4, 2013, from *The New York Times*: www.nytimes.com/2004/11/08/international/08CND_IRAQ.html?_r=0

Fukuyama, F. (2004). *State-Building: Governance and world order in the 21st century*. New York: Cornell University Press.

Galbraith, P. W. (2006). *The End of Iraq*. New York: Simon & Schuster.

Geert, C. (ed.). (1963). *Old Societies and New States: The quest for modernity in Asia and Africa*. New York: Free Press of Glencoe.

Geuss, R. (2001). The State. In R. Geuss, *History and Illusion in Politics* (pp. 14–68). Cambridge: Cambridge University Press.

Glanz, J. (2009, November 11). *U.S. Adviser to Kurds Stands to Reap Oil Profits*. Retrieved March 3, 2014, from *The New York Times*: www.nytimes.com/2009/11/12/world/middleeast/12galbraith.html?_r=0

Going Global. (2014, February 15). *Iraq's Pension Law*. Retrieved February 15, 2014, from Going Global: http://goingglobaleastmeetswest.blogspot.ca/2014/02/iraqs-pension-law-send-pension-law-to.html

Gordon, J. (2010). *Invisible War: The United States and the Iraq sanctions*. Cambridge, MA: Harvard University Press.

Grange, A. D. (2004, June 25). *The Liberation of Baghdad is not Far Away*. Retrieved January 12, 2013, from *Asia Times*: www.atimes.com/atimes/Middle_East/FF25Ak07.html

Hadar, L. T. (1998). Pax Americana's Four Pillars of Folly. *Journal of Palestine Studies, 26*(3), 49–59.

Hagopian, A., Flaxman, A. D., Takaro, T. K., Esa Al Shatari, S. A., Rajaratnam, J., Becker, S., et al. (2013). Mortality in Iraq Associated with the 2003–2011 War and Occupation: Findings from a national cluster sample survey by the University Collaborative Iraq Mortality Study. *PLOS Medicine, 10*(10), 1–15.

Hippler, J. (2002). *Ethnicity, State, and Nation-Building*. Retrieved January 6, 2014, from Jochen Hippler: www.jochenhippler.de/html/ethnicity-_state-_and_nation-building.html

Ismael, J. S., Ismael, T. Y., & Baker, R. W. (2004). Iraq and Human Development: Culture, education and the globalization of hope. *Arab Studies Quarterly, 26*(2), 49–66.

Ismael, T. Y. (2001). *Middle East Politics Today: Government and civil society*. Gainesville: University of Florida Press.

Ismael, T. Y., & Ismael, J. S. (1999). Cowboy Warfare, Biological Diplomacy: Disarming metaphors as weapons of mass destruction. *Politics and the Life Sciences, 18*(1), 70–78.

Ismael, T. Y., & Ismael, J. S. (2004). *The Iraqi Predicament: People in the quagmire of power politics*. London: Pluto Press.

Ismael, T. Y., & Ismael, J. S. (2011). *Government and Politics of the Contemporary Middle East*. London: Routledge.

Jabar, F. A. (1995). *Al-Dawla, al-Mugtam'a al-Madani wa al-Tahawul al-Demokrati fi al Iraq, Markaz Ibn Khaldoun li al-dirasat al-Inma'iyya*. Cairo: Ibn Khaldoun Center.

38 Deconstruction and reconstruction of the state

Jabar, F. A. (2004, April 14). *Formative Forces in the Development of the Modern Iraqi State*. Retrieved from US Institute of Peace: www.usip.org/events/formative-forces-in-the-development-the-modern-iraqi-sta

Jones, G. (1999, July 23). *Iraq—Under-Five Mortality*. Retrieved January 8, 2014, from Federation of American Scientists: www.fas.org/news/iraq/1999/08/irqu5est.pdf

Kadhim, A. (2013, June 19). *Comment: Al-Sistani's triumph*. Retrieved June 19, 2013, from Al-Ahram Weekly: http://weekly.ahram.org.eg/print/2004/706/re6.htm

Kami, A., & Bayoumy, Y. (2012, February 19). *Iraq Sees at Least 9.4 Percent GDP Growth to 2016: Central bank*. Retrieved October 27, 2013, from Reuters: www.reuters.com/article/2012/02/19/us-iraq-economy-gdp-idUSTRE81I07320120219

Kay, J. (2004, December 3). *After Fallujah's Destruction: US occupation force to reach 150,000*. Retrieved January 6, 2014, from World Socialist Website: https://www.wsws.org/en/articles/2004/12/iraq-d03.html

Klein, N. (2004, November 13). *You Asked for My Evidence, Mr. Ambassador. Here it is*. Retrieved January 6, 2014, from *The Guardian*: www.theguardian.com/world/2004/dec/04/iraq.usa

Liu, H. C. (2004, August 18). *Geopolitics in Iraq: An old game*. Retrieved January 12, 2013, from *Asia Times*: www.atimes.com/atimes/Middle_East/FH18Ak02.html

Matthews, W. C. (2011). The Kennedy Administration, Counterinsurgency, and Iraq's First Ba'thist Regime. *International Journal of Middle East Studies, 43*(4), 635–653.

McCarthy, R., & Mansour, O. (2004, December 15). *Seven Killed in Repeat Suicide Attack*. Retrieved January 8, 2014, from *The Guardian*: www.theguardian.com/world/2004/dec/15/iraq.rorymccarthy

Rashid, A. W. (2002). *al-Iraq al-Mu'asir*. Damascus: al-Mada.

Reuters. (2008, January 30). *Iraq Conflict has Killed a Million, Says Survey*. Retrieved January 13, 2014, from Reuters: http://uk.reuters.com/article/2008/01/30/idUKL30488579._CH_.242020080130

Ricks, T. (2006). *Fiasco: The American military adventure in Iraq*. New York: Penguin Press.

Roberts, L., Lafta, R., Garfield, R., Khudhairi, J., & Burnham, G. (2004). Mortality Before and After the 2003 Invasion of Iraq: Cluster sample survey. *The Lancet, 364*(9448), 1857–1864.

Sa'id, A. K. (1999). *Iraq 8 Shibat 1963: Min Hiwar al-Mafahim ila Hiwar ad-Damm, Muraja'at fi Dhakirat Talib Shabib*. Beirut: Dar al-Kunuz al-Adabiyah.

Schmit, E. (2004, December 15). *Cargo Flights Added to Cut Risky Land Trips*. Retrieved January 6, 2014, from *The New York Times*: www.nytimes.com/2004/12/15/politics/15military.html

Schwartz, M. (2004, December 16). *America's Sinister Plan for Fallujah*. Retrieved January 6, 2014, from Truthout: www.truth-out.org/archive/item/51288:michael-schwartz--americas-sinister-plan-for-fallujah

Shahzad, S. S. (2004, December 25). *Mosul Attack "an Inside Job."* Retrieved June 19, 2013, from *Asia Times*: www.atimes.com/atimes/Middle_East/FL25Ak01.html

Sivard, R. L. (1993). *World Military and Social Expenditures 1993*. Washington DC: World Priorities Inc.

Sly, L., & al-Jarrah, H. (2004, November 28). *Shiite Leaders Reject Calls to Delay Iraq Election*. Retrieved January 8, 2014, from *Chicago Tribune*: http://articles.chicagotribune.com/2004-11-28/news/0411280287_1_sunni-heartland-number-of-rebel-fighters-sunni-and-secular-parties

Sørensen, G. (2001). *Changes in Statehood: The transformation of international relations.* New York: Palgrave.

Teresi, D. (2002). *Lost Discoveries: The ancient roots of modern science from Babylonia to Maya.* New York: Simon & Schuster.

Ullman, H. K., & Wade, J. P. (1996). *Shock and Awe: Achieving rapid dominance.* Washington DC: National Defense University Press.

UN Office of the Iraq Programme. (2003, November 21). *Oil for Food: About the programme.* Retrieved January 6, 2014, from UN Office of the Iraq Programme: www. un.org/Depts/oip/background/fact-sheet.html

UN Seeks Probe into Fallujah War Crimes. (2004, November 16). Retrieved January 6, 2014, from Truthout: www.truth-out.org/archive/item/50779:un-seeks-probe-into-fallujah-war-crimes

UNICEF. (1999, August 12). *Iraq Surveys Show "Humanitarian Emergency."* Retrieved January 8, 2014, from UNICEF Information Newsline: www.unicef.org/newsline/99pr29.htm

United Nations Development Programme (UNDP). (2000). *1999–2000 Report, Iraq Country Office.* Retrieved January 6, 2014, from http://mirror.undp.org/iraq/PDF/REPORT.PDF

UNSC. (1991, April 8). *United Nations Security Council Resolution 687—S/RES/687 (1991).* Retrieved January 27, 2014, from Federation of American Scientists: www.fas. org/news/un/iraq/sres/sres0687.htm

US Army Base Hit in Mosul. (2004, December 22). Retrieved January 6, 2014, from Al Jazeera: www.aljazeera.com/archive/2004/12/200849164011766669.html

US Claims Success in Fallujah Offensive. (2004, November 18). Retrieved January 6, 2014, from Raidió Teilifís Éireann (RTÉ): www.rte.ie/news/2004/1118/56918-iraq/

Vick, K. (2004, December 28). *Sunni Party Pulls out of Iraq Vote as Doubts Grow.* Retrieved June 13, 2013, from *The Washington Post*: www.washingtonpost.com/wp-dyn/articles/A28323-2004Dec27.html

Visser, R. (2010a). The Territorial Aspect of Sectarianism in Iraq. *International Journal of Contemporary Iraqi Studies, 4*(3), 295–304.

Visser, R. (2010b). The Kurdish Issue in Iraq: A view from Baghdad at the close of the Maliki premiership. *World Affairs, 43*(1), 77–93.

Visser, R. (2012). The Emasculation of Government Ministries in Consociational Democracies: The case of Iraq. *International Journal of Contemporary Iraqi Studies, 6*(2), 231–242.

Voice of Kurdistan. (2012). *Kurdistan Alliance: If not Talibani and Barzânî what was the Prime Minister of the Dawa Party.* Retrieved February 18, 2014, from Kurdistan Radio: www.kurdistanradio.net/index.php?Page=Articles&cmd=4&id=38270&Lang=En

Watenpaugh, K., Méténier, E., Hansee, J., & Fattah, H. (2003). *Opening the Doors: Intellectual life and academic conditions in post-war Baghdad.* Retrieved January 6, 2014, from The Iraqi Observatory: www.h-net.org/about/press/opening_doors/opening_doors.pdf

Weinstein, M. A. (2004, August 24). *The Iraqi National Conference: Legitimation failure.* Retrieved June 19, 2013, from aliraqi: www.aliraqi.org/forums/showthread. php?t=35808

Whitney, M. (2004). *Firebombing Fallujah.* Retrieved December 10, 2004, from Zmag: http://www.zmag.org/content/showarticle.cfm?SectionID=15&ItemID=6772

3 Killing the state and undermining the nation

From the outset, the invasion and occupation of Iraq in 2003 was defended on the grounds of Iraq's alleged possession of WMDs and its ties to the terrorist organization al-Qaeda. Both claims turned out to be false, and instead the American enterprise in Iraq was retroactively justified as a campaign of regional democratic transformation. In reality, however, it gave rise to an inferno of violence, with Iraqi civilian deaths numbering in the hundreds of thousands.[1] The end of the Ba'thist dictatorship in Iraq did not give way to liberal democracy. Instead, the result was a reconfiguration of Iraqi society and politics on explicitly sectarian lines, with political authority and decision-making modulated by the sectarian balance of power. Regionally, the invasion of Iraq and the unfolding developments amplified sectarian tensions, with Jordanian King Abdullah warning of an incipient "Shia crescent" threatening the region (Black, 2007), while Saudi King Abdullah—in a conversation with his American interlocutor—exhorted an attack on Iran to "cut off the head of the [Shia] snake" (Colvin, 2010). As it happened, American efforts to constrain Iranian regional influence were in fact undermined by its invasion of Iraq, which provided an opportunity for Iranian-affiliated political parties/militias to emerge as the dominant forces in post-invasion Iraq, increasing Iranian regional clout.

From 2010 onward, with popular protest spreading throughout the Middle East, optimism reigned as it appeared a democratic moment had taken the region, resulting in the overthrow of Tunisia's Ben Ali, Egypt's Hosni Mubarak and—with the intervention of NATO—Libya's Gaddafi. Where opposition protests in Syria gave way to violent government repression and resulted in a civil war, the moment of democratic hope receded as militant sectarianism—seen earlier in Iraq—appeared in the Syrian theater, creating a sectarian conflict fanned by Iran, Saudi Arabia and Qatar, and drawing in Iraq, Lebanon and Turkey (Arango, 2012; Sherlock, 2012). In this sense, the sectarian upsurge that emerged in post-invasion Iraq has increasingly engulfed the region.

Thus, the upsurge of sectarianism and religion–state conflict developed into a regional problem with several flashpoints, Iraq most prominently. By December 2011, the US formally ended their "mission" in Iraq, coinciding with the overthrow of the US-client regime in Egypt, headed by Hosni Mubarak. Mubarak was followed by the short-lived tenure of President Mohamed Morsi, whose Freedom and Justice Party had close ties with the Islamist Muslim Brotherhood. In 2013, a military coup removed Morsi from office; however, this move only served to radicalize the Islamist current in Egypt, with violence against the military and police and the bombing of government buildings following (Kirkpatrick, 2014). This radicalization runs parallel to developments throughout the region: the continued descent of Iraq into sectarian chaos; the growth of Iranian influence throughout the region, at cross-purposes with the interests of Saudi Arabia and the Arab Gulf states; the attempt of Turkey to negotiate a path between its Islamic commitments and a desire to play a mediator's role in the region; and the descent of Syria into internecine civil war.

With Iraq at the center of the chaos that engulfed the region in the twenty-first century, it is difficult to comprehend the motivations of American strategic planners that drove that country to its Iraqi campaign. Indeed, Richard Haass, the director of policy planning in the State Department during President Bush's first term, claimed: "I will go to my grave not fully understanding why" (Haass, 2009, p. 234). Haass' disclaimer is reflective of a category of explanation that implies non-rational or irrational causes (i.e. invisible hand of the market, God or Mother Nature; or personal culpability such as insanity or stupidity). Another category of explanation implies totally rational actors with a grand design and long-range goals. Reflecting this approach, one active participant in the Iraqi Shi'i opposition, Faiq al-Shaikh 'Ali, maintained that there was a deliberate US strategy to transfer al-Qaeda from the difficult terrain of Afghanistan to "the flat land [of Iraq]" and

> find a Muslim group to fight the Sunni extremists [...] The sect chosen for this was the Shia, to be helped logistically by Syria and Iran, while it would be made easier for al-Qaeda to penetrate Iraq through the neighbouring countries [...] The US implemented this strategy by keeping the borders of Iraq open and unguarded on all sides in 2003. In addition, both Syria and Iran did everything possible to gather, train and eventually facilitate al-Qaeda's entry into Iraq in order to feed the grinder [...] The Americans overthrew Saddam and delivered the state to the Iraqi Shia, who are agents of Iran, in order to make it possible for them to coordinate with Syria, Iran, and Lebanon in fighting al-Qaeda on behalf of the US; and this is the reason for the overthrow of Saddam.
>
> ('Ali, 2013)

While the question of the motivations behind US policy in invading and occupying Iraq are beyond the scope of this study, this chapter examines the ideological, structural and economic context of the Anglo-American invasion of Iraq, and considers the consequences of developments that arose in the aftermath of the invasion. It begins with a consideration of the ideology of American militarism and the rise of the neoconservative current.

42   *Deconstruction and reconstruction of the state*

American militarism and the neoconservatives

The roots of American militarism can arguably be traced back to the 1898 mine explosion that sank the American battleship *USS Maine* in Havana. Then Assistant Secretary of the Navy, Theodore Roosevelt exploited the event for war propaganda against Spain, and the news media published a series of bellicose articles that seized the American people (Johnson, 2004, p. 40). At the end of his Presidency in 1909, the 16 first-class battleships that constituted the US navy returned home after the longest cruise in naval history, covering 45,000 miles around the world in an ostentatious display of power (Zimmermann, 2002, p. 3). Roosevelt's successor, Woodrow Wilson, who strongly believed that the US had an obligation to spread its principles and way of democracy to the rest of the world, laid the intellectual foundation for America's "global mission" to democratize the world. Wilson also provided the grounding for the rhetoric of humanitarian military intervention and supplied the assumptions and principles for contemporary ideologists who rationalize American imperial power in terms of the exporting of human rights and democracy (Johnson, 2004, pp. 47–48, 51). These were common refrains used by President George W. Bush in his justification of both the Afghanistan and Iraq campaigns more than a century later.

Although the military is an historically important institution of the modern nation-state, it is different from militarism as an ideological disposition, which places the institutional preservation of the armed forces ahead of national security or commitment to the integrity of governmental structure (Johnson, 2004, pp. 23–24). One indicator of militarism is the emergence of a professional army class that glorifies its ideals, a phenomenon that gained visibility in the US following the Vietnam War. On the political front, the leaders of a newly ascendant American conservatism (Reagan and Bush Senior in the 1980s) concluded that the main lesson from Vietnam was to relocate foreign policy to the realm of national security management, which could then operate without a prying media, the oversight of Congress, or the involvement of the public. This ultimately bred a class of professional militarists—both uniformed and civilian that visibly filled the senior level of the Executive, and operated in secrecy. Civilian militarists tend to be ideology-prone and display a ruthless warrior-culture, perhaps in compensation for their lack of genuine military and especially combat experience. This was conspicuous throughout the 2000s, whether in reference to the Iraq war, or the broader "war on terror" (Johnson, 2004, pp. 60–61).

The second hallmark of militarism is the preponderance of arms representatives and military officers in high positions in the government, and the consequent devotion to military preparedness rather than to policies that would prevent military confrontations. The Bush Administration exemplified this phenomenon. While no nation, or even group of nations, has the capacity to confront the US militarily, George Bush, nonetheless, in his inaugural address in 2001, said: "We will build our defenses beyond challenge, lest weakness invite challenge" (Bush, 2001). The Department of Defense budget for fiscal year 2001 was $306,075,000,000 (Executive Office of the President of the United States, 2002); yearly military

Killing the state and undermining the nation   43

expenditures have continued to grow, rising to more than (an estimated) $672 billion by fiscal year 2013 under President Barack Obama (Executive Office of the President of the United States, 2012).

An intricate confluence of constitutive mechanisms ensures the survival of the institution of militarism within the American social fabric. These mechanisms are mutually reinforcing and include, *inter alia*, a pervasive military recruiting apparatus that attracts the young (the age range of recruits lies primarily between adolescence and 24 years) into enlisting in the army, whether for reasons of patriotism, community/family tradition, or for lack of other opportunities (Johnson, 2004, pp. 97–99, 103, 106, 110–112). A second survival mechanism is the Pentagon–Hollywood nexus that goes back to 1927, whereby the film industry produces pro-war films that glorify American military adventures. The third device is the news media–military symbiosis, in which the former cultivates pro-military public sentiment, thwarting in the process potential public scrutiny, in return for the latter's provision of hot news that increases circulation, thereby increasing profits from commercial advertising. The fourth is the "Special Access Program," devoted to secret arms development, whose budget is beyond any public oversight and "whose operational details were known only to a few in the Pentagon, the C.I.A., and the White House" (Hersh, 2004, p. 16). The fifth bolster is comprised of the regional commanders in the four central command structures that gird the planet, and are commonly known as CENTCOM, in the Middle East; PACOM, in the Pacific; EUCOM, in Europe; and SOUTHCOM, in Latin America. These commanders not only exert more influence in their regions of operation than ambassadors and diplomatic missions, but they also shape the key ingredients of foreign policy, draw military strategy, oversee intelligence and supervise arms sales. The enormity of their power is easily adducible from an incident following the 1999 military coup d'état in Pakistan. President Clinton had contacted General Pervez Musharraf, the coup leader, and requested that Musharraf call him back. Instead, Musharraf called the head of CENTCOM, General Anthony Zinni, who most strongly supported Musharraf and who ignored the Congressional ban on aid to governments founded on coups (Johnson, 2004, pp. 112–115, 117–118, 124–126). A more recent example is that of General David Petraeus, who, as commander of US Central Command in Iraq and later as commander of US and ISAF forces in Afghanistan, would in his post-military career be installed as Director of the CIA by a unanimous Senate vote.

However, the institution of militarism cannot reproduce itself without the conditions conducive to continual war, which legitimizes militarism, while also requiring immediate replenishment to equipment and munitions that continuously feeds the arms industry and augments the military–industrial complex. Chris Hedges (2010) describes the current culture of "permanent war" in the US as

> the most effective mechanism used by the power elite to stifle reform and muzzle dissent. A state of war demands greater secrecy, constant vigilance and suspicion. It generates distrust and fear, especially in culture and art, often reducing it to silence or nationalist cant. It degrades and corrupts

44 *Deconstruction and reconstruction of the state*

education and the media. It wrecks the economy. It nullifies public opinion. And it forces liberal institutions to sacrifice their beliefs for a holy crusade, a kind of surrogate religion, whether it is against the Hun, the Bolshevik, the fascist, the communist, or the Islamic terrorist. The liberal class in a state of permanent war is rendered impotent.

(p. 19)

Domination-motivated war is the obverse of militarism, which, as an institution, can concoct and stage world-wide conditions for war, as were the cases of the Cold War, the war on drugs, so-called "humanitarian" wars, the war on terrorism, the democratization invasion of Iraq, and finally the US-led "responsibility to protect" intervention in Libya.[2] Thus, imperialism cannot survive without the support of a strong military machine that subdues resistance and the enabling finance of an economic structure that can sustain an expensive, expansive and unproductive military.

Toward the end of the Vietnam War, all economic indicators pointed toward the worrisome decline of the American economy, which ultimately culminated in turning the US into the largest debtor nation in the world. The US government responded by yielding to the reformulation of the two centuries-old notions of liberal economics into what became known as neoliberalism, the policies in support of which would shortly thereafter reinvigorate globalization. The main thrust of neoliberal thought is encouraging all-encompassing privatization and supporting the global role of multinational corporations (MNCs). As early as 1981, the US's main strategy was to maintain its world prominence by employing international institutions, like the General Agreement on Tariffs and Trade (GATT), the International Monetary Fund (IMF) and the World Bank, to break down trade barriers and state economic enterprises in favor of a neoliberal, global market economy (Johnson, 2004, pp. 259–260, 264, 266, 268–269). During the 1980s, proponents of American hegemony diverged into two groups: one, which the Clinton Administration represents, labeled its global military interventions as "humanitarian intervention," and camouflaged US hegemony under international economic institutions, multilateral military structures and support for the notion of globalization. The Clinton Administration was as militarist as that of Bush (Sr.) (Johnson, 2004, pp. 56, 67, 255, 268–269). The second group, which George W. Bush represents, and is usually referred to as "neoconservatives," advocates unilateral domination by deployment of the US's unmatched military capability. While militarism-based domination was camouflaged under the Clinton Administration, it gained further impetus and overtness from self-righteous notions propounded by neoconservative circles. In the case of President Obama, his foreign policy represents a hybrid, with a reliance on multilateral institution building and intervention and deployment of soft power in the form of lofty rhetoric, on the one hand, and an unabashed unilateralism, as with the accelerated "drone war" in Pakistan and numerous other locations, on the other. In the lead-up to the 2012 election, there proved to be little policy divergence between President Obama and his Republican challenger, then-Governor Mitt Romney, highlighting the fact that

Killing the state and undermining the nation 45

the foreign policy innovations of the Bush Presidency were largely integrated into the US military/security consensus under President Obama (Douthat, 2012).

The neoconservatives, who found themselves in a sort of exile following the collapse of the Soviet Union, re-emerged in the Bush Administration as champions of a post-9/11 global "war on terror," prominently advocating an attack on Iraq. The worldview of neoconservatives tends to be Manichean, in regards to its conception of good and evil, which accords well with both the thinking of the Christian Right and President Bush himself. The moral correctness, and indeed goodness, of the US is thought to be beyond question, and requires a unilateralist policy, lest, by subjecting its will to the wishes or agreements of other countries, or global institutions, the US might otherwise prevent itself from fulfilling its morally inspired, historic mission. They viewed the collapse of the Soviet Union as a new round of American messianism where there was now an opportunity to pursue an idealist policy of shaping the international environment according to American values. Among the neoconservatives, many believed democracy and capitalism to be "transportable and to have a transforming effect; through its implementation, in societies previously tribal or theocratic or otherwise afflicted by divisive and unrepresentative systems [...] populations could be led to become politically enlightened and economically prosperous" (Keegan, 2005, pp. 96–97). This belief was embodied in the work of Francis Fukuyama, who argued in his infamous article "The End of History?" (1989) that liberal democracy is the ultimate end-point of human socio-political development, even if it was not realized in the real world yet. Robert Kagan and William Kristol (2002) claimed the decision to take out Saddam would determine whether or not Fukuyama's thesis would be realized. Writing in January 2002, Kagan and Kristol (2002) argued the decision over whether or not to remove Saddam from power "will shape the contours of the emerging world order, perhaps for decades to come. Either it will be a world order conducive to our liberal democratic principles and our safety, or it will be one where brutal, well-armed tyrants are allowed to hold democracy and international security hostage" (Kagan & Kristol, 2002).[3]

While there may be some nuances in the neocons' application of these tenets, the security of Israel and the platform of its right wing are fundamental to all of them (Lobe, 2003). The policy of the neocons, in essence, reveals the same ideas of nineteenth-century America's "Manifest Destiny" and of its "Good Mission" and domination of the other, but with a further Israeli component. The paradox of the notion that overthrowing Saddam Hussein and instituting a government that would have friendly relations with Israel would have a domino effect on Iraq's neighbors, most notably Iran and Syria, while simultaneously supporting extremist politicians in Israel who opposed relations with Arab states, was not lost on critics. According to John Keegan, liberals and leftists "interpret the contradictions of neoconservative policy as an attempt to establish native versions of American democracy in the unreformed Arab states while supporting a selfishly Zionist regime in Israel" (Keegan, 2005, p. 97). The relationship between the neocons and Israel, in addition to pro-Israel lobby groups that operate in Washington, has been well documented by numerous scholars, including John Mearsheimer

46 *Deconstruction and reconstruction of the state*

and Stephen Walt (2007), who argue that, absent the efforts of Israel and the pro-Israel lobby, America would probably have not gone to war against Iraq at all.

Regime change, Iraq and the politics of hegemony in the Bush Administration

The official position of the Republican Party during the 2000 Republican National Convention called for the full implementation of the Iraq Liberation Act, which was passed by Congress and signed into law by President Clinton in 1998. The Act was a Congressional statement of policy calling for regime change in Iraq. The Republican Party Platform (2000) stated:

> We will react forcefully and unequivocally to any evidence of reconstituted Iraqi capabilities for producing weapons of mass destruction. In 1998, Congress passed and the president signed the Iraq Liberation Act, the clear purpose of which is to assist the opposition to Saddam Hussein [...] We support the full implementation of the Iraq Liberation Act, which should be regarded as a starting point in a comprehensive plan for the removal of Saddam Hussein and the restoration of international inspections in collaboration with his successor. Republicans recognize that peace and stability in the Persian Gulf is impossible as long as Saddam Hussein rules Iraq.

In September of the same year, a document published by the think tank Project for a New American Century (PNAC), *Rebuilding America's Defenses: Strategies, Forces and Resources*, was signed by the incoming Bush Administration and its principal advisers (Vice President Dick Cheney, Secretary of Defense Donald Rumsfeld, Deputy Secretary of Defense Paul Wolfowitz, Secretary of State [and former National Security Adviser] Condoleezza Rice and Vice President Dick Cheney's Chief of Staff Lewis "Scooter" Libby). The report strongly underlined the importance of US global dominance and set about a strategy to increase and maintain it. Furthermore, the document strongly argued the case for maintaining a global US pre-eminence that precluded the rise of any rival power, and for shaping the international order in line with American principles and interests as far into the future as possible, essentially calling for the creation of a global *Pax Americana*. It maintained that one of the primary short-term objectives for the American military was the "fighting and winning [of] multiple large-scale wars" (Project for a New American Century, 2000). The RAD document argued that the US ought to play a permanent and unchallenged role in Gulf regional security for decades.

The logic of the plan to invade Iraq is embedded in the US geopolitical strategy that sees Iraq as central not only to the control of the Gulf's vast oil resources, but central to regional development. By invading Iraq and engineering the emergence of an American-oriented regime, the war planners imagined they could isolate major pockets of opposition to Israel and to American hegemony in the Middle East. The policy was also aimed at subverting Iran to achieve a regime change, as Iran is seen to be a potential regional hegemon, rich in oil and gas, and opposes the policies of the US and Israel in the region. The roots of the plan go back more than a decade. "During the 1990s the notion of toppling Saddam's regime was championed by a circle of neoconservative thinkers, led by Richard Perle, a former assistant secretary of defense for international security policy under President Reagan" (Burrough et al., 2004). The neoconservative framework for US foreign policy was cast in 1990 by a team set up by then Secretary of Defense Dick Cheney after the fall of the Berlin Wall to re-cast American foreign policy in a unipolar world. Membership in this group included Paul Wolfowitz, Lewis Libby and Eric Edelman. Wolfowitz presented a proposal for "Defense Planning Guidance" (DPG), written by Zalmay Khalilzad and Abram Shulsky, that impressed Cheney so much that he "briefed President Bush, using material mostly from DPG, from which George H. W. Bush prepared a major foreign-policy address. But he delivered it on [...] the day that Iraq invaded Kuwait, so nobody noticed" (Lemann, 2002, p. 43). However, when a draft version of the Wolfowitz document itself was leaked to the *New York Times* in 1992, it was met with outrage for its bellicose language and unilateral position. In it, Wolfowitz declared a robust and aggressive US military posture for the post-Cold War era that American journalist Bill Keller (2002) describes as so

> that with the demise of the Soviet Union, the United States doctrine should be to assure that no new superpower arose to rival America's benign domination of the globe. The US would defend its unique status both by being militarily powerful beyond challenge and by being such a constructive force that no one would want to challenge us. We would participate in coalitions, but they would be "ad hoc." The US would be "postured to act independently when collective action cannot be orchestrated." The guidance envisioned pre-emptive attacks against states bent on acquiring nuclear, biological or chemical weapons. It was accompanied by illustrative scenarios of hypothetical wars for which the military should be prepared. One of them was another war against Iraq, where Saddam had already rebounded from his Gulf-War defeat and was busily crushing domestic unrest.

Prior to joining the Bush Administration, Wolfowitz (2000) published an article in *The National Interest* arguing that US power needed to be flexed, "by demonstrating that your friends will be protected and taken care of, that your enemies will be punished and that those who refuse to support you will live to regret having done so." Wolfowitz would later become known as "a major architect of President Bush's Iraq policy and, within the Administration, its most passionate and compelling advocate" (Boyer, 2004).

When Dick Cheney became vice president in 2001, his team, much like him, was made up predominantly of neoconservatives. In addition to Wolfowitz, Libby and Perle, the Cheney team included William Luti, who served under Newt Gingrich, and held the position of the Chief of Middle Eastern Policy in the Pentagon; Stephen J. Hadley, a former member of the first President Bush

48 Deconstruction and reconstruction of the state

Administration; Douglas Feith, former special counsel to Richard Perle when he was Assistant Secretary of Defense under Ronald Reagan, and later Under Secretary of Defense for policy at the Pentagon; and David Wurmser, another Perle associate.[4]

Richard Clarke, who served under seven presidents as a counter-terrorism expert and was the National Coordinator for Security and Counter-Terrorism for both Presidents Clinton and George W. Bush, claimed that Paul Wolfowitz had been pushing for an invasion of Iraq in spite of contradictory evidence from the CIA and other intelligence agencies and that such a link between the Iraqi regime and al-Qaeda was unwarranted. Moreover, Wolfowitz insisted publicly that al-Qaeda was incapable of pulling off a major operation on American soil by itself (Clarke, 2004, pp. 231–232). Clarke (2004, pp. 30, 231–232) pointed out that Wolfowitz maintained the position that al-Qaeda had been sponsored by Iraq, a stance he had held since the 1993 attack on the World Trade Center (WTC), despite the lack of any available evidence.[5] Immediately following the 9/11 attacks on the WTC in 2001, both Rumsfeld and Wolfowitz, along with a handful of supporters, utilized the opportunity to transform the event into momentum for their longstanding objectives in Iraq. Clarke (2004) wrote:

> The administration of the second George Bush did begin with Iraq on its agenda [...] Paul Wolfowitz had urged a focus on Iraqi-sponsored terrorism against the US even though there was no such thing. In 2001 more and more the talk was of Iraq, of CENTCOM [Central Command] being asked to plan to invade.
>
> (p. 264)

Indeed, over a decade after 9/11, accumulated reports suggest that the Administration's obsession with the phantom threat of Iraq blinded it to the very real threat that would arrive in the 9/11 terrorist attacks by al-Qaeda:

> The direct warnings to Mr. Bush about the possibility of al Qaeda attack began in the spring of 2001. By May 1, the Central Intelligence Agency told the White House of a report that "a group presently in the United States" was planning a terrorist operation. Weeks later, on June 22, the daily brief reported that Qaeda strikes could be "imminent" [...] But some in the administration considered the warning to be just bluster. An intelligence official and a member of the Bush administration both told me in interviews that the neoconservative leaders who had recently assumed power at the Pentagon were warning the White House that the C.I.A. had been fooled; according to this theory, Bin Laden was merely pretending to be planning an attack to distract the administration from Saddam Hussein, whom the neoconservatives saw as a greater threat [...] In response, the C.I.A. prepared an analysis that all but pleaded with the White House to accept that the danger from Bin Laden was real.
>
> (Eichenwald, 2012)

Killing the state and undermining the nation 49

The events of 9/11 were viewed by the Bush Administration as an opportunity to pursue a broad strategy for the Middle East, which began with overthrowing Saddam Hussein. According to Scott McClellan, White House Press Secretary from 2003 to 2006, Bush pulled aside Donald Rumsfeld as early as November 2001, only two months post-9/11, and "instructed him to update the Pentagon's war plans for Iraq" (McClellan, 2008, p. 127). It was in this meeting, according to Bob Woodward (2006), that "Bush formally set in motion the chain of events that would lead to the invasion of Iraq 16 months later." McClellan (2008) went on to say:

> [...] what drove Bush toward military confrontation more than anything else was an ambitious and idealistic post-9/11 vision of transforming the Middle East through the spread of freedom. This view was grounded in a philosophy of coercive democracy, a belief that Iraq was ripe for conversion from a dictatorship into a beacon of liberty through the use of force, and a conviction that this could be achieved at nominal cost.
>
> (pp. 128–129)

The following month, in December 2001, Bush instructed Tommy Franks that CENTCOM should start war plans against Iraq, which should include lines of attack, targets for missiles and the composition of a highly mechanized ground force. In March 2002, Bush remarked to Condoleezza Rice, "Fuck Saddam. We're taking him out" (Phillips, 2005, pp. 18–19). Much to the consternation of the Joint Chiefs of Staff, Secretary of Defense Donald Rumsfeld initially suggested an invasion force that comprised only 60,000 troops, even though the officers charged with planning the invasion had recommended a presence of no less than 300,000 soldiers (Schmitt, 2003). A RAND Corporation study went further, claiming there should be 20 occupying forces for every 1,000 citizens, which meant that 500,000 troops would be needed to stabilize Iraq post-invasion. The head of the CPA, Paul Bremer, would later reveal that he sent a copy of the study to Donald Rumsfeld, but never heard back from him regarding the report (Bremer & McConnell, 2006, p. 10). Rumsfeld's tension with military command has been well documented. According to Pentagon adviser Daniel Gouré:

> When Mr. Rumsfeld took over the Pentagon, he was determined to wrest it back from military control, primarily because during the Clinton administration, senior officers became used to having a free hand due to the inexperience and weakness of many of the civilian leaders. Additionally, many senior military officers have come to believe that civilian Pentagon officials don't understand the reality of conflict because they have never served in uniform. Supporters of Mr. Rumsfeld [...] were infuriated by such claims and hit back by denigrating some generals as being almost pathologically cautious and reluctant to commit troops.
>
> (Harnden, 2003b)

50 *Deconstruction and reconstruction of the state*

The *Daily Telegraph* reported that, on March 13, 2003, Secretary Rumsfeld, Chairman of the Joint Chiefs of Staff General Richard Myers, and Myers' deputy, Peter Pace, outlined the Administration's thinking on a potential war against Iraq: a "lightning drive" to Baghdad by a highly mechanized and mobile ground force, bypassing possible confrontations in Iraq's southern cities. The race for the capital would be combined with an intensive bombing campaign, generating what was termed a "shock and awe" assault (Coman, 2003). A compromise was reached for a total of almost 250,000 combat troops, and an intensive, protracted aerial bombardment, which consequently destroyed what was left of Iraqi civilian infrastructures after more than a decade of British and US bombings. This plan, highly dependent upon aerial bombardment, resulted in 41,404 sorties by the US military, which saw 19,948 guided bombs fired and 9,251 unguided bombs dropped; 1,751 of the bombs utilized incendiaries, which scorched extensive areas indiscriminately (Moseley, 2003, pp. 7, 11).

The Anglo-American orchestration for war on Iraq

In spite of America's pre-existing military commitment in Afghanistan, the targeting of Iraq gained momentum in late 2001. There was a concerted campaign to manufacture consent for an American military intervention in Iraq. The key ingredient in this campaign was linking Iraq to the "war on terror" by presenting Iraq as a serious threat to US security and as a source of terrorism. From January 2002, Afghanistan and Bin Laden were replaced by the "threat" posed by Iraq and Saddam Hussein, which were now packaged as the embodiment of "terror." When President Bush then listed Iraq amongst his "Axis of Evil" in the January 29, 2002 State of the Union Address, the media fix on Iraq solidified in an unprecedented wave of uncritical reporting.

The Administration began an orchestrated propaganda campaign as early as September 2002, arguing that Iraq posed a threat to "Western civilization." Central to this case was the claim that Iraq was in possession of significant WMD stockpiles and had an active nuclear weapons program. The Office of Special Plans (OSP)[6] was a unit of the Pentagon established by Paul Wolfowitz and Douglas Feith, and headed by Abram Shulsky, tasked with finding intelligence that would fit the Administration's Iraq policy (Alexandrovna, 2005). The OSP, at least as Paul Wolfowitz conceived it, was to gather intelligence to support claims about Iraqi possession of WMDs and Iraqi connections to al-Qaeda. According to George Packer (2005):

> Just as the new methods of analyzing intelligence evaded the cumbersome old requirements of vetting, this configuration of like-minded officials dispersed on key islands across the national-security archipelago allowed the intelligence "product" and its effect on policy to circumvent the normal interagency process, in which the unconverted would have been among the participants and might have raised objections. It was an efficient way of working if you knew what you wanted to achieve.
>
> (p. 107)

Killing the state and undermining the nation 51

The operation was largely carried out by David Wurmser and F. Michael Maloof who worked "deductively, not inductively: The premise was true; facts would be found to confirm it" (Packer, 2005, p. 107). The OSP was essentially an intelligence agency that relied on data gathered by the other intelligence agencies, foreign governments and Iraqi exiles such as Aḥmad Chalabî and his INC to provide the Administration with intelligence supporting its policies. The rising influence of the OSP was accompanied by a decline in the influence of traditional intelligence agencies including the CIA and the Defense Intelligence Agency (DIA). "By the fall of 2002, the operation rivaled both the C.I.A. and the Pentagon's own Defense Intelligence Agency, the DIA, as President Bush's main source of intelligence regarding Iraq's possible possession of stockpiles of weapons of mass destruction and connection with Al Qaeda" (Hersh, 2004, pp. 207–208). A former CIA task-force leader said that many analysts in the CIA were convinced the Chalabî group's defector-reports were of little value. He added:

> [...] even the DIA could not find any value in it. The people of the OSP and the civilian leadership of the Pentagon have convinced themselves that they were on the side of angels, and everybody else in the government was a fool. The Pentagon and the Office of the Vice-President wrote their own pieces, based on their own ideology. We collected so much stuff that you could find anything you wanted.
>
> (Hersh, 2004)

The OSP reported directly to Paul Wolfowitz and Donald Rumsfeld, and undermined the influence of US intelligence agencies, as well as that of the uniformed officials. Patrick Lang, the former chief of Middle East Intelligence at the Defense Intelligence Agency, said, "The Pentagon has banded together to dominate the government's foreign policy, and they've pulled it off. They're running Chalabî. The DIA has been intimidated and beaten to a pulp. And there's no guts at all in the CIA" (Hersh, 2003). George Tenet (2007, p. 342), former Director of the CIA, later claimed he underestimated how important Iraq was to some in the Bush Administration, claiming the answers given by the CIA never satisfied the neoconservatives, namely Vice President Cheney, Paul Wolfowitz, Douglas Feith and Scooter Libby. According to Tenet, Wolfowitz and Libby "were relentless in asking us to check, recheck, and re-recheck" intelligence as it related to the purported Iraq–al-Qaeda connection and WMDs. Tenet described a meeting between Pentagon officials and members of the CIA that took place in August 2002:

> Feith's team, it turned out, had been sifting through raw intelligence and wanted to brief us on things they thought we had missed. Trouble was, while they seemed to like playing the role of analysts, they showed none of the professional skills or discipline required. Feith and company would find little nuggets that supported their beliefs and seize upon them, never understanding that there might be a larger picture they were missing. Isolated data points

52   *Deconstruction and reconstruction of the state*

became so important to them that they would never look at the thousands of other data points that might convey an opposite story.

(p. 347)

The conviction of the neoconservatives has led some prominent members of the Bush Administration to continue to defend their positions prior to the invasion, which have been proven incorrect by numerous official inquiries. Dick Cheney, for example, remains adamant about Saddam's alleged links to terrorist organizations, writing as late as 2011 that Saddam "was providing a safe haven and financial support to terrorists," a link that was ultimately proved to be false (Cheney, 2011, p. 418).

Under the pretext of an Iraqi threat, the US secured UN Security Council Resolution 1441 on November 8, 2002, calling for the return of UN weapons inspectors to Iraq to ensure the elimination of WMDs. This was a calculated gambit in preparing the legal grounds for military action against Iraq, which accords well with the text of the Downing Street Memo. UN Security Council Resolution 1441 warned of "serious consequences" in case of Iraqi non-cooperation or non-compliance. The notion was that the Iraqi possession of WMDs posed a grave threat to the security of the US, and created a sufficiently powerful moral mandate to wage a war against Iraq. American political calculations appear to have assumed that Iraq would not allow the return of inspectors, and that a direct Iraqi refusal to participate would have established a legal and moral case for war, which the UN would then be forced to authorize after they had failed in drawing Saddam into a confrontation in the fall of 2002. However, Iraq approved the return of the inspection team headed by Hans Blix, and went further than ever before in providing open access for the inspection of sites throughout the country, including presidential palaces, the source of a long controversy between the United Nations Special Commission (UNSCOM) inspectors and the Ba'thist regime. On December 12, 2002, Iraq, as required under Resolution 1441, submitted to the Security Council three copies of an 11,000-page report on the status of its WMD program, along with copies of the documents and invoices from the firms that provided materials and equipment for the purpose of manufacturing biological and chemical weapons. Minutes later, a CIA team arrived, and forced the office of the UN Security Council to hand over all three copies, which were only returned the next day, with thousands of pages missing. The names of all the firms that were involved in supplying the materials and building the manufacturing facilities had been removed (Heikal, 2003). It is quite reasonable to assume that removing the names of the firms from the report was a politically calculated move. The publication of any such information would have allowed the UN to request information regarding the exact extent and location of WMD facilities and equipment through the governments of countries with any firms named in the Iraqi documentation. The weapons, or evidence of their destruction, would then be verifiably located, allowing for either the immediate destruction of prohibited weapons or conclusive evidence of compliance with the Security Council without wasting time in inspections and speculation (Johnson, 2004). Such a diplomatic riposte

Killing the state and undermining the nation 53

would have nullified the urgent call for war, and probably triggered enough world pressure to lift the sanctions and discredit the US agenda.

Allegations of Iraq's supposed WMD program was overwhelming in media coverage, with little attention given to the opposing (and ultimately correct) perspective. For instance, Scott Ritter (2002), the UN chief weapons inspector between 1991 and 1998, gave testimony to the hollowness of the Bush Administration's claims regarding Iraq. He stated:

> We did ascertain a 90–95 percent level of verified disarmament. This figure takes into account the destruction of every factory associated with prohibited weapons manufacture and all significant items of production.
>
> With the exception of mustard agent, all chemical agents produced by Iraq prior to 1990 would have degraded within five years [...] Effective monitoring inspections, fully implemented from 1994–1998 without any significant obstruction from Iraq, never once detected any evidence of retained proscribed activity or effort by Iraq to reconstitute that capability.
>
> (Ritter, 2002)

The United Nations Monitoring, Verification and Inspection Commission's (UNMOVIC) reports, provided to the Security Council in 2002, pointed to increasing Iraqi cooperation with inspectors, although still falling short of expectations in the time frame allowed. Claims that Iraq was importing aluminum tubing to enrich uranium and had tried to buy yellowcake uranium from Niger had been shown to be false before US forces launched their invasion. Dr. Hans Blix, chief weapons inspector, exhaustively detailed to the UNSC in February and again in March 2003 how UNMOVIC inspectors had visited nearly 70 sites in the country without locating any substantial evidence of Iraqi non-compliance that could justify an invasion. While much documentation remained unaccounted for, Blix argued that more inspections would clearly have helped answer the remaining questions. Blix repeatedly asserted that UNMOVIC had found nothing to substantiate US claims and implored US authorities to provide the intelligence for independent verification. Prior to the invasion Blix clearly articulated his belief that by expanding the time frame called for in Resolution 1441 by a few additional months, the inspectors would be able to ensure that Iraq was free of prohibited WMDs. The US and its ally, Britain, rejected the provision of any further time beyond the three months prescribed in Resolution 1441. This rejection decisively laid bare the rift between the Anglo-American political alliance and the rest of the international community. Moreover, opposition to the Anglo-American position expressed itself through the protests of millions of people in street demonstrations all over the world, including Britain and the US itself, on February 15, 2003—the world's largest simultaneous protest ever.

At this stage, the US sought a new UN Resolution in a last-ditch attempt to bestow the necessary legitimizing cover for the invasion in the eyes of the American soldiers, the American public and the international community. However, the world did not "buy" the notion that Iraqi WMDs existed, or that they constituted

54 *Deconstruction and reconstruction of the state*

a legitimate threat. The international community and an overwhelming portion of international public opinion favored "more time to [be given] to the Inspection Committee." Apart from the US, Israel and Kuwait, no country in the world had a majority of their citizens and politicians publically endorse an attack against Iraq in the public discourse (Mearsheimer & Walt, 2007). When Hans Blix dismissed Powell's case for war, based on US satellite "evidence," as a fraud, international opinion sided with the inspectors (Harnden, 2003a).

The failure of Powell's UN venture testified to the ever-increasing gap in perspective between the international community and the US Administration. Hindsight, buttressed by mounting evidence that the rationale of the WMDs was disingenuous, suggests that the ideologues of the Bush Administration entertained the fantasy that, once the world witnessed the destruction of Saddam and his brutal regime, the "righteousness" of the mission would become apparent and the questions of moral legitimacy would dissolve into the annals of history. Moreover, the architects of this strategy seem to have placed an unquestionable faith in the notion that overwhelming military force creates new facts on the ground, compelling countries that had opposed the US war in Iraq, or that remained hesitant to support the occupation, to concede to the new reality. This is quite likely the thinking behind the RAND Corporation report's advocacy for fighting and winning decisive wars. Coinciding with this, there was a volley of derogatory remarks towards "old Europe" by Donald Rumsfeld, and threats to bar all those who opposed the war from participating in lucrative reconstruction contracts. In January 2003, the Administration updated the list of the *casus belli* for the attack to include liberating Iraq from a dictatorship and introducing democracy (BBC, 2003).

Controlling the narrative in the absence of WMDs and the proliferation of chaos

As it became clear in the months following the Anglo-American invasion of Iraq that claims justifying the invasion were unfounded, the focus quickly turned to the role of the media and its coverage in the months preceding the invasion. A poll conducted by the University of Maryland in September 2011, a decade after the 9/11 attacks and over eight years following the invasion of Iraq, found that 46 percent of Americans still believed that Iraq gave al-Qaeda substantial support or thought it was directly involved in 9/11. The same poll found that 47 percent of Americans believed Iraq had actual WMDs or a major WMD program immediately preceding the 2003 invasion (Telhami & Kull, 2011). What is the reason that so many Americans, to this day, cling to false justifications for invading Iraq when overwhelming evidence suggests otherwise? John F. Kennedy, echoing notions espoused by Joseph Goebbels, once said, "No matter how big the lie; repeat it often enough and the masses will regard it as the truth." Media outlets played a key role in repeating official government lines without questioning policy in the lead up to the invasion of Iraq. According to a systematic analysis conducted by Danny Hayes and Matt Guardino of every ABC, CBS

Killing the state and undermining the nation 55

and NBC Iraq-related news story—1,434 in all—in the eight months prior to the invasion, they found that "Bush administration officials were the most frequently quoted sources in the news, the voices of anti-war groups and opposition Democrats were barely audible, and the overall thrust of coverage supported a pro-war perspective" (Hayes & Guardino, 2010, p. 61). A similar study done by FAIR that looked at 393 on-camera sources on four major television networks[7] between January 30, 2003 and February 12, 2003 found that of "all 393 sources, only three (less than 1 percent) were identified with organized protests or anti-war groups" (FAIR, 2003).

Frustrated by the lack of access granted to journalists during the 1991 Gulf War and the 2001 invasion of Afghanistan, as many as 775 reporters and photographers traveled as "embedded journalists" with US and British troops during the 2003 invasion (Powell, 2004). As these journalists depended on the very same troops they were embedded with for their own survival, media coverage naturally lacked objectivity. ABC's Don Dahler, for example, conceded his perspective was limited. He claimed, "I certainly did not get a clear picture of the war because we were so isolated [...] My job was to look at things through a microscope, not the binoculars" (Kurtz, 2003). CBS's Jim Axelrod, embedded with the 3rd Infantry Division, did not necessarily see an issue with the lack of objectivity in his reporting. In a fairly stunning admission, he professed, "This will sound like I've drunk the Kool-Aid, but I found embedding to be an extremely positive experience [...] We got great stories and they got very positive coverage" (Kurtz, 2003). According to Mark Damazer, deputy director of BBC News, "We have got to a situation where our coverage has become sanitised. We are running the risk of double standards, and it is not a service to democracy" (Wells, 2003).

The idea of embedding journalists within military units has been credited to Victoria Clarke, a former Washington office director of the global public relations firm Hill & Knowlton (known for its notorious propaganda campaign during the first Gulf War) and later the Assistant Secretary of Defense for Public Affairs at the Pentagon under Donald Rumsfeld. By all accounts, the effort to "sanitize" the war was remarkably successful. According to former TV reporter Michael Burton:

> [...] the story of war [was] seen through the eyes of the American battalions, but without the real violence. American children see more images of violence on nightly television than they do in this war, because of the deliberate editing at home. Instead, they see a fascination with high tech weapons, battle tactics, and military strategy reporting.
>
> (Schechter, 2003, p. 19)

Geoff Hoon (2003) from *The Times* agrees with Burton that a succession of spectacular images in the media coverage did not contribute toward understanding:

> [...] the understandable thirst for "exciting" images has resulted in a series of disconnected "snapshots" of the conflict. Each, in its own way, may have

56 *Deconstruction and reconstruction of the state*

been informative, but combined they have failed to give the viewer a genuine understanding of "the big picture," and sometimes they have had the opposite effect [...] So while viewers may be "seeing" more than ever before, they may actually be "learning" less, albeit in a more spectacular way.

Information dominance was not, however, simply limited to controlling the narrative at home. As Donald Rumsfeld deemed the proliferation of Iraqi newspapers and emerging "free speech" among the greatest successes after the overthrow of Saddam Hussein, reports leaked about a covert propaganda initiative financed by the Pentagon to pay Iraqi newspapers to publish favorable stories written about US efforts in Iraq. The article claimed, "The military's effort to disseminate propaganda in the Iraqi media is taking place even as US officials are pledging to promote [...] freedom of speech in a country emerging from decades of dictatorship and corruption" (Mazzetti & Daragahi, 2005). This initiative was carried out by a US contractor, The Lincoln Group (formerly Iraqex), who would receive articles written by American troops and translate them into Arabic, later to be placed in a variety of Iraqi newspapers. An intern for The Lincoln Group would later confess: "I had become what I had to admit was the antithesis of a journalist" (Marx, 2006). A later investigation conducted by the Pentagon cleared The Lincoln Group of any wrongdoing, "with Donald Rumsfeld extolling such 'non-traditional' means of fighting terror in Iraq" (Marx, 2006).

On April 8, 2003, a US aircraft bombed the Baghdad bureau of Al Jazeera, which killed a journalist, Târiq Aiyyûb, and wounded another, despite being given the bureau's coordinates prior to the attack. While a US government spokesman claimed the bureau "had never been a target," the attack drew widespread criticism due to a US attack on the Kabul office of Al Jazeera following the US invasion of Afghanistan less than three years prior. A front-page report by *The Daily Mirror* in November 2005 claimed there were discussions between President George Bush and Prime Minister Tony Blair on April 16, 2004 regarding a potential bombing raid on Al Jazeera's world headquarters in Qatar and other locations (Wallis & Khalaf, 2005). The same day of the publication, the UK Attorney General, Lord Goldsmith, warned British papers they would be prosecuted under the Official Secrets Act if they published details of the conversation between the two leaders. According to *The Guardian*, "the government has never prosecuted editors for publishing the contents of leaked documents, including highly sensitive ones about the run-up to the invasion of Iraq" (Norton-Taylor, 2005).

While the idea of bombing a media outlet in an ally country was dismissed by the White House Press Secretary, Scott McClellan, as "absurd," neoconservatives connected to the Bush Administration didn't necessarily agree. Frank Gaffney (2003), former Under-Secretary of Defense for Ronald Reagan and a part of the PNAC, for example, wrote an opinion editorial where he recommended "taking out" Al Jazeera in "one way or another." This opinion wasn't limited to neoconservatives within the US, however. Former British Home Secretary David Blunkett admitted he "urged Tony Blair to break international law and bomb Al Jazeera's Baghdad TV transmitter" during the war (Mirror, 2006).

The combined roles of the INC and OSP

The INC was formed at a conference in Vienna in June 1992. In terms of composition, the INC included Iraq's primary Kurdish parties (the PUK and KDP)—political parties that through the sanctions/no-fly-zone regime of the 1990s and early 2000s ruled over an increasingly autonomous Iraqi Kurdistan detached from Iraqi political and cultural affairs for all practical purposes—and the SCIRI (subsequently the Islamic Supreme Council of Iraq or ISCI) and the Islamic Da'wa—Shi'ite political factions representing (to some degree) particularistic rather than nationalist/civic concerns in Iraq. *In toto*, this opposition coalition represented either secular/military exile factions (with limited connection to current Iraqi affairs) or ethnosectarian factions who, while indigenous to Iraq, were limited in influence to the group they represented.

The chair of the Executive Council was Aḥmad Chalabî, a secular Iraqi Shi'ite Muslim who studied mathematics at the University of Chicago (Pike, 1998). Before taking up business in Britain, he had been the chairman of Petra Bank International in Washington DC and Petra Bank in Jordan, from which he fled after facing charges of fraud, embezzlement and currency-trading irregularities, for which he was convicted in *absentia* by Jordanian authorities and sentenced to 22 years of hard labor. Chalabî's activities between 1989 and 1992 are murky at best, especially his high-level connections within the US government and neoconservative policy-making circles (Allawi, 2007, p. 66). Nevertheless, researchers have unearthed interesting details from this period. Israeli journalist Smadar Peri reported on May 6, 2003 that Chalabî was "pushed into the Americans' arms by Israeli intelligence" after they met with him in London in 1990. The head of the Israel Defense Forces Intelligence Research Branch, Major General Danny Rothschild, met with Chalabî to discuss Israeli efforts to collect information on the fate of Lieutenant-Colonel Ron Arad who had been captured in Lebanon by the Shia Amal militia in 1986. Chalabî promised to use his contacts in Tehran to investigate the issue. In later talks, Chalabî expressed hopes of transforming Iraq into a free and democratic society that would maintain warm ties with Israel and make northern Iraqi oil available through the defunct Haifa pipeline, all of which resonated well with Israel's desire to remove the rejectionist Iraqi regime. Despite some reservations about Chalabî's character within Israeli intelligence circles, Israeli security officials "recommended Chalabi to the American administration and connected him to senior advisers in the [Bush Sr.] White House, the Pentagon and the CIA" (Peri, 2003).[8] In the 1990s, Chalabî became acquainted with Paul Wolfowitz at the behest of nuclear strategist Albert Wohlstetter, Wolfowitz's mentor:

> Ahmed Chalabi's rise to prominence in Washington circles came at the instigation of Albert Wohlstetter, who met Chalabi in Paul Wolfowitz's office. Middle East scholar Bernard Lewis, a friend of Wolfowitz and Wohlstetter, had already talked up the exile to both men, knowing they would see the value of Chalabi's acquaintance. Wolfowitz, Wohlstetter, and Lewis shared

58 *Deconstruction and reconstruction of the state*

similar values and background; each of them secular Jews, defenders of Israel, devoted to reason and to the spread of American values. Wohlstetter and Lewis shared a common fascination with how Kemal Atatürk created the modern, secular Turkish state—seeing it as a model for the new Iraq Chalabi would lead.

(Abella, 2008)

In spite of deteriorating relations with the CIA, which found Chalabî and the INC to be unreliable sources of intelligence, those associated with advocating regime change in Iraq found the contacts invaluable. Iraqi defectors presented by the INC became the primary source for numerous stories that received wide media attention in the mainstream print and electronic media. They purported to provide evidence of expansive Iraqi WMD development and rampant UN delinquency in the conduct of inspections. Almost immediately after 9/11, the INC began to publicize stories of defectors who claimed that they had information connecting Iraq to al-Qaeda (Hersh, 2004). A supporting source of Chalabî was the Jewish Institute for National Security Affairs (JINSA), which saw in him the leader that would pressure the Arab countries towards peace with Israel. Chalabî's leanings for Israel brought him valuable friends in the American Enterprise Institute (AEI) and among journalists in key newspapers such as Jim Hoagland of the *Washington Post*, Judith Miller of the *New York Times* and Claudia Rosset of the *Wall Street Journal* (Phillips, 2005, pp. 71–72).

As if resurrecting the British imperial policy with regards to Baghdad in 1917, Feith, Rumsfeld and Wolfowitz schemed as early as the fall of 2002 to ensure that the future politics of Iraq would fall under the supervision of the Pentagon's civilian militarists, and would exclude the international civil society, the UN and the US State Department. The maneuvering of the Pentagon's neocons excluded many of the most knowledgeable US and international experts on both Iraq and post-conflict reconstruction development. The Pentagon dismissed "The Future of Iraq" project headed by Tom Warrick, which focused on rebuilding Iraq. Judith Yaphe, a former CIA analyst, and an expert on Iraq at the National Defense University, complained:

The Pentagon brass haven't a clue as to what's going on. They don't have plans for a transition in place, they don't know where the money is going to come from, they don't have any organization. And they just don't know anything about Iraq [...] The Office of the Secretary of Defense has no interest in what I do. They've brought in their own stable of people from AEI, and the people at the State Department who worked with the Iraqi exiles are being kept [out].

(Dreyfuss, 2003)

According to the first American Administrator of Iraq, retired General Jay Garner, relations between Pentagon civilian militarists and State Department personnel were both tense and sour because of an interagency rivalry (Associated Press,

2003). Garner rejected imposing privatization and other economic reforms on Iraq and favored free elections, stating: "My preference was to put the Iraqis in charge as soon as we can, and do it with some form of elections [...] I just thought it was necessary to rapidly get the Iraqis in charge of their destiny" (Leigh, 2004). Garner (2004) believed his differences with the Bush Administration are why he was replaced within two months by Paul Bremer, who had never been to Iraq and didn't speak Arabic, and who had no experience with nation building or with a post-conflict society, but who was placed in charge of rebuilding Iraq. At this juncture, the main concern was to keep Iraqi oil underground where American military boots could control it.

In fact, Garner reported that he learned of a detailed study by Secretary of State Colin Powell for postwar Iraq only a few weeks before the war began in March 2003. When he suggested utilizing it, Rumsfeld forbade him (Associated Press, 2003).[9] Paul Bremer, however, enjoyed the unqualified support of President Bush and his neocon administration. Under the administration of Bremer the UN was unable to assume the financial auditing role in Iraq, which the Security Council's Resolution 1483 assigned to it. Years after the fact, a Pentagon audit discovered that an estimated $6.6 billion airlifted to Iraq may have been outright stolen (Richter, 2011), and the bipartisan independent Commission on Wartime Contracting estimated that the "US government's over-reliance on wartime contractors in Iraq and Afghanistan has resulted in as much as $60 billion in waste and fraud" (Arnoldy, 2011).

American credibility: occupation versus liberation

In October 2003, David Kay, who led a 1,400-man team into Iraq to search for Iraqi WMDs, and was a staunch believer in their existence, presented an interim report that stated bluntly that there was no evidence of any WMDs manufactured after 1991. His only finding was one vial of live C. Botulinum Okra B., from which a biological agent could be produced. Bush seized on this single finding, equating it with evidence of WMDs. However, Dr. Glen Rangwala of Cambridge, UK, in analyzing Kay's report, said: "The vial held not the super deadly type A but the less lethal type B and there was no evidence found by Kay's group of any preparations for the extensive process required for weaponization" (Cockburn, 2003).

Further, Botulinum strain B is used for vaccinating livestock and removing wrinkles in cosmetic surgery. It is also used as an antidote to common Botulinum poisoning (Hiro, 2004, p. 434). In January 2004, David Kay also resigned his post and made it clear that he did not believe that there were any WMDs to be found in Iraq. Following Kay's report, the neoconservatives' self-justified imperial project focused on "promot[ing] neo-Wilsonian principles to export and consolidate democracy" (Belloni, 2007).

A comprehensive 107-page report that the Washington-based Carnegie Endowment for International Peace (CEIP) released on January 8, 2004 concluded that the Bush Administration "systematically misrepresented" the threat

60 *Deconstruction and reconstruction of the state*

posed by Iraq's WMDs. The Carnegie analysts found "no solid evidence" of a cooperative relationship between Saddam and al-Qaeda, nor any evidence to support the claim that Iraq would have transferred WMDs to al-Qaeda. Moreover, it reasoned that "the notion that any government would give its principal security assets to people it could not control in order to achieve its own political aims is highly dubious" (Lobe, 2004). The report called for the creation of an independent commission to fully investigate what the US intelligence community knew, or believed to know, about Iraq's WMD program from 1991 to 2003, and to determine whether intelligence was tainted by foreign intelligence agencies or by political pressure. The report's co-author, Joseph Cirincione, told reporters: "It is very likely that intelligence officials were pressured by senior administration officials to conform their threat assessments to pre-existing policies" (Lobe, 2004). Among the supporters of regime change in Iraq, Kenneth Pollack, who had been a Clinton-era National Security Council member, sharply criticized the Bush Administration's justification of the war as at "best faulty, at worst, deliberately misleading" (Regan, 2004). In early January 2004, the Strategic Studies Institute of the US Army War College published a paper entitled *Bounding the Global War on Terrorism*, which found that the Bush Administration's doctrinaire view of the war on terror, which lumped together Saddam's regime and al-Qaeda as a single undifferentiated threat, led the US on a dangerous "detour" into an unnecessary war. The author, Jeffrey Record, a visiting scholar at the Strategic Studies Institute and a former staff member of the Senate Armed Services Committee, claimed that "the global war on terrorism as presently defined and conducted is strategically unfocused, promises much more than it can deliver, and threatens to dissipate US military and other resources in an endless and hopeless search for absolute security" (Regan, 2004).

The American neoliberalization of Iraq

Three weeks after declaring "mission accomplished," on May 22, 2003 the Bush Administration succeeded in securing UN Resolution 1483, which rubberstamped the US occupation and essentially made Iraq a US mandate. The UNSC Resolution minimized the role of the UN, confining it to an advisory financial auditing position, overseeing only the Iraqi Development Fund and other various humanitarian functions.

As administrator of the CPA, Paul Bremer acted as proconsul for neoliberal economic reform. Although Resolution 1483 called for the establishment of an interim Iraqi government, Bremer's first impulse was to ignore it, along with the requirement to establish a UN Advisory Financial Auditing Body to oversee the Iraqi Development Fund (into which Iraq's oil revenues were deposited). Bremer then disbanded the Iraqi army and police forces, banned the Ba'th Party and purged its members from government employment. Under the conditions of Ba'th authoritarian rule, party membership was a necessity for public sector employment and other accrued benefits, which became particularly advantageous under the difficult conditions of first the Iran–Iraq war and then the sanctions

Killing the state and undermining the nation 61

regime in the 1990s. Membership carried strong economic benefits at a time of currency collapse and great economic hardship; for example, section members ('Udu Shu'ba) received a monthly stipend of roughly $250 in 2002, a significant sum. Other benefits included "bonus points for children's educational results in their secondary school examination, vehicles, and greater ease of access to civil service positions and promotions" (Sissons & Al-Saiedi, 2013, p. 5). When the Higher De-Ba'thification Commission began its purges in 2003, it estimated that

> 400,000 Iraqis held the rank of full party members or above. About 150,000 of them worked in the civil service, and about 250,000 were in the defense forces or Ministry of Defense. Of the 150,000 members who were also civil service employees, some 65,000 held one of the top four levels of membership.
>
> (Sissons & Al-Saiedi, 2013, p. 6)

Additionally, disbanding the standing army of 400,000 men, along with its civilian support of 100,000 people (Sanchez & Philips, 2008, p. 184), amplified and spread public dissatisfaction, and provided an endless reservoir of potential recruits for the emerging resistance to occupation. Faiṣal al-Istrabâdî, a member of the American-sponsored Democratic Principles Working Group, claimed, "I don't understand why you take 400,000 men who were highly armed and trained, and turn them into your enemies. Particularly when these are people who didn't fight" (Phillips, 2005, p. 152). Furthermore, when you consider that the average Iraqi family has 6.4 members, the economic impact was felt by roughly 3.2 million Iraqis, or just under 13 percent of the population (WHO, 2008). The lawlessness that permeated the streets following the first few months of the invasion never ceased to exist. Eventually it led criminals, gangs and mafias to take over, which replaced the totalitarian state and the fear it imposed with complete indifference to the idea of an Iraqi nation. "In one fell swoop, Bremer had created a 60 percent unemployment rate" and angered millions of Iraqis (Sanchez & Philips, 2008, p. 184).

The integration of militias within the new Iraqi army, which was formalized under the Anglo-American occupation (by way of CPA Order 91),[10] made it possible for occupied Iraq to field a domestic military presence despite having disbanded 400,000 soldiers. This integration became an established practice during the Anglo-American occupation and continued under Prime Minister Nûrî al-Mâlikî. Cooperation with militias was intended to reduce sectarian divisions, and this argument was made again during the events surrounding the 2014 Fallujah crisis. US Vice President Joe Biden "encouraged the Prime Minister [Mâlikî] to continue the Iraqi government's outreach to local, tribal, and national leaders" (Lobe, 2014) which encompasses the continued integration of militias into the state military. While it is true that militias, in particular the Sahwa militia, played a large role in pacifying rejectionist cities in 2007, they also were a driving force of the sectarian violence that erupted post-invasion in the first place (Alani, 2014). What continues to be discounted is that "the militias that

62 *Deconstruction and reconstruction of the state*

were incorporated into the army did not give their allegiance to the armed forces because they are highly politicised" (Jamal, 2014). An analyst, writing in the *Gulf News* (Jamal, 2014), noted:

> To the best of my knowledge, no militia contributed to the overthrow of the former regime, but we know for sure that since the first day after the top-pling of Saddam Hussain's regime *as a result of the US invasion, several militias, which received their orders from political parties and organisations, did enter the country*. The role of these militias grew after the occupation forces decided to dismantle the Iraqi army and other security forces in Iraq. The Coalition Provisional Authority (CPA), which imposed itself on Iraq, was obliged to recognise these militias rather than clash with them. Hence, it resorted to finding a legal framework for them.
>
> (Emphasis added)

Clearly, the sectarian violence that consumed Iraq was derived, in significant degree, from occupation policy itself (unintentionally or otherwise). Under the Republican and Saddam regimes, the Iraqi military was a force for national iden-tity within Iraq, leading it to become one of the more respected institutions of the state. However, under the Anglo-American occupation, militias were invited to enter Iraq and began to be integrated into the state military—fragmenting its loyalty and aims. Today's Iraq, especially under Prime Minister al-Mâlikî, con-tinues to foster sectarianism by strengthening militias rather than focusing on the recovery of what was once a national symbol of Iraq.

The state had been founded on the army, and the removal of an important symbol of national identity would have enormous consequences that are still manifest today. The Iraqi army, like the Ba'th Party itself, was not synonymous with Saddamism, nor was it an institution that promoted a sectarian agenda. They both, particularly the army, represented efforts to generate Iraqi institutions that transcended sectarian interests and influenced a sense of Iraqi nationalism. Toby Dodge (2005) describes the creation of the Iraqi army under King Faisal:

> Faisal and his Hashemite officers wanted to build an army that would be the personification and instrument of a strong Arab state. To this end they favored a mass conscript army that would act as an institution of, and weapon for, the imposition of national unity. They wanted to build an army through which young Iraqi conscripts would learn Arabic and a Hashemite vision of Iraqi nationalism. Such an army would become a powerful symbol of an independent Hashemite state.
>
> (p. 137)

According to 'Alî 'Allâwî, a member of one of the inner circles of the new Iraqi political class installed in the wake of the American invasion, the Iraqi army "had played an almost mystical role in the narrative of modern Iraqi history [... and] was seen as a preserver of the nation's core values" (Allawi, 2007, p. 155). The efforts

Killing the state and undermining the nation   63

of civic nationalism through state building preceded Saddam Hussein, and efforts to manufacture a sense of Iraqi nationalism continued throughout the Ba'thist era until the 2003 invasion. Thus, once the army and the party's institutions ceased to function, the Iraqi state collapsed, and only the pre-Ba'th primordial social institutions—tribal, religious, communal—re-emerged in the vacuum, precipitating Bremer's loss of control and adding a sectarian dimension to the conflict, which was previously reticent to modern Iraq.

Successive warfare from 1991 through 2003 broke the institutions of state. This lack of Iraqi state capacity only served to allow foreign economic interests and their predatory local agents to expropriate, pillage and render profits gleaned from within the Iraqi market. Paul Bremer was in charge of the task of re-configuring the economic and political bases of Iraq. Of his three major stated priorities, one was to "corporatize and privatize state-owned enterprises [and] wean people from the idea the state supports everything" (Chandrasekaran, 2006, p. 61). Perhaps this was what motivated his poor selections for administrative posts in the CPA, or his support for ineffectual political leadership on the Governing Council. Zaid Al-Ali, examining the residue the CPA left in its wake, argues that "[Bremer's] vision of Iraq [was that] of a country populated exclusively by people who hated each other because of their religion and in which individual behavior was irrelevant" (Al-Ali, 2014, p. 70). Bremer regarded the gasoline, electric and fertilizer subsidies the Iraqi people received under Saddam's regime as being unsustainable and too socialist (Chandrasekaran, 2006, p. 61). According to Rajiv Chandrasekaran (2006, p. 62), "Bremer had come to Iraq to build not just a democracy but a free market. He insisted that economic reform and political reform were intertwined." He followed through by arranging the largest state liquidation sale of economic enterprises since the collapse of the USSR (Klein, 2004). While opening the borders to unrestricted imports, he introduced a set of laws in September 2003 to bring in transnational corporations. Order 37 lowered corporate tax from almost 40 to 15 percent; Order 39 permitted foreign companies to own 100 percent of Iraqi assets; and Order 49 exempted corporations working with the CPA from taxation entirely (Coalition Provisional Authority, 2003a, 2003b, 2004). Foreign companies were also entitled to leases or contracts that could remain in effect for 40 years. Order 40 was designed for foreign banks with the same favorable terms (Coalition Provisional Authority, 2003c). What remained of Saddam's economic policies and laws were the rules that restricted collective bargaining and trade unions. The aggressive economic policies implemented by Paul Bremer under the CPA infuriated Iraq's business class, some of whom responded by funding the insurgency with what little money they had left. Patrick Graham (2004) described the role that Iraq's businessmen played in funding the insurgency:

> A wealthy Sunni in Baghdad told me that some of the [insurgency] groups are being funded by businessmen he knew. They are outraged by the new foreign-investment laws, which allow foreign companies to buy up factories for very little. Their revenues have collapsed, because the country has been

64 *Deconstruction and reconstruction of the state*

flooded with foreign goods, and the increased wages now paid to the public sector are agitating their own, poorly paid workers. The violence, these businessmen realize, is their only competitive edge. It is simple business logic: the more problems there are in Iraq, the harder it is for outsiders to get involved.

Bremer's architectural design for Iraq was a large factor in the escalation of the armed resistance that followed. In the first four months after his arrival, 109 US soldiers were killed and 570 were wounded. When Bremer's shock therapy took effect in the following four months, the number of American casualties almost doubled. Bremer's policies that created half a million jobless people overnight afforded them only "resistance" as an alternative to unemployment. With 67 percent unemployment, the import of foreign products and workers added more fuel for the resistance, as such imports aggravate the suffering that is part of daily Iraqi life.[11]

The occupation authority's project of a utopian free market for Iraq was arrested, however, by international law, which stipulates that occupation forces cannot dispose of the assets of the occupied country in any shape or form. Bremer's belated realization of this block was further compounded by the escalating resistance that rendered the issue of the security vacuum tangible and concrete, which in turn scared away many transnational corporations. Bremer responded by hastily forming the IGC, which consisted of 25 handpicked members, and forced it to agree to the Interim Constitution, alternatively named the TAL. Many Iraqis have dubbed the IGC as "collaborators," primarily because the IGC has no legitimate authority, and does not represent any constituencies within Iraq. In the TAL, Bremer inserted Article 26, stating, "For the duration of the interim government the laws, regulations, orders and directives issued by the Coalition Provisional Authority [...] shall remain in force," and could only be changed after general elections were held in January 2005 (Klein, 2004). According to Naomi Klein (2004):

> Bremer had found this legal loophole: There would be a window—seven months—when the occupation was officially over but before general elections were scheduled to take place. Within this window, the Hague and Geneva Conventions' ban on privatization would no longer apply, but Bremer's own laws, thanks to Article 26, would stand. During these seven months, foreign investors could come to Iraq and sign forty-year contracts to buy up Iraqi assets. If a future elected Iraqi government decided to change the rules, investors could sue for compensation.

By March 2013, a decade after the initial Anglo-American invasion of Iraq, the full scope of occupation policy and the political conditions it gave rise to can be assessed. By 2012 estimates, a near-decade of war and occupation had produced: an Iraqi death toll ranging between 109,000 (2009 estimate from leaked State Department cables, *WikiLeaks*) and over a million (2007 survey data from *Opinion Research Business*); nearly 3 million internally displaced persons; low

Killing the state and undermining the nation   65

levels of press freedom (ranked 150 out of 179 countries by *Reporters without Borders*); and high levels of corruption (ranked 169 out of 176 countries by *Transparency International*). Conversely, access to electricity (which declined to pre-war levels in 2005 and 2006) has gradually risen, from prewar levels of 3,958 megawatts/month to 6,990 megawatts/month by July 2011. Likewise exploitation of oil reserves has continued apace, with oil revenue from exports peaking in fiscal year 2011 at \$82.9 billion before declining to \$45.3 billion in 2012. Hence, while economic indicators in Iraq have stabilized from the 2005–2006 chaos and seen continuous improvement, they came at a tremendous human cost (O'Hanlon & Livingston, 2012). Politically, Iraq's experience over the past decade has been rather cataclysmic.

2005 Iraqi elections and the draft constitution

Iraq's parliamentary elections of 2005, celebrated as Iraq's entry into democratic politics, took place amidst strange circumstances. It was conducted under a state of martial law and foreign occupation, boycotted by 20 percent of the population in the so-called Sunni triangle, and lacked the promised international election monitors. There was virtually no political campaigning by the 7,500 candidates, scattered among 257 lists, and at least 6,000 of them were too fearful to declare their names until Election Day (Iraqis Respond to the Election: Commentary from Imad Khadduri, Tahrir Swift and Munir Chalabi, 2005). Despite the Sunni boycott of the election, the voter turnout on Election Day was reported to be about 58 percent. The voting pattern had two hallmarks: one was the expressed wish of voters that the incoming Iraqi government would insist on the withdrawal of the foreign forces (Potter, 2005); the second was the segmented character of voting which applies with equal weight to the non-voting of the Sunni community. The Shi'ites received a religious edict from Ayatollah 'Alî al-Sistânî as to the imperative of voting for the United Iraqi Alliance; the Kurds voted for the Kurdish list; and the majority of Sunnis obeyed the boycott call of the Sunni Muslim Clerics' [Scholars'] Association. Others, like the Communists or 'Allâwî's list that tried to reach for the votes of Iraqis beyond community barriers, received minimal support at best. Iraqi voting reflected not a nation-state, but segmented communities in an uneasy co-existence (Cole, 2005).

With Sunni political parties boycotting the election, the election was dominated by Shi'ite and Kurdish parties. The Shi'ite United Iraqi Alliance, which was the list put together by al-Sistânî, won 51 percent of the votes and captured 140 seats out of 275. The Kurdish list came second, capturing about 26 percent of the votes and about 75 seats. The loss of the list of Iyâd 'Allâwî was a surprise because 'Allâwî had all the advantages of incumbency. According to Juan Cole, Professor of History at the University of Michigan, 'Allâwî dominated the airwaves in December and January. In addition, he went to Baghdad University and made a variety of promises to the students there, and it was dutifully broadcast. 'Allâwî's list also spent an enormous amount on campaign advertising. The source of these millions is unknown, since Paul Bremer passed a law making disclosure of campaign contributions

66 *Deconstruction and reconstruction of the state*

unnecessary. Despite these enormous advantages, clear American backing, money, etc., 'Allâwî's list won only about 14 percent of the votes (40 seats), and even with outside support, 'Allâwî failed to become the future Prime Minister, which was largely seen as a defeat for the American Administration. According to the Interim Constitution, the formation of a government required a "supermajority" of two-thirds. This stipulation forced the Shi'ites to seek an expedient alliance with the Kurds, who insisted on resolving the problematic demography of the city of Kirkuk and its oil in Kurdish favor even prior to negotiations. These Kurdish demands were a subject of intense negotiations behind closed doors.

The Shi'ite–Kurdish committee, charged with drafting the Iraqi Constitution, attempted to engage the Sunni input in order to lend legitimacy to the draft by presenting it as a national formula and simultaneously undercut the potential of Sunni support to the resistance. However, the Western mainstream media focused on issues of confederation, oil sharing and Kirkuk as the problems that have plagued the process of drawing the draft. Neither the context nor the power agents involved have been discussed, nor has the substance of the draft constitution been analyzed. The Sunni representatives withdrew from the process and disavowed the draft as not representing the aspirations of the Iraqi people, and vowed to turn it down in the referendum. The inter-factional struggle delayed the completion of the draft beyond the deadline of August 15, 2005. Further, the draft was not signed by the Iraqi Parliament, and was only passed as ready for a public referendum in December 2005.

The concrete context in which the constitutional proceedings took place was tainted with so much illegality that this alone could render the constitution illegal under international law. Zaid Al-Ali, a legal expert who oversaw the constitutional process, reported that the US intervened in three basic ways. First, the occupation forces selected the commission that was charged with drafting the permanent constitution. Second, the occupation set up the limits and parameters within which the constitution was to be drafted. Third, the American forces intervened directly in order to safeguard US interests in the context of the constitutional negotiations. An example of such significant American interference was dropping a clause in an earlier draft that forbade foreign military bases in Iraq. Justin Alexander, legal affairs officer for the office of constitutional support with the UNAMI, who oversaw the drafting process, reported that "US ambassador, Zalmay Khalilzad, took an extremely hands-on role," to the point of "Even going so far as to circulate at least one U.S. draft." Dr. Marinos Diamantides, Senior Lecturer in Law at the University of London, said that one could argue that the entire process was a contravention of international law. He explained that "according to the 1907 Convention (the *Convention for the Pacific Settlement of International Disputes*), the occupying power has a duty to maintain the legal system of the country it occupies. This is the first time ever that an occupying power has dismantled the internal law system of the country it occupies" (Jamail, 2005). Furthermore, the very notion that Iraq needed a new constitution, written from scratch, was unnecessary considering Iraq already had a serviceable constitution, which was written in 1970. According to Naomi Klein (2007):

Killing the state and undermining the nation 67

[...] the process of writing a constitution is among the most wrenching any nation can go through, even a nation at peace. It brings every tension, rivalry, prejudice and grievance to the surface. To foist that process—twice—on a country as divided and shattered as Iraq after Saddam greatly exacerbated the possibility of civil strife. The social cleavages cracked open by the negotiations have in no way healed, and may yet result in the partition of the country.

(p. 424)

In every step, from the invasion to drafting the Iraqi Constitution, the US endeavored to lock-in its economic and political interests in Iraq in such a way that they became non-eradicable. The US selected the IGC, which approved Bremer's 100 laws that opened the country to a "fire-sale" of the nation's economic enterprises to foreign corporations, thus paving the way to *de facto* privatization. The election of January 2005 brought in an American-approved cabinet of Shi'ite–Kurdish power agents that had their own agenda that coincided with that of the US. In preparation for drawing the draft constitution, the Iraqi Parliament conducted a massive information campaign that included questionnaires and focus group discussions across the country in order to identify the wish list of the Iraqi people. The wish list emphasized a Scandinavian-style welfare system, with Iraq's wealth spent on upholding every Iraqi's right to education, health care, housing and other social services. Iraq's natural resources would be owned collectively by the Iraqi people, and only Iraqis could operate businesses. Furthermore, when foreign partnership was allowed, it should not exceed 49 percent (Docena, 2005). It was the American list, however, that the draft constitution incorporated because, as Aḥmad Chalabî puts it, "the Americans do not respect the wishes of the Iraqi people because the Iraqi people accepted corruption, no electricity and deficient public services, and did nothing to fix these problems, so why respect them?" (al-Rubai'î, 2013).

The Kurdish and Shi'ite parties, under the ubiquitous presence of US Ambassador Zalmay Khalilzad and the British diplomats, agreed to a document that not only sanctioned the privatization of the state-owned oil industry and the free market restructuring of the economy but also preserved Bremer's laws (Docena, 2005). Article 25 of this document declared "the state shall guarantee the reforming of the Iraqi economy, according to modern economic bases, in a way that ensures complete investment of its resources, diversifying its sources and encouraging and developing the private sector." Article 110, clause 2, of the constitution declared that Iraq's energy resources would be developed by "relying on the most modern techniques of market principles and encouraging investment" (Cogan, 2005). By "reforming," the framers of the constitution meant the usual stock of neoliberal economic policies that include privatizing state-owned enterprises, liberalizing trade, and deregulating the market and opening it up to foreign investors. "Modern techniques of market principles," in Article 110, referred to existing plans to privatize the Iraqi National Oil Company and to open up Iraq's oil reserves to the big oil companies. Former Iraqi Vice President 'Âdil 'Abd-ul-Mahdî referred to such plans as "very promising to the American investors and to

68 *Deconstruction and reconstruction of the state*

American enterprises, certainly to oil companies" (Docena, 2005). By embodying Bremer's laws in the Iraqi Constitution, the framers allowed foreigners to have as much right as Iraqis to ownership of Iraq's national resources, real estate and capital, and paved the way to foreign ownership of Iraqi oil. Providing social services to Iraqis was vaguely mentioned, and the delivery conduit was named the private sector, which opened the way to complete privatization of the social welfare system (Docena, 2005).

The second article of the constitution declared Islam the official state religion and a source of law, and that "no law can be passed that contradicts the established provisions of Islam." The constitution further declared Iraq to be a part of the "Islamic World," thus divorcing the Iraqi people from a national identity that transcends ethnic and confessional allegiances.

This turn towards ethnosectarian identity was examined in a public lecture at the Iraqi Club in Britain in 2014 by Farid Ayyar, a council member from Iraq's first Electoral Commission, who considered that the UN was an active participant in imposing a "sectarian quota to determine the membership of [the Electoral] Commission's council, through [the] presence of Sandra Mitchell,"[12] who at the time was in charge of the elections support team in the UNAMI from 2006 to 2011. "When Sandra Mitchell sat in on interviews that selected the councilors," it implied a UN endorsement for a sectarian policy that became a norm and would eventually serve as the basis of the 2007 law regarding the composition of future councils, and according to Ayyar "had the effect of allowing Iraq's sectarian parties to control the Commission" (Kitabat, 2014a). The "international observers and UN experts [... who] were monitoring the Iraqi political scene" at the time "[met] daily at the US embassy in Iraq to report on the activities of the [Electoral] Commission," implying that the UNAMI staff, among others, acted as an extension of US interests (Kitabat, 2014b). Glowing examples include: Zalmay Khalilzad, former US ambassador to Iraq and the UN, who is now president of Khalilzad Associates, a company that provides advisement to businesses seeking to expand into the Middle East (Gryphon-Partners, n.d.); Peter Galbraith,[13] an adviser to the Kurdistan Regional Government who also works with DNO, a Norwegian oil company who he helped win oil contracts in Kurdistan (Glanz, 2009); and of course Sandra Mitchell, who has been described as the "heroine of rigging the 2010 elections" (Kitabat, 2013) for her role in guiding the preferred candidates of the sectarian parties through the election process while working as a lobbyist of sorts for Iraqi business groups, an activity she retains in spite of her current role working for the United Nations Relief and Works Agency in the Palestinian Territory (Mitchell, n.d.).

The International Republican Institute, a US government-funded entity tasked to build support for free market Iraqi political parties, conducted a survey in July 2005 for the purpose of identifying popular trends. The survey reported that 69 percent of Iraqis from across the country wanted the constitution to establish "a strong central government," and only 22 percent wanted it to give "significant powers to regional governments." In the Shi'ite-majority areas in the south, only 25 percent wanted federalism, while 66 percent rejected it (Docena, 2005).

Iraqis would return to the ballot for the 2010 Parliamentary elections, with the final results granting 91 seats to Iyâd 'Allâwî's al-Iraqiya faction (which was founded in 2009 representing both Shia and Sunni parties), 89 seats to Nûrî al-Mâlikî's State of Law coalition (founded in 2009, predominantly representing Mâlikî's Islamic Da'wa Party), 70 seats to Ibrâhîm al-Ja'farî's National Iraqi Alliance (primarily representing the SCIRI and the Sadrist factions), and 43 seats to the Kurdistan Alliance (representing the PUK and KDP) (Fairfield & Tse, 2010). The final results were highly contested, with the Iraqiya list led by Iyâd 'Allâwî and Nûrî al-Mâlikî's State of Law coalition maneuvering to install their candidate as Prime Minister.

By November 2010, a political resolution finally appeared in reach, with the continuation of Shi'ite al-Mâlikî as Prime Minister, Kurdish Jalâl Țâlabânî as President and Sunni Usâmah al-Nujaifî as Speaker of Parliament. As a concession to Iyâd 'Allâwî, he was designated as head of the newly created Council for Strategic Policy, a body with nominal power to veto legislation; in practice, however, the body will require 80 percent of the council's vote to exercise its veto power, a scenario unlikely given the fractiousness of Iraqi politics. The political failure of 'Allâwî was, by available reports, a US failure as well, as the Obama administration reportedly placed pressure on Mas'ûd Barzânî and Jalâl Țâlabânî to allow the ascension of 'Allâwî to the Presidency. In any case, the effect of the 2010 election was to perpetuate the Shia–Kurdish alliance that has held power since 2005, based on the tenuous support of smaller parties.

The political situation of Iraq has remained fractious and weak, with the alliance between Shia and Kurdish parties threatened by disputes over power-sharing agreements in the Kirkuk region, the degree of federalism that should be allowed in the Iraqi state, the terms of a new oil law and territorial disputes. In 2009, leaked US diplomatic cables warned: "Without strong and fair influence, likely from a third party, these [Arab–Kurdish] tensions may quickly turn to violence after the U.S. Forces withdraw" (Gordon & Lehren, 2010). Since President Obama's formal withdrawal of American troops in December 2011, the political and social situation in Iraq has remained unstable.[14] Furthermore, the volatile nature and sectarian conflict in neighboring Syria has further destabilized an already fragile situation, engendering fear of a return to civil strife unseen since the inferno of sectarian violence in 2005–2006.

Notes

1 For various estimates of Iraqi deaths and methodology discussions and criticism, see Munro & Cannon (2008), Rogers (2010) and Susman (2007).
2 The formalization of the "responsibility to protect" into international law can be seen in paragraphs 138 and 139 of the UN General Assembly's World Summit Outcome (2005).
3 For the historical backdrop on the neoconservative movement, see Heilbrunn (2008) and Mann (2004).
4 For an incisive report on the ideological web behind the Bush Administration, see Burrough et al. (2004).

70 Deconstruction and reconstruction of the state

5 For an alternative perspective on the Iraq–al-Qaeda link see Mylroie (2001). However, the theory put forth by Mylroie is largely unsubstantiated and specious.
6 The OSP was established following the attacks of September 11. Abram Shulsky, the OSP's founding director, had worked on intelligence and foreign-policy issues for three decades, and served in the Pentagon under Assistant Secretary of Defense Richard Pearle during the Reagan Administration, after which he joined the RAND Corporation. William Luti, the Under-Secretary of Defense, oversees the OSP. He is a retired Navy captain, and an early and longstanding advocate of military action against Iraq.
7 The on-camera sources in this study included: *ABC World News Tonight*, *CBS Evening News*, *NBC Nightly News* and PBS's *NewsHour with Jim Lehrer*. The study began one week before and ended one week after Secretary of State Colin Powell's February 5 presentation at the UN.
8 See also Hardy (2004).
9 See also PBS Frontline's *Truth, War and Consequences* (2003) for lengthy interviews with Garner on prewar planning.
10 Annex A and Annex B of Order 91 list the two militias of the Kurdish parties (*Peshmerga*) and seven other mainly religious militias.
11 Perhaps ironically, given the increased violence and the broad rejection of the upcoming election by the Sunni segment of Iraq, on December 15, 2004, Bush presented the Presidential Medal of Freedom to Paul Bremer (Phillips, 2005, p. 221).
12 Before working for the UNAMI, Mitchell worked for non-profits in Bulgaria, Kosovo and Cambodia. Mitchell received her BA from Washington State University before attending the Oklahoma City University School of Law (Mitchell, n.d.).
13 For more on Galbraith, see Chapter 2.
14 As of February 2014, there were less than 6,000 US contractors in Iraq, along with some 200 US military personnel, while the amount of military equipment set to be delivered by the US to Iraq in 2014 has already exceeded $6 billion (Nissenbaum, 2014; RT, 2014).

References

Abella, A. (2008, August 30). *Chalabi, RAND and the Iraq War*. Retrieved February 12, 2013, from *Huffington Post*: www.huffingtonpost.com/alex-abella/chalabi-rand-and-the-iraq_b_99492.html

Al-Ali, Z. (2014). *The Struggle for Iraq's Future: How corruption, incompetence, and sectarianism have undermined democracy*. New Haven: Yale University Press.

Alani, F. (2014, January 16). *Is Oil Iraq's Real Problem?* Retrieved February 5, 2014, from CounterPunch: www.counterpunch.org/2014/01/16/is-oil-iraqs-real-problem/

Alexandrovna, L. (2005, December 2). *Senate Intelligence Committee Stalling Pre-war Intelligence Report*. Retrieved July 13, 2013, from The Raw Story: http://rawstory.com/news/2005/Senate_Intelligence_Committee_stalling_prewar_intelligence_1202.html

'Ali, S. A. (2013, August 3). [*Why the US Overthrew Saddam Hussein*]. Retrieved April 17, 2014, from Voice of Iraq: www.sotaliraq.com/mobile-item.php?id=139993#axzz2z8l0anCX

Allawi, A. A. (2007). *The Occupation of Iraq: Winning the war, losing the peace*. New Haven: Yale University Press.

al-Rubai'î, N. (2013, August 23). [*Iraqi Dialogue*]. Retrieved April 22, 2014, from YouTube: https://www.youtube.com/watch?v=9URYDyELWrM

Arango, T. (2012, September 24). *Syrian War's Spillover Threatens a Fragile Iraq*. Retrieved June 13, 2013, from *The New York Times*: www.nytimes.com/2012/09/25/world/middleeast/iraq-faces-new-perils-from-syrias-civil-war.html?pagewanted=all&_r=1&

Killing the state and undermining the nation   71

Arnoldy, B. (2011, September 1). *US Commission Finds Widespread Waste and Corruption in Wartime Contracts*. Retrieved January 7, 2014, from Christian Science Monitor: www.csmonitor.com/World/Global-News/2011/0901/US-commission-finds-widespread-waste-and-corruption-in-wartime-contracts

Associated Press. (2003, November 26). *Garner: US made major mistakes in Iraq*. Retrieved January 7, 2014, from Fox News: www.foxnews.com/story/2003/11/26/garner-us-made-major-mistakes-in-iraq/

BBC. (2003, January 3). *US Will Liberate Iraq, says Bush*. Retrieved January 29, 2014, from BBC News: http://news.bbc.co.uk/2/hi/2625981.stm

Belloni, R. (2007). Rethinking Nation-Building: The contradictions of the Neo-Wilsonian approach to democracy promotion. *The Journal of Diplomacy and International Relations*, 97–109.

Black, I. (2007, January 26). *Fear of Shia Full Moon*. Retrieved May 15, 2013, from *The Guardian*: www.guardian.co.uk/world/2007/jan/26/worlddispatch.ianblack

Boyer, P. (2004, November 1). *The Believer*. Retrieved January 7, 2014, from *The New Yorker*: www.newyorker.com/archive/2004/11/01/041101fa_fact

Bremer, L. P., & McConnell, M. (2006). *My Year in Iraq: The struggle to build a future of hope*. New York: Simon and Schuster.

Burrough, B., Peretz, E., Rose, D., & Wise, D. (2004, May). *The Path to War*. Retrieved January 7, 2014, from *Vanity Fair*: www.vanityfair.com/politics/features/2004/05/path-to-war200405

Bush, G. W. (2001, January 21). *The Inauguration; Bush Speech: "I will work to build a single nation of justice and opportunity."* Retrieved January 7, 2014, from *The New York Times*: www.nytimes.com/2001/01/21/us/inauguration-bush-speech-will-work-build-single-nation-justice-opportunity.html?pagewanted=all&src=pm

Chandrasekaran, R. (2006). *Imperial Life in the Emerald City: Inside Iraq's Green Zone*. New York: Alfred A. Knopf.

Cheney, D. (2011). *In My Time: A personal and political memoir*. New York: Threshold Editions.

Clarke, R. A. (2004). *Against all Enemies: Inside America's war on terror*. New York: Free Press.

Coalition Provisional Authority. (2003a, September 19). *Order Number 37*. Retrieved January 22, 2014, from The Coalition Provisional Authority: www.iraqcoalition.org/regulations/20030919_CPAORD_37_Tax_Strategy_for_2003.pdf

Coalition Provisional Authority. (2003b, September 19). *Order Number 39*. Retrieved January 8, 2014, from The Coalition Provisional Authority: www.iraqcoalition.org/regulations/20031220_CPAORD_39_Foreign_Investment_.pdf

Coalition Provisional Authority. (2003c, September 19). *Order Number 40*. Retrieved January 22, 2014, from The Coalition Provisional Authority: www.iraqcoalition.org/regulations/20030919_CPAORD40_Bank_Law_with_Annex.pdf

Coalition Provisional Authority. (2004, February 19). *Order Number 49*. Retrieved January 29, 2014, from The Coalition Provisional Authority: www.iraqcoalition.org/regulations/20040220_CPAORD_49_Tax_Strategy_of_2004_with_Annex_and_Ex_Note.pdf

Cockburn, A. (2003, October 11–13). *Kay's Misleading Report*. Retrieved June 24, 2013, from CounterPunch: www.counterpunch.org/2003/10/11/kay-s-misleading-report/

Cogan, J. (2005, August 31). *Iraq's Draft Constitution: A recipe for neo-colonial rule*. Retrieved January 7, 2014, from Global Research: www.globalresearch.ca/iraq-s-draft-constitution-a-recipe-for-neo-colonial-rule/893

72 Deconstruction and reconstruction of the state

Cole, J. (2005, February 13). *SCIRI Sweeps Provincial Elections in South*. Retrieved January 7, 2014, from Informed Comment: http://www.juancole.com/2005/02/sciri-sweeps-provincial-elections-in.html

Colvin, R. (2010, November 29). *Cut off Head of Snake, Saudis Told US on Iran*. Retrieved May 10, 2013, from Reuters: www.reuters.com/article/2010/11/29/us-wikileaks-iran-saudis-idUSTRE6AS02B20101129

Coman, J. (2003, March 30). *Dissent Rounds on Rumsfeld*. Retrieved May 29, 2013, from *The Daily Telegraph*: www.telegraph.co.uk/news/worldnews/northamerica/usa/1426133/Dissent-rounds-on-Rumsfeld.html

Docena, H. (2005, September 1). *How the US got its Neoliberal Way in Iraq*. Retrieved June 9, 2009, from *Asia Times*: www.atimes.com/atimes/Middle_East/GI01Ak01.html

Dodge, T. (2005). *Inventing Iraq: The failure of nation building and a history denied*. New York: Columbia University Press.

Douthat, R. (2012, October 23). *The Missing Debate*. Retrieved July 29, 2013, from *The New York Times*: http://campaignstops.blogs.nytimes.com/2012/10/23/douthat-the-missing-debate/

Dreyfuss, R. (2003, April 9). *Humpty Dumpty in Baghdad: How the Pentagon plans to dominate postwar Iraq*. Retrieved January 7, 2014, from *The American Prospect*: http://prospect.org/article/humpty-dumpty-baghdad

Eichenwald, K. (2012, September 10). *The Deafness Before the Storm*. Retrieved January 7, 2014, from *The New York Times*: www.nytimes.com/2012/09/11/opinion/the-bush-white-house-was-deaf-to-9-11-warnings.html?_r=0

Executive Office of the President of the United States. (2002, February 4). *Fiscal Year 2003: Budget of the United States government*. Retrieved January 11, 2013, from US Government Printing Office: www.gpo.gov/fdsys/pkg/BUDGET-2003-BUD/pdf/BUDGET-2003-BUD.pdf

Executive Office of the President of the United States. (2012, February 13). *Fiscal Year 2013: Budget of the United States government*. Retrieved January 11, 2013, from US Government Printing Office: www.gpo.gov/fdsys/pkg/BUDGET-2013-BUD/pdf/BUDGET-2013-BUD.pdf

FAIR. (2003, March 18). *In Iraq Crisis, Networks are Megaphones for Official Views*. Retrieved May 29, 2013, from Fairness and Accuracy in Reporting: http://fair.org/article/in-iraq-crisis-networks-are-megaphones-for-official-views/

Fairfield, H., & Tse, A. (2010, March 26). *The 2010 Iraqi Primary Elections*. Retrieved September 26, 2013, from *The New York Times*: www.nytimes.com/interactive/2010/03/11/world/middleeast/20100311-iraq-election.html?_r=1&

Fukuyama, F. (1989). The End of History? *The National Interest*.

Gaffney, F. (2003, September 29). *Take out Al-Jazeera*. Retrieved July 1, 2013, from Fox News: www.foxnews.com/story/2003/09/29/take-out-al-jazeera/

Garner, G. J. (2004, March 19). BBC Newsnight Report: General Jay Garner on Iraq (G. Palast, Interviewer). Retrieved January 21, 2014, from G. Palast: www.gregpalast.com/bbc-newsnight-reportgeneral-jay-garner-on-iraq/

Glanz, J. (2009, November 11). *U.S. Advisor to Kurds Stands to Reap Oil Profits*. Retrieved March 24, 2014, from *The New York Times*: www.nytimes.com/2009/11/12/world/middleeast/12galbraith.html?pagewanted=all&_r=0

Gordon, M., & Lehren, A. (2010, October 23). *Tensions High Along Kurdish–Arab Line*. Retrieved January 7, 2014, from *The New York Times*: www.nytimes.com/2010/10/24/world/middleeast/24kurds.html

Graham, P. (2004, June 1). Beyond Fallujah: A year with the Iraqi resistance. *Harper's*.

Gryphon-Partners (n.d.). Retrieved November 14, 2014, from Gryphon-Partners: http:// gryphon-partners.com/?page_id=40

Haass, R. (2009). *War of Necessity, War of Choice: A memoir of two Iraq wars.* New York: Simon and Schuster.

Hardy, R. (2004, May 21). *Analysis: Rise and fall of Chalabi.* Retrieved January 7, 2014, from BBC News: http://news.bbc.co.uk/2/hi/middle_east/3735973.stm

Harnden, T. (2003a, February 15). *Change of Tone as Powell Takes it Personally.* Retrieved June 13, 2013, from *The Daily Telegraph*: www.telegraph.co.uk/news/worldnews/ northamerica/usa/1422172/Change-of-tone-as-Powell-takes-it-personally.html

Harnden, T. (2003b, March 26). *Ex-Generals Fall out With Rumsfeld.* Retrieved June 19, 2013, from *The Daily Telegraph*: www.telegraph.co.uk/news/worldnews/northamerica/ usa/1425722/Ex-generals-fall-out-with-Rumsfeld.html

Hayes, D., & Guardino, M. (2010). Whose Views Made the News? Media coverage and the march to war in Iraq. *Political Communication*, 59–87.

Hedges, C. (2010). *Death of the Liberal Class.* New York: Nation Books.

Heikal, M. H. (2003, October). *Al-kuwat al-Musal'laha fi al-Siyasa al-Amrikiyaa* [*The Armed Forces in American Policy*]. Retrieved October 10, 2013, from Al Jazeera: www.aljazeera.net/wejhat/article.asp?aid=78&ft=1

Heilbrunn, J. (2008). *They Knew They Were Right: The rise of the neocons.* New York: Doubleday.

Hersh, S. (2003, May 5). *Selective Intelligence.* Retrieved January 7, 2014, from *The New Yorker*: www.newyorker.com/archive/2003/05/12/030512fa_fact

Hersh, S. (2004). *Chain of Command.* New York: HarperCollins.

Hiro, D. (2004). *Secrets and Lies.* New York: Nation Books.

Hoon, G. (2003, March 28). *No Lens is Wide Enough to Show the Big Picture.* Retrieved May 19, 2013, from *The Times*: www.thetimes.co.uk/tto/law/columnists/ article2045904.ece

Iraqis Respond to the Election: Commentary from Imad Khadduri, Tahrir Swift and Munir Chalabi. (2005, February 1). Retrieved May 7, 2009, from Occupation Watch: www. occupationwatch.org/article.php?id=9106

Jamal, M. A. (2014, February 3). *Integration of Iraq Militias not a Good Idea.* Retrieved February 5, 2014, from Gulf News: http://gulfnews.com/opinions/columnists/ integration-of-iraq-militias-not-a-good-idea-1.1285907

Jamail, D. (2005, September 6). *UN Official Says US Interfering in Iraq Constitution Process.* Retrieved June 5, 2009, from Antiwar.com: www.antiwar.com/jamail/ ?articleid=7164

Johnson, C. (2004). *The Sorrows of Empire.* New York: Metropolitan Books.

Kagan, R., & Kristol, W. (2002, January 21). *What to do About Iraq.* Retrieved January 21, 2014, from *The Weekly Standard*: www.weeklystandard.com/Content/Public/ Articles/000/000/000/768pylwj.asp

Keegan, J. (2005). *The Iraq War.* New York: Vintage Books.

Keller, B. (2002, September 22). *The Sunshine Warrior.* Retrieved June 12, 2013, from *The New York Times*: www.nytimes.com/2002/09/22/magazine/the-sunshine-warrior. html?pagewanted=all&src=pm

Kirkpatrick, D. (2014, January 24). *Prolonged Fight Feared in Egypt After Bombings.* Retrieved January 29, 2014, from *The New York Times*: www.nytimes.com/2014/01/25/ world/middleeast/fatal-bomb-attacks-in-egypt.html?_r=0

Kitabat. (2013, June 26). [*Back Sandra*]. Retrieved March 23, 2014, from Kitabat: www. kitabat.com/ar/page/26/06/2013/13693/عودة-ساندرا.html

74 Deconstruction and reconstruction of the state

Kitabat. (2014a, March 20). [*How the Election Commission Deliberates*]. Retrieved March 23, 2014, from Kitabat: www.kitabat.com/ar/page/20/03/2014/24894/بختنن-وأ-الننتخب-ل-تائجج-م-عروفةlrm.html

Kitabat. (2014b, March 21). [*Ayyar Accuses the UN*]. Kitabat.

Klein, N. (2004, September). Baghdad Year Zero: Pillaging Iraq in pursuit of a neocon utopia. *Harper's Magazine.*

Klein, N. (2007). *The Shock Doctrine: The rise of disaster capitalism.* Toronto: Random House.

Kurtz, H. (2003, April 28). For Media After Iraq, a Case of Shell Shock; Battle Assessment Begins for Saturating Reporting. *The Washington Post.*

Leigh, D. (2004, March 18). *General Sacked by Bush Says He Wanted Early Elections.* Retrieved January 19, 2014, from *The Guardian*: www.theguardian.com/world/2004/mar/18/iraq.usa

Lemann, N. (2002, April 1). The Next World Order. *The New Yorker.*

Lobe, J. (2003, August 13). *What is a Neo-Conservative Anyway?* Retrieved January 7, 2014, from *Asia Times*: www.atimes.com/atimes/Front_Page/EH13Aa01.html

Lobe, J. (2004, January 10). *Iraqi WMD: Myths and more myths.* Retrieved November 12, 2009, from *Asia Times*: www.atimes.com/atimes/Middle_East/FA10Ak01.html

Lobe, J. (2014, January 10–12). *The Fall of Fallujah.* Retrieved February 5, 2014, from CounterPunch: www.counterpunch.org/2014/01/10/the-fall-of-fallujah/

Mann, J. (2004). *Rise of the Vulcans: The history of Bush's war cabinet.* New York: Penguin Books.

Marx, W. (2006, September). Misinformation Intern: My summer as a military propagandist in Iraq. *Harper's Magazine.*

Mazzetti, M., & Daragahi, B. (2005, November 30). *US Military Covertly Pays to Run Stories in Iraqi Press.* Retrieved May 9, 2013, from *Los Angeles Times*: http://articles.latimes.com/2005/nov/30/world/fg-infowar30

McClellan, S. (2008). *What Happened: Inside the Bush White House and Washington's culture of deception.* New York: Public Affairs.

Mearsheimer, J., & Walt, S. (2007). *The Israel Lobby and US Foreign Policy.* New York: Farrar, Straus & Giroux.

Mirror. (2006, October 12). *Blunkett: We must bomb al-Jazeera TV.* Retrieved June 29, 2013, from *The Mirror*: www.mirror.co.uk/news/uk-news/blunkett-we-must-bomb-al-jazeera-tv-703191

Mitchell, S. (n.d.). *Sandra Mitchell.* Retrieved March 24, 2014, from LinkedIn: www.linkedin.com/pub/sandra-mitchell/20/bb4/421

Moseley, T. M. (2003, April 30). *Operation Iraqi Freedom—By the Numbers.* Retrieved January 17, 2014, from Global Security: www.globalsecurity.org/military/library/report/2003/uscentaf_oif_report_30apr2003.pdf

Munro, N., & Cannon, C. M. (2008, January 4). Data Bomb. Retrieved January 5, 2008, from *National Journal*: http://news.nationaljournal.com/articles/databomb/

Mylroie, L. (2001). *The War Against America: Saddam Hussein and the World Trade Center attacks, a study of revenge* (2nd ed.). New York: HarperCollins.

Nissenbaum, D. (2014, February 3). *Role of U.S. Contractors Grows as Iraq Fights Insurgents.* Retrieved May 5, 2014, from *The Wall Street Journal*: http://online.wsj.com/news/articles/SB10001424052702304851104579361170141705420

Norton-Taylor, R. (2005, November 23). *Legal Gag on Bush–Blair War Row.* Retrieved June 15, 2013, from *The Guardian*: www.theguardian.com/politics/2005/nov/23/uk.topstories3

Killing the state and undermining the nation 75

O'Hanlon, M. E., & Livingston, I. (2012, July). *Iraq Index: Tracking variables of reconstruction & security in Iraq.* Retrieved January 7, 2014, from Brookings: www.brookings.edu/~/media/Centers/saban/iraq%20index/index201207.pdf

Packer, G. (2005). *The Assassins' Gate: America in Iraq.* New York: Farrar, Straus & Giroux.

PBS Frontline. (2003, October). *Truth, War and Consequences.* Retrieved November 12, 2009, from PBS Frontline: www.pbs.org/wgbh/pages/frontline/shows/truth/

Peri, S. (2003, May 6). *Saddam's "Successor" Made Secret Visit to Israel.* Retrieved December 9, 2013, from Israel Behind the News: www.israelbehindthenews.com/bin/content.cgi?ID=1700&q=1

Phillips, D. L. (2005). *Losing Iraq: Inside the postwar reconstruction fiasco.* New York: Basic Books.

Pike, J. (1998, August 8). *Iraqi National Congress (INC).* Retrieved January 7, 2014, from Federation of American Scientists: www.fas.org/irp/world/para/inc.htm

Potter, B. (2005, February 17). Now That They Voted, Iraqis Want US out. *Washington Times.*

Powell, B. A. (2004, March 15). *Reporters, Commentators Visit Berkeley to Conduct In-Depth Postmortem of Iraq War Coverage.* Retrieved January 7, 2014, from UC Berkeley News: www.berkeley.edu/news/media/releases/2004/03/15_mediatwar.shtml

Project for a New American Century. (2000, September). *Rebuilding America's Defenses: Strategy, forces and resources for a new century.* Retrieved January 7, 2014, from Information Clearing House: www.informationclearinghouse.info/pdf/RebuildingAmericasDefenses.pdf

Regan, T. (2004, January 14). *White House's Rush to War was Reckless.* Retrieved November 10, 2009, from Christian Science Monitor: http://www.discussanything.com/forums/showthread.php/47599-White-House-s-rush-to-war-was-reckless

Republican Party Platform. (2000, July 31). *Republican Party Platform of 2000.* Retrieved January 7, 2014, from The American Presidency Project: www.presidency.ucsb.edu/ws/?pid=25849

Richter, P. (2011, June 13). *Missing Iraq Money may Have Been Stolen, Auditors Say.* Retrieved June 14, 2013, from *Los Angeles Times*: http://articles.latimes.com/2011/jun/13/world/la-fg-missing-billions-20110613

Ritter, S. (2002, July 20). *Is Iraq a True Threat to the US?* Retrieved January 7, 2014, from *The Boston Globe*: www.commondreams.org/views02/0721-02.htm

Rogers, S. (2010, October 23). *WikiLeaks: Data journalism maps every death.* Retrieved January 7, 2014, from *The Guardian*: www.theguardian.com/news/datablog/2010/oct/23/wikileaks-iraq-data-journalism

RT. (2014, February 4). *Contractors Flood into Iraq to Give Al-Qaeda a Run for the Money.* Retrieved May 5, 2014, from RT: http://rt.com/news/american-military-contractors-iraq-621/

Sanchez, R., & Philips, D. (2008). *Wiser in Battle: A soldier's story.* New York: HarperCollins.

Schechter, D. (2003). *Embedded: Weapons of mass deception. How the media failed to cover the war on Iraq.* New York: Prometheus Books.

Schmitt, E. (2003, February 28). Pentagon Contradicts General on Iraq Occupation Force's Size. *The New York Times.*

Sherlock, R. (2012, October 24). *Sectarian Rivalry and Syria Politics Divide Lebanon.* Retrieved June 18, 2013, from *Sydney Morning Herald*: www.smh.com.au/world/sectarian-rivalry-and-syria-politics-divide-lebanon-20121023-283cl.html

76 Deconstruction and reconstruction of the state

Sissons, M., & Al-Saiedi, A. (2013, March). *A Bitter Legacy: Lessons of De-Baathification in Iraq.* Retrieved January 7, 2014, from International Center for Transitional Justice: http://ictj.org/sites/default/files/ICTJ-Report-Iraq-De-Baathification-2013-ENG.pdf

Susman, T. (2007, September 14). *Civilian Deaths may Top 1 Million, Poll Data Indicate.* Retrieved January 7, 2014, from *Los Angeles Times*: http://articles.latimes.com/2007/sep/14/world/fg-iraq14

Telhami, S., & Kull, S. (2011, September 8). *The American Public on the 9/11 Decade.* Retrieved January 29, 2014, from The University of Maryland: http://sadat.umd.edu/911Anniversary_Sep11_rpt.pdf

Tenet, G. (2007). *At the Center of the Storm: My years at the CIA.* New York: HarperCollins.

UN General Assembly. (2005, September 15). *2005 World Summit Outcome.* Retrieved January 3, 2014, from World Health Organization: www.who.int/hiv/universalaccess2010/worldsummit.pdf

UNSC. (2003, May 22). *Resolution 1483, S/RES/1483 (2003).* Retrieved January 15, 2014, from United Nations: daccess-ods.un.org/TMP/2229487.44893074.html

Wallis, W., & Khalaf, R. (2005, November 23). *Qatar Shock at al-Jazeera Bombing Report.* Retrieved June 12, 2013, from *Financial Times*: www.ft.com/cms/s/0/92fad322-5c58-11da-af92-0000779e2340.html

Wells, M. (2003, November 6). *Embedded Reporters "Sanitised" Iraq War.* Retrieved May 24, 2013, from *The Guardian*: www.theguardian.com/media/2003/nov/06/broadcasting.Iraqandthemedia

WHO. (2008). *Iraq Family Health Survey (IFHS) 2006/7.* Retrieved January 7, 2014, from World Health Organization: www.who.int/mediacentre/news/releases/2008/pr02/2008_iraq_family_health_survey_report.pdf

Wolfowitz, P. (2000). Remembering the Future. *The National Interest.*

Woodward, B. (2006). *State of Denial: Bush at war part 3.* New York: Simon and Schuster.

Zimmermann, W. (2002). *First Great Triumph.* New York: Farrar, Straus and Giroux.

4 The sectarian state in Iraq and the new political class

The Anglo-American invasion of Iraq in 2003 represented the crescendo of a Western policy that had left Iraq economically crippled, militarily weak and in an ever-present humanitarian crisis. Through comprehensive economic sanctions that were applied by the UN following the 1991 Gulf War, the foundations of Iraq's social infrastructure were crippled, destroying the country's once-esteemed education and health services, and creating a state of desperation among the populace. In hindsight, the goal of the sanctions regime appears to have been to shake the socio-economic foundation of Iraq and, thus, the social coherence of the Iraqi national project that had developed progressively since 1920.

Given the desperate conditions imposed by the sanctions regime, Iraq was singularly unprepared for the military onslaught of Anglo-American forces in 2003, and in the successive years of occupation Iraq has been dominated by forces of sectarian violence, national disarray and factionalism. The violent sectarianism that has since characterized Iraqi politics and society is, however, a modern development. Social sectarianism—represented by competing historical narratives and beliefs, chauvinistic attitudes and social/political resentments—has been variously present in Iraqi and Islamic history, but sectarianism as an explicit and violent political ideology has never before been the norm in Iraqi history. The most prolific sociologist produced by Iraq, 'Ali al-Wardi, saw sectarianism as a very important issue in Iraq and its politics. In elucidating his motives for writing *The History of Sectarian Conflict in Iraq*, al-Wardi (1965) described the influence of sectarianism as

> the most important side of Iraqi society, if not the most important face, as this topic [sectarianism] has a long history in Iraq and deep roots in the Iraqi personality and social culture. I am sure any objective research on sectarian conflict will not be approved by many Iraqis, as they are used to looking at this conflict through a partisan's lens. Every group believes it holds alone the absolute truth, and everything else is folly [...] We are in the most urgent need for a study of this nature as sectarianism has become the most complicated ill that permeates Iraqi society and it may be correct to say that it has ended up as a complex hidden within the inner Iraqi personality. It is natural for this complex to grow and increase as long as it stays in the inner soul and

78 *Deconstruction and reconstruction of the state*

the one sided-arguments go on [...] this complex must someday be studied objectively and consciously, to cure this ill.

(pp. 401–402)

The violent sectarianism that now dominates Iraqi society is a political phenomenon, the outcome of a series of deliberately chosen policies undertaken by Western occupation authorities and their Iraqi allies.

The Iraqi national project, constructed over decades of uneven, often oppressive state building, had nevertheless in large measure suppressed communal factionalism and sectarianism. Resting upon accumulated beliefs and legends of Iraqi nationhood, Islamic and Arab heritage and a historic pride in one's country representing the "cradle of civilization," Iraqi nationalism had been established as the primary credo, even when the country descended into various forms of dictatorial rule. Secular education and secular state building has had, over eight decades, a homogenizing effect, which allowed for the emergence of a sense of Iraqi nationhood or "Iraqi-ness"—a sense of being "Iraqi" that progressively supplanted one's identity as Sunni, Shi'ite, Christian and so forth. It is in light of this evolved social reality that the recent collapse of Iraqi society is so shocking and tragic. This chapter surveys the social conditions and political decisions that gave rise to this state of affairs.

The social setting of pre-invasion Iraq

To understand sectarian forces in contemporary Iraq, it is first instructive to make a distinction between politicized sectarianism and social sectarianism. Folkloric/social sectarianism is used to refer to the manifestations of traditional identifiers and community cohesion, namely concerning matters of cultural/religious practice and ritual, founding myths and shared beliefs that bind a community within the nation. Folkloric sectarianism is especially pronounced in rural areas with homogeneous populations, particularly if these communities are isolated from the cultural multiplicity of modern urban centers; these traditional identities are mitigated and, ideally, give way to civic super-identities that account for variation in social practice and belief. This process is especially marked where the state, as the arbiter of social relations, is perceived as even-handed and neutral. However, where the state is seen as tilted towards one community over another, it risks reawakening feelings of social difference—hence active sectarianism.

Social sectarianism has been observable throughout history. In the case of modern Iraq, forms of social sectarian tension often manifested themselves in conflicts between a secularizing state and religious and tribal and ethnic communities suspicious of secular and nationalist state-building projects. After the emergence of modern Iraq following World War I and the dissolution of the Ottoman Empire, these sectarian tensions were evident in the relations and negotiations between the secular Iraqi state and the Iraqi tribes.[1] In the development of the Iraqi state in the early twentieth century, the structural tension between state and society, on the one hand, and between urban- and rural-based elites, on the other, shaped two interacting, though distinct, Iraqi spheres. One sphere comprised the segmented tribal–rural sectarian-oriented social systems that were cut off from each other and from the main flow of world history; while the other encompassed the urban-based secular-oriented social systems populated with a heterogeneous mix of disaffected old-guard elites, an emerging middle class of state functionaries, professionals and military staff, and a budding working class largely composed of marginalized peasantry migrating into the urban centers for work (Halpern, 1963; Ismael, 1970, pp. 100–121). These two spheres of Iraqi society increasingly interacted with one another, embodied in population migration, casting competing visions of society and politics against one another. Now caught in the main currents of world history following World War I—the collapse of the Ottoman Empire and the retrenchment of Western imperialism—Baghdad, Basra and Mosul became centers where the ideas of modernity, independence, sovereignty, development, tradition, imperialism and exploitation were all juxtaposed against one another. It was in this tumultuous environment of ideas that the secular principles of social equity took root in the popular political culture of urban Iraqi society.

With the establishment of the modern Iraqi state in 1920, a general trend emerged that led the country towards secular development, chiefly through the vehicles of education, the state bureaucracy and the military. The expansion of the bureaucratic state and urbanization, along with the state's role as an architect of re-engineering society through promoting progressive development goals, coalesced to make both religion and tribe less influential as determinants of an individual's life chances, especially in the urban centers. This phenomenon gained much prominence with the establishment of the Republican regime in 1958 and the influx of petro-dollars. Religious fervor subsided in the urban centers and was replaced by the pursuit of secular ambitions, thus gradually closing the gap between Shia and Sunni politico-religious ideologies (al-Wardi, 1954, pp. 259–260). However, this erosion of sectarian feeling was a largely urban phenomenon. In the rural village setting social sectarianism festered, even while the power and authority of the village tribal and religious elite was on the decline. Despite the intensity of this rural-based social sectarianism being ameliorated through state-building projects, sectarian sentiments persisted in the local political cultures. Nevertheless, while sectarianism persisted in its social forms, sectarianism as a political project was rare in contemporary Iraqi history, being ephemeral rather than systematic in nature.

Political sectarianism, on the other hand, describes the institutionalization of social differences through governmental policy, chiefly through the distribution of office, power and resources according to a person or people's affiliations. Having established sectarianism as a norm of governance, political sectarianism replicates itself through society, aggravating in-group/out-group relations—encouraging the use of exaggerated historical narratives to demonize the out group—potentially leading to the formation of sect-exclusive political groupings, armed militias and segmented communities. Political sectarianism erodes notions of citizenship and nationalism, and reduces the state and society to a medley of exclusive sects struggling with each other for power (immaterial and real) and resources.

80   *Deconstruction and reconstruction of the state*

Iraq cannot be understood in isolation from the historical factors that forged the collective memories of external reality, and that set the tempo of transformation. It was the geography of Iraq, with its fertile soil and two rivers, that allowed the emergence of very ancient civilizations and the later emergence of a modern nation. In terms of the social divisions that developed, there are three main factors: (1) conflicting religio-political perspectives; (2) surviving tribal values; and (3) international intervention.

First, with the death of the fourth Caliph, 'Alî Ibn Abî-Ṭâlib, in 661 CE, two oppositional political frames of mind emerged during the Umayyad Dynasty; one supported a political hereditary Caliphate, which the Umayyad had set up, particularly in Greater Syria; the second carried the banner of 'Alî and advocated social justice. The second was heavily propagated in Iraq because of the presence of 148 of the core companions of the Prophet Muhammad and around 850 of the followers of those companions (al-Wardi, 1954, p. 31). During the Umayyad reign and the early period of the Abbasid Dynasty under Abû-Ja'far al-Mansûr (d. 775), the pillars of Islamic jurisprudence supported 'Alî and his lineage as the legitimate rulers, including the famous Sunni jurists, Abû Hanîfah, al-Shafi'î, Anas Ibn Mâlik and Ahmad Ibn Hanbal (al-Wardi, 1954, pp. 233–236). The Abbasids were not different from the Umayyads, who preceded them, in their pursuit of power without the institutionalizing social justice, which in time irreparably widened the gulf between the supporters of 'Alî and the beneficiaries of the hereditary Caliphate. The assassination of al-Husain, the prophet's grandson, by the Umayyads in 680 galvanized 'Alî's supporters into a distinct community that came to be known as the Shi'ite, the partisans of 'Alî and his message. In Shi'ite historical memory, a political-hereditary regime divorced of Islamic social justice was equivalent to oppression and state tyranny. The anti-Shia animosity of some Abbasid caliphs, particularly al-Mutawaqqil (d. 860), was not veiled, and burst into aggression toward the Shi'ites. He and his entourage not only degraded 'Alî and his family publicly but also desecrated the grave of his son, al-Husain, the third Shia Imam, demolished the Shi'ite houses surrounding it and cut the tongues out of those who publicly praised him (al-Wardi, 1954, p. 238).

The quest for social justice, which 'Alî Ibn Abî-Ṭâlib and his son, al-Husain, represented by their martyrdom, has been at the core of Shi'ite social memory and holds them together through the yearly commemorative ceremonies surrounding al-'Azâ' al-Husainî (al-Husain Solace), that takes place on 'Âshûrâ' (the tenth day of Muharram, the first month in the Hijrah calendar). This day marks the day that al-Husain was murdered in 680 CE. According to a distinguished sociologist, who has dedicated most of his life to studying the phenomenon, the first commemoration was probably held in the late seventh century, when Shi'ites congregated around al-Husain's grave, in a pensive mood, to express sorrow for the loss and penitence for forsaking al-Husain on the day of battle (al-Haidarî, 1999, p. 51). The earliest commemoration, thus, in both substance and form, was a sincere expression of mass guilt.

Over time, acculturated accretions of folkloric foreign imports (Turkic tribes and Dervishes) added melodramatic magnitude to the performative commemoration of al-Husain Solace in the late nineteenth century; most notable were al-Tatbîr (sword wounding) and al-Zanjîl (self-flagellation by chains) (al-Haidarî, 1999, p. 456). The Shi'ite Ulama, whether collectively or individually, failed to end this folkloric ritual of self-injury (al-Haidarî, 1999, pp. 451–455). In fact, al-Husain Solace was steadily built up from early times, assuming new dimensions while simultaneously ridding itself from its formulation of mass guilt. This occurred for two reasons. First, Shi'ite opinion makers substituted poetic remembrance of al-Husain's martyrdom, accompanied by a state of induced ecstasy through wailing and self-flagellation for sober reasoning and contemplation, in public performative parades and congregations as early as the eleventh century CE (al-Haidarî, 1999, pp. 52–57). Second, Shi'ite Seminaries (al-Hawzah al-'Ilmiyyah), the highest of Shi'ite religious authorities, dominate every level of Iraqi society, and preach with the unequaled merits of the Prophetic lineage the importance of unconditional obedience and love for the Prophet's household, particularly al-Husain, in anticipation of the return of the Mahdî.[2]

Poets, preachers and storytellers reinforced the religious discourse through evocative myths and legends that became part of the collective thought process of the Shi'ite public (al-Haidarî, 1999, pp. 228–230). In this context, the original sense of guilt was forgotten, projected on the other—that is, the state or the ruler—and the Shi'ites, much like al-Husain, are the oppressed by present circumstances; al-Husain Solace thus evolved into a folkloric, performative, social memory of victimization. Thus, although mechanisms of historical projection and transference have maintained the cohesion of the Shi'ite community, the praxis of recollection emphasizes the form without substance. According to al-Haidarî (1999, p. 460), the noble principles of al-Husain have been reduced to folkloric melodrama, and regressed to mere bodily torture. Although Saddam Hussein used state power and wealth to re-engineer social cohesion and forge a secular national identity, he, for this reason perhaps, allowed the observance of al-Husain Solace to continue. In allowing Shi'ite folkloric practices under the state's patronage, he conveyed a subtle message that he was the leader of all Iraqis, no matter their cultural, religious or tribal affiliations. He was thus able to be dismissive of dissenting Shi'ite cohorts (al-Haidarî, 1999, pp. 75–79).

Second, unlike any other country in the Arab world, Iraq has been a recipient of frequent tribal migrations from the Syrian Desert and the Arabian Peninsula. For example, the Ghazâ'il tribe moved into Iraq around 150 years ago, Ka'b around 100 years ago, Rabî'ah around 70 years ago and the Zubaid around 60 years ago (al-'Alawî, 2009, p. 42). According to the distinguished Iraqi sociologist 'Ali al-Wardi (al-'Alawî, 2009, p. 132), many such tribes were originally Sunni, but under the influence of Shi'ite missionary zeal, they adopted the socio-political orientation as it resonated with their tribal social complexes and cultural traits. Prominent among Bedouin values is warriorship, which is not only necessary for survival in the desert but also to resist submission and oppression. The ethos of warriorship is primary not only in relating the tribesmen's mindset to the Shi'ite narrative of historical state tyranny but also in arousing strong empathy with Shi'ite socio-political grievances against the state. Chivalry, solidarity and protection stand out in the Bedouin

82 Deconstruction and reconstruction of the state

cultural pattern and were equally valued practices among the Shi'ite community after it withdrew from public life, and insulated the community from the state following the disappearance of the Twelfth Imam, Muhammad al-'Askarî, in the tenth century. From that time onwards, the Shi'ite jurists cemented the community by addressing its needs through an ongoing process of Ijtihad while becoming economically independent from the state; Shi'ite jurists lived on religious taxes and public contributions went to the Shi'ite clerics, whereas Sunni jurists, since Hârûn al-Rashîd (d. 809), were co-opted into the state machinery as salaried employees, thus countenancing state practices, much to the revulsion of Bedouin values. The connection between the Shi'ite socio-political narrative and Bedouin value complexes, which have not fully disappeared, made it difficult and time consuming for the modern Iraqi state to build a permanent political infrastructure.

Third, Iraq suffered the mismanagement, discrimination and corruption of the Ottoman state machinery for 400 years as well as the horrors of the Ottoman–Safavid wars, which were waged on Iraqi soil in the context of state religious bigotry. Four religious wars were launched by the Shi'ite Safavids in Iran and the Sunni Ottomans between 1508 and 1638, which massacred hundreds of thousands of people. The Iranians killed Sunni Ottomans and Iraqis en masse, and ravaged Sunni monuments; the Ottomans mass-murdered Iranians and Shi'ite Iraqis, and demolished Shi'ite shrines. Memories of the ravages of war have lingered on, bolstering Shi'ite opposition to the tyrannical state. The Sunnis, under Ottoman suzerainty, discriminated against the Shi'ites more, whom they perceived as the phalanx of Iranian domination. Each community was so entrenched in partisanship and defensiveness that rationality and reasoning gave way to myths and folk traditions unfounded in religion, particularly among the laity, resulting in a schizoid culture (al-'Alawî, 1996, pp. 51–56).

This was the social environment that predated (1915–1918) the British incursion and eventual occupation of Iraq, which in turn precipitated two revolts. One is known as the Jihad Movement, which the Shi'ite jurists and the Shi'ite community had led, and in which they suffered heavily warding off foreign forces. The second is known the Great Revolt of 1920, which included Iraqis from all denominations, and culminated in enthroning King Faisal I, creating the façade of an independent Iraq. Reviewing the political literature of the Jihad Movement in 1915 makes it clear that the Shi'ite jurists and their followers were politically self-conscious of their Arabo-Muslim identity. After the British quelled the movement and preceding the Great Revolt, Shi'ite jurists, such as Muhammad Taqiyyi al-Hâ'irî al-Shîrâzî, addressed the British occupation, in seven messages, to clarify their political agenda for future governance. These underscored the principles of full independence under an Arab–Islamic government headed by an Arab–Muslim King whose authority would be checked by a publicly elected parliament (al-'Alawî, 2009, pp. 62–69, 79–80, 111–122). The Shi'ite resistance during the Jihad Movement and their leadership in the Great Revolt aroused British intransigence regarding an Islamic government because it would mean intractable Shi'ite hegemony in Iraq by way of Islamic jurists serving in the absence of the *de jure* Imam; this is what came to be known as the custodianship of jurists. It was the

British occupation that precluded this possibility, which in turn gave rise to the secular modern Iraqi state following the 1920 Revolt.

In the aftermath of World War I and the collapse of the Ottoman Empire, British mandatory rule over Iraq invested rural-based semi-feudal tribal chiefs (sheikhs) with political authority mediated by external power. The British tactic of "divide and rule" had a legal instrument, the Law of Land Settlement, which the British implemented by appointing an adjudicating panel headed by a Briton to resolve disputed land rights. The strategic objective was to reward Britain's collaborators and punish Iraqi opposition by depriving dissenting Iraqis from land rights, thus luring self-interested Iraqis into Britain's service. For example, Hasan Suhail al-Tamîmî, a British spy, was working as a peddler selling thorn and thistle bundles in the street. The British rewarded him with enough land to elevate him to one of the wealthiest in the country. 'Alî Sulaimân al-Dulaimî was also in service of the British, fighting against the Iraqi nationalists during the 1920 Revolt; his reward was the territory that extended from north of Ramadi to the environs of Baghdad (al-Rasafî, 2007, pp. 46–48). The British policy was to divide Iraq by engineering tension between the encapsulated rural population under semi-feudal tribal allies and an urban world populated with a heterogeneous mix of disaffected old-guard elites. In this milieu a state-engineered class of bureaucrats, professionals, military staff and a skilled working class emerged (Halpern, 1963; Ismael, 1970, pp. 100–121). Against the backdrop of a receding Western imperialism, Baghdad emerged within Iraq as a center of cosmopolitan and modern values that bred political activism and a struggle for citizenship and social reform.

With the retrenchment of British imperialism and its mandatory rule over Mesopotamia—Iraq was granted nominal independence in 1932—a number of political upheavals and intrigues would follow, though a general trend emerged leading the country towards secular education at all levels. The expansion of the bureaucratic state, along with its added role of re-engineering society towards progressive development goals, created a public perception of rewarding careers in state departments and state-sponsored projects. The fact that such careers existed for state school graduates gradually reduced the importance of religious and tribal affiliations. This turn toward the state as a prime institution rather than the ethnosectarian community accelerated especially during the Republican regime. The differences between Shi'ite and Sunni politico-religious ideology became less of a feature in daily life for Iraqis as they embraced a secular national identity (al-Wardi, 1954, pp. 259–260). The Iraqi people were the beneficiaries of this turn, as was the nascent nation-state. In sum, the tangential overlapping of Bedouin values and the Shi'ite socio-political narrative did not produce segmented Sunni/Shi'ite communities, which could otherwise have led to a sectarian societal structure. Bedouin values straddled both communities in varying degrees; as Bedouins settled in the rural areas and moved into urban centers they began to supplement their core traits with rural and urban ways of living. Settlement adumbrated desert Bedouin values, and as they enmeshed into the Shi'ite narrative the result was cultural ambivalence, not a sectarian culture. The Sunni/Shi'ite difference is one of politically interpreted historicity. The Abbasids, much like the Shi'ite Imams,

84 *Deconstruction and reconstruction of the state*

are descendants from the Prophetic bloodline. The former had, in many ways, deprived the latter from government offices and employed Sunni jurists (Ulama), which, with the passage of centuries, became associated with state tyranny in Shi'ite historical memory. Because there are no religiously embodied differences, we can find a mix of Sunnis and Shi'ites in cities and tribes, where people live peacefully. This is exemplified by Deyala City in the middle of the Euphrates, as well as Zubair City, Abu al-Khaseeb and Nassiriyah, all in southern Iraq (al-Wardi, 1954, pp. 252, 254, 259, 260).

Modern Iraqi politics and the development of Iraq's political diaspora

Iraqi politics in the second half of the twentieth century was characterized by a vast state-engineered project to inculcate nationalist sentiment through the construction of an elaborate Iraqi public sector and political vision, as well as through varying levels of political oppression and social reconstruction. Under the Ba'thist regime, particularly with the ascension of Saddam Hussein to power in 1979, the Ba'th Party and the state became synonymous and engaged in campaigns of mass repression, with the goal of destroying all organized opposition. These policies created the conditions that gave rise to a diaspora class of political elites that tended to represent narrow parochial interests and became vulnerable to the influence of external actors. Of the Shia opposition groups, one of the more significant that developed during the exile period was SCIRI. Founded in Iran by Mohammad Bâqir al-Ḥakîm in November 1982, its paramilitary wing, the Badr Brigade, was trained and financed by Tehran to fight alongside Iranian troops during the Iran–Iraq war (1980–1988). SCIRI included mainly Shia Islamists and aimed to take over a post-Saddam Iraq. During this same period, Britain attempted to engineer an anti-Khomeini Shia bloc that could be deployed should one of the warring parties—Iraq or Iran—be vanquished. This bloc was composed of a pro-West religious Marji'iya,[3] without Khomeini's jurisprudent custodianship,[4] which was prepared to fill an anticipated power vacuum. Many such disaffected expatriates flocked to London during this period. Prominent on the list were Ibrâhîm al-Ja'farî and Muwaffaq al-Rubai'î from the Da'wa Party and Al-Sayyid Muḥammad Baḥr al-'Ulûm and Ḥussain al-Shâmî from Iran, all of whom went to London in the mid-1980s and obtained British passports (al-'Alawî, 2009, pp. 218–219; Allawi, 2007).[5]

Along with SCIRI, the most significant exile movement to develop in the pre-invasion period was the Da'wa Party. The Da'wa fragmented into four splinter groups located, respectively, in London, Syria, Iran and Iraq. In the 1980s, Britain's attempt to build a surrogate Shia religious Marji'iya in London that could elicit Shia loyalty ultimately failed. This led Britain to enlist the support of an anti-Khomeini religious luminary, Grand Ayatollah Murtaḍâ al-'Askarî, who quickly rejected Britain's overtures (al-'Alawî, 2009, pp. 79–80). Nevertheless, an ambitious group of religious activists remained in Britain, with visions of seizing power in Iraq, who responded to Britain's failed plan by forming the al-Khoe'i

Foundation, an "international charity for educational and religious works under the supervision of the Marji'iya" (Allawi, 2007, p. 75). The foundation marked the beginning of a new current within the political Shia diaspora. Ali Allawi (2007), an exiled Iraqi businessman whose ties to Gulf and Western governments paved the way to his appointment in 2003 to the Iraqi Interim Government, where he has continued on as an adviser to al-Mâlikî, described the transformation:

> In the summer of 1992, the [al-Khoe'i] Foundation hosted a seminar on "The Shi'a of Iraq at the Cross-roads" [...] for the first time, a federal structure for the Shi'a of Iraq was proposed as a solution for their disempowerment. The seminar had a very powerful impact in the Iraqi Shi'a diaspora, as it was the first time that the spotlight was focused [...] on the specific problem of the Shi'a of Iraq. It elicited broad support for its claim that they were now united in adversity against the idea of a central state [in Iraq] [...] It was no longer considered forbidden or bad form to discuss the problem in a candid way.
>
> (p. 75)

With the end of the Iran–Iraq war in 1988, and in spite of Iraq having accrued an insurmountable national debt, Saddam Hussein attempted to project an image as the defender of Arab nationalism and as the last line of defense against Iran and radical Shi'ism. The invasion of oil-rich Kuwait in August 1990 brought Hussein into direct conflict with US regional interests. A US-led military coalition led to the expulsion of Iraq's army from Kuwait in January 1991 and widespread destruction of the Iraqi military and the country's infrastructure. The US-led coalition vanquished Iraq's military forces, effectively rendering it an impotent regional power, and subsequently imposed, through the UN, a costly sanctions regime that impoverished the Iraqi population.

In anticipation of the Ba'thist regime's demise, the 1990s saw intense regional and international attempts to form opposition blocs, groups of Iraqi exiles, that could fill the vacuum of a post-Saddam Iraq. A common denominator among all such groups was their exile from Iraq for three to four decades, which left them without an indigenous base of support, and thus dependent on the support of foreign actors who could install them in power as a new political class of "carpetbaggers."[6]

Throughout the 1990s, Iraqi exile movements increasingly coordinated their activities with foreign and regional powers. In 1990, Damascus, which was ideologically opposed to Saddam Hussein's wing of the Ba'th Party, formed an opposition front that comprised five irreconcilable factions from the Lajnat al-'Amal al-Mushtarak, or Joint Action Committee (JAC), consisting of the Arab Socialist Ba'th Party's Syrian Branch, the Iraqi Communist Party, the Da'wa Party, SCIRI and the Kurdish Front. Except for the Kurdish Front, these opposition groups were subject to direct Syrian and Iranian influence. Likewise, Saudi Arabia attempted to develop an opposition front, though it never directly hosted Iraqi opposition exiles. A high-ranking Saudi intelligence figure, Brigadier Muḥammad al-'Utaibî, sought the help of a UNICEF manager in Riyadh, Ṣabâḥ

86 *Deconstruction and reconstruction of the state*

'Allâwî, the brother of Iyâd 'Allâwî (a former Ba'thist, an activist with ties to the CIA and MI6 and the future Prime Minister of the Iraqi Interim Government). Iyâd 'Allâwî recruited Salah 'Umar al-'Alî, an ex-Iraqi minister, UN ambassador and former Ba'th Regional Command member, to join him in Saudi Arabia, thus heightening his stature (al-Zubaidi, 2009). In November 1990, the two men were in Saudi Arabia where they received their first check from Saudi intelligence to found the Iraqi National Alliance (INA), which comprised both ex-Ba'thists and ex-military officers (al-Zubaidi, 2009). Soon after that, coinciding with US strategy, the INA split into two factions: a Sunni faction led by al-'Alî and a Shi'i faction led by 'Allâwî ('Ali, 2013).

Between November 1990 and March 1991, a new and dangerous political principle was established by the five members of the JAC and the two Saudi-sponsored factions.[7] The principle was called "al-Tawafuq" or "al-Muhassah," which signifies, in English, consensus among political leaders as to the allocation of power/government positions among themselves (al-Zubaidi, 2009). The principle of agreeing on the apportioning of political positions, a formula concocted by the Syrian and Saudi-sponsored Iraqi exiles to distribute political power in a post-Saddam Hussein Iraq on an ethnosectarian basis, gained strong support from regime-change advocates in the US. This support only emboldened the diaspora of political elites to further lobby the US to help them implement their goal of taking power in Iraq. According to one of the most active and well-informed mouthpieces of the Iraqi exiles, Faiq al-Shaikh 'Ali (2013), they had only one aim in mind:

> We in the opposition were not interested in finding a legitimate justification for overthrowing Saddam; all that we wanted and worked for was to overthrow him [...] We, the true opposition, aimed to overthrow Saddam regardless of who ruled after him as we believed that the problems of Iraq were personified by the tyrant himself, Saddam Hussein, and none other, and when he fell everything was to be simple [...] We did not think we could overthrow him [...] nobody in this world would dare or be able to overthrow him except the US.

Because there was an alliance between the US and the engineered "Shi'i opposition" when the US decided to pursue regime change, the Shi'i opposition were told in December 2002 that the US "is now serious in overthrowing Saddam." According to Faiq al-Shaikh 'Ali, when some of the opposition members asked "What about the future form and nature of the government in Iraq?," the US representative responded:

> Don't worry; all that you are required to do is to hold your conference and come up with a formal, final pronouncement in accordance with your power-sharing consensus [al-Tawafuq/al-Muhassah] agreed upon in your June, 1992 Vienna conference and November, 1992 Salahaldin conference.
>
> ('Ali, 2013)

The March–April 1991 uprising in Iraqi Kurdistan enjoyed the organizational leadership and battle-readiness of the Peshmerga paramilitaries, which allowed it to withstand Saddam Hussein's heavily armed military assault. The Western imposition of a no-fly zone over Iraq's three Kurdish provinces forced the Iraqi military into retreat, and allowed the Kurdish leaders of the KDP and PUK to negotiate a cease-fire with Saddam Hussein's regime from a position of strength. Throughout the 1990s, the Kurds—who endured a fratricidal civil war between the PUK and KDP (1993–1998)—nevertheless enjoyed administrative autonomy and Iraqi Kurdistan served as a safe haven for other Iraqi opposition factions.

Unlike the success of Iraq's Kurds, the southern uprising in March 1991 was spontaneous, unorganized and without political or religious leadership, which hastened its bloody demise (Allawi, 2007, pp. 46–50). Nonetheless, during the Beirut conference of March 1991, where Saudi Arabia paid $4 million to organize the 5 + 2, the Islamist groups under Iranian control stymied the conference with turgid propaganda extolling their leadership of the Shia uprising in Iraq, thereby silencing other voices of opposition, including the two Saudi-sponsored organizations of Iyâd 'Allâwî (Iraqi National Accord) and Sa'd Ṣâliḥ Jabr (Free Iraqi Council, based in London). In this manner, the Iranian-sponsored Islamist groups, chiefly SCIRI, dominated the proceedings in an attempt to demonstrate their power within the Iraqi opposition movement. As a result, Saudi Arabia withdrew its funding of the JAC, and Iyâd 'Allâwî began to seek new foreign patrons, capitalizing on his links to MI6 which he had cultivated after he fled Iraq for Britain in 1971. Likewise, the US withdrew their support from Jabr, considered to have been "America's ally, friend, and the dean of Iraqi opposition," who had been working for a long time against the Ba'thist regime. Under the guidance of the US, he had almost succeeded in pulling off a coup against Saddam in the early 1990s, according to Faiq al-Shaikh 'Ali (2013). The coup was aborted by the US, when they informed Saddam of details of the conspirators' plan. 'Ali emphatically claims that the US abandoned Jabr in favor of their own opposition groups, which he dubs "the Shi'i politicians." Between 1990 and 1992 about 100 opposition exile factions were established, though none could compete with the finances or external support of the JAC and develop an alternative opposition umbrella (Allawi, 2007, p. 52; al-Zubaidi, 2009).

Through its public relations arm Rendon Company, the CIA was concurrently responsible for founding and funding the INC, headed by Aḥmad Chalabî, which held its first meeting in Vienna in April 1992. Between 1992 and 1996, the CIA had paid it $12 million. This investment increased substantially in later years, however. Figures from the US Government Accountability Office (GAO) report even higher figures, claiming that, from March 2000 through September 2003, the INC received a total of $33 million.[8] The US found in Chalabî's ambitions a working façade for mobilizing Iraqi expatriates to replace the Hussein regime following its overthrow (Chossudovsky, 2004; Dizard, 2004; Peri, 2003; SourceWatch, 2010). In 1992 the Clinton Administration attempted to market Chalabî and the INC in the Arab world as a legitimate opposition to Saddam Hussein, while pressuring Saudi Arabia to officially host him and his two close associates, Layth Kubba and Muhammad Ali. Although they were issued Saudi entry visas, no Saudi official

88 *Deconstruction and reconstruction of the state*

met with them (al-Zubaidi, 2009). In October 1992 an opposition meeting was held in Salahuddin, Iraqi Kurdistan, under the tutelage of PUK leader Jalâl Ṭâlabânî and KDP leader Mas'ûd Barzânî. Both SCIRI and the Iraqi Da'wa Party attended the meeting and developed a leadership structure and executive council whose composition was based on an explicit principle of ethnosectarianism (Allawi, 2007, p. 53). Communications between Chalabî and powerful American officials, such as Richard Perle (chair of the Pentagon's Defense Policy Board Advisory Committee), appear to have allowed him to extract a written commitment from the Clinton Administration to help overthrow Saddam Hussein, namely the Iraqi Liberation Act, which was signed in October 1998. The Act referred to "democratic parties," which included the KDP, PUK, SCIRI, INC, the Islamic Movement of Kurdistan (IMK) and the Constitutional Monarchy Movement (CMM). However, no Arab country recognized this umbrella organization (Allawi, 2007, pp. 67–68). Subsequently, in October 1999, the US organized the New York Conference, and invited about 350 delegates. Among the attendees were members of the INA, INC, PUK, KDP and CMM. The conference was chaired by Sharif Ali Ibn al-Hussein and resulted in the formation of a 65-member executive council and 7-person leadership council (Allawi, 2007, p. 69).

The second round of voting by delegates at the INC conference in New York provided an indicator of the future direction of ethnosectarian politics in Iraq. Of the 65-member executive council, Iyâd 'Allâwî's INA won 21 seats, Chalabî's INC 15 and the Kurdish parties 15, while 14 seats were left for future members among Iraq's Sunni Arabs and other ethnic/religious groups (al-Zubaidi, 2009). Subsequently, SCIRI was integrated within the US-backed opposition bloc, with the stature of SCIRI leader Bâqir al-Ḥakîm overshadowing other prominent figures (Allawi, 2007, pp. 69–70, 73). An important stumbling block during this period was that Iraqi Islamists in Iran, whether SCIRI or Da'wa, envisioned an Iranian-tinged political Islam. For these groups to be included, the US set as a condition that they "renounced terrorism and modified their political platforms," to which the two parties swiftly agreed (Allawi, 2007, p. 74). At the London conference held in December 2002, the leaders of Da'wa and SCIRI suitably presented themselves as "English gentlemen" as opposed to turbaned jurists (al-'Alawî, 2009, p. 184). Nevertheless, during the meeting the attendees endorsed the *I'lan Shi'at al-'Iraq*, or the *Declaration of the Shia of Iraq*,[9] which was written by Muwaffaq al-Rubai'î, 'Alî 'Allâwî and Sahib al-Ḥakîm (Allawi, 2007, p. 75). Building on the theme of the al-Khoe'i Foundation's 1992 seminar, it was essentially based on the notion that Iraqi Shias had a special identity and collective consciousness that must be projected and embodied in the political sphere. Allawi (2007) described the turning point:

> The Shi'a had always sought to express their political aspirations through any number of ideologies that variously included Arab nationalism, Islamism, liberalism, communism, and even Iraqi "antivism"—but never specifically in Shi'a form. There had been an avoidance of expressing or discussing sectarianism.
>
> (p. 74)

The manifesto, which over 120[10] attendees signed, "stressed that the Iraqi state was inherently sectarian in nature" (Allawi, 2007, p. 75). Furthermore, the declaration encouraged regionalism within Iraq, which would later be incorporated in the 2005 Iraqi Constitution. Allawi (2007) described the impact of US intervention in the Gulf from 1990:

> The involvement of the USA in the affairs of Iraq after the Gulf War had changed all the rules. The USA believed the formal opposition, broadly supportive of US objectives in Iraq, would be an important adjunct to its own drive to isolate and contain the country. It also gave the opposition the means to propel their activities to an altogether different plane.
>
> (p. 76)

The Shia opposition, within and outside of Iraq, had, before their Western orientation, engaged in a variety of ideologies to express their political aspirations, but it was not until the impetus of an Anglo-American-sanctioned Iraqi opposition that Shia groups, specifically SCIRI and Da'wa, had the means to seize and promote an explicitly sectarian policy for their vision of a post-Saddam Iraq.

The occupation of Iraq and the engineering of political sectarianism

Though US designs in Iraq have not proceeded without significant opposition, the political environment engineered in Iraq is presided over by a political class of carpetbaggers that had been nurtured in the West for decades prior to the 2003 Anglo-American invasion and occupation of Iraq. Under conditions of occupation, two primary phenomena emerged within Iraq. First, occupation authorities deployed a series of legal/political, cultural and constitutional machinations designed to create a particular Iraqi state and society, which is fragmented, weak and sectarian in nature. This has, in particular, resulted in the institutionalization of sectarian politics through the electoral system, preventing the emergence of a strong nationalist form of Iraqi politics that is able to resist American strategic objectives in Iraq, with access to oil resources figuring particularly prominently. Second, neighboring Iran has emerged as the most significant regional power in shaping Iraqi affairs, and has used its influence to preclude the emergence of a strong Iraqi state, primarily through Shia Islamist proxies in the political and paramilitary realms. Thus, contemporary Iraqi politics is dominated by a class of "carpetbagger" politicians who lack any strong indigenous base of support and depend, paradoxically, upon the simultaneous patronage of the US and Iran. Although the US's and Iran's objectives in Iraq differ greatly, they both share the goal of a fragmented and sectarian Iraqi government beholden to external support. These developments have played themselves out against a backdrop of sectarian violence, political paralysis and foreign military occupation.

From the onset of the occupation, Anglo-American authorities embodied sectarianism in the CPA, headed by proconsul L. Paul Bremer. The CPA

90 *Deconstruction and reconstruction of the state*

imposed a 25-member IGC on Iraq whose composition was explicitly sectarian, with a ratio of thirteen Shia representatives, five Sunni Arabs, five Kurds, one Turkmen and one Assyrian. The Shi'is of the governing council established a caucus called *al-Bayt al-Shi'i*, or the Shia House, which sought to coordinate the efforts of the IGC with the demands of the Marji'iya of Najaf (Allawi, 2007; Bremer & McConnell, 2006). The caucus would soon become a proxy for the top religious clerics, specifically Ayatollah 'Alî al-Sistânî, who refused to meet with the occupation authorities. According to 'Alî 'Allâwî, al-Sistânî viewed the occupation as a historic opportunity to redress the balance of power within Iraq in favor of the Shia majority. As some mistook his restrained demeanor and quietist tone as a continuation of the passive political stance of his spiritual mentor 'Abul-Qâsim al-Khu'î, this indeed was not the case. Through the grassroots effort of Sistânî's "Hawza Civic Association," his efforts to enhance the structure of civil society, independent from the state but dependent on Iraqi Shias, underscores his political influence at all levels of Iraqi society (Rahimi, 2007). This influence has only grown through the following decade. A case in point is Grand Ayatollah al-Sistânî's response to the ISIS occupation of Mosul in June 2014, after which he issued a fatwa citing "the legal and national responsibility of whoever can hold a weapon to hold it to defend the country, the citizens and the [Shi'i] holy sites" (Rubin et al., 2014). This prompted a warning from Ali al-Amin, the distinguished Lebanese Marji, who rebuked the fatwa and called upon the Marji'iya of Iraq to "refrain from issuing fatwas calling for military mobilizations that fuel sectarian conflicts," and reminded them that "the role of the Marji'iya demands that they call for the end of bloodshed, and work to unite all Muslims, keeping them from temptation and calling them away from violence and weapons [...]." He concluded by saying that "the issuance of fatwas like this will only be met by the same from the other sects [...] fanning the fires of sectarianism in Iraq" and the Muslim world at large (Al-Annahar, 2014).

Not only was the distribution of seats premised on sectarian identification, the first time a governing body in Iraq had been formed along explicitly ethnosectarian lines, but the IGC's members were drawn largely from exile groups, which lacked a natural constituency or firm grounding in Iraqi society. This fundamentally altered the orientation of those selected to govern, undermining any pretense to their representing all Iraqis, forcing them to enhance and amplify their sectarian credentials and ability to deliver to a segment of Iraqi society at the detriment of any other such factions. This process necessarily radicalized political actors and removed moderate or minority candidates as, "[s]uddenly, only those who claimed to speak for a specific linguistic or religious group would be invited to play a role in government. And the more extreme their position, the more likely that they would be seated at the front of the table" (Al-Ali, 2014, p. 65). Thus, the new class of politicians was forced to build support through appeals to tribe or sect, rather than constructive visions of national reconstruction and/or Iraqi nationhood. This early configuration of Iraqi affairs presaged the emergence of sectarianism as the primary locus of post-2003 Iraqi politics.

The formalization of sectarian identity politics as praxis has become enshrined within Iraqi elections. Several structural factors have stifled the development of electoral democracy beyond regular national polls, concentrating power within the hands of unaccountable leaders and detracting from the formation of political parties that genuinely encourage regular input from the entire populace. With the high levels of political violence and the overwhelming need of candidates to have the appeal of mass media exposure, campaigning has proven difficult in all of Iraq's post-2003 elections. While the elections themselves have received enormous international media coverage and prodigious security mobilization has allowed for the successful conduct of the polls, campaigning has become increasingly dangerous as rival militias and factions target candidates for assassination. While candidates may well be willing to brave such conditions, citizens desiring to participate in rallies or to meet their candidate first hand are kept from such a banal and yet essential basis of democratic politics through legitimate safety concerns. This has heightened the need for candidates to access the resources afforded by the state to incumbent political leaders, in particular security forces, the electoral process, state media networks and funding, all in addition to their own privately held finances and media outlets, or those of their patrons.

Moreover, the electoral process itself has favored the concentration of power, especially through incumbency. Having adopted a modified version of the Sainte-Laguë method for the 2013 local elections (and continued in the 2014 Parliamentary elections), the Iraqi electoral system has yet to be made more open to smaller parties emerging, apart from those who were handed their authority during the occupation. Iraqi polls since 2003 have allowed both individuals as well as party lists to compete for voter preferences through an amended formula to allot the votes not directly tied to winning candidates. While seemingly providing greater choice to the electorate, the process has been hijacked through elite-level machinations that allow for the concentration of power and anti-democratic outcomes. Without a single nation-wide electoral constituency, as used in 2005, it was nonetheless assumed that the 2013 change would allow for increased numbers of minority candidates, or candidates representing smaller constituencies, to be elected. However, in point-of-fact, it has not allowed for such increased diversity because the required number of votes has risen, albeit slightly, dampening the hopes of political movements whose dispersed support across the country precludes them from gaining sufficient numbers to achieve electoral success in any one constituency. The current practice, rather, has allowed for elected members to achieve status as Members of Parliament (MPs), only to barter their seat to the highest bidder, providing an outsized advantage to incumbent parties capable of securing government largesse. Candidates were thereby less responsible to electorates beyond their own narrow patronage networks—or those that could be crafted for them by more powerful actors.

Efforts to alter the electoral law as well as develop legal infrastructures for political parties have been stymied by the executive and judicial branches. Prime Minister al-Mâlikî has been highly effective in enticing candidates from opposing party lists in joining his faction. Efforts to stymie this manner of political malfeasance first emerged in 2010, aiming to regulate the sources of party finances and forbid political parties from foreign financial connections or the use of mosques/schools for political purposes. Further articles of the draft law sought to regulate the manner in which one could join or leave a party, party funding, party organization and party conduct. This proposal, which aimed at curbing the worst abuses then being practiced to empower incumbency and prevent reforms, did not proceed, and "business as usual" would remain the order of the day, as displayed in the lead-up and aftermath of the 2014 Parliamentary elections (Mamouri, 2014). Efforts in 2013 again saw dismissal of sweeping reforms, aside from the change away from the "largest remainder" method to that of the Sainte-Laguë method for calculating seats, whereby proportional representation was dealt a further blow. The informal legal status of electoral law and the mode by which it may be altered has put efforts to bring about change in spite of the major parties' agreement in parliament. This saw the proposed 2013 revisions scrapped due to the Iraqi Supreme Court's predilection to strike down any laws not drafted and proposed by the executive branch, arguing that the sole authority to suggest new laws rests in the Prime Minister's and President's offices and not parliament, according to Article 60 of the Constitution. However, such challenges are required, and should be part of an open process to encourage greater inclusion and participation in an emergent democracy such as Iraq, or indeed in any democratic polity. Thus, while the 2013 changes allowed for the alteration of the method used to decide how to allot votes, calls for changes to the constituencies, a brake on campaign funding from outside Iraq, as well as a ban on religious institutions being utilized as political platforms, were all rejected by the incumbent executive powers. While all electoral systems will change over time, through three national elections since 2003 Iraq has seen the systemic blocking of non-sectarian parties. Unable to achieve sufficient popular support in the existing constituencies, a great many such small parties are thereby denied any room for growth, and their alternative to sectarian identity and corrupt officeholders left largely silent in a national media supportive of incumbent power.

Even beyond MPs elected on their own merits, this is largely the result of the weak party discipline evident in post-election maneuvers, which allow individuals to negotiate where their parliamentary loyalty will be directed if they are willing to abandon the myriad coalitions, or party "lists," formed prior to the election campaign. These lists allow multiple parties to run as a conglomerate group to increase their chances of electoral success through greater exposure and cross-pollinated affinities. Voters who have taken the time to decipher where an individual candidate or smaller party is situated, thereby casting their vote for the list upon which their preferred candidate resides, may then see their candidate switch to an alternative list in an effort to secure patronage rather than to establish coherent factions and opposition parties. Thus, individuals running independently are clearly allowed to join, or abandon, the coalitions and political alignments they espoused during the election campaign. Similarly, those elected on a party ticket may likewise alter allegiances once seated in parliament. Such fluidity has opened post-election racketeering, as MPs maneuver to be part of a winning coalition that may end up not representing their electorate's desires. Efforts to encourage the formation of new parties, to allow for alternatives to achieve representation and the requisite platform to present that alternative to the broader electorate, have yet to be established. The incumbent parties, especially the State of Law coalition led by Prime Minister al-Mâlikî, have proven adept at manipulating the system to peel individual MPs away from smaller parties, or even larger competitors, through patronage and the provision of access to the perks of incumbency. Thus, al-Mâlikî has both adroitly outmaneuvered his current opponents but, at one and the same time, closed the political system to emergent voices and those current forces not pre-positioned for success under the occupation regime.

Running parallel to the creation of new political norms within Iraq was the imposition of a set of "edicts" and legal mechanisms that redefined the nature of the Iraqi state, creating a vast culture of political corruption, on the one hand, and reinforcing sectarian tendencies, on the other. These are the predominant features of the failed Iraqi state, sectarianism and corruption, factors that cooperate and feed into one another. Fakhari Karim, a former long-time member of the Iraqi Communist Party and veteran opponent of the Saddam Hussein regime, later a senior adviser to Iraqi President Jalâl Ṭâlabânî, and finally the owner of a media conglomerate and the publishing house Almada, has aptly commented on the relationship between sectarianism and corruption under Anglo-American occupation. In an Almada editorial, he observed:

> The American military operation, and before that political activities, were based on preconceived foundations that considered Iraq as an area of a conflict between sectarian, religious, and ethnic groups, with particular reference to the Sunni and Shi'ite tensions. The Americans are still mesmerized by this distorted understanding of Iraq, and it is on this basis that the American government, its agencies, and the American mass-media's conduct with Iraq and its complexities is based. It's no strange thought, then, that the American mass-media now explains Maliki's adventurous policies as representing the interests of the Shi'ites and reflects their aspirations for state control, while marginalizing the Sunnis and accusing them of premeditated terrorism. This is what informs the American government leaders and intelligence's beliefs. Whether it was intentional or not, sectarian violence is something that can appear at any moment and around any corner [...] The US has to realize that this is an apocalyptic crisis in [Iraq] and the conflict will not serve the interest of the Shi'ites in their struggle against the Sunnis. Rather this fight to control leadership is a front to protect corruption, waste the country's wealth and all groups struggling in the process, to different degrees, are partners in what is happening and dominate this shambling political environment.
>
> (Karim, 2014)

The nexus of sectarianism and corruption was embodied in the restructuring of state institutions through the veneer of "de-Ba'thification." First, the 400,000-man Iraqi army was dissolved, creating a mass of trained and unemployed combatants. Next came the large-scale dismissal of Iraq's civil servants. In both cases, the joint

94 *Deconstruction and reconstruction of the state*

measures constricted the Iraqi state and its ability to provide social services, creating a security and welfare vacuum that was rapidly filled by paramilitary groups affiliated with the sectarian parties, chief among them SCIRI's Badr Brigade.

Under the conditions created by these political decisions by occupation authorities, Iraq was thrust into a climate of politicized sectarianism. The absence of a functioning Iraqi state facilitated the emergence of sectarian organizations as the central political units in post-invasion Iraqi society. Consequently, the Iraqi elections conducted in 2005 were organized around sectarian political blocs, the most significant of which was the National Iraqi Alliance, a Shia super-bloc dominated by SCIRI and the Da'wa Party. Under these conditions, Iraqi politics operated not on the basis of pursuing national Iraqi objectives, but rather, on the advancement of narrow sectarian objectives of small groups of political actors. Iraq's security forces came to be staffed by the Shia militias of the Badr Brigade, who engaged in a policy of wide-scale ethno-confessional cleansing, including a concerted effort to drive Sunni and Christian Iraqis out of different Baghdadi neighborhoods in order to expand the territory under the Brigade's control (Casey, 2014). This in turn prompted the proliferation of competing paramilitary forces. Iraq thus became engulfed in a massive wave of communal violence that continues and is even seen as necessary by Iraqi politicians, considering statements like those from Ḥanân al-Fatalâwî, an MP who could be considered as al-Mâlikî's female spokesperson, who said in an interview with Al-Sumaria (2014, April 5) that "if seven [Shi'ite] soldiers die, we should line up seven Sunnis to shoot" (al-Aidroosa, 2014).

Needless to say, the maelstrom of sectarian violence did not proceed without the notice of American occupation authorities. As a key element of occupation policy, the US exploited sectarian tensions through the use of Shia and Kurdish paramilitary forces to subdue an anti-occupation insurgency. In 2004, "US command dispatched 2000 Kurdish Peshmerga militia-men to Mosul, and five battalions of Shia troops, with a smattering of Kurds to police the Sunni-majority town of Ramadi in Al-Anbar Province, subsequently expanding the presence of sectarian-motivated paramilitaries to Samara and Fallujah as well" (Porter, 2010). The stimulation of sectarian tendencies and forces within Iraq took the country to extreme levels of violence, peaking in the months preceding the 2007 US military surge. The subsequent decline in violence, widely celebrated as a confirmation of the surge, is revealed in recently leaked documents to have owed much to social exhaustion following years of internecine warfare, and hence a temporary willingness to abide by a cease-fire and work within the political system (Tavernise, 2010).

This strategy was particularly evident with the use of the "Wolf Brigade," a police-commando unit formed by SCIRI official Abû Walîd (*nom de guerre*). The Wolf Brigade, largely Shia in composition and affiliated with the Badr Corps, was widely known to be involved in the torture of Sunni detainees. Recent leaks have demonstrated that this torture was treated, in large measure, with indifference by occupation authorities, with US "FRAGO" (fragmentary order) 242 indicating that, "provided the initial report [of torture] confirms US forces were not involved in the detainee abuse, no further investigation will be conducted unless directed by HHQ [Higher Headquarters]" (Fisk, 2010). Worse than merely tolerating torture by sectarian forces, military cables from 2004 demonstrate that US forces in Iraq handed over detainees to the Wolf Brigade, purportedly on the basis that the US's paramilitary allies would be more "effective" in their interrogations, i.e. not bound by the Uniform Code of Military Justice and prohibitions on torture. Interrogations by the US's Iraqi allies involved techniques such as whippings, burning by cigarettes, electrocution of feet and genitals, and rape (Davies, 2010). It is very difficult to know the extent to which any real religious sectarianism has taken hold within these forces or how far the impression of religious sectarianism has been deliberately deployed as a strategy of conflict. What is clear, however, is that the mischaracterization of the counterinsurgency campaign as an inter-communal sectarian conflict was deeply embedded from the outset of the occupation in the widespread rubric that the Ba'th Party had ruled on behalf of a minority Sunni Arab community and that that community constituted the core of the politico-military resistance to occupation.[11]

As sectarian violence reached its climax in 2006, the US maintained detailed logs on the extent and character of the violence, most dramatically in the aftermath of the bombing of a Shia shrine in Samarra, with active US soldiers detailing the ongoing killings, including the discovery of 47 bodies in a mass grave in Baghdad on February 23, 2006. While the extent of sectarian violence following the Samarra incident is now reasonably documented, at the time US Pentagon and occupation authorities denied its occurrence. General George W. Casey, then the commanding general of US forces in Iraq, denied that Iraq was "awash in sectarian violence," instead claiming to see "a lot of bustle, [and] a lot of economic activity." US Secretary of Defense Donald Rumsfeld, for his part, criticized reports that an estimated 1,300 (since determined to have been an under-estimation) had been killed in Baghdad in the days following the Samarra bombing, characterizing them as "exaggerated reporting" (Knickermeyer, 2010a). The scope of sectarian violence in Iraq, actively denied during its worst period, has since been revealed by the US military's own documents, highlighting the occupation authorities' simultaneous collaboration with sectarian forces—as with the use of the Badr-dominated Wolf Brigade—and an unwillingness to control, or even account for, their violence (Knickermeyer, 2010b).

The emergence of a Lebanese-style confessional system that structures political authority on a sectarian quota basis sparked a dispute, with the 'Allâwî-led Iraqiya bloc walking out of the initial parliamentary session that engaged in assigning political positions. 'Allâwî characterized the power-sharing program as "a joke." According to a report in *al-Sharq al-Awsat*, 'Allâwî had agreed to join the power-sharing program, and accept his diminished role within it, on the condition that three Iraqiya members who had been disqualified by the Justice and Accountability Commission (i.e. De-Ba'thification Committee) be reinstated, a condition the new government apparently initially reneged upon (Cole, 2010). While the Iraqiya bloc subsequently relented and accepted its fate, ongoing controversies do not bode well for the cohesion and functioning of the new Iraqi

96 *Deconstruction and reconstruction of the state*

government (Fadel, 2010). Indeed, the alliance between Shia and Kurdish parties that forms the basis of the al-Mâlikî government is highly tenuous, and leaked US diplomatic cables have revealed there was anxiety that, without a strong moderating force in the wake of the US military departure, disagreements between the parties could quickly turn violent (Gordon & Lehren, 2010b).

In the run-up to the April 2014 federal election it appears that this tenuous partnership may be approaching its end as al-Mâlikî's campaign adopted a markedly sectarian tone. In a speech unveiling his campaign platform at a Rule of Law Alliance rally in Najaf on April 9, 2014, al-Mâlikî announced that the attempted national sectarian partnership had been a failure and that his next term must take the "form [of] a majority government, without the participation of other political parties in the country"—a sectarian agenda for which he called on all Iraqis to "rally around [him] in order to establish the state of Ahl al-Bayt [the People of the Prophet's House]." In other words, he aims to establish a state founded upon the Ja'afri school of Shi'ism. Al-Mâlikî described those who oppose him, such as the Anbar protesters,[12] as followers of Muawiya, a reference to the roots to the Sunni–Shia schism in the seventh century when, according to Shia beliefs, the Caliphate was illegitimately seized from the House of the Prophet. In effect, al-Mâlikî was attempting to portray himself as the historical redeemer of Shia right to rule (Kitabat, 2014a; Mamouri, 2014). Al-Mâlikî's historic/political claim—Shi'ism as forming the basis of legitimate governance in Iraq—represented an unusually stark declaration of the sectarian basis of politics in post-invasion Iraq.

Sectarianism and the patrimony of Iraq's oil

When President Barack Obama declared the Iraq war officially over on August 31, 2010, Simon Jenkins (2010) of *The Guardian* observed:

> As his troops return home, Iraqis are marginally freer than in 2003, and considerably less secure. Two million remain abroad as refugees from seven years of anarchy, with another 2 million internally displaced. Ironically, almost all Iraqi Christians have had to flee. Under western rule, production of oil—Iraq's staple product—is still below its pre-invasion level, and homes enjoy fewer hours of electricity. This is dreadful.
>
> Some 100,000 civilians are estimated to have lost their lives from occupation-related violence. The country has no stable government, minimal reconstruction, and daily deaths and kidnappings. Endemic corruption is fuelled by unaudited aid. Increasing Islamist rule leaves most women less, not more, liberated. All this is the result of a mind-boggling $751bn of US expenditure, surely the worst value for money in the history of modern diplomacy.

Under the control of Anglo-American occupation authorities, the Iraqi state and society have been reconfigured, and a class of exile politicians who depend on external patronage and lack a credible, indigenous basis of support has been empowered. Thus, Iraq has become a dependent and compliant state within a highly strategic region with vast energy resources.

Commenting on this reality, the former chair of the US Federal Reserve, Alan Greenspan, observed that he was "saddened that it is politically inconvenient to acknowledge what everyone knows: The Iraq war is largely about oil" (Patterson, 2007). Indeed, as American authorities have rejected any accusation that US policy was designed to secure and restructure Iraq's oil sector, the American management firm Bearing Point was tasked to collaborate with the US State Department in the drafting of a then hypothetical Iraqi oil law that would legalize production sharing agreements (PSAs) (Faucon, 2006).

In the aftermath of the US "surge" of 2007, a series of "success benchmarks" were proposed, included among them the passing of a hydrocarbon law, which was endorsed as a draft law on February 27, 2007 by Iraqi Prime Minister Nûrî al-Mâlikî. However, as the public came to learn from domestic trade unions and oil experts that it exposed 80 percent of Iraq's proven reserves of 120 billion barrels of cheap-to-extract oil to potential control by foreign oil giants (Energy Intelligence Group, 2008), it became stalled in the Iraqi parliament, as it had become politically expedient for MPs to vote against it. In response to this episode the al-Mâlikî government shifted away from parliamentary and legislative measures to control energy policy to unilateral control through the executive. Measures to dent public opposition, including the prohibition of public protests, would also be utilized to subvert the democratic process in an effort to advance the proposed contracts with international oil companies (IOCs).

In 2008, Ḥussain al-Shahristânî, then oil minister in Iraq, removed the Director General of the South Oil Company (SOC), Jabbâr al-Lu'aibî, who opposed the oil policies of the al-Mâlikî government. On June 30, 2008, the Iraqi Oil Ministry announced that foreign oil companies would be invited to bid for long-term "technical service contracts" for six of the largest existing oil fields. As a consequence of Bremer's de-Ba'thification policy,[13] the Iraqi oil expertise that had accumulated over more than 70 years was mostly lost (Chalabi, 2009), necessitating dependence on IOCs to modernize and repair Iraq's oil infrastructure, left dilapidated by wars and sanctions. Thus, while Iraq owns its oil in a strict legalistic sense, in fact all the real control over oil decisions has been transferred to foreign companies for the first time in decades.

In June 2009, during the first round of contract bidding, six oil-producing fields were auctioned to IOCs. The strict terms of the contracts—a per-barrel price at around $1.15 and $1.40 for the IOCs (Walt, 2009), subject to a 35 percent tax (Ministry of Oil, Iraq, 2010), and no profit-sharing in the economic rent[14]—have deterred many profit-driven Western IOCs from pursuing exploration contracts on top of the contracts companies such as BP, Exxon and ENI won to refurbish and manage Iraq's largest existing oil fields. These exploration contracts, instead, attracted state-owned Chinese, Korean and Russian oil companies as a hedge to guarantee future access (Arango & Krauss, 2013).[15]

The first round of contracts have been followed by the signing of many other oil contracts with IOCs across four rounds of auctions, with more to come, in

98 *Deconstruction and reconstruction of the state*

al-Shahristânî's "big push" oil development strategy, wherein production capacity is to be developed as rapidly as possible to an expected 9 million barrels per day in 2020 (Jiyad, 2012; Lee, 2014). Such an unprecedented rush to grant energy contracts to IOCs has called into question the sustainability and desirability of such growth, as the Iraqi constitution stipulates in Articles 111 and 112 that the management of and investment in oil fields must be in the best interest of Iraqis, respecting their collective ownership. However, of the contracts approved by the Iraqi Ministry of Oil, none have been ratified by parliament nor verified to be in the "best interest" of the Iraqi people, making the legality of these contracts dubious. Nor is there any sort of capital gains tax, a norm in most countries, attached to these contracts should holdings in them ever be sold to another company (a likely prospect given the length of the contracts) (al-Sayeh, 2014; Jiyad, 2011, 2014). The development of Iraqi oil, while certainly profitable, has not necessarily been conducted in a manner respecting the best interest of Iraqis, many of whom live in squalor while corrupt politicians reap the profits.[16] Thus IOCs who gain contracts not only set the course for development, as the largest source of technically competent and employable skilled labor, but also have an incentive to support the current political order in Iraq. For Iraq, these contracts, in conjunction with the rampant corruption in Iraqi politics (Chapter 5), represent an erosion of public control of the country's economic lifeblood and the reversal of modern Iraq's development trajectory based on a public oil sector.

Iranian strategic depth and Shia political forces

A paradoxical consequence of the Anglo-American invasion of Iraq has been the emergence of Iran as a dominant player on the Iraqi political stage. In the pursuance of their aims within Iraq, occupation authorities seem to have underestimated the capacities of Iran within the country or perhaps felt confident that they could mitigate any Iranian adventures. Whatever the case, it is certain that occupation planners did not foresee the growth of Iranian power as an outcome; strangely, however, while the US and Iran are battling for influence within Iraq, on various issues there is a congruence of perspective between the two countries. Like the US, Iran views the emergence of a strong, centralized Iraqi government as an obstacle. Instead, Iran prefers a decentralized state whose Shia factions can be manipulated for the purposes of Iranian strategic interests. A Shia regime beholden to Iran is, from an Iranian perspective, an attractive option (Porter, 2008). As a policy, the Iranian message to its Iraqi clients (SCIRI [which later changed its name to ISCI], Da'wa and others) was not to provoke the invasion forces (Allawi, 2007, p. 303). Iran's policy was premised on extending its calibrated support to all entities across the political spectrum, including the Kurds, the Sadrists and secular Shias, such as Iyâd 'Allâwî and Ahmad Chalabî. Through this, Iran sought to ensure and maintain the political ascendancy of its Shia allies, and achieve strategic depth, thereby balancing US influence in Iraq. In tandem with such support, Iran has signed many trade and economic agreements with Iraq, provided the latter with electricity and flooded the Iraqi market with inexpensive basic commodities. However, surreptitiously, Iran has established an all-encompassing intelligence network staffed by Iraqis to provide it with timely, on-the-ground reports. In fact, in June 2006, the CIA reported that most Shia insurgents (militia) were being funded by Iranian intelligence, and that many of Iraq's politicians and civil servants were affiliated with such insurgents, fueling violence and sectarian strife (Allawi, 2007, pp. 306, 312–313; CIA, 2006; Porter, 2007; Shoamanesh, 2010).

The unchallenged success of Iranian policy in Iraq became of critical concern to the US in late March 2008. As a result, the US pressured the al-Mâlikî government to rein in the powerful Shia militias. Al-Mâlikî's government, in preparation for provincial elections in the fall of 2008, focused on Muqtadâ al-Ṣadr's militia, the Mahdi army, which controlled Iraq's major port and outlet for Iraqi oil—the port of Basra. On March 23, 2008, al-Mâlikî ordered the Iraqi army to launch a campaign, "The Knights' Assault," against the Mahdi army. US Special Forces and the Air Force provided support for the attack, which, against all expectations, dragged on for a week, wreaking havoc on both sides. The attack brought about such fierce resistance that it led the Bush Administration to deny taking any part in it. It became clear that the US did not wield any power to end the military confrontation. At this point Iran intervened and, within 24 hours, the intra-Shia fighting ended on March 29–30 (Cole, 2008; Porter, 2008, 2009; Reuters, 2008; Strobel & Fadel, 2008).

In US diplomatic cables leaked in 2010, confidential American accounts and suspicions of Iranian activity in Iraq were laid bare. The cables reported that Iran was providing weaponry, including rockets, magnetic bombs and explosively formed penetrators (EFPs) to allied Shia militias in Iraq. In addition, the cables discuss collaboration between Iran's Quds Force with Iraqi forces to "assassinate" designated Iraqi officials, noting as well that Iranian intelligence officials working within the Badr Corps were "influencing attacks on ministry officials in Iraq." At the political level, the leaked cables document concerns in 2005 that "Iran is gaining control of Iraq at many levels of the Iraqi government" (Gordon & Lehren, 2010a).

Indeed, the US is right to be concerned, as the growth of Iranian influence in Iraq has coincided with the concomitant decline of US influence, a fact publicly flaunted by Iraqi politicians. Sâmî al-ʻAskarî, an ally of Prime Minister al-Mâlikî, commented in October 2010 that "Iraqi politicians are not responding to the U.S. like before. We don't pay great attention to them [...] The weak American role has given the region's countries a greater sense of influence on Iraqi affairs." Mahmoud Othman, a prominent Kurdish lawmaker, responding to a visit by the US Vice President in late October 2010, commented that the "Iranian ambassador has a bigger role than Biden" and speculated that the Americans "will leave Iraq with its problems, thus their influence has become weak" (Jakes & Abdul-Zahra, 2010). Sunni lawmaker Usâmah al-Nujaifî (later to become Speaker of the Iraqi Parliament) commented that, as the Americans "begin to withdraw their military, the Iranians are taking advantage of the empty space, and are ready to fill the vacuum" (Jakes & Abdul-Zahra, 2010).

100   Deconstruction and reconstruction of the state

At the center of this growing influence is the leader of the Quds Force, Qassem Suleimani, who has masterminded both political and armed resistance to the US in Iraq. Both Shia and Sunni militias received arms, funding and advisory support from the Quds Force, which served as tools Suleimani could apply to foster sectarian violence and division (Mamouri, 2013). According to General George Casey, who served as the senior coalition commander in Iraq from 2004 to 2007, "the Iranian role in training and equipping the Iraqi militias is a major factor in sustaining sectarian violence in Iraq from 2006 to 2008 and frankly it continues today"; thus through the efforts of Suleimani, Iran has been "directly and purposefully fomenting sectarian violence to destabilize Iraq" (Casey, 2014).

Politically, Suleimani's influence has been felt from the beginning as well, as Ryan Crocker, a US diplomat who has been involved in Iraqi affairs including selecting members of the Governing Council and who would later serve as the US Ambassador to Iraq in 2007, indirectly vetted candidates with Suleimani, saying: "The formation of the governing council was in its essence a negotiation between Tehran and Washington" (Filkins, 2013). In fact, the political depth of Suleimani's networks reached "active social factions, from the religious to the media to civil society organizations representing Iraq's different ethnicities and confessions"; few who "participate in the Iraqi government [do so] without a direct or indirect understanding [...] with Suleimani" (Mamouri, 2013). Even though Suleimani obviously works for Iran's best interest, he is difficult to resist because, as one official put it, "When we say no, he makes trouble for us. Bombings. Shootings. The Iranians are our neighbors. They've always been there, and they always will be. We have to deal with them" (Filkins, 2013).

After the elections on March 7, 2010, in which no electoral bloc won the necessary 163 parliamentary seats to form the government, *Al-Jazeera* reported that on June 23, 2010 al-Mâlikî claimed that foreign interference was the obstacle to the creation of a new government. Former Iraqi national security adviser Muwaffaq al-Rubai'î, who belongs to the INA led by 'Ammâr al-Ḥakîm, made explicit reference to regional and international meddling in Iraqi affairs, particularly in the formation of the new Iraqi government, while Aḥmad Chalabî explained that "domestic [political] forces are nothing more than fronts for foreign interests" (al-Rubai'î, 2013). On July 29, 2010, *Al-Sharq Al-Awsat* (2010a) quoted one of the leaders of the INA, saying, "Iran has relayed to us that we should accept al-Maliki [as Prime Minister] even though he might abuse us."[17] In the months before a coalition government was formed, "Suleimani invited senior Shiite and Kurdish leaders to meet with him in Tehran and Qom, and extracted from them a promise to support al-Mâlikî, his preferred candidate" (Filkins, 2013). Likewise, 'Allâwî, Barzânî and al-Mâlikî were invited to the US embassy where President Obama and Vice President Biden made it clear to them, over the phone, that Iran and the US both expected al-Mâlikî to become the Prime Minister (al-Rubai'î, 2013). *Al-Sharq Al-Awsat* further reported on July 31, 2010 that Iran had reduced its funding to the ISCI by 50 percent in order to pressure it into supporting al-Mâlikî's candidacy as Prime Minister (Al-Sharq Al-Awsat, 2010b). In November 2010, al-Mâlikî—and Iran by proxy—had triumphed, not merely with the continuation of

The sectarian state in Iraq 101

al-Mâlikî as Prime Minister, but also with having undermined the Iraqiya bloc led by Iyâd 'Allâwî, the largest parliamentary bloc, who was denied the prime ministership or presidency, and instead having to settle for becoming president for a proposed Council for Strategic Policy, which never formed. On this 'Allâwî felt he could have become the Prime Minister if he had the support of the US as a counterpoint to the support al-Mâlikî had from Iran: "I needed American support, but they wanted to leave, and they handed the country to the Iranians. Iraq is a failed state now, an Iranian colony" (Filkins, 2013). The "Obama Administration concluded that backing Allawi would be too difficult if he was opposed by Shiites and by their supporters in Iran" (Filkins, 2014).

The invasion and occupation of Iraq, aside from its immense human tragedy, has been deeply ironic. The US, who invaded Iraq to reorient the Middle East and to shore up their position within the region, inadvertently fed the growth of Iranian regional power. While Suleimani successfully pressured the Shi'ite blocs to stand behind the Da'wa Party in the 2005 and 2010 elections, al-Mâlikî lost the support of his former partners—ISCI, the KRG and the Sadrists[18]—in the run-up to the 2014 election, and it appears that Iran has in turn decided to withdraw their support for him as well (Kitabat, 2014b).[19] Even the highest-ranking marja' in Iraq, Grand Ayatollah al-Sistânî, has refused to meet with al-Mâlikî because his government has "failed to deal with the security situation, create social peace, ensure access to public services; and had created factionalism within the Shi'ite alliance through discrimination," and in effect "called on Iraqi voters to dismiss him through elections" (Kitabat, 2014a; Mamouri, 2014). Grand Ayatollah Bashir al-Najafi was much more scathing in his remarks, issuing a fatwa that banned followers from voting for anyone from al-Mâlikî's Rule of Law Alliance list (Mustafa, 2014). This is the first time that the Marji'iya have so openly involved themselves in politics, breaking from the tradition of public non-alignment. While Articles 2 and 3 of Iraq's constitution make Islamic jurisprudence the basis of the state, al-Najafi's fatwa has moved Iraq further down the path of an Islamic state. In effect, the Grand Ayatollahs (the highest religious authority in Shi'ism), as well as Iran's Supreme Leader (the highest-ranking Shi'ite religious and political authority in Iran), have rejected al-Mâlikî's claim to champion the Shi'i and have dissociated themselves from his politics. Through the course of the Anglo-American occupation, and following the withdrawal of American troops, Iran has hedged its bets by providing support for multiple factions in Iraq, never casting its lot with one faction to the exclusion of all others. And while the fortunes of its proxies have risen and fallen, on balance, Iranian influence in post-invasion Iraq has been prominent.

It is this prominence of Iranian influence that prompted al-Mâlikî to travel with "Ibrahim al-Jaafari and Khodair [al-Khozaei]," on the eve of the 2014 elections, "on a secret mission to Tehran to persuade it [to pressure] the blocs [...] to form a new government with Prime Minister Nuri al-Maliki" once again (Al-Baghdadia, 2014). Even while splitting its bet among Iraq's candidates, the priority for Iran remains "the survival of [Iraq's] 'National Alliance' in its current form, and not to risk fragmentation" (Kitabat, 2014d), an aspiration that al-Mâlikî has hoped to

102 *Deconstruction and reconstruction of the state*

appeal to in his attempt to portray himself as "strongman," and the only candidate able to deal with the divisive violence Iraq now faces (Arango & Gordon, 2014; Shaoul, 2014). "Iraqis know who is supporting the rebuilding of the country and democracy, and who is supporting terrorism and seeking to destroy the country," al-Mâlikî declared in a campaign speech (Arango & Gordon, 2014). Meanwhile, Sheik 'Abdul Halim al-Zuhairi, the so-called "godfather" of al-Mâlikî's second term, has been dispatched to Najaf to negotiate with the Grand Ayatollah al-Sistânî to ensure he does not reject the possibility of a third term for al-Mâlikî. Thus, it appears that in advance of the horse-trading that comes with creating a government in Iraq (as seen in the prior elections), al-Mâlikî is hard at work to curry the favor of Iran and the Shia leadership in Iraq (Abbas, 2014).

In the final analysis, the US failed to achieve many of its aims in Iraq; while they removed the regime of Saddam Hussein and dramatically improved the position of Western oil giants vis-à-vis Iraqi oil, the government that ultimately rose to power in Iraq is not the reflexively pro-American regime occupation authorities had envisioned, but a regime that increasingly tilts towards Iran. The engineering of a fragmented sectarian Iraqi state, while beneficial in the short term to the US in the realm of oil, has had peculiar consequences in terms of regional politics. This has very serious implications for the US in the long term.

Conclusion

Sectarianism in Iraq, while long manifested in social habit and belief, had rarely acquired an explicitly political content. In the aftermath of the 2003 Anglo-American invasion and occupation of Iraq, the country degenerated into a frenzy of sectarian violence, with sectarian political parties and their militias emerging as the most powerful political units in contemporary Iraq. As a result, the Iraqi state has become fragmented and weak, leaving it dependent on the patronage of external forces, chiefly the US and, increasingly, Iran. At the head of the new post-2003 political system is a class of political exiles, carpetbaggers, who willingly allowed themselves to be variously nurtured and co-opted by foreign patrons, in exchange for acquiring power in the "new" Iraq. The negative consequences of these arrangements for Iraq are legion, and are evident in wide-scale violence, the progressive loss of national control over the country's oil riches and the compromising of the nation's political independence. Such fragmentation became evident with the loss of state authority across Anbar province in early 2014, and was capped by the Iraqi military and security apparatus' withdrawal from Mosul, Iraq's second largest city, ahead of occupation of that city by ISIS militiamen from Syria who had allied with Iraqi tribes and local authorities displeased with the al-Mâlikî regime on June 10.

In the face of the failures to anticipate the extent of popular opposition in Western Iraq, nor the onslaught of ISIS in its ousting of Iraqi security forces from Mosul, al-Mâlikî was forced by the combined efforts of local, regional and international forces to abandon his efforts to form a third government. In the waning days of his administration, as a new government was being crafted by

Haidar al-Abadi, al-Mâlikî used his executive authority to appoint a number of his Da'wa Party members, staffers, family and political allies to positions of influence throughout the state. This effort enmeshed them into the post-al-Mâlikî body politic, protected them from any past abuses with legal immunity and saw them in position to influence the state in a manner to his future benefit. For instance, despite not holding so much as a high school diploma and therefore not meeting the legal prerequisites for the position, Áli al-Moussawi, former media adviser for the Prime Minister's Office (under al-Mâlikî), was appointed as Director-General at the Ministry of Foreign Affairs. Similarly, Áli Alfalh was appointed Chief of Trustees at the Iraqi Media Network. Such appointments went beyond patronage for long-standing Da'wa Party cadres, but instead veered towards the naked corruption so endemic in the post-2003 state (Kitabat, 2014e). As the decrees flowed during the days taken to establish a new "inclusive" government, they grew to exceed political appointments. Al-Mâlikî granted the titles to public parks to members of the military and security apparatus. Parliament reacted by pledging to investigate (Kitabat, 2014f).

This amplification of sectarian logic encroached on security efforts as well. Militias, private expressions of power beholden to local and often sectarian authority, were empowered in an effort to defend Baghdad from ISIS's advance. That al-Mâlikî had moved against such sectarian actors in his expansion of executive authority in 2008's "Operation Knight's Charge" demonstrated the abandonment of any remaining pretense of his administration's commitment to national institutions. The militias called into service, armed and supported logistically through state resources, further undermined the military and security institutions' function as bedrocks of state authority and comity. This melding of the state's own security apparatus, lavishly supported by both the Anglo-American occupation and then the post-2011 al-Mâlikî government, abandoned any pretense of it being a national institution. That the militias were seen to be responding to the religious edict of Grand Ayatollah Sistani, as he called on Shi'i men of military age to defend Baghdad and the shrine cities of the south from ISIS, only amplified the sectarian divide.

Notes

1   For the details and history of sectarianism in Iraq, see al-'Alawî (1996), Allawi (2007), al-Wardi (1954), Davies (2005, pp. 29–148) and Mahmûd (1987a, 1987b).
2   The Twelfth Imam is regarded as having been in occultation since 873 CE, awaiting the time when Allah has decreed for his return. It is believed he will lead the fight against the forces of evil and prevail and rule the earth with justice and peace for a number of years, before the return to earth of Isa Al-Maseeh (Jesus Christ) and other Imams, including Husain, prophets and saints.
3   The hierarchical institution of Shia religious representatives.
4   In Shia Islam emerged the concept of the Guardianship of the Jurist, *Wilayat al Faqih*, the rule by knowledgeable Shia clerics/jurists until the return of the Twelfth Imam. This concept is most clearly embodied in the Islamic Republic of Iran, with the clerical authority of the "Supreme Leader," the "Assembly of Experts" and the courts.
5   Hussain al-Shâmî became the Imam of the Dar al-Islam Foundation in London, and currently serves as a cultural aide to Nûrî al-Mâlikî.

104 *Deconstruction and reconstruction of the state*

6 "Carpetbaggers" originated as a term in the American South during the era of reconstruction (1865–1877) following the American Civil War (1861–1865), denoting northern Republicans who migrated south to reconstruct and administer the defeated South. It has since acquired a colloquial meaning to describe a politician running for office in a region where they have a limited natural constituency. In this case, it refers to exiled figures who returned to Iraq as politicians despite often being decades removed from the country and having since developed external allegiances. For a more elaborate discussion on the notion of carpetbaggers, see Ismael & Ismael (2010).

7 These groups, which came to be known as the 5 + 2, became the major political players in preparing, with their foreign patrons, for a post-Saddam Hussein Iraq.

8 US State Department, "Issues Affecting Funding of Iraqi National Congress Support Foundation," *US Government Accountability Office* (April 30, 2004).

9 The *Declaration of the Shia of Iraq* is reprinted in Appendix 1 as translated by Al-Bab (2002).

10 'Allâwî has exaggerated the number of signatories as surpassing 400.

11 For example, see Dickey (2004): "They can punish Iraq's Arab Sunnis, who are about 20 percent of the country's population and at least 90 percent of the insurgents […] a decisive role running the country […] is what [Sunnis] were used to under Saddam Hussein." This essentially superimposed sectarian discourse was of course thoroughly embedded in the massively repeated phrase: the Sunni Triangle.

12 See Chapter 8 for more on the Anbar protests.

13 See Chapter 3 for more on de-Ba'thification.

14 That is to say in this case that, of each barrel produced by an oil field in Iraq, the contracted IOC gets at most $1.40, which is then subject to a 35 percent income tax. The full difference between this per-barrel fee and the actual value of a barrel on the market (the economic rent) goes to Iraq.

15 Of the 18 IOCs awarded contracts in the 2009–2010 bidding rounds, only eight were from Western countries, and only two of those from the US.

16 See Chapter 5 for many examples of corruption in Iraq.

17 See also Al-Jazeera, *Al-Maliki: Intervention hindered forming the government* (2010a) and *Al-Rubai'i: The US and Iran hinder Iraq* (2010b).

18 According to Kitabat (2014c), "al-Sadr and al-Hakim told the Iranians clearly that they will not accept a third term for [al-Mâlikî], while […] Barzani was very frank with Iraqi leaders and the Iranian ministry in the recent past and told them firmly that the Kurdish leadership would strongly consider seceding from Iraq if al-Mâlikî wins a third term."

19 Another report indicates that Suleimani and Supreme Leader Ali Khamenei still favor a third term for al-Mâlikî; however, President Hassan Rohani and other reformers in Tehran oppose this, believing that al-Mâlikî will prove too troublesome in the future (Abbas, 2014).

References

Abbas, B. (2014, May 7). [*Zuhairi, Godfather of the State, Begins to Move to Support Maliki's Third Term*]. Retrieved May 6, 2014, from Al-Hayat: http://alhayat.com/Articles/2193861/ الزهيري-عراب-الدولة-المالكي-الثاني-أدب-ة-التحرك-لتأمين-ولاية-الثالثة

al-Aidroosa, R. O. (2014, April 5). [*To Permit Hanan al-Fatlawi*]. Retrieved April 9, 2014, from Kitabat: http://www.kitabat.com/ar/page/05/04/2014/25720/فكيك-لتصريح-جح-والتفل-حنان.html

al-'Alawî, H. (1996, November/December). Al-Judhûr al-Târîkhiyyah Lil-T â'ifiyyah fî al-'Irâq. *Dirâsât 'Arabiyyah*(1/2).

The sectarian state in Iraq 105

al-'Alawî, H. (2009). *Shi'at al-Sulta wa Shi'at al-'Iraq*. London: Dar al-Zawrâ'.

Al-Ali, Z. (2014). *The Struggle for Iraq's Future: How corruption, incompetence, and sectarianism have undermined democracy*. New Haven: Yale University Press.

Al-Annahar. (2014, June 15). [*From Ali al-Amin to the Marji'iya in Iraq*]. Retrieved June 16, 2014, from Al-Annahar: www.annahar.com/article/141921-ددسي-من-السي-العلأا-نيمن-ىلال-ىلال-مرمجعة-نيدلا-في-العارق

Al-Baghdadia. (2014, May 3). *Maliki Sends Jaafari and Al-Khozaei on a Secret Mission to Tehran*. Retrieved May 3, 2014, from Al-Baghdadia News: www.albaghdadianews. com/politics/item/51634-lzhde-aklakkn-nnjd-akvijen-nakgeain-jn-lml%D8%A9-yoen%D8%A9-ako-zmeal.html

al-Haidarî, I. (1999). *Trâjidiya Karbal'a*. London: Dar al-Sâqî.

'Ali, F. A. (2013, August 3). [*Why the US Overthrew Saddam Hussein*]. Retrieved April 17, 2014, from Voice of Iraq: www.sotaliraq.com/mobile-item. php?id=139993#axzz2z8l0anCX

Al-Jazeera. (2010a, June 23). *Al-Maliki: Intervention hindered forming the government*. Al-Jazeera [Arabic].

Al-Jazeera. (2010b, June 30). *Al-Rubai'i: The US and Iran hinder Iraq*. Retrieved August 1, 2010, from Al-Jazeera [Arabic]: www.aljazeera.net/NR/exeres/5EB90546-BA73-4255-8E9A-A57FBCCA9563.htm

Allawi, A. A. (2007). *The Occupation of Iraq: Winning the war, losing the peace*. New Haven: Yale University Press.

al-Rasafî, M. (2007). *Al-Resâlah al-'Irâqiyyah fî al-Siyâsah wa al-Dîn wa al-'Ijtimâ*. Germany: al-Kamel Verlag.

al-Rubai'î, N. (2013, August 23). [*Iraqi Dialogue*]. Retrieved April 22, 2014, from YouTube: https://www.youtube.com/watch?v=9URYDyELWrM

al-Sayeh, A. H. (2014, April 22). *Corruption in the Oil Ministry*. Retrieved April 22, 2014, from Al-Baghdadia: www.albaghdadia.com/fail-years/item/28781-21-4-2014

Al-Sharq Al-Awsat. (2010a, July 29). *Al-Hakim: Iran informed us to accept al-Maliki, even if he hit us on our heads*. Retrieved August 1, 2010, from Al-Sharq Al-Awsat [Arabic]: www.aawsat.com/details.asp?section=4&article=580164&issueno=11566

Al-Sharq Al-Awsat. (2010b, July 31). *Al-Hakim: Iran decreased its support to US by half*. Retrieved August 1, 2010, from Al-Sharq Al-Awsat [Arabic]: www.aawsat.com/ details.asp?section=4&article=580445&issueno=11568

al-Wardi, A. (1954). *Wu'âz al-Salatîn: Ra'i Sarîḥ fî Ṭārīkh al-Fikr al-Islāmī fî Ḍaw' al-Manṭiq al-Hadīth* [*The Preachers of the Sultan*] (2nd ed., 1995). London: Dar Kufân.

al-Wardi, A. (1965). *Dirâsahfî Ṭabî'at Al-Mujtama' Al-'Irâqî* [*A Study into the Nature of Iraqi Society*] (2nd ed., 1995). London: Kufaan Publishing.

al-Zubaidi, I. (2009, December 16). Safahât Matwiyya min Ayyâm al-Mu'aradah al-'Iraqiyya al-Sabiqa [The Forgotten History of the Ex-Iraqi Opposition]. *Elaph*.

Arango, T., & Gordon, M. R. (2014, April 29). *Amid Iraq's Unrest, Maliki Campaigns as Strongman*. Retrieved May 3, 2014, from *The New York Times*: www.nytimes. com/2014/04/30/world/middleeast/unrest-in-iraq-narrows-odds-for-maliki-win. html?ref=middleeast&_r=0

Arango, T., & Krauss, C. (2013, June 2). *China is Reaping Biggest Benefits of Iraq Oil Boom*. Retrieved February 7, 2014, from *The New York Times*: www.nytimes. com/2013/06/03/world/middleeast/china-reaps-biggest-benefits-of-iraq-oil-boom. html?pagewanted=all

Bremer, L. P., & McConnell, M. (2006). *My Year in Iraq: The struggle to build a future of hope*. New York: Simon and Schuster.

106 Deconstruction and reconstruction of the state

Casey, G. W. (2014, May 1). *April 25, 2014, Phoenix, AZ—Gen. George Casey, 36th Chief of Staff of US Army, speaking at a Conference: "Countering Iran's Nuclear, Terrorist Threats."* Retrieved May 6, 2014, from YouTube: https://www.youtube.com/watch?v=x2SAvJ8lrsg

Chalabi, M. (2009, July 16). *Iraqi Oil: The influence of the 1st bid round on the Future of Iraq's national oil and gas industries.* Retrieved August 1, 2010, from ZCommunications: https://zcomm.org/znetarticle/iraqi-oil-the-influence-of-the-1st-bid-round-on-the-future-of-iraqs-national-oil-and-gas-industries-by-munir-chalabi/

Chossudovsky, M. (2004, May 21). *Who is Ahmad Chalabi?* Retrieved August 1, 2010, from Global Research: www.globalresearch.ca/articles/CHO405D.html

CIA. (2006, June 8). *US Iraq Intelligence Summary—Iran—Shia—COA Scimitar—Karbarla (June 8, 2006).* Retrieved August 1, 2010, from WikiLeaks: http://wikileaks.org/wiki/US_Iraq_Intelligence_Summary_-_Iran_-_Shia_-_COA_Scimitar_-_Karbarla_(June_8,_2006)

Cole, J. (2008, March 30). *Mahdi Army Unsubdued: Iran asks for end to fighting.* Retrieved August 1, 2010, from Informed Comment: www.juancole.com/2008/03/mahdi-army-unsubdued-iran-asks-for-end.html

Cole, J. (2010, November 14). *Sunni Arabs Return to Parliament but Shiite–Kurdish Ascendancy Holds: Ahmadinejad congratulates his candidate, al-Maliki.* Retrieved November 20, 2010, from Informed Comment: www.juancole.com/2010/11/sunni-arabs-return-to-parliament-but-shiite-kurdish-ascendancy-holds-ahmadinejad-congratulates-his-candidate-al-maliki.html

Davies, E. (2005). *Memories of State: Politics, history and collective identity in modern Iraq.* Berkeley and London: University of California Press.

Davies, N. (2010, October 22). *Iraq War Logs: Secret order that let US ignore abuse.* Retrieved November 1, 2010, from *The Guardian*: www.theguardian.com/world/2010/oct/22/iraq-detainee-abuse-torture-saddam

Dickey, C. (2004, November 19). Make or Break. *Newsweek.*

Dizard, J. (2004, May 4). *How Amad Chalabi Conned the Neocons.* Retrieved August 1, 2010, from Salon: www.salon.com/news/feature/2004/05/04/chalabi

Energy Intelligence Group. (2008, October 6). *Terms Take Shape for Iraqi Bid Rounds.* Retrieved August 1, 2010, from Energy Intelligence: www.energyintel.com/DocumentDetail.asp?document_id=241186

Fadel, L. (2010, November 14). *Sunni-Backed Bloc Agrees to Role in Iraqi Government.* Retrieved November 20, 2010, from *The Washington Post*: www.washingtonpost.com/wp-dyn/content/article/2010/11/13/AR2010111304273.html

Faucon, B. (2006, April 28). *USAID Provides Adviser to Iraq Government on Oil Law.* Retrieved June 20, 2014, from Dow Jones Newswire: http://new.dowjones.com/

Filkins, D. (2013, September 30). *The Shadow Commander.* Retrieved March 26, 2014, from *The New Yorker*: www.newyorker.com/reporting/2013/09/30/130930fa_fact_filkins?currentPage=all

Filkins, D. (2014, April 28). *What We Left Behind.* Retrieved April 28, 2014, from *The New Yorker*: www.newyorker.com/reporting/2014/04/28/140428fa_fact_filkins?currentPage=all

Fisk, R. (2010, October 24). *The Shaming of America.* Retrieved November 1, 2010, from *The Independent*: www.independent.co.uk/voices/commentators/fisk/robert-fisk-the-shaming-of-america-2115111.html

Gordon, M., & Lehren, A. (2010a, October 22). *Leaked Reports Detail Iran's Aid for Iraqi Militias.* Retrieved November 1, 2010, from *The New York Times*: www.nytimes.com/2010/10/23/world/middleeast/23iran.html?_r=0

The sectarian state in Iraq 107

Gordon, M., & Lehren, A. (2010b, October 23). *Tensions High Along Kurdish–Arab Line.* Retrieved January 7, 2014, from *The New York Times*: www.nytimes.com/2010/10/24/world/middleeast/24kurds.html

Halpern, M. (1963). *The Politics of Social Change in the Middle East and North Africa.* Princeton: Princeton University Press.

Ismael, J. S., & Ismael, T. Y. (2010). The Sectarian State in Iraq and the New Political Class. *International Journal of Contemporary Iraqi Studies, 4*(3), 339–356.

Ismael, T. Y. (1970). *Government and Politics of the Contemporary Middle East.* Homewood: Dorsey Press.

Jakes, L., & Abdul-Zahra, Q. (2010, October 21). *US Sway Dwindles in Iraq.* Retrieved January 8, 2014, from NBC News: www.nbcnews.com/id/39788625/ns/world_news-mideastn_africa/

Jenkins, S. (2010, August 31). *A Trillion-Dollar Catastrophe. Yes, Iraq was a headline war.* Retrieved August 31, 2010, from *The Guardian*: www.guardian.co.uk/commentisfree/2010/aug/31/trillion-dollar-catastrophe-iraq-war

Jiyad, A. M. (2011, June 11). *Inaccurate and Partial Interpretation of the Constitution (comment in reply to "Debate Continues on Legality of Kurdistan's Petroleum Contracts").* Retrieved February 8, 2014, from Iraq Business News: www.iraq-businessnews.com/2011/06/07/debate-continues-on-legality-of-kurdistans-petroleum-contracts/comment-page-1/#comment-52789

Jiyad, A. M. (2012, September 10). *Inside Iraq's Energy Revolution: An Interview with Ahmed Mousa Jiyad* (R. Tollast, Interviewer). Retrieved February 7, 2014, from Global Politics: http://global-politics.co.uk/blog/2012/09/10/Iraq_energy_revolution/

Jiyad, A. M. (2014, February 10). *Capital Gain Tax on IOCs Operating in Iraq.* Retrieved February 11, 2014, from Iraq Business News: www.iraq-businessnews.com/2014/02/10/capital-gain-tax-on-iocs-in-iraq/

Karim, F. (2014, January 14). *Can the White House Comprehend What is Happening in Iraq?* Almada.

Kitabat. (2014a, April 10). [*Maliki Calls for "National Household," al-Sistani Refuses to Receive Him*]. Retrieved April 10, 2014, from Kitabat: www.kitabat.com/ar/page/10/04/2014/26070/المالكي-يدعو-لبناء-دولة-ال-ه أ-لبلا ت-والسياتني-يرفض-استقباله.html

Kitabat. (2014b, April 12). [*Iranian Official: We will not support Maliki's attempt for a third term*]. Retrieved April 12, 2014, from Kitabat: www.kitabat.com/ar/page/12/04/2014/26201/مسؤول-ايراني--لن-ندعم-تشرح-أ-المالكي-لولاية-ثالثة.html

Kitabat. (2014c, April 19). [*Newspaper Analyzes the Attitudes of Politicians on a Third Term for Maliki*]. Retrieved April 19, 2014, from Kitabat: www.kitabat.com/ar/page/19/04/2014/26662/صحف-تحلل-تبست-تحلل-مواقف-السياسيين-من-والية-المالكي-الثالثة.html

Kitabat. (2014d, May 4). [*Maliki Makes a Pilgrimage to Tehran to Arrange the Alliance That Will Save His Job*]. Retrieved May 4, 2014, from Kitabat: www.kitabat.com/ar/page/04/05/2014/27557/المالكي-يحج-الى طهران-لترتيب-تحالفات-بقائه-بمنصب ه.html

Kitabat. (2014e, September 2). [*Maliki Appoints His Media Advisor to be the Director-General of Foreign Affairs*]. Retrieved on September 3, 2014, from Kitabat: www.kitabat.com/ar/page/02/09/2014/33876/المالكي-يعين-مستشاره-الاعلامي-مديرا-عاما-في-الخارجيةبشهادة-مزورة.html

108 *Deconstruction and reconstruction of the state*

Kitabat. (2014f, September 7). [*Parliament Investigates Granting of Parks to Senior Officials*]. Retrieved September 7, 2014, from Kitabat: www.kitabat.com/ar/page/07/09/2014/34190/مجلس-النواب-يحقق-بمنح-المالكيي-ضباط-كبار-ارضي-متنزهات-بغداد.html

Knickermeyer, E. (2010a, October 25). *WikiLeaks Exposes Rumsfeld's Lies*. Retrieved November 1, 2010, from The Daily Beast: www.thedailybeast.com/articles/2010/10/25/wikileaks-shows-rumsfeld-and-casey-lied-about-the-iraq-war.html

Knickermeyer, E. (2010b, October 27). *Blood on our Hands*. Retrieved January 8, 2014, from Foreign Policy: www.foreignpolicy.com/articles/2010/10/25/Blood_on_Our_Hands

Lee, J. (2014, January 29). *Iraq, Iran Plot Oil Revolution, Challenge Saudi*. Retrieved March 16, 2014, from Iraq Business News: www.iraq-businessnews.com/2014/01/29/iraq-iran-plot-oil-revolution-challenge-saudi/

Mahmûd, N. (1987a, March). Al-Judhûr al-Târîkhiyyah Lil-Nizâm al-Tâ'ifî fî al-'Irâq [Part 1]. *Al-Ghad*(20).

Mahmûd, N. (1987b, November). Al-Judhûr al-Târîkhiyyah Lil-Nizâm al-Tâ'ifî fî al-'Irâq [Part 2]. *Al-Ghad*(21).

Mamouri, A. (2013, October 13). *The Enigma of Qasem Soleimani and His Role in Iraq*. Retrieved March 26, 2014, from Al-Monitor: www.al-monitor.com/pulse/fr/contents/articles/originals/2013/10/the-enigma-behind-qassem-suleimani.html

Mamouri, A. (2014, April 15). *Sistani Calls on Iraqi Voters to "Choose Wisely."* Retrieved April 17, 2014, from Al-Monitor: www.al-monitor.com/pulse/originals/2014/04/sistani-call-change-iraq-elections-maliki.html

Ministry of Oil, Iraq. (2010, February 15). *The Law of Income Taxation on Foreign Oil Companies*. Retrieved February 7, 2014, from Republic of Iraq Ministry of Oil: http://oil.gov.iq/en/upload/upfile/44The%20Law%20of%20Income%20Taxation%20on%20Foreign%20Oil%20Companies%20Working%20in%20Iraq%20and%20its%20regulation.pdf

Mustafa, H. (2014, April 30). *Najafi's Prohibition Against Electing al-Maliki Does Not Conflict With al-Sistani's Position*. Retrieved April 30, 2014, from Al-Sharq Al-Awsat: www.aawsat.net/2014/04/article55331362

Patterson, G. (2007, September 16). *Alan Greenspan Claims Iraq War was Really for Oil*. Retrieved August 1, 2010, from *The Sunday Times*: www.timesonline.co.uk/tol/news/world/article2461214.ece

Peri, S. (2003, May 6). *Saddam's "Successor" Made Secret Visit to Israel*. Retrieved December 9, 2013, from Israel Behind the News: www.israelbehindthenews.com/bin/content.cgi?ID=1700&q=1

Porter, G. (2007, July 26). *Bush Line Distorts Iran's Real Interest in Iraq*. Retrieved January 8, 2014, from Antiwar.com: www.antiwar.com/porter/?articleid=11351

Porter, G. (2008, December 17). *Iran's Regional Power Rooted in Shia Ties*. Retrieved August 1, 2010, from Antiwar.com: www.antiwar.com/porter/?articleid=13917

Porter, G. (2009, July 13). *A US/Iraq Conflict on Iran*. Retrieved August 1, 2010, from CounterPunch: www.counterpunch.org/porter07132009.html

Porter, G. (2010, November 5). *US "Exploited" Iraq Communal Strife*. Retrieved January 8, 2014, from Al-Jazeera: www.aljazeera.com/indepth/features/2010/11/2010115112630560418.html

Rahimi, B. (2007, June). *Ayatollah Sistani and the Democratization of Post-Ba'athist Iraq*. Retrieved January 8, 2014, from United States Institute for Peace: www.usip.org/sites/default/files/sr187.pdf

Reuters. (2008, April 4). *Iran Helped End Iraq Fighting: Iraq party adviser*. Retrieved January 8, 2014, from Reuters: www.reuters.com/article/2008/04/04/idUSL04611687

Rubin, A., al-Salhy, S., & Gladstone, R. (2014, June 13). *Iraqi Shiite Cleric Issues Call to Arms*. Retrieved June 16, 2014, from *The New York Times*: www.nytimes.com/2014/06/14/world/middleeast/iraq.html?_r=0

Shaoul, J. (2014, May 5). *Iraq Election Sets Stage for Protracted Civil Strife*. Retrieved from May 5, 2014, from World Socialist Web Site: www.wsws.org/en/articles/2014/05/05/iraq-m05.html

Shoamanesh, S. S. (2010, March 8). *Iraq Election 2010: Neighours eye Iraq election*. Retrieved January 8, 2014, from Al-Jazeera: www.aljazeera.com/focus/iraqelection2010/2010/03/201037123914357815.html

SourceWatch. (2010, August 12). *Iraqi National Congress*. Retrieved January 8, 2014, from SourceWatch: www.sourcewatch.org/index.php?title=Iraqi_National_Congress

Strobel, W. P., & Fadel, L. (2008, March 31). *Iranian who Brokered Iraqi Peace is on US Terrorist Watch List*. Retrieved August 1, 2010, from McClatchy DC: www.mcclatchydc.com/2008/03/31/32141/iranian-who-brokered-iraqi-peace.html

Tavernise, S. (2010, October 23). *Mix of Trust and Despair Helped Turn Tide in Iraq*. Retrieved December 1, 2010, from *The New York Times*: www.nytimes.com/2010/10/24/world/middleeast/24surge.html

The Declaration of the Shia of Iraq. (2002, July). Retrieved January 22, 2014, from Al-Bab: www.al-bab.com/arab/docs/iraq/shia02a.htm

Walt, V. (2009, December 19). *U.S. Companies Shut Out as Iraq Auctions Its Oil Fields*. Retrieved February 7, 2014, from *Time Magazine*: http://content.time.com/time/world/article/0,8599,1948787,00.html

5 The hallmark of the new state
Political corruption

The Anglo-American invasion of Iraq, beyond its immediate justifications of having resting on false claims of Iraqi possession of WMDs and in its providing support to al-Qaeda terrorists, purportedly sought to make the Middle East safe for democracy, and to craft Iraq as a model of a tolerant and liberal regime in the heart of the Arab world. The democratization of Iraq and assumed spread of democracy throughout the region would vindicate the liberal democratic "end of history" presupposed by the collapse of the Soviet Union and the end of the Cold War. These justifications, while popular with the American public, did not survive first contact with reality on the ground. Democracy requires more than open and free elections—although even here, it is dubious that Iraq has crossed this benchmark. Rather, the rule of law, government transparency and the protection of rights allow for the emergence of a civil society, separate from the state and market, as a vehicle for the enrichment of democratic life.

On the measure of transparency and the rule of law, Iraq "the model" has performed terribly, and the dominant feature of Iraqi civic life would become corruption. So much so that over a decade following the end of Ba'thist rule, a new compact was asserted in the guise of the "National Conference" of September 19, 2013. Responding to broad public derision of the new regime, the Vice President of the Republic, Khiḍr Al-Khûzâ'î, presented a document calling for "honor and social peace." The conference was attended by Prime Minister Nûrî al-Mâlikî, Parliament Speaker Usâmah al-Nujaifî, head of the Islamic Supreme Council 'Ammâr al-Ḥakîm, and head of the National Alliance Ibrâhîm al-Ja'farî, who declared in a televised speech during the opening of the conference that "corruption is a culture in Iraq." Such a pact was hoped to be a solution to the sectarian violence that plagues post-invasion Iraq, although prominent opposition leaders like Iyâd 'Allâwî refused to attend (Al-Baghdadia, 2013).

Scholarly and legal discourse on corruption and its connection to both state building and democracy promotion identifies it as both cause and effect of failed efforts across the developing world—often in isolation from any comparative examination of corruption in the developed world, or in the exchange between developed and developing states and economies. While corruption existed under Ba'thist rule and especially the burdens of the sanctions era, current scholarship remains largely silent on its growth under Anglo-American occupation in Iraq.

The hallmark of the new state   111

This period is foundational to the modes and methods adopted in the new state, allowing for corruption to be increasingly manipulated by the new political class implanted through Anglo-American military intervention. For our purposes a useful heuristic is provided by Transparency International, an organization that measures levels of perceived corruption, where corruption is defined, generally, as "the abuse of entrusted power for private gain" (Transparency International, n.d.). This straightforward definition underpins various types of corruption: grand corruption, petty corruption and political corruption. Grand corruption is defined as "acts committed at a high level of government that distort policies or the central functioning of the state, enabling leaders to benefit at the expense of the public good." Contrary to grand corruption, petty corruption "refers to everyday abuse of entrusted power by low and mid-level public officials in their interactions with ordinary citizens." The primary locations petty corruption occurs in are hospitals, schools, police departments and other agencies that have day-to-day interaction with the populace. Lastly, political corruption is defined as "a manipulation of policies, institutions and rules of procedure in the allocation of resources and financing by political decision makers, who abuse their position to sustain their power, status and wealth." While such classifications of corruption are germane to every system of governance, democratic and autocratic alike, some governments are incidentally corrupted, with corrupt officials regularly prosecuted, while some governments are foundationally corrupt. The new Iraqi state represents the latter classification, for while corruption was not an unknown feature of Iraqi politics under Ba'thist rule, the political corruption of contemporary Iraq is notable in that it is fundamental (i.e. inseparable) to the current political system and broadly beyond prosecution or oversight. This endemic nature was cited by Ziad Al-Ali (2014) when explaining his frustration as

> [b]y the end of 2010, it had been clear to me for some time that [...] I was essentially wasting my time trying to assist a state that was led by the worst elements in society. What was the point of negotiating anti-corruption frameworks with mid-level officials, when ministers and other high-ranking officials were robbing the state in broad daylight? [...] In the 1970s, Iraqis generally eschewed corruption and theft [...] By the time Nouri al-Maliki's second government had formed in November 2010, [... there was] an understanding that anything that was not stolen would just be wasted or gobbled up by the political parties anyway.
>
> (p. 9)

Moreover, by the standards provided by Transparency International, all three classifications of corruption are applicable to the contemporary Iraqi state.

Corruption in post-conflict societies can be more destructive to citizens and civil society, destabilizing development efforts and promoting rent-seeking behaviors. According to Mark Phillip (2008), this impact of such perniciousness is wide in scope:

112   *Deconstruction and reconstruction of the state*

> In post-conflict societies its [corruption's] impact is potentially still more serious, because it can undercut the emergence of stable expectations and the processes by which they are legitimated, it can maintain or further exacerbate situations in which outcomes lack legitimacy, making it difficult for any serious form of authority to emerge, it can lead to the squandering of aid and external political will, and it can make the weak weaker, the poor poorer and the vulnerable still less secure.
>
> (p. 314)

The conditions created by the re-engineering of Iraqi state and society not only created an environment of mass violence, but also an environment in which corruption would encompass all levels of Iraqi state and society. Embezzlement, money laundering and bribery have become standard operating procedures, as indicated in a 2007 report by Walter Pincus, which not only outlines corruption on a wide scale, but also sketches the absence of independent investigation into these crimes, with prosecution becoming politicized:

> The quashed CPI [Commission on Public Integrity] probes include investigations of Central Bank employees who released $14.7 million despite an Agriculture Ministry letter opposing that action; Oil Ministry personnel who manipulated bids for $2.5 million in contracts for pumps and fuel equipment; and others at the Oil Ministry who stole 33 trucks loaded with petroleum. The Electricity Ministry also had bidding irregularities in a $3 million contract, the Youth and Sport Ministry had $3.5 million in contract irregularities, and the Supreme Electoral Commission was being investigated for a $5 million illegal advertising contract.

Complementary to the findings of other NGO and journalist investigations, corruption and waste are not exclusive to a certain ministry or to certain politicians, but have become standard operating procedures. A report from Iraq's Ministry of Planning details how, in the past decade, the federal bureaucracy has ballooned 300 percent, now employing 6 million people who, on average, work 17 minutes out of their 6-hour workday (Al-Mada, 2014b). Meanwhile, the majority of Iraq's political elite, regardless of affiliation, have accumulated billions of dollars illegally (Al-Baghdadia, 2014a). The aforementioned blocked cases involved alleged corruption at 11 ministries, not to mention the Central Bank of Iraq (CBI) (Pincus, 2007). Furthermore, corrupt political practices have become universal among the most senior policymakers within the government and state apparatus. For the year 2009 alone, Iraq's CPI issued 152 arrest warrants against officials at the rank of Director General or above (Iraq, Commission of Integrity, n.d.). Even Iraq's national budget lacks adequate transparency, as in excess of $400 billion has been spent by the Iraqi government since 2004, yet a detailed disclosure of public spending has yet to emerge (Parker, 2012). In 2014 the estimated total amount of laundered funds that have been invested outside of Iraq has surpassed $1 trillion (Kitabat, 2014l). The proliferation of corruption in modern Iraq

The hallmark of the new state   113

has become so pervasive that, during the height of the insurgency and sectarian conflict, government officials considered corruption to be a greater threat to the stability of a future Iraqi state than sectarian violence. This opinion is consistent with the seminal study done by Knack and Keefer (1995), which showed that corruption has a greater adverse effect on economic growth than political violence.

Sectarian violence and corruption, however, are not mutually exclusive in the contemporary Iraqi context, but rather mutually reinforcing. Uncontrolled levels of corruption have become a catalyst for sectarian violence as political actors survive and prosper through economic rents. According to the former Deputy Prime Minister of Iraq, Barham Ṣâliḥ, "The political economy of this conflict is very much rooted in the alarming levels of corruption that we're dealing with […] A lot of money from many sectors of the economy is diverted to sustain the violence" (Negus, 2006). Many alliances and political blocs are able to impose their agendas by the force of sectarian militias, funded through corruption and illicit behavior, exacerbating communal differences at the expense of national interests. Iraq is caught in a cycle whereby negative developments are self-reinforcing. According to Robert Looney (2008), these cycles often continue until an exogenous factor comes and stops, or reverses the cycle.

The corrupt political order in Iraq begs the question: How did Iraq "the model," launched as a liberatory project through US-led intervention, see Iraq becoming comparable to countries such as Somalia and Sudan with regards to corruption? Political corruption in post-invasion Iraq did not emerge indigenously, as a function of cultural norms tolerating corruption, but through the exogenous imposition of a corrupt political class. As we have seen, the political class that came to rule post-invasion Iraq was nurtured in exile, particularly in the 1990s, when there were international and regional efforts to formulate a post-Saddam ruling elite.

Through the occupation's efforts to fill the vacuum created through regime change, a new political caste was parachuted into Iraq representing either a rootless exile class ("carpetbaggers")[1] or sectarian party-militias with narrow social bases. Such actors were necessarily lacking in any desire to expand their legitimacy or responsibility to the broader Iraqi society for competing political actors not associated with the occupation and who were more well known to Iraq's population were they to displace them. Rent-seeking behavior from the exiles provided ample support for their narrow base, who quickly gained positions and influence in the new government, while Iraqi state institutions built up over the previous eight decades were conflated with their former Ba'thist masters. This pitted the exiles against not only the remnants of the former regime, but also the broader Iraqi state institutions, in a society desperately in need of expanded institutional capacity. Former exiles would often be chosen to lead ministries for which they had no prior experience or technical expertise. In an effort to cement their rule and continued role, they would populate their assigned ministries with cronies, who were patently unsuited for the positions of power they were awarded, but rather selected for their loyalty. According to Ali Allawi (2007, p. 349), "Failed former petty traders became senior advisers; adventurers and bankrupts ended up in charge of huge departmental budgets." The incompetence resulting from a lack of expertise and the future

114   *Deconstruction and reconstruction of the state*

corrupt practices that would follow were highly predictable. A few months prior to the Anglo-American invasion, an Iraqi civil servant made a somber but telling prediction: "The exiled Iraqis are the exact replica of those who currently govern us […] with the sole difference that the latter are already satiated since they have been robbing us for the past 30 years" (Cockburn, 2013a). The Ba'th regime, while fleecing and repressing the Iraqi populace, maintained Iraq's social institutions while protecting Iraqis from extreme economic deprivation. Such controls existed, in part, to maintain political legitimacy, but they were also a reflection of what was politically acceptable in Iraqi political culture.

Hence, the state that emerged post-invasion was weak and fragmented, with the new political elite dependent on external support for its authority, chiefly the US and Iran. As this new political class lacked an indigenous basis of support, they would legitimate their rule through appeals to subnational ethnic and sectarian client groups, as opposed to Iraqi civic concerns. Consequently, this weak and sectarian political authority was rife with corruption, encompassing Iraq at every level: external (corruption in allocation of American reconstruction funds), internal (pursuit of private interests by Iraqi public figures), and the intersection in between (cooperation of external and internal actors in joint corruption). This corruption would infect Irazq at the political, economic, social and cultural levels.

At the political level, Paul Bremer's CPA, effectively sanctioning the new political class through the *dictat* of proconsul rule, initiated the corrupt order. Like the British administration of Iraq following World War I, which also sought to legitimate its rule through Iraqi faces, the CPA sought legitimacy through the creation of the IGC. Crucially different, however, was that while the British ruled Iraq through a chimera of indigenous authority, relying on existing Iraqi tribal elites, the American occupation instead attempted to legitimate its rule through an Iraqi exile class, whose connections to Iraq were either weak or highly particularistic. The new political class, the "carpetbaggers," were parachuted into a weak and fragmented post-invasion environment, with the goal of creating a highly pliable Iraqi regime and state apparatus, controllable and dependent on external support. That planners desired for this to be American in design failed to dissuade regional actors such as Iran, Turkey and Saudi Arabia from aggressively pursuing their own allies and dependent proxies.[2] The political culture characterized by the IGC would shape the political formations and alliances moving forward in the lead-up to the 2005 parliamentary election, establishing political sectarianism as a defining feature of the post-invasion Iraqi state.

In order to clear the path for this highly corruptible and pliable political elite, all elements of Iraq's inherited political culture were disassembled.[3] Exiles and occupation authorities removed all political competition from the embryonic state institutions they were constructing. In doing so they also denied all input from Iraqi society that would not align with the new order, going so far as to openly define who was an Iraqi and who was not. Those opposing the occupation were thereby dismissed as "anti-Iraqi," and their political agency was unwelcome in the development of any new political regime. In addition, the confined ideological mindset of the CPA rendered its objectives contrary to the practicalities of both daily life and any future democratic society. Disassociated from the enormous levels of human suffering and destruction wrought through the war and sanctions surrounding them, planners engaged in a re-engineering of society without inputs from Iraqis. Campaigns, such as that to privatize Iraq's public sector, were futile efforts, because those responsible for doing so "lacked the baseline belief in the public sphere that is required for the complex task of reconstructing a state from the ground up" (Klein, 2007, p. 426). For the CPA, staffed with young conservatives with strong Republican credentials, virtually none of whom had Foreign Service experience, ideological precepts trumped political acumen and common sense. As violence increased and rocket attacks and suicide bombings became an all too frequent occurrence, those senior CPA staffers with Foreign Service experience left Iraq for safer assignments, leaving the political appointees ascendant. "In short order, six of the new young hires found themselves managing the country's $13 billion budget, making decisions affecting millions of Iraqis" (Cha, 2004). While being young and inexperienced didn't necessarily guarantee failure for the CPA, their animosity and opposition to the very notion of government had little use when it came to building public institutions, something they intrinsically despised.

Replacing tyranny with anarchy and claiming it was order

Measures of corruption in Iraq, both systematic and anecdotal, reveal a country whose state and civic institutions operate in a complete absence of meaningful transparency or lawful supervision. What oversight is present is largely through the efforts of civil society, with independent journalists featuring prominently, often at great personal risk. Journalists are frequently killed (Abbas, 2013b),[4] and there are still no effective laws to guarantee the protection of journalists or reasonable access to state information (Mamouri, 2014b). While dozens of media outlets have come on to the scene in the New Iraq, filling the void left by heavy censorship during the Ba'th regime, they by and large have political, ethnic and sectarian affiliations that exacerbate the divisions within the country (Hasan, 2014; Kitabat, 2014d). Even the official state television station, Al-Iraqiyya, which had aspirations to match the BBC in terms of quality and independence, has come under fire as a heavily biased mouthpiece for al-Mâlikî, with opposition MPs calling for its funding to be cut from the state budget (Hasan, 2014). Common themes in Iraqi journalism are

> fragmenting the news to present only the part that is in line with the policies of each channel or newspaper, editing news clips and manipulating copy, stirring emotions in line with the channel's orientation [...] when one follows the main Iraqi news outlets, one sees an often monotonous picture of either governmental accomplishment versus arbitrary aggression against the government by its adversaries who represent the enemies of the Iraqi nation, or a failed Iraqi political project since 2003 versus alternative revolutionary projects.
>
> (Mamouri, 2014b)

116 *Deconstruction and reconstruction of the state*

The state of journalism in Iraq is in disarray, dominated by rumor, speculation and empty spin, falling short of any sort of integrity. "The truth is that you never really know what is going on behind the scenes. Each media outlet in Iraq is directed by its political affiliations" (Mamouri, 2014b). However, Al-Baghdadia, an Iraqi television station broadcast from Cairo so that it can remain independent and outspoken, stands out as one journalistic voice that has remained largely independent (Hasan, 2014). Three of its popular programs, *Studio 9* (hosted by Anwar al-Hamdani), *Qadhiyat Ra'i A'mm* (hosted by I'mad al-I'badi) and *Hewar Iraqi* (hosted by Najim al-Rubai'i), in which members of parliament, particularly the Chairman of the Parliamentary Integrity Committee, Bahâ' al-A'rajî, discuss cases of state corruption, stand out as great examples of journalistic integrity. Al-Baghdadia has also sponsored a civil society movement in the fourth quarter of 2013, known as *Haquona* (Our Rights), under the slogan of "combating terrorism, looting and corruption," and "in order to bring to justice those thieves." *Haquona* established coordinating committees in each of Iraq's governorates and has circulated a petition that obtained over two million signatures from Iraqi intellectuals, lawyers, teachers, Majarii' and students. Al-A'rajî says he participates often to emphasize the lack of action from the Commission of Integrity, who, despite their occasional successes, regularly neglects to follow through on the recommendations or investigation requests of the Committee. According to Judge Rahîm al-'Uqailî, a former head of the Commission, even "the inspector generals, who are supposed to audit each ministry to ensure it complies with standard procedural and accounting practices and remains free of corruption, are all senior officials of the Da'wa party and facilitators of corruption" (Al-Baghdadia, 2014a). Al-A'rajî identifies political corruption as the basis of corruption in Iraq, remarking:

> We have people inside our political parties who direct institutions and companies and receive commissions in return. Every ministry chases commissions and is willing to turn a blind-eye to others. This is why Ibrahim Al-Jaafari declared that "corruption in Iraq is a culture," because he is close enough to smell it and because [Iraq] is a state of [corrupt] political parties and not [public serving] institutions.
>
> (Studio 9, 2013)

Thus, al-A'rajî concluded that corruption is protected by comity between political parties. Transparency International ranked Iraq 169 out of 176 countries in their 2012 survey (Transparency International, 2012). This represents a level of corruption that sets Iraq in the company of countries like Somalia, North Korea, Afghanistan and Sudan—in other words, international "outlaw" regimes representing disorder and dictatorship, which is an inconvenient reality in light of the claim made by President Bush that Iraq would serve as a "beacon of democracy" for other countries in the Middle East to follow. With the American mission in post-invasion Iraq now officially "over," the country has in fact become emblematic of "a culture of lawlessness," identified by Farîd Jâsim Hammûd, dean of the

The hallmark of the new state 117

College of Law at the University of Kirkuk, as being "rampant in Iraq" (Reuter, 2013, p. 3).

Outside the formally "political," corruption has become ubiquitous in Iraq's economic affairs, extending to external actors through the allocation of reconstruction funds and the activities of Western contractors within Iraq, internal actors through the bribery and graft of/by Iraqi public officials, and the intersection between two spheres that has witnessed a culture of lawlessness permeating the dealings of the Iraqi government with regional and international forces. Fundamental to the postwar regime initiated by the CPA was an absence of accountability and democratic Iraqi control over developments within its borders. Indeed, CPA Order 17 (Coalition Provisional Authority, 2004b) declared that the Multi-National Force (MNF), the CPA, foreign liaison missions, their personnel, property, funds and assets, as well as "all International Consultants[,] shall be immune from Iraqi legal process" and "immune from any form of arrest or detention other than by persons acting on behalf of their Sending States" (Coalition Provisional Authority, 2004a).

The lack of oversight or observance of international legal norms that characterizes private contractors operating within Iraq also extends to financial matters. A report authored by Stuart Bowen, the SIGIR, concluded that of the $60 billion in reconstruction funds deployed in Iraq, $8 billion was simply "wasted," an astonishing figure that he described as merely a "conservative" estimate in a later interview (Ackerman, 2013). Within Iraq, a watchdog agency—the Board of Supreme Audit—estimated that "$800 million in profits from illicit activities was being transferred out of Iraq each week, effectively stripping $40 billion annually from the economy" (Smith, 2013).

Beyond private contractors, the financial matters of the US occupation's administration of its own funds were highly suspect, with tens of billions of dollars operating within a legal vacuum and an unaccountable black hole. Unsurprisingly, in its final report, the SIGIR claimed that "it could not find reliably complete information showing what US construction funds accomplished" and that "the full story on the use of billions of US dollars for reconstructing Iraq will forever remain incomplete" (al-Sayegh, 2013). At the outset of the invasion, the US Government flew an estimated $12 billion into Iraq, 363 tons of shrink-wrapped packets of $100 notes, which were distributed throughout Iraq without any oversight or controls. This represented a scheme in which wide-scale corruption was, at minimum, highly predictable. In a 2005 US House Committee on the scheme, payments of dubious legality were described: "One contractor received a $2m payment in a duffel bag stuffed with shrink-wrapped bundles of currency. Auditors discovered that the key to a vault was kept in an unsecured backpack" (Pallister, 2007). The report concludes:

> Many of the funds appear to have been lost to corruption and waste [...] thousands of "ghost employees" were receiving pay cheques from Iraqi ministries under the CPA's control. Some of the funds could have enriched both criminals and insurgents fighting the United States.
>
> (Pallister, 2007)

118 *Deconstruction and reconstruction of the state*

Hence it described an intrinsically absurd intersection of corruption between external and internal actors, where hundreds of millions—if not billions—were distributed by the occupation regime throughout Iraq's government ministries without any oversight or accountability, inevitably funneling money to Iraqi ministries (such as the Interior Ministry) which were implicated in the violence of (often American-trained) party-militias, including torture centers:

> "They [the US and Iraqi Ministry of Interior] worked hand in hand," said General Muntadher al-Samari, who worked with [US Colonel] Steele and [US Colonel] Coffman for a year while the commandos were being set up. "I never saw them apart in the 40 or 50 times I saw them inside the detention centres. They knew everything that was going on there [...] the torture, the most horrible kinds of torture."
>
> (Mahmood et al., 2013)

The function of this engineered political order—sectarian, fragmented, weak and pliable—was to generate an Iraqi political regime that was limited in its ability to oversee Iraqi affairs and establish legitimate national policy. Instead, the new regime dedicated itself to personal enrichment or to the service of rent-seeking subnational ethnosectarian communities within Iraq. In this weak political environment, Iraqi economic policy—particularly in the energy sector—was shaped by American planners as a policy of "disaster capitalism," or what Naomi Klein (2007) dubbed the "shock doctrine." Amidst this chaos, Iraq's economy was subject to the precepts of CPA Order 39 (Coalition Provisional Authority, 2003), permitting foreign firms up to 100 percent ownership of Iraqi assets, with an absence of Iraqi capital controls or taxation policy. Hence while the Iraqi government was carved into ethno-sectarian fiefdoms, economic policy would be shaped through this American-imposed "shock doctrine." The oil sector, of course, was the prize jewel in this post-war economic order. Historically, Iraq's oil wealth had served as the fulcrum for national development, financing an extensive public sector (health, education and public works) aimed at engineering an Iraqi identity that took precedence over sect or tribe. Under this new regime, Iraqi revenues were disproportionately awarded to American firms:

> Of contracts for more than US$5 million, 74% went to US companies, with most of the remainder going to US allies, Only 2% went to Iraqi companies [...] Kellogg, Brown, and Root (KBR), a subsidiary of Halliburton, received over 60% of all contracts paid for with Iraqi funds, although it was repeatedly criticized by auditors for issues of honesty and competence.
>
> (Gordon, 2013)

Corruption and graft in occupied Iraq took various forms, ranging from outright theft, to misallocation of resources, to overcharging, to projects that were never completed or completed so poorly as to render the project a waste. At the most innocent level of failure, funds that simply failed to achieve their desired result, one considers the approximately $8 billion spent improving Iraq's power and water supply. By 2011, eight years after the initial invasion, Iraqi households averaged only 7.6 hours of electricity per day, which has in fact decreased in recent years (Ackerman, 2013). Power outages have a particularly devastating impact on the Iraqi economy. In September 2013, Iraq's Oil and Energy Committee published a report indicating that Iraq is losing around $40 billion annually due to the power outage crisis (Khadduri, 2013). Citizens are thus forced to use generators, increasing costs to every sector of the emergent economy, and contributing heavily to environmental pollution. While the energy crisis impacts ordinary Iraqis on a day-to-day basis, it is not the only crisis facing the energy sector in Iraq. The emergence of two different oil industries, one controlled by the federal government and the other controlled by the Kurdistan Regional Government (KRG), has yet to be resolved. This situation may be exacerbated even more so should the Kurdistan region begin exporting oil directly to Turkey without the federal government's approval, which ultimately would be a violation of the Iraqi constitution (Khadduri, 2013).

In many instances, such failures could be attributed to either incompetence or lack of genuine concern. For instance, in the aftermath of the 2003 assault, the occupation authorities committed themselves to rebuilding a key bridge across the Tigris River necessary for oil pipelines. Initially priced at $5 million, the project was revised for "security purposes" (the pipelines would now be built underground), raising the estimated cost fivefold. Although warned that the soil was not appropriate for underground pipelines,

> neither the [US] Army Corps of Engineers nor the main contractors at the site, Kellogg, Brown and Root [formerly a subsidiary of Halliburton], heeded the warning. As a result, "tens of millions of dollars [were] wasted on churning sand" [...] By the time the digging effort was halted [...]—more than three years later—the bill had reached more than $100 million.
>
> (Smith, 2013)

In a survey of US reconstruction projects from 2003 onward, the SIGIR (2008) report concluded: "40 percent of the 116 in-progress and 54 finished projects that SIGIR evaluated (worth almost $2.1 billion) had 'major deficiencies.'" Other fundamental problems in reconstruction included "the practice of paying contractors/subcontractors far more than the project's value," the Iraqi and US governments' "failures to coordinate with one another" and "tolerance of rampant corruption that occurred on both the Iraq and U.S. sides" (Coleman, 2013). Iraq's oil industry, which is the lifeblood of its economy, has been similarly pilfered, with an estimated 30 percent smuggled out of Iraq and sold on the black market (SIGIR, 2008, p. 211).

Worse still were instances of outright fraud resulting from weak oversight, typically in the form of overcharging by contractors. In one instance highlighted by the SIGIR report, a subcontractor "overcharged Iraqi projects by thousands of dollars for supplies, including $900 for a control switch valued at $7.05, and

120 *Deconstruction and reconstruction of the state*

$80 for a pipe that should cost $1.41" (Ayesh, 2013). Likewise, "a firm based in Dubai managed to keep around $4 billion in Pentagon construction contracts [...] despite routinely marking up [prices] [...] between 3,000 and 12,000 percent" (Smith, 2013).[5] Such questionable practices by private contractors, in fact, represent a general trend. According to the Comptroller General of the US GAO, David Walker, between 1991 and 2005 there has been "an explosion in [military] contracting, while at the same point in time we have seen a contraction of those engaged in oversight of contracting matters." This has led to a series of contracts that cannot be effectively monitored to ensure they deliver value for money. Among these was the contract awarded to KBR (Kellogg, Brown and Root), a former subsidiary of Halliburton, from 2001 to 2007, an uncapped cost-plus contract wherein KBR would be reimbursed for their costs plus 3 percent of the total expenditures. Thus, "the fact that LOGCAP [Logistics Civil Augmentation Program] is cost-plus means that KBR benefits from accepting the most expensive offer," and instances of extraordinary markups in the price of equipment, such as the above, are institutionally incentivized (Rose, 2007).

In another instance of corruption, the Iraqi government spent up to £75 million British pounds ($114 million USD) on ADE651 bomb detection devices, with the British contractor charging Iraqis between £23,548.37 ($36,064.33 USD) and £34,702.86 ($53,147.43 USD) each, even though the real cost of the devices is no more than £61.97 ($94.91 USD), according to a senior official (Reuters, 2011). It was subsequently determined that the devices—meant to detect bombs at security checkpoints and elsewhere—were fake. As a result, numerous suicide bombers passed through checkpoints undetected, resulting in the killing of hundreds of Iraqi civilians (Booth & Jones, 2013). Most troubling, however, is that while these bomb detectors were identified as being defective and Jim McCormick, the British businessman responsible for selling them to Iraq, was convicted and sentenced to an eight-year jail term in the UK, the detectors continued to be used in Baghdad. A number of Iraqi officials have even defended their use, with one official claiming that only "a few of them are defective" and they require the "operator to be in the right frame of mind" (Beaumont, 2013). While the issue was first raised in 2010 by 'Aqîl al-Ṭuraiḥî, now the inspector general of the Ministry of the Interior (MOI), his predecessor attempted to grant immunity to those responsible for the corrupt deal. According to al-Ṭuraiḥî, "there were officials who knew they weren't effective but still did the deal anyway" (Beaumont, 2013). Among these officials is Fadel Dabbas, the owner of the United Bank of Investment in Iraq, the agency that arranged the deal for the fake detectors. Dabbas had been exonerated by al-Mâlikî in 2013, and was later given $120 million to organize the Iraq Coalition, a list of Sunni businessmen who were to run in Iraq's 2014 federal election. Each candidate running under Dabbas received $4 million in campaign funding through this arrangement. Following the election, and having won 6 seats, the Iraq Coalition announced its allegiance to al-Mâlikî (Ahrar News, 2014; Al-Aalem, 2014).

Beyond the contracting process, petty corruption amongst public servants in state bureaucracies is rampant in Iraq. The Iraqi Commission of Integrity, which was created by the Interim Governing Authority (IGC) on the authority of CPA Order 55 (2004), is the body tasked with investigating and prosecuting corruption. The results of a survey conducted by the Commission of Integrity in 2011 were analyzed, along with the results of two similar surveys, in cooperation with the United Nations Office on Drugs and Crime (UNODC) in a 2013 report. The report found that, in the 12 months preceding the surveys, 11.6 percent of Iraqis had paid approximately four bribes each to a public official. Of these bribes, roughly 65 percent were requested by a public official themselves (UN Office on Drugs and Crime, 2013, pp. 5–6, 10). Despite the importance of the Commission's research, its effectiveness has been hampered by Prime Minister Nûrî al-Mâlikî's consolidation of power; each of the judges who have led the Commission have been forced to resign and "have had fabricated charges placed against them" (Al-Sharq Al-Awsat, 2014). Judge Hamzah Râdhî al-Râdhî, head of the Commission of Integrity until 2007, resigned in response to the limiting of the Commission's scope by al-Mâlikî: "I cannot just sit in my place and see corruption eating the Iraqi state, so I asked for retirement" (Rubin, 2007). Following his resignation, Râdhî was granted political asylum in the US. Subsequently, Rahîm Hassan al-'Uqailî, who headed the Commission of Integrity until 2013, would likewise be constrained to resign in dismay, "sharply critici[zing] interference in his inquiries." He had previously described "the fight over stealing the money of the state and its property [as an] unspoken part of the struggle for power in Iraq today" while accusing the Iraqi government of "trying hard to resist the tools and mechanisms of accountability and transparency," concluding that "no committee fighting corruption can work actively and efficiently without sufficient political support" (Iraq Business News, 2011). According to 'Uqailî, at one meeting he attended with the inspector generals from all the ministries and al-Mâlikî, they were instructed by al-Mâlikî to "overlook any incident of corruption in which the amount taken was less than ten percent of the total transaction" (Al-Baghdadia, 2014a). In November 2013 a warrant for 'Uqailî's arrest was issued over charges of corruption and terrorism, but it has been revealed by a source within the judiciary that the warrant was issued without any evidence of corruption having been submitted to the judge for review (Al-Sharq Al-Awsat, 2014; Kitabat, 2014j). 'Uqailî's problems with al-Mâlikî began when he investigated the practice of torturing suspects to extract confessions. It was further noted that "the warrant [that] was issued by parties involved in a plot create an exclusionary political scene in Iraq […] [The same] judges that have participated in this plot are also behind the coerced confessions gained from cutting the throats of hundreds of innocent people. These are mock trials and do not meet the basic rules of justice" (Kitabat, 2014j). 'Uqailî was convicted in absentia in March 2014, with a verdict of one year's imprisonment issued.

On January 25, 2014, a member of the Parliamentary Integrity Committee, Shirwân al-Wâ'ilî, revealed on an episode of *Hewar Iraqi* that currently there are over 500 corruption cases investigated by the Parliamentary Committee and sent to the Commission of Integrity that are still waiting to be acted upon; effectively any investigation into each case has stalled indefinitely. That there are even

122 Deconstruction and reconstruction of the state

500 reported corruption cases is remarkable in light of the allegation of *Studio 9* (2014b) that "the Court of Information and Publications is a special court that anyone who criticizes the government will eventually find themselves in front of and arrested under the orders of its corrupt judges."

Ṣabâḥ al-Sa'dî, a member of the Parliamentary Integrity Committee, told *Studio 9* on January 29, 2014 that the operating budgets of Iraq's political parties come from the proceeds of corruption: "These parties have embraced financial and administrative corruption, and they seek to cover it up." Al-Sa'dî was himself offered one million dollars per day to stop exposing government corruption, according to 'Uqailî, who was present when the offer was made (Al-Baghdadia, 2014a). Corruption permeates every ministry in Iraq, especially the Ministries of Education, Health, Commerce, Oil, Industry, Municipalities, Defense and the Interior; as well as the religious endowment trusts (Awqaf) of both Sunni and Shia. Al-Mâlikî has managed to position members of the Da'wa Party at the helm of every government office and independent commission (Al-Baghdadia, 2014a). Sawaiba Zangana, the former deputy minister of commerce who resigned after four years of service in protest at the corruption, told Al-Baghdadia (2014a) that al-Mâlikî interferes in the affairs of the ministry and used to send merchants and contractors "in droves" to the ministry to get contracts. She concluded by saying that al-Mâlikî is

> worse than Saddam, as he directly gets involved in the affairs of every ministry for the purpose of achieving private gains [...] the ministries are headed by ministers, but in every case the real administrator is al-Maliki, through his chief of staff [...] the Ministry of Commerce became a ministry of looters, where everyone steals from the ration of the people for the Da'wa party.
>
> (Al-Baghdadia, 2014a)

The aforementioned Judge Râdhî was quoted as identifying the contracting process as "the father of all corruption issues in Iraq." As contracts are awarded to companies run by, or friendly to, senior politicians, large sums of money are awarded without taking bids and lacking viable documentation, most of which occurred prior to projects being started. In essence, money is being awarded and the beneficiaries simply move on. Such was the case with the former Minister of Electricity (2003–2005), Ayham al-Sâmirrâ'î, who was arrested following the Commission of Integrity's findings that he was responsible for "financial and administrative irregularities by approving contracts for electricity projects [...] misappropriating millions of dollars" (Pravda, 2006). Al-Sâmirrâ'î escaped prison in December 2006 with the help of a mercenary group and fled to the US where he currently resides (Environmental News Service, 2007).

Of all the cases Judge Râdhî prosecuted while serving as head of the Commission of Integrity, the most egregious cases occurred from 2004 to 2005 and involved nearly $1.3 billion in Ministry of Defense funds. According to Judge Râdhî, the funds were diverted by then-Minister of Defense Ḥâzim al-Sha'lân, in collaboration with the head of the procurement department, Zaid Qattân. Qattân,

The hallmark of the new state 123

who by his own admission had no experience with weapons procurement, claimed that he previously sold "water, flowers, shoes, [and] cars—but not weapons. We didn't know anything about weapons" (Moore & Miller, 2005). Sha'lân claimed the money was going to be used to build a quick reaction force (QRF) to respond to the growing insurgency and appealed to then-Prime Minister Iyâd 'Allâwî to circumvent the legal standard to publicly solicit bids for the project. 'Allâwî, claiming imperative national defense contracts required secrecy, granted approval to Sha'lân and waived all legal requirements with regards to purchases for the QRF. According to a report by SIGIR, Qattân accepted bribes and paid out the full $1.3 billion prior to any deliveries being made. Goods that were later delivered were of such poor quality that they were obsolete on arrival. For example, "The QRF contracts included the purchase of 24 Russian helicopters for $10 million [... which] turned out to be more than 30 years old and in such bad condition that the Iraqi military refused to accept them." By the time the Integrity Commission figured out that $1.3 billion was missing, Sha'lân and his associate Qattân had fled the country and "were living comfortably abroad" (SIGIR, 2012a, p. 106).

The corruption that overtook Iraq was similarly noted by Najib Salhi, a general who fled Iraq during the Saddam years and aided the opposition. Returning to post-Saddam Iraq, Salhi resumed his military post until he was compelled to resign under pressure from the al-Mâlikî government in 2009, in response to his frequent appearances in the media exposing corruption, where he described the Ministry of Defense as beset by low morale and unprofessionalism. According to Salhi, as a result of CPA Orders 1 and 2, which instituted de-Ba'thification and disbanded the Iraqi army, most of Iraq's professional officers were cleared out from the military. In the newly constituted army, many of Iraq's militias were incorporated and members of Iraq's new political class recruited their friends, family and co-religionists/sectarians to serve as officers, most of whom had no prior military experience, bypassing the constitutionally required parliamentary approval for ranks of colonel and higher. This practice sidestepped the professional officers that had served in the old army and instituted nepotistic practices that have led to the post-Saddam Iraqi army as having more generals than any other military of its size in the world. Further, Judge 'Uqailî, the successor of Judge Râdhî, also found the Ministry of Defense to be "one of the fattest cows of corruption," uncovering dubious contracts with "exaggerated budgets" that, for instance, payrolled soldiers who existed only on paper. The money of such contracts is generally split between the commanding officers involved and whichever militia is supposedly supplying the soldiers. Another source of income for officers is demanding protection money, like organized criminals, or levying tolls at checkpoints. Unsurprisingly, officer positions are also for sale—it costs only $1 million to become a divisional commander in the army (Cockburn, 2014). In 2007, al-Mâlikî ordered the Integrity Commission to cease investigating the Ministry of Defense, citing national security concerns. This lack of oversight and ease of skimming contract money is most evident in the fact that the majority of Iraq's defense ministers since 2003 have followed the pattern of looting the Ministry's budget and fleeing the country with their newfound riches (al-Sayeh, 2014c). The

124 *Deconstruction and reconstruction of the state*

costs of corruption have been steep for Iraq's military; it is reported that "whole battalions" have deserted—some because they have not been paid, others because they have not received food or ammunition while deployed (Cockburn, 2014).

Another case which garnered international notoriety was that against 'Abd-ul-Falâḥ al-Sûdânî, the Minister of Trade from 2006 to 2009. A member of the Da'wa Party, and former Education Minister under the Iraqi Transitional Government, al-Sûdânî resigned on May 14, 2009 amidst allegations of stealing public money, mismanaging the Trade Ministry and populating his ministry with relatives, including his two brothers. The Ministry, responsible for a near $6 billion budget, is responsible for the import of grain, seeds and construction materials, amongst other things (Karim, 2009). Al-Sûdânî was accused of "selling food instead of giving it to its intended recipients and of letting foodstuffs go bad in ministry warehouses" (Bloomberg, 2009). A month after a shootout between al-Sûdânî's staff and investigators, al-Sûdânî attempted to leave the country and was briefly jailed. While al-Sûdânî was tried and sentenced in June 2009 to seven years in prison, the trial and judgment were held in absentia, as he fled the country subsequent to being released on bail. Almost a year later, a judge dismissed the case against him. This case had implications for the most senior Iraqi political officials, including Prime Minister al-Mâlikî. Sheik al-Wakil, General Secretary of the Islamic Accord Movement, identified the former convicted Minister of Trade al-Sûdânî as being a partner of al-Mâlikî. According to al-Wakil, al-Sûdânî threatened to "spill the beans" on al-Mâlikî, something that former Judge 'Uqailî recalls Sûdânî as saying would "implicate three-quarters of [Iraq's] political elite," which is the reason al-Sûdânî was allowed to flee the country and eventually go to Britain, where he is a citizen (Al-Baghdadia, 2014a). This is why another judge was found who would release al-Sûdânî on bail, fully aware that he would not come back to be tried in court (al-Ruba'ie, 2014a). The example of the case against al-Sûdânî, among others, emphasizes the weakness of Iraq's judicial system and highlights the lack of commitment to impose the rule of law against corrupt officials.

The Ministry of Industry and Minerals has likewise seen corruption. On May 13, 2014, the Integrity Commission issued a warrant for the arrest of Ahmed al-Karbouli, the Minister since 2011, and his brother Jamal al-Karbouli, the head of the al-Hal political bloc (the National Movement for Development and Reform) and an MP since 2009, for "stealing medicine, children's food, medical equipment, eight ambulances valued at $50 million donated by the Saudi Red Crescent to its Iraqi counterpart, and cash donations totaling $150 million from international NGOs given to the organization in Oman." Jamal has already been convicted in one other legal case out of seven outstanding cases under investigation, one of them involving the attempted assassinations of ten separate general directors in the Ministry of Industry (three of the assassinations were successful). The Karbouli brothers are believed to have acted together in all of these crimes and fraudulent transactions. The whistleblower at the Red Crescent, Radhwan al-Sa'dî, was murdered three days after he divulged the thefts (Kitabat, 2014p).

Ḥussain al-Shahristânî, the oil and energy czar of Iraq from 2006 to 2010 and the Deputy Prime Minister for Energy since 2010, is at the center of another

The hallmark of the new state 125

high-profile corruption scandal. He is aligned with the Da'wa Party and is a leading member of al-Mâlikî's Rule of Law Alliance, and has been described by al-Mâlikî himself as a close, personal friend. Ḥussain al-Shahristânî is also considered to be the representative of the marji'iyyah in the government. His name has come up often in connection to corrupt oil contracts. The most recent incident was a deal in which he awarded a $6.5 billion USD contract to build an oil refinery, something that normally should not exceed $2 billion according to experts, in the Maysan Governorate (in the South of Iraq) to a Swiss shell corporation, that happened to be owned and managed by Ridhâ al-Shahristânî, his brother (al-Sayeh, 2014a; Kitabat, 2013). This was discovered by Iraqi-expatriate oil professionals living in Switzerland, and was confirmed through leaks from senior officials in the Ministry of Oil. The contract was signed on behalf of the Iraqi government by Ḥussain al-Shahristânî himself, with the blessing of the Prime Minister, al-Mâlikî. This is but one example of corruption that has led one expert to say: "In Iraq, mafioso already run [...] almost the entire oil output of the south of the country" (Fisk, 2014). The scandal roused the attention of even the marji'iyyah. Thus, Jawâd al-Shahristânî (a cousin of the al-Shahristânî brothers), the son-in-law and international representative of the Grand Ayatollah, 'Alî al-Sistânî, was dispatched from Iran, where he has lived in exile for the past 35 years, to go to Najaf for a meeting with representatives from al-Mâlikî and the marji'iyyah. At the meeting, the parties determined that al-Mâlikî, in exchange for squashing the scandal, would receive the support of the marji'iyyah for a third term as Prime Minister (Kitabat, 2013). According to Kitabat (2013), a respectable news outlet:

> [Of the $6.5 billion], $1 billion has gone to Maliki's Da'wa party, $1 billion to the Independent Bloc (*Mistaquloon*) led by Mohammad Reza al-Sistani (the son of the Grand Ayatollah), and Hussain al-Shahristani received 10% of the whole amount.

Scandals of this sort have misdirected billions of dollars from improving Iraq's oil infrastructure, and are to blame for the delay in returning to and exceeding the pre-invasion export levels (2.4 million barrels per day)—a benchmark that was not achieved until 2014. Yet, even with these high exports, the refining capacity has not recovered, and Iraq is expected to remain dependent on importing oil derivatives for at least four more years, according to the former Iraqi oil minister and internationally regarded oil expert, Issam Chalabi (al-Sayeh, 2014a).

Staggering corruption has been revealed within the ministries of Education and Higher Education. Since the Anglo-American invasion, the Ministry of Education has demolished 700 schools on the basis of structural concerns. Contracts to replace the schools were awarded to four different contractors, and 60 percent of the value for each contract was paid out as an advance; all four contractors disappeared with the money and the schools have yet to be replaced. For example, in 2010 the Ministry of Education contracted the Ministry of Industry to build 49 schools in Najaf Governorate within 8 months, "but until now they have not been completed," according to Luay Yassiri, the head of the Governorate

126 *Deconstruction and reconstruction of the state*

Council, who has asked the Integrity Commission to investigate (Kitabat, 2014q). The added student population at Iraq's schools has created a great strain—class sizes are significantly larger, dropout rates higher, and classes are now organized around three distinct blocks, in the morning, afternoon and evening. The selling of government jobs has become common practice and continues to the present. It is common knowledge that jobs in the Ministry of Education are for sale, teaching jobs in particular. The current minister, Mohammad al-Jabouri, has built on the "legacy" of his predecessors in this regard, whereby people can go to a used car lot in Kirkuk, the capital of his home governorate, and pay $700 to become a teacher. Meanwhile at the Ministry of Higher Education it has become a common practice to accept bribes from students wishing to have their grades improved, according to the Ministry's former deputy inspector general, Raghad al-Dulaimi. Further, al-Dulaimi discovered that many government officials are enrolled in graduate studies despite the requirement that students in Master's and PhD programs commit to a full-time residency. An example includes the Minister of Higher Education, Ali al-Adeeb, who obtained his MA in Psychology from Al-Mustansiryah University in 2009 while he was serving as an MP (al-Sayeh, 2014b; Ministry of Higher Education, n.d.). Iraq's universities were considered the most prestigious in the Arab world during the 1960s and 1970s, and now rank among the world's worst (Mamouri, 2014c).

The impact of corruption in the Ministry of Education can also be seen in the negligence of the so-called "school biscuit scandal" that erupted in mid-January 2014 when Al-Baghdadia's *Studio 9* program interviewed Dr. Ra'd Ḥâjzîn, chairman of the Jordanian Parliamentary Committee on Health, on January 13. Ḥâjzîn disclosed that a journalist contacted his committee regarding the falsification of the expiry date on biscuits purchased by the Iraq Ministry of Education from the World Food Programme as a food supplement for students. According to the documents presented by the journalist, the biscuits were past their specified date of expiry, and the Iraqi contractor in Jordan (where they were being shipped from) was extending the date of expiration by two years at the request of the Iraqi Deputy Minister of Education in order to satisfy health requirements in Iraq. This disclosure led to the seizure of the biscuit shipment by the Jordanian Organization of Food and Medicine, forcing the Iraq Minister of Education to fly to Amman to investigate this with the Jordanian authorities. Soon after, the Iraqi Parliamentary Legal Committee also flew to Amman to investigate the issue. The Iraq Minister of Health subsequently insisted that no tainted biscuits entered Iraq. However, the Governor of Naynawa announced that over 260 tons of the tainted biscuits were already in their storage facilities, and the Governor of Diwaniya announced that 300 tons of the tainted biscuits had already been distributed to their students. Despite these revelations, the Prime Minister's Office has remained silent on the issue (Studio 9, 2014c) to the chagrin of the public.

The al-Mâlikî government has—according to critics and investigators—developed an elaborate regime of corrupt patronage, allocating contracts to supporters, while beneficiaries of contracts "are threatened with investigation and exposure if they step out of line" (Cockburn, 2013a). Al-Mâlikî's efforts to monopolize

The hallmark of the new state 127

power have alienated not only Sunni and Kurdish lawmakers, but many among Iraq's powerful Shi'ite community as well. The marji'iyyah "have come to see the Prime Minister as a provoker of crises that discredit Shi'ism and may break up the country" (Cockburn, 2013b). Complaints about corruption are frequently ignored as these companies are protected by the very same politicians who are responsible for awarding the contracts in the first place (Dodge, 2013). Through dubious deals and the fake projects being awarded, including "one of the most flagrant examples of the financial and administrative looting of public funds, the $500 million opera house project that was tendered to a Turkish company that simply does not exist," one part of a series of vaporous construction projects commissioned by the Ministry of Culture to make "Baghdad the cultural capital of the Arab world" according to the Senior Deputy Minister of Culture, money laundering has become a growing challenge that has resulted in a massive waste of resources and an increasing wealth gap between the masses and the political elite (Kitabat, 2014m). According to Aḥmad al-Jabûrî, a member of the Commission of Integrity, money laundering operations make up to $9 billion per year, representing around 20 percent of Iraq's investment budget (al-Shaher, 2013b). Much of this money is subsequently smuggled outside of Iraq to establish projects overseas as well as to purchase real estate investments.

Al-Mâlikî's corrupt patronage is also prevalent in the Ministry of Health, as evidenced by the frequency by which contracts for medical supplies and facility construction projects are paid for but left unfulfilled. The General Inspector of the Ministry, 'Âdil Muḥsin, who has been in the position since the occupation began in 2003 and is responsible for the integrity of the contacts, supplies and purchasing, has admitted that "We've uncovered some problems, mostly with the contracts," and implied things are not as prevalent as has been described by Iraqi medical professionals (Reilly, 2009). However, the credibility of Muḥsin's statement is dubious given continued supply problems in Iraqi hospitals and clinics that have been documented by the Parliamentary Integrity Committee; and he has avoided charges and arrest numerous times in Baghdad. However, in 2013, he was placed under arrest by the Integrity Commission judge of Najaf (Hussein, 2013), but was released on bail shortly after. Al-Ṣadr, a prominent opposition voice in Iraq, has also accused Muḥsin of being in league with al-Mâlikî, who uses the Ministry of Health as one of his money-laundering enterprises (Sadah, 2013b). The credibility of al-Ṣadr's accusation is strengthened given that Muḥsin has been, from the beginning, a close ally of al-Mâlikî and a member of the Da'wa Party executive leadership. Further, Muḥsin had also appointed his wife to be in charge of medical contracts in the Ministry of Health. Following his release on bail, Muḥsin fled Iraq, something that is difficult without help from high places, and his whereabouts are presently unknown.

Meanwhile, an arrest warrant has been issued for the former Deputy Minister of Health (2006–2007), Hakim al-Zamili, for leading militias during his tenure as the Deputy Minister; these militias were implicated in the killing of Sunnis who were kidnapped from hospitals and ambulances, as well as the kidnapping of two of his rivals in the ministry, Ammar al-Saffar (Da'wa) and Ali al-Mahdawi

128 *Deconstruction and reconstruction of the state*

(whose whereabouts remain unknown). He also stands accused of selling the bodies of the militias' victims back to their families for burial. The profits from these activities were used to finance the Sadrists. Al-Zamili is also charged with extorting businessmen after threats of assassination since having been elected to parliament, as part of the Sadrist bloc, and then being appointed to its Security and Defense Committee in 2011 (Kitabat, 2014n). Al-Zamili had been arrested in 2007 by US forces, to whom he confessed to all charges, but was released after being turned over to Iraqi authorities, subsequently running for parliament in the 2010 elections. Such crimes coming from government officials are common, although they rarely are charged unless it is politically expedient for al-Mâlikî.

Another feature of "patronage" within post-invasion Iraq has been the manner in which al-Mâlikî rewards his supporters, conferring upon them military and police ranks, a power predicated upon CPA Order 91 (Kitabat, 2014b). A collection of leaked documents reveals that many within al-Mâlikî's inner circle—few of whom have prior military experience—have received an officer rank; among them is Adnan al-Asadi, a former minimarket employee in Denmark by his own admission (Studio 9, 2014e) and now the Deputy Interior Minister,[6] who, in a document dated March 25, 2008, gave himself the rank of General within the Iraqi police force (Kitabat, 2014b). The problems facing the legitimacy of the Iraqi military are compounded by the fact that al-Asadi has been in charge of a selection of Shia militias, affiliated with the Da'wa Party, since 2004 as part of the so-called integration policy (al-'Assaf & Jawad, 2013, pp. 290–296). Not only are those personally loyal to al-Mâlikî given military rank, but are also placed in charge of militias. The collection of documents shows that "the period of al-Mâlikî's tenure in office between 2006 to present [2014] shows the greatest wave of distributing military ranks to his inner-circle, especially those affiliated with the militias loyal to him" (Kitabat, 2014b). For unknown reasons, al-Asadi rescinded his rank in a document dated September 14, 2009, although it was likely a decision made by al-Mâlikî (Kitabat, 2014b).

Nepotism is yet another common example of corruption in Iraq. The appointment of relatives to government offices occurs frequently. Often the children or immediate relatives and in-laws of Da'wa Party leadership are posted to embassies outside Iraq offering their families security and good pay. A case in point is the appointment of Vice President Khodair al-Khozai's two children to the Iraqi Embassy in Canada, the children of the leader of the Rule of Law Alliance, Khalid al-'Atiyah, to the Iraqi embassy in London (Al-Baghdadia, 2014a), and the Military Chief of Staff of the Prime Minister's Office Farouq al-Araji's daughter, Huda, and her husband to the Iraqi Embassy in London as well, where they serve as an accountant and an administrator in the military attaché's office, respectively (H. A. Karim, 2014). Other prominent members of the Da'wa or friends of their friends have also followed suit, appointing their unqualified children to embassies around the world (al-Baghdadi, 2014). Special benefits are another face of nepotism. Madhi Hadi al-'Ameri, the son of the Minister of Transportation, Hadi al-'Ameri, who is a member of al-Mâlikî's Rule of Law Alliance and now the leader of the Badr Brigade and who has filled most of the senior positions in

The hallmark of the new state   129

his ministry with his family and clansmen (Kitabat, 2014f), was in Beirut and running late for a flight back to Baghdad on Middle East Airlines. Since he was absent at the departure time, and having announced his name several times along with his bodyguard, the flight had to leave without him, as is normal procedure. Upon hearing of this departure, al-'Ameri called the Baghdad Airport Authority and notified them to not allow the flight to land without him. This is exactly what happened. There was an uproar in Iraq and Lebanon over this row in the mass media and social media, forcing his father to call the Minister of Transportation in Lebanon to apologize, while al-Mâlikî ordered the arrest of the deputy director of the Baghdad Airport Authority (Kitabat, 2014e). It is unsurprising that al-Mâlikî has also been accused of nepotism, as according to Al-Sharq Al-Awsat (2014) he

> legalized the sale of state property for the benefit of his party and relatives. Among these sales includes the Bakr University, which he sold to a Da'wa party leader for a nominal price. The buyer made it into the Imam Sadiq University, a private, for-profit university, and made himself the chairman of the board of governors. Maliki's family took over all the state property in the Green Zone, placing under the control of his son, as well as the Muthanna airport in the heart of Baghdad.

Further, al-Mâlikî's office is filled with members of his own family, in addition to those serving elsewhere in the government. In the 2014 election five members of al-Mâlikî's family ran for parliament under his banner, and won with high proportions of the votes in their respective ridings. These include two sons-in-law (one of whom was his private secretary and the other his chief of security), one nephew and two cousins (Al-Mada, 2014a). Additionally, between April 2014 and May 2014, al-Mâlikî, his inner circle and their families transferred $4.3 billion outside of Iraq according to a report issued by an Iraqi anti-corruption and human rights NGO, Al-Salam, in "cooperation with officials in the Integrity Commission and the Office of Financial Supervision." They reported that "the money was laundered through private companies under the knowledge of the Ministry of Finance itself," thus bypassing the Central Bank of Iraq, spurred by "fears of the possibility of Maliki being unable to secure a third term." The majority of the money was routed across the Arab world, with Egypt being the top destination followed by Jordan and Lebanon, while in the West Britain was the top destination followed by Greece; an additional $300 million was also directed to Iran (Kitabat, 2014o).

One of the chief mechanisms to ensure that top government officials do not skim money is a mandatory annual financial disclosure, which became law in 2011; however, like the majority of other anti-corruption measures in Iraq this too is ineffectual and poorly enforced. For example, only four (out of 15) governors, two (out of three) deputy prime ministers and 153 (out of 325) MPs have disclosed their financial assets for 2013 (Agator, 2013; Al-Baghdadia, 2014b).

Parliamentarians receive many benefits, the latest of which were established on February 3, 2014 when the Iraqi parliament passed a controversial retirement bill, drafted by a committee headed by Hussain al-Shahristânî that has

130 *Deconstruction and reconstruction of the state*

given lavish salaries to many in Iraq's imported political class (Hussein, 2014; J. Karim, 2014). The law gives Iraqi presidents a $50,000 monthly pension, while prime ministers and speakers of parliament will be entitled to receive a $40,000-a-month pension. Members of parliament will also receive incredibly lavish pensions, valued at 70 percent of their current $11,000-a-month salaries, in addition to other benefits (Kitabat, 2014a).[7] The retirement law also creates a jihadi benefit, wherein Iraqis who lived in exile during the Saddam regime are considered *mujahideen* (people doing jihad) and entitled to a doubling of their standard pension. All that is required to gain recognition as a *mujahid* is a letter of recognition from any of the political parties currently in power (Studio 9, 2014d). Such laws are possible because of the legal precedents set in the CPA orders, many of which remain in effect.

While Humâm Hammûdî, head of the Foreign Relations Committee, described the retirement law as a "step towards achieving social justice" (Hussein, 2014), it is important to note that MPs can gain the above benefits after only four years of service, while government bureaucrats must be over 50 and have served for over 30 years before qualifying for a meager pension of $325 monthly (Kitabat, 2014a). Citizens in 13 governorates protested the retirement law while it was being drafted, and the law remains unpopular (Kitabat, 2014a). There has been significant confusion as to how and why this law was even passed. Of the parliament's 325 members, only 173 attended the session to vote on this law. Of those present, only 2 voted against the law and 8 abstained (Studio 9, 2014d). Following the passage of the law two MPs, Hanân al-Fatalâwî (Rule of Law Alliance), head of the parliamentary Sub-Committee of Human Resources, and Mahâ al-Dûrî (*al-Ahrar* [Sadri Bloc]), held a press conference to denounce the law—however, remarkably, they both voted in favor of it according to *Studio 9* (2014d). Another member of the Sadri Bloc, Jawâd al-Shuhailî, has expressed his intention to challenge the jihadi benefit in court; he also voted in favor of the law (J. Karim, 2014). Anwar al-Hamdânî, a *Studio 9* anchor who had interviewed many MPs who criticized the law only to vote in favor of it, expressed his frustration, saying: "Who the hell, then, is against this?" (Studio 9, 2014d).

The outcry over the new retirement law has been enormous. Anger has filled the street, and clerics, including 'Alî al-Sistânî, have called on followers to boycott MPs who voted for the law in the upcoming federal election. Moreover, Muqtadâ al-Ṣadr has completely resigned himself from politics, stating: "al-Maliki is a dictator [...] who leads the previously exiled hungry wolves that now govern Iraq [...] on behalf of the Shi'ites behind the defenses of the [Baghdad] Green Zone," adding that this goes on while everyday Iraqis live in fear of assassination if they speak out against the central government (Kitabat, 2014c). Many of the 40 MPs from the Sadri Bloc voted in favor of the retirement law, to the disappointment of al-Ṣadr, who has closed all his political offices to turn his full attention to his cultural and charitable organizations instead (Abbas, 2014). Over 18 MPs from the Sadri Bloc have followed suit, also resigning (Shafaaq, 2014). This shift has left a large void in the Iraqi parliament, while also seriously diminishing government approval ahead of elections.

Corruption within Iraq would be described in American diplomatic cables as the "norm," spreading throughout Iraq's ministries (Corn, 2007). The Ministry of the Interior, which oversees Iraqi security forces, has been widely implicated as "dysfunctional and sectarian," and is described in American cables:

> "Untouchable by the anticorruption enforcement infrastructure of Iraq," it says. "Corruption investigations in the Ministry of Defense are judged to be ineffectual." The study reports that the Ministry of Trade is "widely recognized as a troubled ministry" and that of 196 corruption complaints involving this ministry merely eight have made it to court, with only one person convicted.
>
> (Corn, 2007)

The Central Bank of Iraq, which oversees monetary policy in Iraq, has been similarly caught in accusations of corruption and political intrigue. In October 2012, a warrant was issued by the Iraqi government against Central Bank Chief Sinân al-Shabîbî, accusing him of corruption, specifically negligence resulting in millions of fraudulent withdrawals, with funds being smuggled into Syria and Iran (al-Shaher, 2013a). Shabîbî, while denying corruption charges, nevertheless suggested that

> some political parties are giving cover to some private banks in Iraq to withdraw foreign currency from the Central Bank with false documents [...] The proof is that these figures [Iraqi politicians] have valuable accounts and real-estate properties outside Iraq.
>
> (al-Shaher, 2013a)

The decision to replace Shabîbî came amid allegations that the CBI's role in supervising the banking system had been compromised and corrupt practices were reaching every level of the government. Political opponents of Prime Minister al-Mâlikî asserted that Shabîbî's dismissal "was an attempt to bring the CBI and its $63 billion in reserves under executive branch control" (SIGIR, 2012b).

In the al-Mâlikî government, the executive branch has become the dominating force. According to *Qadhiyat Ra'i A'mm* (2014), the parliament is now the sole-contested ground between political factions as al-Mâlikî has successfully used his powers of appointment to fill the Judiciary with judges loyal to him. Among these loyal judges are former members of Saddam Hussein's regime, including Medhat al-Mahmoud, who had worked as Saddam's legal adviser for three years before becoming a cabinet adviser in the Ba'th regime. Mahmoud became the Chief Justice of Iraq and the Head of the Supreme Judicial Council in 2005.[8] Mahmoud's loyalty to al-Mâlikî was cemented following an attempt by the Justice and Accountability Commission to remove Mahmoud from his post as Head of the Supreme Judicial Council on the grounds of de-Ba'thification. The move was successfully reversed in an appeal to the cassation panel, who failed to find any evidence of Mahmoud's connections to the Ba'th regime. This episode

132 *Deconstruction and reconstruction of the state*

affirmed al-Mâlikî's control over the judiciary through Mahmoud (Sadah, 2013a). Any confrontation between parliament and Prime Minister al-Mâlikî is referred to the Federal Court, which is presided over by one of al-Mâlikî's political allies.

Judicial corruption goes as far as the local courts and is, in fact, embedded within the legal/political apparatus of post-invasion Iraq. One of the more corrupting practices, introduced by Anglo-American occupation authorities and later integrated into Iraqi legal practice, is the allowance of secret evidence to be presented in court, in which evidence is presented against the defendant without them having an opportunity to challenge it, let alone review it. This has rendered a farce of the Iraqi justice system and the norm of a fair trial. Beyond this fundamental layer, corruption underpinning the post-invasion Iraqi legal system is the reality, where it has become dangerous for Iraqi lawyers to challenge the state. One lawyer conveyed to *Qadhiyat Ra'i A'mm* (2014) how he had brought a man who had been tortured and left disabled by state police, overseen by the Ministry of the Interior. The judge suggested to the lawyer that it would be in his best interest to withdraw the case. According to 'Uqailî (2014), this is possible because the judiciary

> has lost its conscience and has sold everything in order to keep its unjust control over the constitution and the law. One of the most vicious weapons used against judges [who resist] is to transfer them to places [...] that are dangerous. If the judge is a Shia he will be transferred to a Sunni area, and the Sunni judge to a Shia area, thus endangering the life of the judge and his family. The Iraqi judiciary is now in a great crisis [...] the misconduct of the current administration in devoting the judiciary and the law towards the purpose of political gains for an exclusive group.

These maneuvers have given al-Mâlikî the ability to enforce discipline outside the Da'wa Party's Rule of Law Alliance. Al-Mâlikî has successfully used his influence to politically discredit opposition within the Accountability and Justice Commission, an instrument of de-Ba'thification, and the judiciary; in effect, adding political opponents, whether an incumbent or prospective candidate, to the Iraqi Election Commission's list of banned candidates. It is difficult to overturn such a decision because the appeals go to the cassation court, whose judges are appointed by Medhat al-Mahmoud, and thus loyal to al-Mâlikî. An example of this practice can be seen in the banning of Rafi al-Issawi, the former Finance Minister, from running in the 2014 elections. Issawi, who led a boycott of the Iraqi cabinet in December 2011 and called on al-Mâlikî to resign, asserts that his being banned from running in the 2014 election is "politically motivated" (Kitabat, 2014g). The December 2011 boycott was spurred by the arrest warrant issued by the Ministry of the Interior for Tariq al-Hashimi on December 18 as the last of the US forces withdrew from Iraq (Carlstrom, 2011). Hashimi was Iraq's Vice President from 2006 to 2012 and had been leader of the Sunni Iraqi Accord Front before moving to the secular Iraqiya bloc in 2010 as part of his continued bid to oppose al-Mâlikî, who he believes excludes Sunnis from political dialogue

(Wicken, 2012, p. 1). With the Iraqiya bloc gaining two more seats than the Rule of Law Alliance, Hashimi had become a serious challenger to al-Mâlikî. The warrant was based on dubious charges linking Hashimi to a failed plot to bomb al-Mâlikî and the parliamentary speaker, Usâmah al-Nujaifî. Hashimi has since fled to Turkey where he continues to live. It is unclear if the judges who issued the warrant had even reviewed evidence before acting, with others noting that this is only another example of al-Mâlikî "leverag[ing] the judiciary to consolidate power and sideline rivals" (Wicken, 2012, pp. 2–3).

Manipulation of the power of the judiciary has been a recurring feature of al-Mâlikî's rule. For instance, he has already exerted his influence in the judiciary to overturn a law passed by parliament that placed a term limit on prime ministers to clear the way for his re-election in 2014 (Morris, 2014; Shaoul, 2014). This is also demonstrated in the manner in which loyal judges of the judiciary will refer political adversaries to the Iraqi Election Commission, citing poor conduct to have them banned from running for office,[9] as has happened in the run-up to the 2014 election. This has been a common strategy to deal with disloyal members of the Da'wa Party, rising opponents in other parties—including 38 candidates from Ayad Allawi's bloc (who had actually gained more votes in the 2010 elections than al-Mâlikî's bloc)—and as a way to discredit members of the Parliamentary Integrity Commission who spoke out against al-Mâlikî's corruption (Kitabat, 2014g, 2014h; Morris, 2014; Sabah, 2014; Shaoul, 2014).

Al-Mâlikî's abuse of the "good conduct" qualification for election candidates sparked outrage, as many candidates and incumbents who opposed him found themselves on the Election Commission's list of banned candidates. This led to a parliamentary review of Election Commission Law No. 45 (2013), Article 8, which contains the list of qualifications a candidate must have to run for Iraqi parliament. To clarify the intent of the article, parliament unanimously decided that a candidate cannot be disqualified on grounds of poor conduct unless they have a criminal conviction, and ordered the Electoral Commission to follow this advisory, despite orders to the contrary from the judiciary (Kitabat, 2014i). The councilors of the Iraqi Election Commission resigned en-masse following this decision by parliament, stating: "The Commission is under considerable pressure stemming from conflicting interpretations of the legislative and judicial branches on [the good conduct clause] that each expects the Commission to comply with, despite the conflict. The Commission does not want to be a party to this dispute" (Kitabat, 2014k). However, a short time later, the Commission withdrew their resignations and returned to work under the lead of Muqdad al-Sharifi, a member of the Da'wa Party.

In a similar vein, al-Mâlikî has also been using Iraq's Court of Publishing and Media to attack detractors. The court issued two warrants in February 2014, "the first against Judge Munir Haddad, who approved the death sentence of Saddam Hussein; and the second against Iraqi journalist Sarmad al-Tai, a known critic of the government's political and economic performance" (Mamouri, 2014a). Both are accused of defaming al-Mâlikî. In Iraq, as a holdover of the former regime, it is illegal to criticize public servants. The laws enshrining this facet of Iraqi

134   *Deconstruction and reconstruction of the state*

politics have not been repealed, and reprisals for violations are often harsh—for instance, a journalist who lampooned Massoud Barzânî in 2010 was shortly thereafter abducted and murdered (Human Rights Watch, 2014). It is clear that in Iraq freedom of speech is in jeopardy.

This centralization of power within the office of the Prime Minister has been a particularly prominent feature of lawlessness in post-invasion Iraq. This is most visible, perhaps, with regard to the security apparatus of the state. Al-Mâlikî—as Prime Minister—was granted the title/status of Commander-in-Chief, creating in the Prime Minister's Office extensive executive power over the entirety of the security apparatus (military, police, intelligence) without any legally delineated limits of power or authority. This is in addition to his having formally "[taken] on the roles of minister of defense, interior and national security" following the 2010 elections (Morris, 2014), placing some "930,000 security personnel at his disposal" (Shaoul, 2014). This unaccountable executive power in security/military matters has been compounded by the fact that al-Mâlikî has banned all ranking military officers from appearing before parliament to answer questions (a practice he likes to follow himself), has granted military promotions unilaterally, and has expanded the mandate of the military to include domestic command and control, allowing the Prime Minister to deploy the military in domestic affairs without any clearly understood legal parameters (Filkins, 2014).[10] Thus, al-Mâlikî has become emboldened to refuse to cooperate with anyone who is not, directly or indirectly, loyal to him even in matters of national security and public safety. Since early April 2014 Baghdad has been suffering with water shortages while much of its westernmost suburb, Abu Gharab, has been flooded after the Islamic State of Iraq and the Levant (ISIS) took control of Fallujah Dam and closed its gates. According to Ali Mohsen al-Tamimi, the Governor of Baghdad and a member of the Sadrist Party, al-Mâlikî has refused to meet with him on this issue and others. Al-Tamimi has even been banned from communicating with the military, and says that this is how al-Mâlikî treats anybody who is not a member of his party or from his immediate loyal circle (al-Ruba'ie, 2014b). Thus, as "Insurgents have [...] asserted control over vast rural areas west and south of the capital" (Pasha, 2014) and "levies taxes in cities such as Mosul and Tikrit" north of Baghdad (Cockburn, 2014), the military stands by and, most dispicably, as reported by Human Rights Watch in May 2014, has acted as of late only to hinder "residents from leaving areas where fighting is taking place and impeding aid from getting in [...] government forces shoot residents [...] trying to leave or return to Anbar, killing some of them."

Al-Mâlikî has also created within his office the Bureau of the General Commander of the Armed Forces, a near replica of Saddam Hussein's Revolutionary Command Council, through which he has created offices staffed by loyal employees to parallel the civilian government cabinet positions. Any challenge to al-Mâlikî's centralization of power within the Office of Prime Minister, namely judicial independence, was undermined when al-Mâlikî managed to "[secure] a decision from the Iraqi High Court that gave him the exclusive right to draft legislation" (Filkins, 2014), effectively shielding al-Mâlikî's parallel deep state from any oversight. In view of these seemingly extralegal practices, al-Mâlikî has refused to appear in parliament for questioning.

When asked why corruption is endemic within Iraq, the answer many Iraqis provide is: "UN sanctions destroyed Iraqi society in the 1990s and the Americans destroyed the Iraqi state after 2003" (Corn, 2007). Indeed, in the aftermath of the 1991 Gulf War and the crippling sanctions regime, Iraq saw the utter collapse of its social infrastructure (health and education), a dramatic rise in infant mortality and malnutrition rates, and the re-emergence of tribal social systems to fill the vacuum left by the anemic state. With the American invasion of 2003 and subsequent occupation, the infrastructure of the Iraqi state was dismantled under the banner of de-Ba'thification and reconstituted by sectarian militia-parties whose allegiance lay not in the notion of Iraqi citizenship, but with their particular ethno-religious communities. In this highly sectarian environment, Iraq's factions "are engaged in sometimes cooperative, sometimes competitive efforts to extract rents from not only private citizens, but also from [each other]" (Gunter, 2013, p. 48). This oscillation between cooperation and competition necessitates a contradictory acceptance for and disdain of corruption, leading the factions to expose one another's misdoings when it is advantageous. The purpose is not to deal with the fundamental issues of a corrupt state, but to remove rival factions in efforts to overtake influential positions.

A spoils system?

The future progress of limiting sectarian strife and corruption is not promising, as Iraq's electoral system has been partly to blame for the growing gap between politicians and ordinary citizens. Iraq's 2005 parliamentary elections were conducted according to a "closed-list" form of party-list proportional representation.[11] Under such a system, ballots bore party and coalition names as opposed to the names of individual politicians. Each party received a number of seats, proportional to the percentage of votes it received. The assignment of those seats was left solely to party leaders. Furthermore, for the purposes of the election, Iraq was, in effect, a single constituency, which disproportionately had a devastating impact on the representation of Iraq's Sunnis. Under the continued US presence and perceived assumption that the election was unfair, the vast majority of Sunnis boycotted the elections. Voters who went to the polls chose lists that represented their specific sectarian group, and naturally, Shi'ites and Kurds emerged dominant. In effect, individual MPs were not accountable to the local-level constituencies, but exclusively to party leaders, which would later be illuminated in parliament. 'Aliâ Naṣîf and Jawâd al-Bazzûnî, for example, were dismissed from their respective coalitions for taking positions in parliament that differed from their blocs (Abbas, 2013a). What should not be overlooked in this political arrangement is that Iraq does not have a presidential election. The Council of Representatives (COR), its members appointed by party leaders, has the responsibility to elect the President, who then nominates the Prime Minister from the membership of the majority coalition. The power of Iraq's Council of Representatives in choosing Iraq's

136 *Deconstruction and reconstruction of the state*

President, and indirectly the Prime Minister, makes it even more crucial that parliament be representative of the Iraqi population.

To overcome the increasing sectarian rift between Iraq's major ethnic groups, an agreement to adjust Iraq's electoral process in order to make the COR more representative of Iraq's demography was needed. A new electoral law was adopted in 2009, which increased the size of the Council of Representatives from 275 members to 325, divided Iraq into 18 constituencies representing Iraq's provinces and changed Iraq's closed-list system to a semi-open-list system. The open list allows voters to see the names of individual candidates as well as their party and/ or coalition affiliations. While many COR members leaned toward a closed-list system, those who wanted an open list ultimately prevailed. The 2010 election, while making some progress toward representative democracy, was marred by the disqualification of more than 500 candidates by the Justice and Accountability Commission (JAC) over their alleged ties to the banned Ba'th Party.[12] The executive director of the JAC, 'Alî Faiṣal al-Lâmî, was known for his close ties to Iran as well as to the former head of the De-Ba'thification Commission, Aḥmad Chalabî (Lake, 2010). Some politicians have noted that the banned candidates were exclusively secularists and no excluded names belonged to religious parties (RFE/RL, 2010). Other allegations regarding the corruptibility of Iraq's elections have emerged from Mushtaq Hussain al-A'li (2014), who described in an episode of Al-Baghdadia's *They Wrote the Press* that an innovative new wave of corruption is sweeping Iraq, centered around "senior leaders in the state who sell cabinet positions and other government, military and policing jobs" as a way to raise money to pay contractors whose job it is to guarantee votes for certain candidates/ incumbents in specific parties.

Conclusion

In this collapse of civic and citizenship norms, transparency and the impartial rule of law was not possible. A decade and $2 trillion in military expenses later, Iraq has suffered a regime of incinerating violence, communal strife and widespread corruption. While Iraq exhibits some of the institutional characteristics of parliamentary democracy, Iraq's polity remains controlled by a small political elite, centered on its current Prime Minister. Prime Minister al-Mâlikî's government, in many respects, continues the personalistic style that has characterized Iraqi politics since independence. The modern uses of media and repression developed by the Ba'thist dictatorship are re-emerging, with a plurality of personalities as opposed to a commitment to citizenship.

Recent studies on corruption don't offer much of a positive outlook. On the contrary, Iraqi citizens are disillusioned with the current political process. According to a UN Office on Drugs and Crime report in conjunction with the UNDP, released in January 2013, 54 percent of Iraqi citizens believed corruption was more widespread than it had been two years prior. While the American presence in Iraq has receded, with the occupation formally ending in summer 2010, the political order initiated by the Anglo-American invasion and occupation has

The hallmark of the new state 137

not. Iraq remains in the thrall of weak, corruptible and highly sectarian political forces, where corruption is the business of government and legal authorities are highly limited in their ability to prosecute offenders. Corruption, however, is not an end in itself, but has become the means of doing politics. Corruption has become the opaque zone in which politics takes place, far removed from the input of ordinary Iraqis. Deeply entrenched officials, operating outside state channels, impede any notion of accountability, exacerbating the cleavage between the political elite and those they represent. The rentier nature of the Iraqi state, in which elites hold political clout that surmounts their popularity levels, precludes a loyalty to constituents and instead makes Iraqi politicians rely on elaborate patronage networks, largely developed outside of Iraq, to financially support them. According to Sheik Ṣabâḥ al-Sa'dî, who appeared on Al-Baghdadia's *Studio 9* program on January 19, 2014, these "corruption mafias [...] permeate every part of the state, and every ministry without any sort of limit to their reach. They are international and local in their scope, aim, and activities." These mafias are "administrated by political groups [...] political parties hide corruption because it is the source of their funding" (Studio 9, 2014a). In effect, this new feature makes modern Iraqi politics different from any period since the establishment of the Iraqi state, given that previous regimes all maintained at least some illusion of popular sovereignty. In this sense, the regime that calls itself the Iraqi government is broadly unaccountable to the Iraqi population, its authority instead resting on appeals to subnational communities, on the one hand, and the support of external patrons, on the other. As a former Iraqi minister noted, "the Iraqi government is an institutionalized kleptocracy" (Cockburn, 2013a). While the Arab region saw the emergence of mass protests from 2010 onward that saw the overthrow of multiple regimes, the experience of Iraq has served, not as a "model," but as a grim warning.

Notes

1 For a more elaborate discussion on the notion of "carpetbaggers," see Chapter 4 and Ismael & Ismael (2010).
2 For a further discussion on the role of regional and international actors, see Chapter 3.
3 For an examination of the policies that led to the destruction of the Iraqi state, see Chapter 3.
4 162 journalists confirmed killed according to the Committee to Protect Journalists (2014).
5 Consider the comments of Barrington Godfrey, a contract management executive: "A thousand percent [markup] is common" for contracts in Iraq, with "500 percent routine. I have never seen a markup of less than 100 percent." However, in the US "the average markup under government contracts is 10 percent, and anything more than 12 percent will usually be rejected when the government conducts audits. If your profit margin on a government contract conducted outside Iraq is more than 10 percent, you may well be accused of committing fraud" (Rose, 2007).
6 Al-Asadi makes millions of dollars annually; however, it has been revealed by a Danish paper, *Ekstra Bladet* (2009), that his wife and three children still reside in Denmark (where al-Asadi retains citizenship), and are dependent upon welfare for their survival.

138 *Deconstruction and reconstruction of the state*

The paper reached out to Peter Miller, a director of the Ishoej Municipality, for a comment: "His [al-Asadi's] behavior [is] deeply immoral and a subversion of the Danish social security system."

7 MPs get diplomatic passports, a $50,000-per-month bodyguard allowance and a housing allowance. Their health benefits are also generous, with some MPs admitting having spent up to $50,000 in a single month on personal health services. In retirement, MPs enjoy a $10,000 monthly allowance for bodyguards, in addition to being able to qualify for additional monetary benefits based on their positions while MPs (Kitabat, 2014a).

8 Article 91 of Iraq's constitution stipulates that the Chief Justice must be approved by parliament; however, Mahmoud has never been subject to this process.

9 Among the qualifications one must possess to run for parliament in Iraq is that they "must be known for [their] good conduct" (Article 6, Election Law No. 16, 2005). This is reiterated in the later Election Commission Law No. 45 (2013), Article 8.

10 There is even a commonly held opinion on the Iraqi street that any employee (civilian or military) will be "fired or penalized if they don't vote for the Rule of Law Alliance" in any election (F. Karim, 2014).

11 For a more elaborate discussion on the evolution of Iraq's electoral system see Dawisha (2010).

12 The Justice and Accountability Commission was the successor to the De-Ba'thification Commission responsible for purging former Ba'thists from any role in the new government.

References

Abbas, M. (2013a, August 30). *Iraq's Missing Parliament*. Retrieved September 28, 2013, from Al-Monitor: www.al-monitor.com/pulse/originals/2013/08/iraq-parliament-role-king-makers.html

Abbas, M. (2013b, December 10). *Iraqi Authorities Fail to Protect Journalists*. Retrieved February 19, 2014, from Al-Monitor: www.al-monitor.com/pulse/originals/2013/12/journalists-iraq-targeted-government.html

Abbas, M. (2014, February 17). *Sadr's Sudden Retirement Shakes Up Iraqi Politics.* Retrieved February 19, 2014, from Al-Monitor: www.al-monitor.com/pulse/originals/2014/02/sadr-retires-iraq-politics-confusions-frustration.html

Ackerman, S. (2013, March 6). *Over $8B of the Money You Spent Rebuilding Iraq was Wasted Outright*. Retrieved January 8, 2014, from Wired: www.wired.com/dangerroom/2013/03/iraq-waste/

Agator, M. (2013, April). *Iraq: Overview of corruption and anti-corruption*. Retrieved April 18, 2014, from Transparency International: www.transparency.org/files/content/corruptionqas/374_Iraq_overview_of_corruption_and_anticorruption.pdf

Ahrar News. (2014, February 8). *Secret Bloc Led by Fadel Dabbas, Supported by Al-Maliki*. Retrieved June 4, 2014, from Ahrar News Agency: www.ahrarnewsagency.com/index.php?option=com_content&view=article&id=2086:2014-02-08-08-56-50&catid=28&Itemid=174#.U5XdxvldWjt

Al-Aalem. (2014). *120 Million Dollars to Form a List Allied With Al-Maliki*. Retrieved June 4, 2014, from Al-Aalem: www.alaalem.com/index.php?aa=news&id22=13914

al-A'li, M. H. (2014, January 30). "Contracts for Electoral Votes," They Wrote the Press. *Al-Baghdadia*.

Al-Ali, Z. (2014). *The Struggle for Iraq's Future: How corruption, incompetence, and sectarianism have undermined democracy*. New Haven: Yale University Press.

al-'Assaf, S. I., & Jawad, S. N. (2013). *Al-Mar'ah Al-'Irâqiyyah bayna Al-Ihtilâl Al-Amrîkî wa Mabda' Al-Tadakhkhul Al-Insânî*. Amman, Jordan: Dar Al-Jinân.

al-Baghdadi, S. (2014, April 16). [*Currency Counterfeiting by Leaders of the Da'wa*]. Retrieved April 16, 2014, from Kitabat: www.kitabat.com/ar/page/16/04/2014/26457/ الحقيقة-الغائبة-عن-خفايا-أو-تزوير-العملة-العراقية-من-قبل-قادة-حزب-الدعوة-الإسلامية.html

Al-Baghdadia. (2013, September 19). *Leaders of Political Blocs to Sign a Code of Honor and Social Peace and Affirm Commitment to its Terms*. Retrieved September 22, 2013, from Al-Baghdadia: www.albaghdadia.com/thenews/iraq-news/item/19355-jAD%D8%A9-AkKbk-AkYOnAYOn%D8%A9-nNjINl-IkO-LnVAj-AkyoEJ-NAkYOkL-AkAvbLAIn-NnTKDNl-AkAkbeAL-BBlNDm?tmpl=component&print=1&ml=1

Al-Baghdadia. (2014a, April 5). *Years of Failure*.

Al-Baghdadia. (2014b, April 17). [*Integrity Commission: Only 4 Governors and 153 MPs Comply with Financial Disclosure*]. Retrieved April 17, 2014, from Al-Baghdadia: www.albaghdadianews.com/politics/item/50773-AkleAm%D8%A9-4-LGAJznl-JjZ-N153-lASBA-KyoJNA-Il-dLLmL-AkLAkn%D8%A9.html

Allawi, A. A. (2007). *The Occupation of Iraq: Winning the war, losing the peace*. New Haven: Yale University Press.

Al-Mada. (2014a, April 24). [*Candidates from Maliki's Family with Generous Propaganda*]. Retrieved April 24, 2014, from *Al-Mada Newspaper*: www.almadapaper. net/ar/news/463554/٥-مرشح-من-نحين-أسرة-المالكي-يدورون-دعاية-سخ

Al-Mada. (2014b, June 14). [*Attention Please ... in Iraq, Six Million Employees Work Only 17 Minutes a Day!*] Retrieved June 15, 2014, from *Al-Mada Newspaper*: www. almadapaper.net/ar/news/466273/انتباه-رجاء--في-العراق-ستة-ملايين-موظف-م

al-Ruba'ie, N. (2014a, January 18). Hewar Iraqi. *Al-Baghdadia*.

al-Ruba'ie, N. (2014b, May 4). *Iraqi Dialogue—Ali Mohsen Al-Tamimi*. Retrieved May 5, 2014, from Al-Baghdadia: www.albaghdadia.com/hewar/item/29124-3-5-2014

al-Sayegh, H. (2013, March 17). *Political Conflict Keeps a Muzzle on Iraq's Economic Enthusiasm*. Retrieved January 8, 2014, from *The National*: www. thenational.ae/business/industry-insights/economics/political-conflict-keeps-a-muzzle-on-iraqs-economic-enthusiasm

al-Sayeh, A. H. (2014a, April 22). *Corruption in the Oil Ministry*. Retrieved April 22, 2014, from Al-Baghdadia: www.albaghdadia.com/fail-years/item/28781-21-4-2014

al-Sayeh, A. H. (2014b, April 23). *The Corruption of the Ministries of Education and Higher Education*. Retrieved April 23, 2014, from Al-Baghdadia: www.albaghdadia. com/fail-years/item/28817-22-4-2014

al-Sayeh, A. H. (2014c, April 24). Corruption in the Ministry of Defense. Retrieved April 24, 2014, from Al-Baghdadia: www.albaghdadia.com/fail-years/item/28845-23-4-2014

al-Shaher, O. (2013a, March 6). *Iraqi Politician Attacks Central Bank Corruption*. Retrieved January 8, 2014, from Al-Monitor: www.al-monitor.com/pulse/originals/2013/03/iraq-banks-bypassing-sanctions.html

al-Shaher, O. (2013b, August 21). *Money Laundering in Billions, Iraqi Official Estimates*. Retrieved January 8, 2014, from Al-Monitor: www.al-monitor.com/pulse/originals/2013/08/money-laundering-corruption-iraq.html

Al-Sharq Al-Awsat. (2014, March 25). [*Iraq—Lost to Corruption and Terror*]. Retrieved March 25, 2014, from Al-Sharq Al-Awsat: www.aawsat.com/details.asp?section=4&article=765953&issueno=12901

140 *Deconstruction and reconstruction of the state*

Ayesh, M. (2013, March 15). *US Companies and Kurds: The biggest gainers in Iraq.* Retrieved October 4, 2013, from Al Arabiya News: http://english.alarabiya.net/en/business/2013/03/15/U-S-companies-and-Kurds-the-biggest-gainers-in-Iraq.html

Beaumont, P. (2013, April 23). *Fake Bomb Detectors Were Being Used in Iraq as Recently as Last Month.* Retrieved January 8, 2014, from *The Guardian*: www.theguardian.com/world/2013/apr/23/fake-bomb-detectors-used-iraq?guni=Article:in%20body%20link

Bloomberg. (2009, May 26). *Iraq Trade Minister Quits Amid Corruption Allegations.* Retrieved September 30, 2013, from *Sydney Morning Herald*: www.smh.com.au/business/iraq-trade-minister-quits-amid-corruption-allegations-20090526-bkz9.html

Booth, R., & Jones, M. (2013, April 23). *UK Businessman Found Guilty of Selling Fake Bomb Detectors to Iraq.* Retrieved January 8, 2014, from *The Guardian*: www.theguardian.com/uk/2013/apr/23/somerset-business-guilty-fake-bombs

Carlstrom, G. (2011, December 18). *Political Crisis in Iraq as US Withdraws.* Retrieved March 17, 2014, from Al-Jazeera: www.aljazeera.com/news/middleeast/2011/12/2011121865543438111.html

Cha, A. E. (2004, May 23). *In Iraq, the Job Opportunity of a Lifetime.* Retrieved January 8, 2014, from *The Washington Post*: www.washingtonpost.com/wp-dyn/articles/A48543-2004May22.html

Coalition Provisional Authority. (2003, September 19). *Order Number 39.* Retrieved January 8, 2014, from The Coalition Provisional Authority: www.iraqcoalition.org/regulations/20031220_CPAORD_39_Foreign_Investment_.pdf

Coalition Provisional Authority. (2004a, January 27). *Order Number 55.* Retrieved January 16, 2014, from The Coalition Provisional Authority: www.iraqcoalition.org/regulations/20040204_CPAORD55.pdf

Coalition Provisional Authority. (2004b, June 27). *Order Number 17 (Revised).* Retrieved January 8, 2014, from The Coalition Provisional Authority: www.iraqcoalition.org/regulations/20040627_CPAORD_17_Status_of_Coalition__Rev__with_Annex_A.pdf

Cockburn, P. (2013a, March 4). *Iraq 10 Years on: How Baghdad became a city of corruption.* Retrieved January 8, 2014, from *The Independent*: www.independent.co.uk/news/world/middle-east/iraq-10-years-on-how-baghdad-became-a-city-of-corruption-8520038.html

Cockburn, P. (2013b, March 6). *The Shia are in Power in Iraq—but not in Control.* Retrieved January 8, 2014, from *The Independent*: www.independent.co.uk/news/world/middle-east/the-shia-are-in-power-in-iraq--but-not-in-control-8523280.html

Cockburn, P. (2014, May 5). *Foreign Jihadists in Syria Pledge Their Own 9/11.* Retrieved May 8, 2014, from CounterPunch: www.counterpunch.org/2014/05/05/foreign-jihadis-in-syria-pledge-their-own-911/

Coleman, I. (2013, March 6). *Corruption and Mismanagement in Iraq.* Retrieved January 8, 2014, from Council on Foreign Relations: http://blogs.cfr.org/coleman/2013/03/06/corruption-and-mismanagement-in-iraq/

Committee to Protect Journalists. (2014). *162 Journalists Killed in Iraq since 1992/Motive Confirmed.* Retrieved February 19, 2014, from Committee to Protect Journalists: www.cpj.org/killed/mideast/iraq/

Corn, D. (2007, August 30). *Secret Report: Corruption is "norm" within Iraqi government.* Retrieved January 8, 2014, from *The Nation*: www.thenation.com/blog/156346/secret-report-corruption-norm-within-iraqi-government

Dawisha, A. (2010). Iraq: A vote against sectarianism. *Journal of Democracy, 21*(3), 26–40.

Dodge, T. (2013). State and Society in Iraq Ten Years After Regime Change: The rise of a new authoritarianism. *International Affairs, 89*(2), 241–257.

Environmental News Service. (2007, November 1). *Iraqi Electricity Crisis: Baghdad suffers worst cuts.* Retrieved February 1, 2014, from Environmental News Service: www.ens-newswire.com/ens/nov2007/2007-11-01-01.asp

Filkins, D. (2014, April 28). *What We Left Behind.* Retrieved April 28, 2014, from *The New Yorker:* www.newyorker.com/reporting/2014/04/28/140428fa_fact_filkins?currentPage=all

Fisk, R. (2014, April 20). *The Middle East We Must Confront in the Future Will be a Mafiastan Ruled by Money.* Retrieved 24 April, 2014, from *The Independent:* www.independent.co.uk/voices/comment/the-middle-east-we-must-confront-in-future-will-be-a-mafiastan-ruled-by-money-9272265.html

Gordon, J. (2013, March 25). *America's Other Dark Legacy in Iraq.* Retrieved January 8, 2014, from Foreign Policy in Focus: http://fpif.org/americas_other_dark_legacy_in_iraq/

Gunter, F. R. (2013). *The Political Economy of Iraq: Restoring balance in a post-conflict society.* Northampton: Edward Elgar Publishing.

Hasan, H. (2014, January 28). *Iraqi "Ninth Studio" Avoids TV's Sectarian Divide.* Retrieved February 19, 2014, from Al-Monitor: www.al-monitor.com/pulse/originals/2014/01/search-non-sectarian-media-iraq.html

Human Rights Watch. (2014, May 4). *Iraq: Government Blocking Residents Fleeing Fighting.* Retrieved May 5, 2014, from Human Rights Watch: www.hrw.org/news/2014/05/03/iraq-government-blocking-residents-fleeing-fighting

Hussein, A. (2013, July 3). *Integrity Commission in Najaf Releases General Inspector of MoH on Bail.* Retrieved February 1, 2014, from Iraqi News: www.iraqinews.com/baghdad-politics/integrity-commission-in-najaf-releases-general-inspector-of-moh-on-bail/

Hussein, A. (2014, February 3). *Urgent ... 16 Articles of Retirement Law Approved.* Retrieved February 5, 2014, from Iraqi News: www.iraqinews.com/baghdad-politics/urgent-1-articles-of-retirement-law-approved/

Iraq Business News. (2011, September 13). *Ex-Iraq Official Slams Leaders Over Graft.* Retrieved January 8, 2014, from Iraq Business News: www.iraq-businessnews.com/2011/09/13/ex-iraq-official-slams-leaders-over-graft/

Iraq, Commission of Integrity. (n.d.). *Annual Report for 2009.* Retrieved January 8, 2014, from Integrity Commission: www.nazaha.iq/pdf_up/189/p03.pdf

Ismael, J. S., & Ismael, T. Y. (2010). The Sectarian State in Iraq and the New Political Class. *International Journal of Contemporary Iraqi Studies, 4*(3), 339–356.

Karim, A. (2009, May 25). *Iraq Trade Minister Resigns Amid Corruption Claims.* Retrieved September 30, 2013, from The Free Library: www.thefreelibrary.com/Iraq+trade+minister+resigns+amid+corruption+claims-a01611880368

Karim, F. (2014, April 27). *[Al-Maliki, His Team, and Society].* Retrieved April 27, 2014, from *Al-Mada Newspaper:* http://almadapaper.net/ar/news/463713/م-سيلةةداراإلاريوزتوداسفلا-مأوتةيروراتاكدلا

Karim, H. A. (2014, June 1). *Corruption in the Prime Minister's Office.* Retrieved June 2, 2014, from Voice of Iraq: www.sotaliraq.com/mobile-item.php?id=160606#axzz33SD9ATZs

Karim, J. (2014, February 5). *Government Reveals Retirement Law that Adds Benefits for Parliamentarians.* Retrieved February 5, 2014, from Azzaman: http://www.azzaman.com/?p=60781

Khadduri, W. (2013, September 24). *Electricity Shortage Costs Iraq Economy $40 Billion a Year.* Retrieved January 8, 2014, from Al-Monitor: www.al-monitor.com/pulse/business/2013/09/iraq-oil-energy-crisis.html#

142 Deconstruction and reconstruction of the state

Kitabat. (2013, December 25). [*Sistani to Guarantee Maliki Third Term for Shahristani Scandal Coverup*]. Retrieved February 1, 2014, from Kitabat: www.kitabat.com/ar/ page/25/12/2013/20996/صهر-الساستيني-لتطويق-فضيحة-الاخوان-الشهرستاني-وولاية-ثالثة-للمالكي-شرط.html

Kitabat. (2014a, February 4). [*Iraqi MPs Deceive the People and Spend to Give Themselves a Huge Retirement*]. Retrieved February 5, 2014, from Kitabat: www.kitabat.com/ar/ page/04/02/2014/22691/نواب-العراقي-يخدعون-الشعب-وقضائه-ويمنحون-أنفسهم-تقاعدا-ضخما.html

Kitabat (2014b, February 13). [*Al-Asadi Discovered to Grant Himself Rank of General: Revoked for unknown reasons*]. Retrieved February 13, 2014, from Kitabat: www. kitabat.com/ar/page/13/02/2014/23076/الكشف-عن-منح-عدنان-الاسدي-رتبة-لواء-نفسه-ثم-سحبها-السباب-مجهولة.html

Kitabat. (2014c, February 18). [*An Unjust Handful Govern Iraq in the Name of Shi'ism*]. Retrieved February 19, 2014, from Kitabat: www.kitabat.com/ar/ page/18/02/2014/23304/الصدر-ثلث-الظلمة-تحكم-العراق-بأسم-الشيعة-والتشيع.html

Kitabat. (2014d, March 5). [*More than 130 Radio Stations Fill Political, Religious Space in Iraq*]. Retrieved March 6, 2014, from Kitabat: www.kitabat.com/ar/ page/05/03/2014/24058/130-اذاعة-تملآ-الفضاء-العراقي-بالسياسي-والديني-والترفيهي.html

Kitabat. (2014e, March 7). [*The Spoiled Son of the Minister*]. Retrieved March 7, 2014, from Kitabat: www.kitabat.com/ar/page/07/03/2014/24164/الابن-المدلل-للوزير--ضرورة-السياقة-حفظ-اظهر-للكرامة.html

Kitabat. (2014f, March 8). [*Naked Women Don't Wear Clothes: Resign*]. Retrieved March 8, 2014, from Kitabat: http://kitabat.com/ar/page/08/03/2014/24218/هادي-العامري-العاري-لايلبس-ثيابا-أستقل--الصقك-الكاملة.html

Kitabat. (2014g, March 17). [*Issawi: Political motives behind the exclusionary elections*]. Retrieved March 17, 2014, from Kitabat: http://kitabat.com/ar/page/17/03/2014/24754/ العيساوي-دوافع-سياسية-وراء-استبعادي-من-الانتخابات.html

Kitabat. (2014h, March 17). [*Saadi: The elimination allows only supporters of Maliki to stand for election*]. Retrieved March 18, 2014, from Kitabat: http://kitabat.com/ar/ page/17/03/2014/24752/الساعدي--القضاء-يعدل-عن-عدم-داعم-المالكي-وحده-مه-التزحرح-للانتخابات.html

Kitabat. (2014i, March 19). [*Iraqi Parliament to Prevent Exclusion of Candidates for Election*]. Retrieved March 20, 2014, from Kitabat: www.kitabat.com/ar/ page/19/03/2014/24856/البرلمان-العراقي-يمنع-استبعاد-مرشحين-عن-الانتخابات. html

Kitabat. (2014j, March 19). [*Uqaili Sentenced to Year in Prison for Plot to Create Exclusionary Election*]. Retrieved March 20, 2014, from Kitabat: www.kitabat.com/ ar/page/19/03/2014/24855/العكيلي-عن-حكم-حبسه-عاما--انه-مؤامرة-لاستبعادي-عن-المشهد-السياسي.html

Kitabat. (2014k, March 25). [*Election Commission Councilors Submit Mass Resignation*]. Retrieved March 25, 2014, from Kitabat: www.kitabat.com/ar/page/25/03/2014/25174/ اعضاء-مجلس-مفوضية-الانتخابات-يقدمون-استقالة-جماعية-دفعة-للجرح.html

Kitabat. (2014l, March 31). [*Iraq Funds Smuggled Abroad Surpass One Trillion Dollars*]. Retrieved April 7, 2014, from Kitabat: www.kitabat.com/ar/page/31/03/2014/25455/ الأموال-العراقية-المهربة-للخارج-ترليون-و14-مليون-دولار.html

Kitabat. (2014m, April 17). [*Jabri and Aides Accuse al-Dulami, the Minister of Culture, of Corruption*]. Retrieved April 17, 2014, from Kitabat: www.kitabat.com/ar/ page/17/04/2014/26555/الجابري-يتهم-الدليمي-ومساعديه-بوزارة-الثقافة-بالفساد.html

Kitabat. (2014n, April 22). [*Supreme Judiciary Asked to Lift Zamili's Immunity*]. Retrieved April 22, 2014, from Kitabat: www.kitabat.com/ar/page/22/04/2014/26858/و-ثقي-تنف رد-اهب--كاتابات--القضاء-الأعلى-يطلب-رفع-الحصانة-عن-النائب-الزامي-ل تق-مهمتب-ةمكاحمل.html

Kitabat. (2014o, May 14). [*Iraq Officials Have Taken $4.3 Billion Before the Formation of the New Government*]. Retrieved May 14, 2014, from Kitabat: www.kitabat.com/ar/page/14/05/2014/28070/مسؤولون-عراقيون-هربوا-43-م-رايلم-رالود-لبق-تشكيل-ةموكحلا-ةديدجلا.html

Kitabat. (2014p, May 15). [*Integrity Commission: The Growth of Karbouli's Illegally Gained Funds Outside of Iraq is Behind His Arrest Warrant*]. Retrieved May 15, 2014, from Kitabat: http://kitabat.com/ar/page/15/05/2014/28126/.html

Kitabat. (2014q, May 26). [*Corrupt Construction Contracts for 49 Schools in Najaf*]. Retrieved May 27, 2014, from Kitabat: www.kitabat.com/ar/page/26/05/2014/28595/فجنلاب-ةسردم-49-ءانب-يف-داسف-قيقحت-ةوعد.html

Klein, N. (2007). *The Shock Doctrine: The rise of disaster capitalism.* Toronto: Random House.

Knack, S., & Keefer, P. (1995). Institutions and Economic Performance: Cross-country tests using institutional measures. *Economics and Politics, 7*(3), 207–227.

Lake, E. (2010, February 17). *US General: 2 Iraqi election chiefs linked to Iran.* Retrieved September 17, 2013, from *Washington Times*: www.washingtontimes.com/news/2010/feb/17/us-general-2-iraqi-election-chiefs-linked-to-iran/?page=all

Looney, R. E. (2008). Reconstruction and Peacebuilding Under Extreme Adversity: The problem of pervasive corruption in Iraq. *International Peacekeeping, 15*(3), 424–440.

Mahmood, M., O'Kane, M., Madlena, C., & Smith, T. (2013, March 6). *Revealed: Pentagon's link to Iraqi torture centres.* Retrieved January 8, 2014, from *The Guardian*: www.theguardian.com/world/2013/mar/06/pentagon-iraqi-torture-centres-link

Mamouri, A. (2014a, February 7). *Human Rights Watch Condemns Situation in Iraq.* Retrieved June 4, 2014, from Al-Monitor: www.al-monitor.com/pulse/originals/2014/02/iraq-human-rights-situation-bad-hrw.html

Mamouri, A. (2014b, February 13). *Iraqi Media Also Characterized by Political, Sectarian Bias.* Retrieved February 19, 2014, from Al-Monitor: www.al-monitor.com/pulse/originals/2014/02/iraq-media-truth-authority-propaganda.html

Mamouri, A. (2014c, May 23). *Iraqi Higher Education Continues Decline.* Retrieved May 23, 2014, from Al-Monitor: www.al-monitor.com/pulse/originals/2014/05/iraq-higher-education-quantity-growth-qualitative-decline.html

Ministry of Higher Education. (n.d.). *Curriculum Vitae of His Excellency Minister of Higher Education and Scientific Research, Mr. Ali Al-Adeeb.* Retrieved April 26, 2014, from the Ministry of Higher Education and Scientific Research: www.en.mohesr.gov.iq/PageViewer.aspx?id=13

Moore, S., & Miller, T. C. (2005, November 6). *Before Rearming Iraq, He Sold Shoes and Flowers.* Retrieved January 8, 2014, from *Los Angeles Times*: http://articles.latimes.com/2005/nov/06/world/fg-cattan6

Morris, L. (2014, April 27). *Iraq Gears Up for Bitter, Bloody Election Battle.* Retrieved May 3, 2014, from *The Washington Post*: www.washingtonpost.com/world/iraq-gears-up-for-bitter-bloody-election-battle/2014/04/28/61824c7b-9e34-4ee4-bf41-099fefb322fa_story.html

Negus, S. (2006, November 16). *Corruption is "Fuelling Iraqi Conflicts."* Retrieved January 8, 2014, from *Financial Times*: www.ft.com/cms/s/0/dac4bb6a-75ab-11db-aea1-0000779e2340.html#axzz2eX4nsB5v

144 Deconstruction and reconstruction of the state

Pallister, D. (2007, February 8). *How the US Sent $12bn Cash to Iraq. And watched it vanish*. Retrieved January 8, 2014, from *The Guardian*: www.theguardian.com/world/2007/feb/08/usa.iraq1

Parker, N. (2012, March/April). *The Iraq We Left Behind*. Retrieved January 8, 2014, from Foreign Affairs: www.foreignaffairs.com/articles/137103/ned-parker/the-iraq-we-left-behind

Pasha, M. (2014, April 29). *ISIS Insurgents Have Almost Surrounded Baghdad*. Retrieved May 3, 2014, from Vice: www.vice.com/read/ISIS-Iraq-jihadists-Anbar-Fallujah-Bagdhad

Phillip, M. (2008). Peacebuilding and Corruption. *International Peacekeeping, 15*(3), 310–327.

Pincus, W. (2007, June 25). *Shhh... There is Corruption in Iraq*. Retrieved August 1, 2010, from *The Washington Post*: www.washingtonpost.com/wp-dyn/content/article/2007/06/24/AR2007062401301.html

Pravda. (2006, September 26). *Arrest Warrants Issued for 88 Former Iraqi Officials on Corruption Charges*. Retrieved February 1, 2014, from Pravda.ru: http://english.pravda.ru/news/world/26-09-2006/84684-corruption-0/

Qadhiyat Ra'i A'mm. (2014, January 21). *Al-Baghdadia*.

Reilly, C. (2009, May 17). *Iraq's Once-Envied Health Care System Lost to War, Corruption*. Retrieved February 1, 2014, from McClatchy DC: www.mcclatchydc.com/2009/05/17/68193/iraqs-once-envied-health-care.html

Reuter, C. (2013, March 20). *Iraq's Model City: Kirkuk thrives in a sea of corruption and chaos*. Retrieved January 8, 2014, from Spiegel Online: www.spiegel.de/international/world/kirkuk-thrives-despite-corruption-and-sectarian-violence-in-iraq-a-889611.html

Reuters. (2011, February 17). *Iraq Police Official Charged in Bomb Device Scandal*. Retrieved January 8, 2014, from International Business Times: www.ibtimes.com/iraq-police-official-charged-bomb-device-scandal-268213

RFE/RL. (2010, January 28). *What Do We Know About the Election Crisis in Iraq?* Retrieved September 22, 2013, from Radio Free Europe/Radio Liberty (RFE/RL): www.rferl.org/content/What_Do_We_Know_About_The_Election_Crisis_In_Iraq_/1942557.html

Rose, D. (2007, November). *The People vs. the Profiteers*. Retrieved May 1, 2014, from *Vanity Fair*: www.vanityfair.com/politics/features/2007/11/halliburton200711

Rubin, A. J. (2007, September 7). *Blaiming Politics, Iraqi Antigraft Official Vows to Quit*. Retrieved January 8, 2014, from *The New York Times*: www.nytimes.com/2007/09/07/world/middleeast/07iraq.html?_r=1&

Sabah, M. (2014, March 18). *[Regarding the Write-off of Candidates]*. Retrieved March 18, 2014, from *Al-Mada Newspaper*: http://almadapaper.net/ar/news/461250/ معلومات-عن-شطب-١٣-مرشح-جديد-بينهم-وزير

Sadah, A. A. (2013a, February 18). *Iraqi Judicial Reforms Include Removal of Chief Justice*. Retrieved March 17, 2014, from Al-Monitor: www.al-monitor.com/pulse/originals/2013/02/judiciary-changes-iraq.html

Sadah, A. A. (2013b, March 5). *Sadr Attacks Iraq's Integrity Committee*. Retrieved February 1, 2014, from Al-Monitor: www.al-monitor.com/pulse/originals/2013/03/iraq-sadr-maliki-integrity.html

Shafaaq. (2014, February 16). *18 Members of the Sadr Bloc Announce Their Resignation, Following Head*. Retrieved February 19, 2014, from Shafaaq: www.shafaaq.com/sh2/index.php/news/iraq-news/72624--18-.html

The hallmark of the new state   145

Shaoul, J. (2014, May 5). *Iraq Election Sets Stage for Protracted Civil Strife*. Retrieved May 5, 2014, from World Socialist Web Site: www.wsws.org/en/articles/2014/05/05/iraq-m05.html

SIGIR. (2008). *Hard Lessons: The Iraq reconstruction experience*. Retrieved January 8, 2014, from Special Inspector General for Iraq Reconstruction (SIGIR): http://usiraq.procon.org/sourcefiles/hard_lessons12-08.pdf

SIGIR. (2012a, January 30). *January 2012 Quarterly Report to Congress—Section 4: Developments in Iraq*. Retrieved January 8, 2014, from Special Inspector General for Iraq Reconstruction (SIGIR): http://psm.du.edu/media/documents/us_research_and_oversight/sigir/quarterly_reports_eng/us_sigir__report_to_congress_january_2012.pdf

SIGIR. (2012b, October 30). *Quarterly Report to the United States Congress*. Retrieved January 8, 2014, from Special Inspector General for Iraq Reconstruction (SIGIR): http://psm.du.edu/media/documents/us_research_and_oversight/sigir/quarterly_reports_eng/us_sigir_report_to_congress_oct_2012

Smith, R. J. (2013, March 19). *Waste, Fraud and Abuse Commonplace in Iraq Reconstruction Effort*. Retrieved January 8, 2014, from NBC News: http://investigations.nbcnews.com/_news/2013/03/19/17362769-waste-fraud-and-abuse-commonplace-in-iraq-reconstruction-effort?lite

Studio 9. (2013, September 19). *Corruption has Become Protected by Law*. Retrieved September 21, 2013, from Al-Baghdadia: www.albaghdadia.com/programs/politics-prog/studio9/item/19394-YObNDnN-AkbAYOI%D8%A9-BbAEng-19/9/2013

Studio 9. (2014a, January 19). *Al-Baghdadia*.

Studio 9. (2014b, January 30). *Al-Baghdadia*.

Studio 9. (2014c, January 13, 15, 17, 20, 21). *Al-Baghdadia*.

Studio 9. (2014d, February 4). *Al-Baghdadia*.

Studio 9. (2014e, February 11, 12, 14). *Al-Baghdadia*.

Transparency International. (2012). *Corruption Perceptions Index 2012*. Retrieved January 8, 2014, from Transparency International: www.transparency.org/cpi2012/results

Transparency International. (n.d.). *FAQs on Corruption*. Retrieved September 28, 2013, from Transparency International: www.transparency.org/whoweare/organisation/faqs_on_corruption

UN Office on Drugs and Crime. (2013, January). *Corruption and Integrity Challenges in the Public Sector in Iraq*. Retrieved January 8, 2014, from UN Office on Drugs and Crime: www.unodc.org/documents/publications/2013_Report_on_Corruption_and_Integrity_Iraq.pdf

'Uqailî, R. H. (2014, April 6). [*Intimidate and Subdue the Judges*]. Retrieved April 12, 2014, from Kitabat: www.kitabat.com/ar/page/06/04/2014/25761/ورةيع-القلاةاخ-واضعامه.html

Wicken, S. (2012, September 11). *The Hashimi Verdict and the Health of Democracy in Iraq*. Retrieved March 17, 2014, from Institute for the Study of War: www.understandingwar.org/sites/default/files/ISWPoliticalUpdate_Hashemi-Verdict-Democracy-Iraq.pdf

Part II
People in the quagmire

6 Children of the occupation
A decade after the invasion

Consideration of the impact of conflict on children has been on the global agenda at least since 1993 when the 48th session of the UN General Assembly adopted Resolution 48/157, entitled "Protection of children affected by armed conflicts," in which it requested the Secretary-General to appoint an expert to undertake a comprehensive study with the support of the Centre for Human Rights and UNICEF. The expert's report was submitted to the UN General Assembly on August 26, 1996 (UN, 1996). A decade after the report, UNICEF initiated a strategic review, published in 2009, which noted that although "there is increased global awareness about deliberate violations against children in armed conflict [...] appalling consequences that stem from the complex interplay of conflict, poverty and discrimination are often overlooked" (UNICEF, 2009, p. iv). These reports provide a backdrop to the examination of UN and international civil society discourse on the plight of Iraqi children from 1990 to 2013. In this period, Iraqi children were caught in a cycle of impoverishment and conflict spearheaded by the US and channeled through the UN Security Council to provide international legitimacy to its actions in Iraq. Our purpose is first to use this discourse to describe the circumstances of life and death for Iraqi children under occupation and, second, to critically reflect on the description that emerges from the approach.

Approach to topic

The topic "Children of the occupation" is inherently problematic for it begs the question of when the occupation began. The commonplace perspective is that the occupation of Iraq followed upon the invasion of Iraq in 2003. However, many argue that the occupation actually began with the imposition of draconian sanctions in 1990 (Democracy Now, 2010). As Marcus Aurelius, Roman emperor (161–180 CE) and philosopher, observed, "Everything we hear is opinion, not a fact. Everything we see is a perspective, not the truth." In order to cast the subject of "Children of the occupation" in an inclusive framework to capture alternative perspectives, this chapter will approach the topic as a timeline with three stages anchored around the 2003 Anglo-American invasion of Iraq: sanctions, invasion and post-invasion military occupation.

150 *People in the quagmire*

The three stages of the timeline provide the framework for an examination of selected UN and international civil society reports on the plight of Iraq's children. The reports were selected to represent the prevalent discourse, as time and space did not allow a more detailed examination. The UN and civil society discourse on Iraq's children is extensive, as indicated in Table 6.1, some of which this survey will draw upon.

Table 6.1 UN and civil society discourse on the children of Iraq

Report citation (author/title)	Issuing agency	Year
International Study Team on the Gulf Crisis www.cesr.org/downloads/Health%20and%20 Welfare%20in%20Iraq%20after%20the%20 Gulf%20Crisis%201991.pdf	UNICEF	1991
Situation Analysis of Children and Women in Iraq http://citeseerx.ist.psu.edu/viewdoc/download;jsess ionid=7CF85122251211F840520947FB947D12?d oi=10.1.1.194.4798&rep=rep1&type=pdf	UNICEF	1998
Multiple Indicator Cluster Survey for the Year 2000: Baghdad, Iraq www.childinfo.org/files/iraq1.pdf	UNICEF	2001
The Situation of Children in Iraq http://www.casi.org.uk/info/unicef0202.pdf	UNICEF	2002
Iraq Watching Briefs: Overview Report www.unicef.org/evaldatabase/files/Iraq_2003_ Watching_Briefs.pdf	UNICEF	2003
The Human Costs of War in Iraq www.cesr.org/downloads/Human%20Costs%20 of%20War%20in%20Iraq.pdf	Center for Economic and Social Rights	2003
Country Cooperation Strategy for WHO and Iraq 2005–2010 www.who.int/countryfocus/cooperation_strategy/ ccs_irq_en.pdf	World Health Organization	2006
Gilbert Burnham, Shannon Doocy, Elizabeth Dzeng, Riyadh Lafta and Les Roberts, *The Human Cost of the War in Iraq: A Mortality Study 2002–2006* http://web.mit.edu/cis/pdf/Human_Cost_of_War. pdf	Bloomberg School of Public Health, Johns Hopkins University, School of Medicine, Al Mustansiriya University in cooperation with the Center for International Studies, MIT	2006
Iraq's Children: A Year in their Life www.unicef.org/infobycountry/files/Iraqs_ Children_2007.pdf	UNICEF	2007
State of the World's Children www.unicef.org/sowc/	UNICEF	1980– 2013

Sanctions context (1990–2003)

The sanctions context covers the period from the Security Council's imposition of sanctions in 1990 to the US's declaration of war against Iraq in 2003. A snapshot of the rapid deterioration in the quality of life in Iraq and direct impact of this rapid transition on children is reflected in Table 6.2.

As Table 6.2 indicates, child, infant and maternal mortality rates more than doubled within four years. Throughout the 1970s and 1980s, Iraq enjoyed some of the highest health and educational indicators in the Middle East and was among the most industrialized nations in the region. Iraqi children enjoyed healthy home lives and excellent education, and were well nourished. Despite more than 250,000 Iraqi deaths and significant damage to Iraq's civilian infrastructure during the Iran–Iraq War, Iraq's health, education and other social programs continued to advance throughout the 1980s. Just prior to the 1990–1991 Gulf War, the UN described Iraq as a high-middle-income country, with a modern social infrastructure. In 1989, Iraq's GDP stood at 75.5 billion US dollars for a population of 18.3 million. GDP growth from 1974 to 1980 averaged 10.4 percent, and by 1988, during the last year of the Iran–Iraq War, Iraq's GDP per capita totaled 3,510 US dollars (UN, 1999). Although Iraq's oil production declined precipitously throughout the 1980s as a result of their ongoing war against Iran, two years after the war's end, in July 1990, Iraq achieved oil production of just less than 3.5 million barrels per day, almost matching their peak output in the year preceding the war (Crude Oil Production, Iraq, n.d.).

In 1990, the Iraqi government accused Kuwait of pumping oil from Iraq's side of the border as well as increasing oil exports, which drove down the cost of petroleum and devastated the Iraqi economy. As diplomatic negotiations between the two countries failed to end the standoff, Iraq invaded and annexed Kuwait, effectively making it the nineteenth province of Iraq. This led to a US-led coalition and war against Iraq, resulting in the expulsion of Iraqi forces from Kuwait and the heavy bombing of Iraq. Following the end of the war, on April 3, 1991, UNSC Resolution 687 was applied, later known as the economic sanctions regime. Numerous rounds of sanctions were imposed over the next two years, but Security Council Resolution 687 was the most devastating. While the primary objectives of Resolution 687 were to charge Iraq with the dismantling of its WMDs and the

Table 6.2 Infant and child mortality: impact of the sanctions regime

Child population (millions, 0–15), 1990/1996	8.3	9.23
Under-5 mortality rate (per 100,000 live births), 1990/1994	52	140
Infant mortality rate (per 1,000 live births), 1990/1994	31.7	111.7
Maternal mortality rate (per 100,000 live births), 1990/1994	117	310

Source: UNICEF, 1998, p. iii.

152 *People in the quagmire*

facilities used to manufacture them, a comprehensive economic embargo was also imposed, which froze all of Iraq's financial assets and banned both imports and exports. The resolution itself gave no clear conditions to have the sanctions lifted, and successive US administrations, supported by Congress, were able to use this omission to maintain the sanctions regime, regardless of Iraqi compliance with the stipulations of the resolution (Global Policy Forum, n.d.). In fact, while import restrictions were reduced once the Anglo-American coalition gained administrative oversight of Iraq in 2003, the sanctions were only lifted in their entirety in December 2010 (BBC, 2010).[1]

During the Cold War era, economic sanctions had a lesser effect on countries than in the years following. When one side imposed economic sanctions, the other side undermined them (e.g. the US embargo on Cuba was mitigated by the Soviet Union). With the collapse of the Soviet Union, however, sanctions became an increasingly effective tool with regards to achieving political objectives. Iraq's economy, being heavily dependent on oil exports and the import of consumer goods, was particularly vulnerable to the effects of economic sanctions. The major destruction caused to Iraq's infrastructure during the First Gulf War (January 17– March 3, 1991) was highlighted in a UNSC report on humanitarian needs written by the former President of Finland, Martti Ahtisaari, following the war:

> The recent conflict has wrought near-apocalyptic results upon the infrastructure of what had been, until January 1991, a rather highly urbanized and mechanized society. Now, most means of modern life support have been destroyed or rendered tenuous. Iraq has, for some time to come, been relegated to a pre-industrial age, but with all the disabilities of post-industrial dependency on an intensive use of energy and technology [...] With the destruction of power plants, oil refineries, main oil storage facilities and water related chemical plants, all electrically operated installations have ceased to function. Diesel-operated generators were reduced to operating on a minimum basis, their functioning affected by lack of fuel, lack of maintenance, lack of spare parts and nonattendance of workers.
>
> (UNSC, 1991)

Subsequent declassified documents reveal that US-led forces deliberately destroyed Iraq's water treatment capacity, knew that the necessary chemicals were blocked by sanctions, and fully understood the implications for Iraqis (Arbuthnot, 2000; Barrett, 2002; Nagy, 2001, pp. 22–25). The Pentagon's Defense Intelligence Agency (DIA) identified Iraq's water treatment systems as vulnerable because of their reliance on foreign materials already blocked by sanctions. According to a DIA report (1991):

> With no domestic sources of both water treatment replacement parts and some essential chemicals, Iraq will continue attempts to circumvent United Nations Sanctions to import these vital commodities. Failing to secure supplies will result in a shortage of pure drinking water for much of the population. This

could lead to increased incidences, if not epidemics, of disease and to certain pure-water-dependent industries becoming incapacitated, including petro chemicals, fertilizers, petroleum refining, electronics, pharmaceuticals, food processing, textiles, concrete construction, and thermal powerplants.

While US policymakers and academics alike claimed that the civilian devastation caused by the Gulf War and the sanctions regime were unintended consequences (UN Oil-for-Food Programme, n.d.), evidence points to the contrary. Severe damage to Iraq's civilian infrastructure was a deliberate strategy of war. Many of these infrastructure facilities were categorized as "dual-use targets" and deliberately targeted. In an article written in the US Air Force Journal, *Air and Space Power Journal*, Colonel Kenneth Rizer (2001) explained the legal and strategic justifications for such attacks using precision munitions:

A key example of such dual-use targeting was the destruction of Iraqi electrical power facilities in Desert Storm. While crippling Iraq's military command and control capability, destruction of these facilities shut down water purification and sewage treatment plants. As a result, epidemics of gastroenteritis, cholera, and typhoid broke out, leading to perhaps as many as 100,000 civilian deaths and a doubling of the infant mortality rates [...] the US Air Force has a vested interest in attacking dual-use targets so long as dual-use target destruction serves the double role of destroying legitimate military capabilities and indirectly targeting civilian morale. So long as this remains within the letter if not the spirit of the law [...] the Air Force will cling to the status quo.

US intelligence documents, observing that the degradation of Iraq's water supply under the bombing continued, noted the particular impact this had on children (Nagy, 2001, p. 24). Within months of the war, the UN Secretary General's envoy reported that Iraq was facing a water and sanitation crisis, predicting an "imminent catastrophe, which could include epidemics and famine, if massive life-supporting needs are not rapidly met"; US intelligence agreed (Tyler, 1991). In October 1991, the International Study Team sent a task force of 87 researchers and professionals specialized in a wide variety of disciplines—including medicine, health care and child psychology—to conduct a comprehensive study concerning the impact the 1991 Gulf War had on Iraqi civilians, particularly children. The study covered all of the Iraqi governorates without interference or supervision from the Iraqi government. The study was based on 9,000 household interviews in more than 300 locations. The study pointed to: an increase in infectious diseases correlated with contaminated water supplies; malnutrition caused by a collapse in crop production and the inability to import sufficient food; a sharp increase in infant and child mortality immediately following the war; and severe impacts on the social and psychological well-being of women and children (International Study Team, 1991, pp. 18 (137), 4 (74), 2 (37), 1 (120), 3 (165)). With the sanctions in place, the crisis of the health care system, which the war created, was further exacerbated.

154 *People in the quagmire*

The study reported an immediate and startling increase in child mortality rates associated with the destruction of the physical infrastructure and the collapsing of the health care system, the capacity of which the protracted sanctions regime greatly diminished. The study estimated that the mortality rate for children under 5 years old increased 380 percent after the onset of the war: for children 1 year old and under, the increase in mortality rate was 350 percent (International Study Team, 1991, pp. 1 (2), 2 (3)). The study estimated that there could be as many as 170,000 excess deaths among children under 5 years old in 1991 (International Study Team, 1991, p. 6 (125)). The International Study Team, using the practices established by the US National Center for Health Statistics, investigated the level of malnutrition, designating children as "malnourished" where they fall 2 standard deviations (–2 SD) from the median reference value (International Study Team, 1991, p. 3 (4)). The Study Group observed the percentage of children below –2 SD: 24.7 percent for stunting, 14.2 percent for underweight and 3.6 percent for wasting, as determined by weight-for-height comparisons (International Study Team, 1991, pp. 15–16 (28–29)).[2]

The mental health of the children was no better than their physical well-being. In-depth interviews with children of primary school age from the Amariyah shelter and from Basrah revealed high levels of anxiety and stress, as well as pathological behavior, which the psychologists had not seen in their ten years of field work in war-ravaged countries (International Study Team, 1991, p. 3 (165)). Nearly two-thirds of the children interviewed believed that they would not survive to become adults. Eighty percent reported experiencing daily fear of losing their families through death or separation. Nearly 80 percent also reported having been subjected to shelling at close range (International Study Team, 1991, pp. 9–10 (171–172)). The intrusive thoughts of war had emotionally traumatized children, according to the study. All efforts on the part of the child to block the thoughts were futile: "I try every day, but it is impossible not to think about it" was cited as a common refrain amongst the children interviewed (International Study Team, 1991, p. 5 (167)). It was found that 50 percent of the children continued to dream about the war, 66 percent found it difficult to sleep because of the event, 63 percent found it difficult to concentrate and 75 percent felt sad and needed the company of older people (International Study Team, 1991, pp. 6–8 (168–170)).

Though the US and Britain made no efforts to investigate, Iraqi doctors suspected a fourfold increase in cancer in children. By the late 1990s, Western evidence was offering support for the suspicions of those Iraqi doctors. The likely culprit was depleted uranium (DU), a by-product of the enrichment of natural uranium. It contains significantly less of the fissile U^{235} (hence depleted), yet retains 60 percent of the radioactivity of uranium. A 1991 internal document, given by Britain's Atomic Energy Authority to the military, stated that if "8 per cent of the DU fired in the Gulf War was inhaled, it could cause '500,000 potential deaths'" (Pilger, 2002, p. 95). It added that it would be unwise for people to stay close to large quantities of DU and that this would obviously be a concern for the local population. As British Middle East correspondent Robert Fisk noted more than seven years later, no one bothered to even suggest a cleanup. This was the first time that DU-tipped munitions had

Children of the occupation   155

ever been used in warfare. The consequences of ingesting DU dust are considered comparably worse than the serious health hazards associated with lead, another toxic heavy metal. Conservative estimates put the amount of DU debris scattered across the 1991 Gulf War battlefields at 300 tons (Fisk, 1998a, 1998b; Kelly, 2003, p. 122). In early 2003, the *San Francisco Chronicle* reported from Baghdad that the increased incidence of malignant tumors was killing children, a fact which Iraqi doctors attributed to the presence of DU in the soil. The Pentagon was swift to deny any relation between DU and the incidences of cancer, citing a lack of any definitive scientific evidence. From 1990 to 2003, incidences of cancer increased by five-fold among Iraqi children, congenital birth defects and leukemia tripled, and overall cancer rates among all Iraqis rose by 38 percent, according to the Iraqi government (Collier, 2003). American official statements about the military purpose of DU may explain the reasons behind the denial of the DU and cancer correlation. For example, Defense Department spokeswoman Barbara Goodno argued that DU is

> an important component in the U.S. arsenal. Despite being engaged multiple times [during the Gulf War] often at close range, by Iraqi tanks and anti-armor weapons, not a single U.S. tank protected by DU armor was penetrated or knocked out by hostile fire.
>
> (Collier, 2003)

The consensus among military experts is that the defensive and offensive advantages afforded by the density of DU are too great to leave unutilized (Hambling, 2000).

However, Doug Rokke, PhD, a retired physics professor from Jacksonville State University in Alabama and former director of the US Army's Depleted Uranium Project, affirmed that all Americans who came in contact with DU dust during the 1991 War were contaminated, and most of them suffered serious health problems in the following years, including death. He identified the health woes among residents of southern Iraq and his own colleagues as "the direct result" of DU exposure (Arnove, 2003). Nevertheless, the US was quick to dismiss these reports as "anecdotal," as they argued evidence is lacking to make definitive conclusions directly linking DU to devastating health outcomes. Steve Leeper, co-director of the Global Association for Banning DU Weapons, however, suggests:

> The reason there is no proof of causality between DU and any particular disease is that no one has seriously looked for it, the biggest problem with radiation, especially involving a low level radiation source that is also a toxic chemical, is that it can get you in so many ways. Which disorder you contract depends on where the DU ends in your system and what sort of damage it does to what sort of cells. To really find an effect, the government would have to study all the veterans, especially the 205,000 that have applied for medical help from the Veterans Administration, and the people of southern Iraq and test for uranium in their urine, organs and bones, then look for correlations with various pathologies.
>
> (Arnove, 2003)

156   *People in the quagmire*

However, the US government is resistant to test its own soldiery, let alone the dying children of Iraq.

Douglas Westerman reported in April 2006 that Dr. Asaf Durakovic, a former US Army Colonel, who founded the Uranium Medical Research Center (UMRC), was asked by the US Veterans' Administration to lie about the risks of incorporating DU in the human body. However, Dr. Durakovic resisted, saying:

> Yes, uranium does cause cancer, uranium does cause mutation, and uranium does kill. If we continue with the irresponsible contamination of the biosphere, the denial of the fact that human life is endangered by the deadly uranium isotope, then we are doing disservice to ourselves, disservice to the truth, disservice to God and to all the generations who follow.
>
> (Westerman, 2006)

In his report, Westerman noted that DU has a half-life of 4.7 billion years, which means that thousands upon thousands of Iraqi children will suffer for tens of thousands of years to come (Westerman, 2006). He quoted the head oncologist at Saddam Teaching Center, who was educated in Britain, Dr. Jawad al-Ali, who stated in a conference in Japan that:

> Two strange phenomena have come about in Basra which I have never seen before. The first is double and triple cancers in one patient, for example, leukemia and cancer of the stomach. We had one patient with two cancers—one in his stomach and another in the kidney. Months later, primary cancer was developing in his other kidney—he had three different cancer types. The second is the clustering of cancer in families. We have 58 families in personal circles with more than one person affected by cancer. Dr Yasin, a general Surgeon, has two uncles, a sister and cousin affected with cancer. Dr Mazen, another specialist, has six family members suffering from cancer. My wife has nine members of her family with cancer. Children in particular are susceptible to depleted uranium poisoning. They have a much higher absorption rate as their blood is being used to build and nourish their bones and they have a lot of soft tissues. Bone cancer and leukemia used to be diseases affecting them the most, however, cancer of the lymph system, which can develop anywhere on the body, and has rarely been seen before the age of 12, is now also common. At one point after the war, a Basra hospital reported treating upwards of 600 children per day with symptoms of radiation sickness; 600 children per day?
>
> (Westerman, 2006)

Because DU bonds with the DNA, and causes it to mutate, it raises the incidence of various types of cancer. The unborn children of Iraq are being asked to pay the highest price, the integrity of their DNA. The US mainstream media has, nevertheless, largely maintained an uncanny silence on the correlation between DU and incidences of cancer despite the thousands of afflicted

American soldiers, whose symptoms were dubbed "the Gulf War Syndrome." A taboo seemingly surrounds discussion of the subject. Moreover, this taboo has allowed the US government to remain unaccountable for the contamination of Iraq and the hazard DU poses to the Iraqi people. Unfortunately, the problem of DU also escapes attention within the Iraqi government, who have yet to put in place any sort of national program to clean any of the hundreds of sites in Iraq contaminated by DU (al-Ansari et al., 2014).

The unraveling of the Iraqi state, precipitated by the devastating bombing campaign, was exacerbated by the imposition of a draconian sanctions regime, which compounded the precipitous decline and impoverishment of Iraq's social and economic infrastructure.[3] Predictably, the brunt of the sanctions regime imposed on Iraq following the Gulf War was borne by the people. Per-capita income precipitously declined, while domestic agricultural productivity collapsed and food imports were blocked, leading to the tremendous inflation of food prices (Ismael et al., 2004).[4] As a result, the incidence of malnutrition in Iraqi children under five years of age almost doubled from 1991 to 1996, contributing to increasing morbidity and mortality rates (UNICEF, 1998). Due to the overall breakdown of Iraq's health care system, including maternal and child care facilities, deaths of Iraqi children under the age of five during the time of the sanctions ranged from 5,000 to 7,000 per month, which is generally considered to be a conservative estimate given that births in rural areas were not registered immediately, and therefore if a child died, the birth was never recorded (Halliday, 1999). Table 6.3 provides evidence of the increasing vulnerability of Iraqi children to morbidity and mortality as a direct result of the impact of sanctions.[5]

Invasion context

The invasion context spans the period from March 20, 2003, when the US unleashed the "Shock and Awe" air bombardment on Iraq, to May 1, 2003, when US President George Bush declared the combat over. Shock and awe (also known as Rapid Dominance) is a military doctrine proposed by Harlan Ullman and James Wade at the US National Defense University in 1996 and operationalized on Iraq in 2003. This doctrine makes use of a huge amount of firepower to destroy large amounts of physical infrastructure in a short space of time. The objective is to

Table 6.3 Malnutrition and deaths in Iraqi children under five years of age

	1990/1991	*1996*
% subject to chronic malnutrition	18	31
% who died when they had diarrhea	0.2	1.7
% who died when they had pneumonia	1.6	12

Source: UNICEF, 1998, p. 25.

158 *People in the quagmire*

destroy not only the enemy's physical infrastructure, but also their psychological will to fight. The Shock and Awe campaign against Iraq included the massive air bombardment of Iraq's major cities, which entailed approximately 41,404 air sorties (Moseley, 2003), setting off the social chaos and the looting and burning of Iraq's historical and educational infrastructure.[6] The air bombardment destroyed the physical and public infrastructure—electrical power, sanitation, transportation and communication. Ullman and Wade describe the Shock and Awe tactic as an "all-encompassing" approach that requires "the ability to control the environment and to master all levels of the opponent's activities to affect will, perception, and understanding. This could include means of communication, transportation, food production, water supply, and other aspects of infrastructure" (Ullman & Wade, 1996, p. xxvii). The authors claim that the result the Shock and Awe campaign seeks to impose is "the non-nuclear equivalent of the impact that the atomic weapons dropped on Hiroshima and Nagasaki had on the Japanese" (Ullman & Wade, 1996, p. xxvi). Commenting on this in her seminal book *The Shock Doctrine*, Naomi Klein (2007, pp. 403–404) observed: "When the war began, the residents of Baghdad were subjected to sensory deprivation on a mass scale. One by one, the city's sensory inputs were cut off; the ears were the first to go […] Next to go were the eyes […]" The looting and burning of Iraq's museums, libraries and educational institutions destroyed the country's historical heritage and educational infrastructure. Occupying forces understood that, for Iraq to be remade into a weak and malleable state, the human and cultural memory of what it meant to be Iraqi must be eradicated. Consequently, "state destruction in Iraq entailed more than regime change and more than political and economic restructuring. It also required cultural cleansing, understood in the Iraqi case as the degrading of a unifying culture" (Baker et al., 2010, p. 6).

The Shock and Awe campaign targeted government facilities and densely populated areas. According to the Landmine Monitor Report (2003), the coalition's use of cluster munitions was confirmed in Baghdad, Basra, Hillah, Kirkuk, Mosul and Nasiriyah among other towns (Landmine and Cluster Munition Monitor, 2003). Analysis carried out by Iraq Body Count (IBC) found that, of Iraqis killed from air raids, 39 percent were children. In addition, of all Iraqi fatalities resulting from mortar attacks by invasion forces, 42 percent were children (Sengupta, 2009). The traumatization of Iraq's youngest generation constitutes a foremost challenge to the future of Iraq. Dr. Haithi al-Sady, Dean of the Psychological Research Center at Baghdad University, estimates that around 28 percent of Iraqi children suffer some degree of post-traumatic stress disorder (PTSD), and the numbers are progressively rising (Chelala, 2009).

The use of DU was not limited to the 1991 War, but was relied on in the 2003 invasion as well. On March 16, 2004 (one year after the US invasion of Iraq), Lawrence Smallman (2003) reported from Baghdad an explosive increase in leukemia among all ages in Iraq. Baghdad alone received 200 tons of DU, out of the 1,700 tons dropped on Iraq, which has irreversibly mixed with the soil. This condition alarmed Dr. Aḥmad Ḥardân, a special scientific adviser to the World Health Organization and the Iraqi Ministry of Health. The effects are already seen in Baghdad—"every form of cancer has jumped up at least 10 percent with the exception of bone tumors and skin cancer, which have only risen 2.6 percent and 9.3 percent respectively" (Smallman, 2003). To manage the health disaster, Dr. Ḥardân solicited international medical expertise. He arranged for a delegation from Japan's Hiroshima Hospital to come and contribute their knowledge on the radiological-related diseases that are likely to become more prevalent in Iraq over time. He also invited a world-famous German cancer specialist. The Americans, however, refused permission for either of them to enter Iraq, fully knowing the nature of their mission (Smallman, 2003).

According to a letter written by Iraqi and British doctors petitioning the UN to investigate the alarming rise of birth defects in Fallujah hospitals resulting from DU:

> Young women in Fallujah [...] are terrified of having children because of the increasing number of babies being born grotesquely deformed, with no heads, two heads, a single eye in their foreheads, scaly bodies or missing limbs. In addition, young children in Fallujah are now experiencing hideous cancers and leukemias.
>
> (Koehler, 2010)

The *International Journal of Environmental Research and Public Health* published an epidemiological survey corroborating these claims. The report found that Fallujah is experiencing higher rates of cancer, leukemia and infant mortality than Hiroshima and Nagasaki did in 1945 (Busby et al., 2010). Calls to ban the use of these weapons has fallen on deaf ears (Weir, 2012). When asked about Iraq's complaints about the impact of DU shells, Colonel James Naughton of the US Army Material Command claimed in a Pentagon briefing that "they want it to go away because we kicked the crap out of them" (Considine, 2013). Compounding the devastation resulting from the use of DU was the "US's persistent refusal to release the data that could have helped facilitate effective assessment and clearance work" (Zwijnenburg, 2013). Perhaps unaware of their hypocrisy, the US and UK were appalled at the use of similar weapons in Syria, in which the Obama Administration viewed the use of chemical weapons against civilians as constituting a "red line" that would be met with US intervention. Similarly, British Foreign Secretary William Hague argued that the use of chemical weapons against the Syrian rebels is "not something that a humane or civilized world can ignore" (Jolly, 2013).

The post-invasion military occupation context

The post-invasion military occupation context spans the period from May 1, 2003, when US President George Bush declared the combat over, to December 2011, when the US proclaimed the pullout of its troops was complete. The Anglo-American invasion and subsequent occupation of Iraq in 2003 triggered increasing violence and exposed Iraqi households to a state of entrenched insecurity and instability.[7] Five emergent patterns signify this state of insecurity and instability:

160 *People in the quagmire*

1   The two major responses to increasing resistance/insurgency towards the occupation were military siege and detention. Between 2003 and 2006, the occupying forces of the US military launched about 14 battles against Iraqi cities and towns. Fallujah was the first, and all the battles followed the same modus operandi of laying siege to the center and then going street by street, house by house, in search of any resistance. In addition, there was a massive increase in detentions. In 2010, the International Committee of the Red Cross reported that about 16,000 detainees were held in detention centers in Iraq, the most infamous being Abu Ghraib. How many children were held is difficult to determine, but the 2011 *Report of the Secretary-General on Children and Armed Conflict in Iraq* remarked that between 2008 and 2010 "a large number of children were detained [...] on suspicion of posing a threat to security" (UNSC, 2011, p. 7).

2   Sectarian incidents—such as bombings of holy sites—began early in the occupation, and increased in frequency and scale in tandem with the upward spiral of resistance and military suppression. Women and children were victims of this violence—killed and disabled. Sectarian violence has had a profound effect on Iraq's social fabric. From March 2006 to March 2008, 52,000 civilians died as sectarian-inspired killings peaked (IBC, 2013). The number of sectarian deaths declined in 2008 and 2009; a resurgent wave of sectarian violence, to some degree influenced by the Syrian Civil War, made July 2013 the deadliest month in Iraq in over five years, with 1,057 civilian deaths (Tawfeeq, 2013).

3   Mixed neighborhoods in Baghdad, such as Washash and Ghazaliya, were cleansed of Sunni Arabs, most commonly by factions of Jaish al-Mahdi, the militia loyal to Muqtaḍā al-Ṣadr, an Iraqi political figure. The cleansing of ethnic and religious minorities was not limited to Baghdad, however, as cleansing of Arabs and other ethnic and religious minorities, largely in retaliation for Saddam's Arabization project, was carried out in Kirkuk ahead of a planned census scheduled to take place in 2010. The census was continuously delayed, and ethnic tensions continued.[8]

4   By 2012, about 2 million Iraqis were internally displaced and about 1.4 million were externally displaced as refugees (IDMC, 2012). Over 80 percent of the displaced population were women and children (MIT Center for International Studies, n.d.). The destruction of public infrastructure and degradation of services, siege warfare and sectarian violence have all contributed to the displacement of Iraqis on a massive scale.

5   Children were profiled as a security threat, in effect portraying them as potentially dangerous enemies and legitimating their detention or worse. According to a UNSC report (2011) covering the period from January 2008 to December 2010, children have been used to "spy and scout, transport military supplies and equipment, videotape attacks for propaganda purposes, plant explosive devices and actively engage in attacks against security forces and civilians." In addition, the report identified children as suicide bombers used by insurgency groups, most frequently by al-Qaeda in Iraq. According to the report,

children were used as suicide bombers "because they arouse less suspicion and it is considered to be easier for them to move through security checkpoints than for adults." According to the report, the "Birds of Paradise," or al-Qaeda's youth wing in Iraq, was made up of children under the age of 15 recruited for such missions. While the report admitted that information on the Birds of Paradise was scarce, nevertheless it reported that al-Qaeda in Iraq targeted vulnerable children for its youth wing, particularly orphans, homeless children and mentally disabled children (UNSC, 2011).

Following 13 years of economic sanctions, the impact of eight years of occupation was devastating on the Iraqi population in general, and children in particular, as they foreshadow the future. The ramifications include the following:

- *Increased mortality*: Analysis carried out for the research group Iraq Body Count found that 39 percent of those killed in air raids by the US-led coalition were children. Fatalities caused by mortars, used by American and Iraqi government forces as well as insurgents, were 42 percent children (Sengupta, 2009).
- *Unaccompanied children*: UNHCR surveys in 2009 stated that 20 percent of internally displaced persons (IDPs) and 5 percent of returned refugees reported children to be missing. The total internally displaced population as of November 2009 was estimated to be up to 2.76 million persons or 467,517 families. A simple calculation shows that more than 93,500 children of internally displaced families are missing (Adriaensens, 2011).
- *Orphaned children*: There was a drastic increase in the number of orphans in Iraq during the war and occupation. There are five million Iraqi orphans as reported by official government statistics. About 500,000 of these orphans live on the streets (al-Azzawi, 2010). Approximately one in six Iraqi children under the age of 18 is an orphan (Sponsor Iraqi Children Foundation; UN General Assembly, 2013). Many orphans beg on the streets or sell water to help poor widowed mothers or siblings. They are very vulnerable to arrest for begging as well as to recruitment or abuse by criminals, extremists and human traffickers.
- *Disabled children*: Casualties from failed cluster submunitions rose between 1991 and 2007 from 5,500 to 80,000; 24 percent were children under the age of 14. Both UNICEF and the UNDP believe these figures are an underestimation (War Victims Monitor, 2011). This last decade the Al Munthanna and Basra provinces of Iraq have challenged Angola for the highest proportion to total population of children amputees (Anonymous, 2011).
- *Post-traumatic stress in children*: According to the UN World Health Organization (WHO), the fourth-leading cause of morbidity among Iraqis older than five years is "mental disorders," which ranked higher than infectious disease. A study by the Iraqi Society of Psychiatrists in collaboration with the WHO found that 70 percent of children (sample 10,000) in the Sha'ab section of North Baghdad are suffering from trauma-related symptoms (al-Daini, 2012).

162   *People in the quagmire*

In 2006 some studies on the prevalence of mental disorders of children were completed in Baghdad, Mosul and Dohuk. In the first study it was found that, of the 47 percent of primary school children reporting exposure to a major traumatic event during the previous two years, 14 percent had PTSD (Razokhi et al., 2006). In the second study in Mosul, adolescents were screened for mental disorders. Thirty percent had symptoms of PTSD. There was a higher rate of PTSD in the older adolescents. Another study, conducted at the Child Psychiatric Department of the General Pediatric Hospital in Baghdad in 2005, found: anxiety disorders (22 percent), behavioral problems (hyperkinetic and conduct disorders) (18 percent), non-organic enuresis (15 percent), stuttering (14 percent), epilepsy (10 percent) and depression (1.3 percent) (Budosan et al., 2010).

Discourse versus policy

While the discourse of UN agencies and international civil society documented and bemoaned the plight of Iraqi children, the US and Britain, backed by the UN Security Council, continued the pursuit of policies directly causing their plight, with some modest attempts to ameliorate the impact on civilians in general, and children in particular (such as the Oil-for-Food Programme).[9] However, at the policy level of power politics, acceptance of child suffering as an inevitable consequence of war is nothing new. Officially and journalistically children are treated as a lamentable but integral part of so-called "collateral damage"—a term which sanitizes civilian casualties as an unintended consequence of a natural phenomenon and ignores the Geneva Conventions relative to the protection of civilians in times of war (Geneva Conventions, 1949). This underlying acceptance of child suffering as a legitimate cost of war was impenitently demonstrated in May 1996 by Madeleine Albright (then US Ambassador to the UN) toward Iraqi children in an interview on the popular national news show *60 Minutes* that addressed the impact of the draconian sanctions regime the UN Security Council imposed on Iraq since 1990. Asked by the interviewer, "We have heard that half a million children [in Iraq] have died. I mean, that's more children than died in Hiroshima. […] is the price worth it?," Albright replied, "This is a very hard choice, but […] we think the price is worth it" (Democracy Now, 2004).[10] She was not alone in her dismissal of the plight of Iraqi children. The former US Ambassador to the UN, Bill Richardson, also claimed the sanctions that were responsible for killing half a million Iraqi children was the "correct policy" (Shah, 2005). In effect, these statements were a direct reflection of US policy in Iraq.

A UNICEF (1999) report, *Iraq Child and Maternal Mortality Surveys*, concurred with these earlier estimates of the effects of the UN sanctions regime, finding they were responsible for the deaths of approximately 500,000 Iraqi children (Ali et al., 2003; Jones, 1999). The report charted the difference between mortality rates during sanctions based on UNICEF surveys and what the situation would have been based on an extrapolation of the declining mortality trend established in the 1980s before sanctions (Jones, 1999; see Figure 6.1).

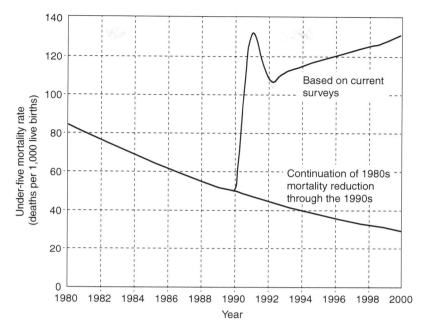

Figure 6.1 Iraq: under-five mortality rate disparities

Source: Jones, 1999, p. 3.

The UNICEF report, and Albright's earlier justification of the death toll, set off a fire-storm of controversy (Sadiq & Tiller, 2002), as the NGO community condemned US policy on sanctions (Richman, 2004) and the US State Department and public relations media either condemned the report as methodologically flawed (Cortright, 2001) or condemned Saddam Hussein's obstructionism for the high mortality rates (US Department of State, 1999).

Denis Halliday, former UN Humanitarian Administrator in Iraq from 1997 to 1998, used the word "genocide" in a 1999 speech to describe the catastrophic situation he had witnessed during his 13 months in Iraq under the sanctions regime. While genocide has become an acceptable term to use in Western democracies with regards to Rwanda, Darfur and Kosovo, the use of the word has been absent from US discourse regarding the impact of sanctions on Iraqi civilians. Halliday (2000) argues that this

> indicates a belief that only other nations commit genocide, that somehow we Western democracies do not. This perception is self-serving, coming from nations that once ran the transatlantic slave trade, undertook the massacre of American Indians, and enabled the slaughter of the aboriginal peoples of Australia.

164   *People in the quagmire*

Following Halliday's resignation, Hans-Christof von Sponeck, UN Assistant Secretary General, took over as UN Humanitarian Coordinator for Iraq. In 2000, he and Jutta Burghardt, head of the UN World Food Programme in Iraq, resigned for much the same reason as Halliday. Commenting on the impact of sanctions imposed on the Iraqi people in his book *A Different Kind of War*, Sponeck (2006) argued:

> All parties to this conflict, including the UN Secretariat, had options. The fate of a nation could have been different—more humane and consistent with internationally defined standards of life—had the protagonists opted for dialogue and honest intentions. The United Nations could have emerged as a winner by helping to resolve a crisis. International law would have been confirmed as the universally acceptable basis for international relations. The world would have been less confused and a more secure place today.
>
> (p. 2)

The UN sanctions regime was a morally shameful affair, revealing "international law" to be a façade, a legal pretense to advance the interests of the world's powerful at the expense of the weakest—in this instance, Iraq's children. The purported objective of the sanctions regime, to force Iraq's disarmament of WMDs—as stated in Resolutions 661 and 687—now look quite hollow, as Iraq had, in fact, substantively disarmed in accordance with the resolutions. And while no nation would be "prepared" for the Anglo-American military assault that was unleashed in 2003, Iraq—having been beggared over the preceding decade—was in a state of humanitarian disaster, the subsequent military invasion tipping it over the abyss. The legacy of the 1990s and the years preceding the 2003 Anglo-American invasion, thus, reflect very poorly on the UN, representing a total negation of its stated principles.

Conclusion

A child born in Iraq during the 1990s was about 3.5 times more likely to die in infancy than one born in the 1980s. If the child survived infancy, she or he was more than 2.5 times likely to die before reaching their fifth birthday than a child born in the 1980s. If the 1990s child survived early childhood, she or he was about 30 percent less likely to enroll in school than a child born in the 1980s. By the time of the invasion in 2003, the children born in 1990 that had survived the perils of infancy and early childhood were 13 years old; and by the time of the tenth anniversary of the invasion, they were 23, and no longer children. There are about 16 million survivors born since 1991. The number of children born between 1990 and 2013 who did not survive war, sanctions, invasion or occupation very likely exceeds a million (Cole, 2013). Nevertheless, the youth component in Iraq is the fastest growing in the country. Iraq's median age, 20.9, makes it the second-youngest population by country in the Middle East and North Africa. In today's Iraq, 16.6 million, or over 50 percent of the Iraqi population, are under the age of 18, which means half of Iraq's population has never experienced life in the absence of devastating economic sanctions, war or both. The situation for these 16.6 million children has not greatly improved across any of UNICEF's metrics, as indicated by their latest *Annual Report for Iraq* (2012). Some 5.3 million children experience multiple deprivations, with wasting having increased from 21 to 23 percent and stunting from 5 to 7 percent from 2006 to 2011 (UNICEF, 2012, pp. 1–2). The under-five mortality rate is nearly unchanged at 37 per 1,000, and infant mortality is now 32 per 1,000 live births (UNICEF, 2012, p. 2). Education stands out as a small glimmer of hope, with elementary enrollment having increased to 93 percent; however, upper-level (ages 15–17) enrollment is only 21 percent. Distance to schools, violence experienced on the way to or at school, and lack of classroom space contribute to this low enrollment level (UNICEF, 2012, p. 2). "Protracted violence and on-going regional disagreements continue to impede development" in Iraq (UNICEF, 2012, p. 1).

Notes

1 See Chapter 2 for more on the sanctions regime.
2 See Chapter 7 for more on malnutrition.
3 See www.questia.com/library/politics-and-government/international-relations/ international-organizations/united-nations/u-n-sanctions-against-iraq for a list of articles and books, with previews, on sanctions against Iraq. Accessed August 6, 2013.
4 Imported food had supplied two-thirds of demand prior to the war, and Iraq's own agricultural sector was quickly overburdened as stockpiles of parts and fertilizers diminished because of the sanctions regime. For more on the effects of the sanctions regime on agriculture and sanitation in Iraq, see Chapter 2.
5 See Chapter 7 for mortality rates based on the 1999 UNICEF report.
6 See Chapter 2 for more on the cultural pillaging of Iraq.
7 For a picture of daily life under the occupation see Adriaensens (2012), al-Araji et al. (2008) and Wrigley-Field & Ross (2009).
8 See Chapter 4 for more on ethno-confessional cleansing in Iraq.
9 For an overview of the program, see UN Office of the Iraqi Programme Oil-for-Food (UN n.d.), www.un.org/depts/oip/background/; accessed August 11, 2013. For a critique of the program see Zurbrigg (2007).
10 Albright has since revised that opinion (Democracy Now, 2004).

References

Adriaensens, D. (2011). *Always Someone's Mother or Father, Always Someone's Child: The missing persons of Iraq.* Retrieved August 12, 2013, from *Brussels Tribunal*: www.brusselstribunal.org/pdf/Disappearances_missing_persons_in_Iraq.pdf

Adriaensens, D. (2012, November 29). *Child Kidnapping in Iraq: Another legacy of US military occupation.* Retrieved August 8, 2013, from Global Research: www.globalresearch.ca/child-kidnapping-in-iraq-another-legacy-of-us-military-occupation/5313358

al-Ansari, N., Knutsson, S., & Almuqdadi, K. (2014, March). Engineering Solution for Radioactive Waste in Iraq. *Journal of Advanced Science and Engineering Research, 4*(1), 18–36.

166　*People in the quagmire*

al-Araji, F., Jarrar, R., & Jarrar, K. (2008). *The Iraq War Blog: An Iraqi family's inside view of the first year of occupation.* Second Chance Publishing.

al-Azzawi, S. N. (2010, March 19). *Violation of Iraqi Children's Rights.* Retrieved August 13, 2013, from Global Research: www.globalresearch.ca/violations-of-iraqi-children-s-rights/18205

al-Daini, A. (2012, January 5). *The Plight of Iraqi Children.* Retrieved August 13, 2013, from Dissident Voice: http://dissidentvoice.org/2012/01/the-plight-of-iraqi-children/

Ali, M. M., Blacker, J., & Jones, G. (2003). Annual Mortality Rates and Excess Deaths of Children Under Five in Iraq, 1991–98. *Population Studies, 57*(2), 217–226.

Anonymous. (2011, December 4). *Iraq—landmines, bombs, depleted uranium—devastation—children amputees. How you can help.* Retrieved August 13, 2013, from Independent Media Centre Australia: www.indymedia.org.au/2011/12/04/iraq-%E2%80%93-landmines-bombs-depleted-uranium-%E2%80%93-devastation-%E2%80%93-children-amputees-how-you-can-hel

Arbuthnot, F. (2000, September 17). *Allies Deliberately Poisoned Iraq Public Water Supply in Gulf War.* Retrieved January 11, 2014, from *Sunday Herald*: www.commondreams.org/headlines/091700-01.htm

Arnove, A. (ed.). (2003). *Iraq Under Siege.* Cambridge: South End Press.

Baker, R., Ismael, S., & Ismael, T. Y. (2010). Ending the Iraqi State. In R. Baker, S. Ismael & T. Y. Ismael (eds), *Cultural Cleansing in Iraq: Why museums were looted, libraries burned and academics murdered.* London: Pluto Press.

Barrett, G. (2002, August 7). 12 Years Later, Sanctions Targeting Saddam Hussein Strike Civilians. *Gannet News Service.*

BBC News. (December 15, 2010). UN Lifts Sanctions Against Iraq. Retrieved November 15, 2014, from BBC News: http://www.bbc.co.uk/news/world-middle-east-12004115

Budosan, B., Jeffrey, L., & Al-Obaidi, A. K. (2010). Child and Adolescent Mental Health in Iraq: Current situation and scope for promotion of mental health policy. *Intervention, 8*(1), 40–51.

Busby, C., Hamdan, M., & Ariabi, E. (2010). Cancer, Infant Mortality and Birth Sex-Ratio in Fallujah. *International Journal of Environmental Research and Public Health, 7*(7), 2828–2837.

Chelala, C. (2009, March 5). *Iraqi Children Bear the Costs of War.* Retrieved July 15, 2013, from Common Dreams: www.commondreams.org/view/2009/03/05-0

Cole, Juan. (2013, October 17). *The American Genocide Against Iraq: 4% of population dead as a result of US sanctions, wars.* Retrieved February 3, 2014, from Informed Comment: www.juancole.com/2013/10/american-population-sanctions.html

Collier, R. (2003, January 13). *Iraq Links Cancers to Uranium Weapons/U.S. Likely to Use Arms Again in War.* Retrieved January 17, 2014, from SFGate: www.sfgate.com/news/article/Iraq-links-cancers-to-uranium-weapons-U-S-2686745.php

Considine, C. (2013, August 29). *US Depleted Uranium as Malicious as Syrian Chemical Weapons.* Retrieved December 29, 2013, from *Huffington Post*: www.huffingtonpost.com/craig-considine/us-depleted-uranium-as-ma_b_3812888.html

Cortright, D. (2001, November 15). *A Hard Look at Sanctions.* Retrieved August 14, 2013, from *The Nation*: www.thenation.com/article/hard-look-iraq-sanctions#

Crude Oil Production, Iraq. (n.d.). Retrieved July 10, 2013, from Economagic: www.economagic.com/em-cgi/data.exe/doeme/paprpiq

Children of the occupation   167

Democracy Now. (2004, July 30). *Democracy Now! Confronts Madeline Albright on the Iraq Sanctions: Was it worth the price?* Retrieved July 29, 2013, from Democracy Now: www.democracynow.org/2004/7/30/democracy_now_confronts_madeline_albright_on

Democracy Now. (2010, September 1). *Invisible War: How thirteen years of US-imposed economic sanctions devastated Iraq before the 2003 invasion.* Retrieved August 5, 2013, from Democracy Now: www.democracynow.org/2010/9/1/invisible_war_how_thirteen_years_of

DIA. (1991, January). *Iraq Water Treatment Vulnerabilities.* Retrieved November 15, 2014, from GulfLink: http://www.gulflink.osd.mil/declassdocs/dia/19950901/950901_511rept_91.html

Fisk, R. (1998a, May 28). The West's Poisonous Legacy. *The Independent (London)*, p. 13.

Fisk, R. (1998b, October 16). The Evidence is There—We caused cancer in the Gulf. *The Independent (London)*, p. 4.

Geneva Conventions. (1949, August 12). *Convention (IV) Relative to the Protection of Civilian Persons in Time of War.* Retrieved July 27, 2013, from International Committee of the Red Cross: www.icrc.org/applic/ihl/ihl.nsf/INTRO/380

Global Policy Forum. (n.d.). *Sanctions Against Iraq.* Retrieved August 6, 2013, from Global Policy Forum: https://www.globalpolicy.org/previous-issues-and-debate-on-iraq/sanctions-against-iraq.html

Halliday, D. (1999). The Impact of the UN Sanctions on the People of Iraq. *Journal of Palestine Studies, 28*(2), 29–37.

Halliday, D. (2000). The Deadly and Illegal Consequences of the Economic Sanctions on the People of Iraq. *Brown Journal of World Affairs, 7*(1), 229–233.

Hambling, D. (2000, May 18). *Why Deadly Depleted Uranium is the Tank Buster's Weapon of Choice.* Retrieved February 3, 2014, from *The Guardian*: www.theguardian.com/world/2000/may/18/armstrade.kosovo

IBC. (2013, March 19). *The War in Iraq: 10 years and counting.* Retrieved August 12, 2013, from Iraq Body Count (IBC): www.iraqbodycount.org/analysis/numbers/ten-years/

IDMC. (2012, December 31). *Internally Displaced Persons in Iraq.* Retrieved August 31, 2013, from Internal Displacement Monitoring Centre: www.internal-displacement.org/middle-east-and-north-africa/iraq/figures-analysis

International Study Team. (1991, October). *Health and Welfare in Iraq After the Gulf Crisis: An in-depth assessment.* Retrieved January 11, 2014, from Center for Economic and Social Rights: www.cesr.org/downloads/Health%20and%20Welfare%20in%20Iraq%20after%20the%20Gulf%20Crisis%201991.pdf

Ismael, T. Y., Ismael, J. S., & Ismael, S. (2004). Social Deconstruction: Social development under siege. In T. Y. Ismael & J. S. Ismael, *The Iraqi Predicament: People in the quagmire of power politics.* London: Pluto Press.

Jolly, D. (2013, August 23). *Russia Urges Syria to Cooperate in Chemical Weapons Inquiry.* Retrieved December 29, 2013, from *The New York Times*: www.nytimes.com/2013/08/24/world/middleeast/syria-chemical-attack.html?_r=1&

Jones, G. (1999, July 23). *Iraq—Under-Five Mortality.* Retrieved January 12, 2014, from Federation of American Scientists: www.fas.org/news/iraq/1999/08/irqu5est.pdf

Kelly, K. (2003). Raising Voices: The children of Iraq, 1990–1999. In A. Arnove (ed.), *Iraq Under Siege.* Cambridge: South End Press.

Klein, N. (2007). *The Shock Doctrine: The rise of disaster capitalism.* Toronto: Random House.

168 *People in the quagmire*

Koehler, R. (2010, July 29). *The Suffering of Fallujah*. Retrieved December 28, 2013, from *Huffington Post*: www.huffingtonpost.com/robert-koehler/the-suffering-of-fallujah_b_663545.html

Landmine and Cluster Munition Monitor. (2003). *Landmine Monitor Report 2003—Iraq*. Retrieved January 17, 2014, from Landmine and Cluster Munition Monitor: www.the-monitor.org/index.php/publications/display?url=lm/2003/iraq.html

MIT Center for International Studies. (n.d.). *The Human Cost of the War in Iraq*. Retrieved August 8, 2013, from Iraq: The Human Cost: http://web.mit.edu/humancostiraq/

Moseley, T. M. (2003, April 30). *Operation Iraqi Freedom—By the numbers*. Retrieved January 17, 2014, from Global Security: www.globalsecurity.org/military/library/report/2003/uscentaf_oif_report_30apr2003.pdf

Nagy, T. J. (2001, September). *The Secret Behind the Sanctions: How the US intentionally destroyed Iraq's water supply*. Retrieved January 11, 2014, from The Progressive: http://progressive.org/mag/nagy0901.html

Pilger, John. (2002). *The New Rulers of the World*. Brooklyn, New York: Verso Books.

Razokhi, A., Taha, I., Taib, N. I., Sadik, S., & Al Gasseer, N. (2006). Mental Health of Iraqi Children. *The Lancet, 368*(9538), 838–839.

Richman, S. (2004, January 1). *Iraqi Sanctions: Were they worth it?* Retrieved August 14, 2013, from The Future of Freedom Foundation: http://fff.org/explore-freedom/article/iraqi-sanctions-worth/

Rizer, K. (2001). Bombing Dual-Use Targets: Legal, ethical, and doctrinal perspectives. Retrieved July 17, 2013, from *Air & Space Power Journal*: www.airpower.au.af.mil/airchronicles/cc/Rizer.html

Sadiq, S., & Tiller, S. (2002, November). *The Debate Over UN Sanctions*. Retrieved August 14, 2013, from PBS Frontline/World: www.pbs.org/frontlineworld/stories/iraq/sanctions.html

Sengupta, K. (2009, April 16). *Iraq Air Raids Hit Mostly Women and Children*. Retrieved July 14, 2013, from *The Independent*: http://www.independent.co.uk/news/world/middle-east/iraq-air-raids-hit-mostly-women-and-children-1669282.html

Shah, A. (2005, October 2). *Effects of Iraq Sanctions*. Retrieved August 5, 2013, from Global Issues: www.globalissues.org/article/105/effects-of-sanctions

Smallman, L. (2003, October 30). *Iraq's Real WMD Crime*. Retrieved January 17, 2014, from Al Jazeera: www.aljazeera.com/archive/2003/10/2008410163515321636.html

Sponeck, G. H. (2006). *A Different Kind of War: The UN sanctions regime in Iraq*. Germany: Berghahn Books.

Tawfeeq, M. (2013, August 12). *Suicide Bombing at Iraq Coffee Shop; 12 Dead*. Retrieved August 12, 2013, from CNN: www.cnn.com/2013/08/12/world/meast/iraq-violence

Tyler, P. E. (1991, June 3). US Officials Believe Iraq Will Take Years to Rebuild. *The New York Times*.

Ullman, H. K., & Wade, J. P. (1996). *Shock and Awe: Achieving rapid dominance*. Washington DC: National Defense University Press.

UN. (1996, August 25). *Promotion and Protection of the Rights of Children: Impact of armed conflict on children*. Retrieved January 11, 2014, from UNICEF: www.unicef.org/graca/a51-306_en.pdf

UN. (1999, March 30). *Report of the Second Panel Established Pursuant to the Note by the President of the Security Council of 30 January 1999 (S/1999/100), Concerning the Current Humanitarian Situation in Iraq*. Retrieved July 10, 2013, from Campaign Against Sanctions on Iraq (CASI): www.casi.org.uk/info/panelrep.html

Children of the occupation 169

UN. (n.d.). *Office of the Iraqi Programme Oil-for-Food*. Retrieved August 11, 2013, from UN: www.un.org/depts/oip/background/

UN General Assembly. (February 25, 2013). Human Rights Council A/HRC/22/NGO/138. Retrieved November 15, 2014, from Geneva International Centre for Justice: http://www.gicj.org/NOG_REPORTS_HRC_22/children.pdf

UN Oil-for-Food Programme (n.d.). *The United Nations Oil-for-Food Programme: Focus on humanitarian relief*. Retrieved February 3, 2014, from United Nations: www.un.org/News/dh/iraq/oip/human_relief.htm

UNICEF. (1998, April 30). *Situation Analysis of Children and Women in Iraq*. Retrieved August 13, 2013, from Penn State: http://citeseerx.ist.psu.edu/viewdoc/download;jsessionid=7CF85122251211F840520947FB947D12?doi=10.1.1.194.4798&rep=rep1&type=pdf

UNICEF. (1999, July). *Results of the 1999 Iraq Child and Maternal Mortality Surveys*. Retrieved January 11, 2014, from Federation of American Scientists: www.fas.org/news/iraq/1999/08/irqscont.pdf

UNICEF. (2003, July). *Iraq Watching Briefs*. Retrieved July 9, 2013, from UNICEF: www.unicef.org/evaldatabase/files/Iraq_2003_Watching_Briefs.pdf

UNICEF. (2009, April). *Children and Conflict in a Changing World*. Retrieved July 7, 2013, from UN: www.un.org/arabic/children/conflict/pdf/MachelReviewBanners.pdf

UNICEF. (2012). *UNICEF Annual Report 2012 for Iraq, MENA*. Retrieved February 20, 2014, from UNICEF: www.unicef.org/about/annualreport/files/Iraq_COAR_2012.pdf

UNSC. (1991, March 20). *Report to the Seretary-General on Humanitarian Needs in Kuwait and Iraq in the Immediate Post-Crisis Environment by a Mission to the Area Led by Mr. Martti Ahtisaari, Under-Secretary-General for Administration and Management, Dated 20 March 1991*. Retrieved August 4, 2013, from UN: www.un.org/depts/oip/background/reports/s22366.pdf

UNSC. (2011, June 15). *Report of the Secretary-General on Children and Armed Conflict in Iraq*. Retrieved August 8, 2013, from Security Council Report: www.securitycouncilreport.org/atf/cf/%7B65BFCF9B-6D27-4E9C-8CD3-CF6E4FF96FF9%7D/CAC%20S%202011%20366.pdf

US Department of State. (1999, September). *Saddam Hussein's Iraq*. Retrieved August 14, 2013, from George Washington University: http://www2.gwu.edu/~nsarchiv/NSAEBB/NSAEBB167/13.pdf

War Victims Monitor. (2011, April 11). *Iraq: Moving ahead to improve lives of Iraqis affected by landmines*. Retrieved August 13, 2013, from War Victims Monitor: http://warvictims.wordpress.com/2011/04/11/iraq-moving-ahead-to-improve-lives-of-iraqis-affected-by-landmines/

Weir, Doug. (2012). *Precaution in Practice: Challenging the acceptability of depleted uranium weapons*. Retrieved February 2, 2014, from International Coalition to Ban Uranium Weapons: www.bandepleteduranium.org/en/docs/195.pdf

Westerman, D. (2006, April 17). *The Real WMD's in Iraq—Ours*. Retrieved January 11, 2014, from Information Liberation: www.informationliberation.com/test.php?id=9712

Wrigley-Field, E., & Ross, J. (eds). (2009). *Iraqi Girl: Diary of a teenage girl in Iraq*. Chicago: Haymarket Books.

Zurbrigg, S. (2007). Economic Sanctions on Iraq: Tool for peace, or travesty? *Muslim World Journal of Human Rights, 4*(2), 3–63.

Zwijnenburg, W. (2013, January). *In a State of Uncertainty: Impact and implications of the use of depleted uranium in Iraq*. Retrieved January 11, 2014, from IKV Pax Christi: www.ikvpaxchristi.nl/media/files/in-a-state-of-uncertainty.pdf

7 Iraqi women under occupation
From tribalism to neo-feudalism

With demonstrable progress in the five decades following Iraqi independence in 1932, Iraqi women secured *de jure* status and accumulated tangible advances in women's rights, education and socio-economic participation across Iraqi society. However, over the last three decades they have endured dictatorship, three major wars, the draconian economic deprivation of the international sanctions regime from 1990 to 2003, and the yoke of occupation. With the 2003–2011 military occupation by Anglo-American forces, foreign-based actors and ideas initiated a process that has brought about profound alterations to status and developmental matters directly relevant to Iraqi women. Over the past decade, the progress towards emancipation that Iraqi women had struggled for in the five preceding decades has been rolled back more than a century. In the face of a so-called "liberation" of Iraq, virtually every international convention on human rights generally and on women in particular has been flagrantly violated, and Iraqi women have been effectively enslaved in institutionalized patriarchy by the political reconstruction of Iraq in the twenty-first century. This chapter examines the struggle of Iraqi women over the course of the twentieth century and sketches their historical trajectory from emancipation to bondage.

Emergence of women onto the stage of modern Iraqi history

Like the history of many societies in the Global South, there is very little information available in the public records on women in Iraq prior to World War II. As feminist historians have revealed, history generally represents the narrative of "his-story," and contemporary feminist scholarship on "her-story" has therefore had a significant impact on our understanding of history (Ashby & Ohrn, 1995). To compensate for the invisibility of women in historical records, literature has been utilized in contemporary research to provide a representation of women in social history (Goodman, 1996). Drawing on this tradition, Shuja Muslim al-Ani studied early twentieth-century Iraqi literature to identify a number of recurrent themes in the representation of women, including: (1) popular antipathy toward the education or employment of women; (2) general acceptance of the inferiority of women and their subordination to men; (3) lack of women's rights in matters of marriage and divorce (a male prerogative); (4) cultural acceptance that the killing of women was legal under codes of honor killing, a practice based on pre-Islamic tribal custom; (5) general acceptance of the practice of polygamy as a man's right; and (6) women's segregation from men in both the private and public domain (al-Ani, 1972).

A graphic illustration of the repressive cultural conservatism toward women was reflected in what became known as the 1904 Baghdad census incident. As a modernizing effort, the Ottoman Governor of Baghdad, Abd-ul-Wahab Pasha, attempted to have women registered so as to include the female population in the census. He was confronted by a protesting crowd of males incited by representatives of the traditional elite, including Ahmad Ifindi al-Naqib, representing the city's dignitaries, and al-Saiyyid Muhammad Jamalu-d-Din al-Naqib, representing the enormously influential class of *sdah*, direct descendants of the Prophet.[1] The protesting crowd engaged the gendarmerie, forcing the governor to halt the entire census process. The same scenario took place in Mosul, where the census was protested against as representing a "dishonor to women" (al-'Umari, 1969). Such protests can be understood in the social context of widespread illiteracy (male literacy was less than 1 percent in the early twentieth century); urban squalor with virtually no public health services or education; an official acquiescence of tribal-clan dominance within society; and a cultural acceptance that saw superstition and tribal tradition serving as a primary justification for social practice. These were the conditions that prevailed in the early decades of the twentieth century (Izz-il-Din, 1960, pp. 16–18, 65), and are being resuscitated in the twenty-first century with the institutionalization of patriarchy (as delineated in the course of this chapter).

In spite of such reactionary responses that confronted the Governor of Baghdad in 1904, there were strong reformist trends already stirring across the region. The plight of women in the Arab world was brought to light with the diffusion of enlightenment thought by Arab intellectuals in the late nineteenth century—in particular, the social reform movement advanced by Muhammad Abduh (Imarah, 1972), a prominent Egyptian religious reformer, who argued that Islam upheld women's equality to men and who supported the rights of women to education and employment. Qasim Amin's *The Liberation of Women*, published in Cairo in 1899, illustrates the scope of these reformist currents. Egyptian and Syrian newspapers were widely circulated among Iraq's intelligentsia, propagating women's rights and challenging the reactionary nature of many existing social practices, as well as religious interpretations that supported the oppression of women (Izz-il-Din, 1960, p. 239).

The winds of change in Iraq were reflected at the turn of the century with the 1899 founding of a school for girls in Baghdad (Izz-il-Din, 1960, p. 47), *Onath Rushdiyah Makatabi*.[2] By 1918 there were three institutions for girls' education, and pressure from an emerging civil society to expand such opportunities further (Daud, 1958, p. 45). A 1918 letter from the resolute orientalist Gertrude Bell, adviser to the British High Commissioner of Iraq from 1917 to 1926, provided an oblique indicator of women's awakening in Iraq. Commenting on a tea party she hosted for "the ladies of Baghdad," Bell (1927) observed:

172   *People in the quagmire*

> It's odd, isn't it, that the success of a party should depend on the absence of that element [men]. One woman, the wife of the Director of Religious Bequests (Moslem of the Moslem), said that "if only they [women] could see one another and meet more in company, life would be quite different."
>
> (p. 457)

Iraq fell under British occupation in 1917, and the occupation acquired a veneer of legitimacy under a League of Nations mandate (1920–1932). Following a nationalist revolt in 1920 Iraq received nominal independence in 1921; however, Britain remained in effective control of the state until 1932 when Iraq joined the League of Nations. During its occupation, Britain aligned itself with conservative tribal and feudal forces advocating maintenance of the status quo. Its support for traditional authority was a bulwark set against the reform efforts of the later Ottoman era and the progressive aspects of pan-Arab nationalist forces advocating change and modernization. British machinations were designed to block reforms and the expression of Iraqi popular sovereignty. However, as examined by Philip Ireland (1937/2005) in his definitive study of Britain's role in the creation of the modern state, *Iraq: A study in political development*, British rule rearticulated traditional authority to suit its imperial interests. Britain sought to reinforce and strengthen tribal feudal organization as "a method of control," exercising control over Iraq through the tribal sheikhs by recognizing their suzerainty over the land. In effect, the tribal sheikhs were transformed from community leaders into large landowners (Ireland, 1937/2005, p. 95).

At the same time, Iraqi agriculture was coming into increasing contact with the world market, as reflected by the increase of Iraq's grain exports from 65,000 tons in the early 1890s, to 120,000 tons in the years 1909–1913, and to 380,000 tons in the years 1934–1939. The profits associated with this burgeoning export trade stimulated the acquisitive dispositions of the sheikhs, and led them to amass still larger holdings of cultivable land (Warriner, 1975, pp. 101–109). Thus, tribal sheikhs joined the class of large landowners established under Ottoman rule, thereby becoming vassals in liege to the British administration (Hasan, 1966, p. 172).[3] The sheikhs' rise, however, resulted in Bedouins and small landholders increasingly becoming enmeshed within a landholding system incorporated within the legal apparatus of the new state. Previously more independent of any such state authority, Bedouin and other rural populations found themselves increasingly dominated by these tribal sheikhs. Moreover, robust efforts by the government to settle these semi-nomadic populations through landholding policy led to sedentarization and increasing migration to urban areas, bringing the formerly independent Iraqi Bedouin population within the confines of state authority.

Thus, in spite of its charge as mandatory power to shepherd the newly established Iraqi state to independence in the interests of its people, British colonial practices drove decision making based on logic benefiting the imperial power. Instead of Iraqi indigenous voices being empowered under British suzerainty, what emerged in Iraq was a quasi-feudal system under large landowners drawn from two distinct strata of the population. While traditional elites were found in the urban environs of Baghdad, Mosul and Basra, a new elite emerged to manage rural areas. Traditional authorities, former-Ottoman urban notables, whose land-holdings predated the twentieth century, were largely absentee, using the lands as a store of wealth (al-Zahir, 1946, pp. 17–21). In contrast, tribal authorities, supported by the mandatory state, were determined to profit from the productive output of their holdings. Hanna Batatu, the premier political historian of modern Iraq, differentiated the landed tribal sheikhs into four categories based on their relationship to the cultivators: (1) leaders of tribal freeholding farmers; (2) own-ers of estates or village land tenanted by sharecropping peasants from their own tribes; (3) sheikhs owning estates tilled partly or largely by client or extraneous tribesmen; and (4) *aghas* possessing village land cultivated by nontribal serf-like *miskins* ("miserables"). Batatu's (1978) characterization of the relationship reveals the quasi-feudal nature of land tenure in Iraq:

> The first type of chiefship, which was of infrequent occurrence, rested on kinship, and approached the patriarchal ideal. The authority of the third type of tribal leaders, which grew out of ties of patronship or ties essentially eco-nomic in character, could be very arbitrary; but most oppressive was the power of the *agha* [Kurdish tribal chiefs] of a *miskin* village.
>
> (p. 79)

While the quasi-feudal system, undercut through the Ottoman modernization efforts of the *Tanzimat* (reorganization policy), predated the British mandate, the tribalization of the system occurred at the behest of the British. Indeed, through their efforts, tribalism was built into the nascent institutions of the state, and long-standing efforts to sedentarize the rural populations achieved success. In 1918, the British enshrined tribal customary law (*al-Sawani*) into a Tribal Civil and Penal Code (*Qanun Da awi al- Asha'ir*) (Hasanayn, 1967).[4] In effect, such efforts for-malized in the written laws of the state the imposition of inherently misogynous tribal laws that dominated the lives of rural women as well as now extending their application to the more progressive women of urban areas. Thus, at the same time that reform movements were stirring in Baghdad, tribal customs were codi-fied and empowered by the British-controlled state apparatus. In tribal custom, women's sexual purity was a matter of tribal honor, and tribal law not only held women responsible for any transgression, real or imagined, that might cause dis-honor, but also tightly controlled access to females through gender segregation and female seclusion. The 1918 penal code legalized such tribal customs as *al-tahjir*, *al-nahwa* and *al-hasham*. *Al-tahjir* referred to the assertion by the son of a girl's paternal uncle of his right to marry his cousin (al-Azzawi, 1937, p. 414). She had the right to refuse, although if she did, he then had the right to declare *al-nahwa* (that is, preventing her from marrying anyone else). *Al-hasham* related to the settlement of serious disputes with compensation, and by *al-hasham* women could be used in payment of compensation (Hasanayn, 1967, pp. 45–95).[5]

Facing such patriarchal impositions at the heart of the state-building enterprise, Iraqi women nonetheless propelled emancipation forward. In spite of British,

174　*People in the quagmire*

religious and tribal opposition, female education in the cities rapidly expanded—in effect reflecting the strength of reformist currents in general, and the emergence of a nascent urban-based women's movement in particular (Ismael & Ismael, 2000, pp. 186–189). Thus, between 1920–1922 and 1930–1931 the number of primary schools for girls rapidly increased from 3 to 45, and female enrollments increased from 462 to 7,046 (Daud, 1958, pp. 61, 242). In 1923, *Nadi al-Nahda al-Nisa'iyya* was founded, representing the first women's organization established to mobilize the participation of Iraqi women for the pursuit of solutions to social issues (such as female education) (Daud, 1958, p. 175). Commenting on "a women's club which is just coming into being," Gertrude Bell (1927, p. 679) recorded in her journal in 1924 that "it's the first step in female emancipation here." Through this period of British dominance, a plethora of political parties emerged—including *al-Taqaddum, al-Umma, al-Sha'b, al-Nahda* and *al-Watani*—however, none supported women's rights, nor female emancipation. Thus, formal politics under the mandatory state successfully reflected British efforts to suppress local authority, self-government and progressive efforts at reform. As noted by the social historian Khairi al-'Umari (1969, p. 143), "despite the fact that they called for constitutional freedoms and revision of treaties and agreements [with the British], they took a negative stand on social issues and ignored women's emancipation." Instead of a political debate about women's rights, al-'Umari noted that the women's issue crystallized around the issue of veiling, erupting into a heated debate in the Baghdad press in the 1920s. Papers for and against the veil contested the issue. Al-'Umari reported that, among Baghdad's major newspapers of the period, *al-Bada'i'* consistently denigrated unveiling, *al-Iraq* supported women's unveiling and *al-Alam al-Arabi* published articles by advocates of both positions. However, according to al-'Umari, the women's magazine *Laila*, founded by Bilina Hassun "for the sake of the awakening of Iraqi women" (Daud, 1958, pp. 204–205)[6] in 1923, did not adopt an explicit position on the veil, perhaps reflecting that veiling was not as significant an issue to Iraq's women as it was to the men (Weber, 2003).[7] The proponents of veiling, championed by the conservative religious establishment, argued that unveiling was tantamount to sensual invitation and dishonor of tradition. The proponents of unveiling, on the other hand, maintained that the Qur'an established that women were created equal, and that nothing in the Qur'an or Sunna called for the veil. The veil only symbolized the segregation of women and social backwardness. Further, they argued, women were the principal guides and instructors of children, and unless they were educated guides, Iraqi society would remain rigid and backward. The mandatory state's institutionalizing of patriarchal norms and the framing of debate as being one of control over women's bodies through the veil thereby obfuscated grassroots efforts at more tangible reforms. The debate reverberated, with the schism between Islamic modernizers and traditionalists foreshadowing the emergence of the secular nationalist tide that would sweep across the Arab world in the 1950s (al-'Umari, 1969, pp. 104, 110–115, 117, 132).

In March 1929, the first Arab Women's Congress was held in Cairo, and Asma' al-Zahawi, president of *Nadi al-Nahda al-Nisa'iyya*, was invited to send

Iraqi women under occupation 175

a delegation of Iraqi women to participate. In her response to the invitation, al-Zahawi was forced to decline, writing that "the government is unable to help women against the reactionary forces which flex their muscles to threaten our progress and terrorize the club so that we are unable to name even one Iraqi woman to attend the conference" (al-Bayati, 2007). This reflected, on the one hand, the strength of conservative and reactionary opposition to change. Nevertheless, on the other hand, three years later the 1932 Arab Women's Congress was held in Baghdad, reflecting the tidal force of historical change sweeping through Iraq. As across much of the formerly colonial world, women's emergence into public life was initiated with their participation in the nationalist struggle for Iraq's independence. Noting the widespread participation of Iraqi women in the 1920 revolt against British occupation, Sabihah al-Shaikh Daud, the first to chronicle the women's movement in Iraq, observed that "the 1920 revolution destroyed the major barrier which impeded women's development and laid the foundation for their march" (Daud, 1958, p. 35). However, this did not result in any substantive political gains for Iraqi women of the period. The nominally independent monarchy, established in 1921, did not accord women political rights in the first constitution of 1925.[8] Nevertheless, women's participation in civil society continued to grow and they were politically active on the issue of women's rights. This happened in spite of the opposition of the state, as indicated by the failure of some women's groups to be granted approval to form associations via Iraq's Ministry of the Interior. Noga Efrati (2004, pp. 153–173) describes the steady growth of women's social service organizations throughout the 1930s and 1940s, as well as to the emergence of two women's political organizations—the Women's League Against Nazism and Fascism founded in 1943 and the Iraqi Women's Union founded in 1945. Noting that there are only two detailed accounts of the Iraqi women's movement in that period, she observes that "these sources construct what might be called an 'official' history of the women's movement. Both often disregard continual governmental reining in of the women's movement and ignore oppositional activities" (Efrati, 2004, p. 170).

The Iraqi Communist Party, established in 1934, was the first political organization to address the issue of women, establishing "the protection of motherhood" as one of its four principal objectives (al-Juburi, 1977, p. 111). From its beginning, women were active in the Communist Party, among them Amina al-Rahhal, who represented Iraqi women in the first eastern women's congress held in Damascus in July 1930. In March 1952 the Iraqi Communist Party established the *Rabitat al-Difa An Huquq al-Mar'a al- Iraqiyya* (League for the Defense of Iraqi Women's Rights). The League's by-laws and programs "connect[ed] the struggle for the liberation of women with the struggle against imperialism and war," and established communications with the international conferences of social-democratic women (Khairi & Khairi, 1984, p. 189). The League's programs promoted democracy, national freedom and welfare for children, and the realization of women's rights. It remained an underground organization under the monarchy. To forward women's status, the Iraqi Women's Union was founded in 1945. An umbrella organization associated with reform-oriented upper-class women,

176   *People in the quagmire*

it strove to unite those women's associations and clubs that had achieved state sanction. Reflecting the degree of political mobilization of the women's movement on the eve of the Republican revolution, in March 1958 the Iraqi Women's Union petitioned the government to amend the constitution to enshrine women's political rights. Iraqi Prime Minister Nûrî al-Said accepted these demands, and on March 23, 1958 announced that "among the new principles required for the socio-political development of Iraq is the granting of political rights to Iraqi women" (Daud, 1958, p. 235). Broader support for women's emancipation emerged during this period as well. During the second half of the 1940s, five new political parties were licensed, and while three of those faded away, the two that remained— the National Democratic Party and al-Istiqlal Party—formally advocated for women's rights. Thus, by 1958, such ideas gained sufficient traction to undergird the first post-revolutionary constitution. Indeed, the 1958 constitution emerged as not merely a binding statement of non-discrimination and legal gender equality, but also the embryogenesis of women's socio-political and economic rights that continued to evolve across the subsequent constitutions of 1968 and 1970, as well as the draft constitution of 1991 (Efrati, 2012, pp. 82–84).

Qâsim and the revolution of 1958

The popular revolt of 1958, led by Brigadier-General 'Abd-ul-Karîm Qâsim, toppled the Hashemite monarchy and established a republic. Under Qâsim's regime, "the power of the tribes, clans, sectarian and feudal forces was severely challenged by progressive policies such as land reforms and legal reforms of family law, and by ideological politics" (Zubaida, 2003). Citizenship replaced sectarian affiliation (tribal, religious or ethnic) in the identity politics of the state, and a vibrant civil society emerged. Describing Iraqi society in the Qâsim period, Sami Zubaida (2003) observed:

> It was the world of government functionaries, intellectuals, teachers, journalists, artists, the modern sectors of business, traders and financiers and the professions and, in some instances, extending to sectors of the "common people" such as organised elements of the working classes who consciously linked themselves to the national and international situation.

Consistent with the relatively open social climate of the new republic, and highlighting the centrality of the issue of women's emancipation on the new regime's agenda, the Qâsim government moved swiftly. Within the first six months following the revolution, they licensed the League for the Defense of Iraqi Women's Rights, and Qâsim, now Prime Minister, gave the keynote speech at its inaugural congress on March 8, 1959. In 1959 Naziha Dulaimi, the head of the League, was appointed Minister of Municipalities, becoming the first woman in the Arab world to hold a cabinet-level position (Mamouri, 2014). In its first year, the League initiated a literacy campaign and opened 78 literacy centers; 550 volunteer teachers were recruited and 3,503 women enrolled. In addition, 111 centers for teaching sewing were opened, while roving health clinics were established to provide health care services to rural women. The League's membership soared from 20,000 in 1959 to 42,000 in 1960. More significant in terms of the entrenchment of women's rights, shortly after establishment of the new republic, a commission was appointed to create a unified code of personal status for all Iraqis to replace the Sunni–Shia specificity of family law under the monarchy. Thereby, Personal Status Law 188 (1959) established the legal framework for women's rights under the new republic. Examining the new law, J. Anderson (1960) observed that

> the Revolutionary regime brought to an end a controversy regarding the codification of the law of personal status which had ebbed and flowed in Iraq for more than twelve years; and it is significant that it produced, in the event, a code which was much more radical than anything which had previously been proposed.
>
> (p. 542)

A "statement of objects and reasons" that accompanied the code explained that one of the primary aims of the republican regime was the

> promulgation of a unified personal status law which will become the foundation on which the structure of Iraqi family in its new era will be built, and which will guarantee its stability and ensure to women their legal rights and family independence.
>
> (Qanun al-Ahwal al-Shakhsiyya wa Ta Dilatuhu
> [The Personal Status Law and its Amendments], 1978, pp. 64–65)

The new constitution implicitly recognized women's rights for political participation (Articles 3 and 7), while Article 9 read, "Iraqis are equal in access to public rights and duties according to the law; discrimination based on gender, race, language or religion is prohibited by the law." Finally, on December 29, 1958, Iraqi women were legally recognized as active political participants in society.

The significance of the Personal Status Law to women's rights was in the fundamental limitations it imposed on the subjugation of women to sectarian tribal authority. This was accomplished by replacing the role of family law based on religious sectarianism and tribal practice with a unified code of law consistent with the Islamic reformist principles of Abduh and Amin. A major step was the replacement of Sunni and Shia courts with the establishment of a Court of Personal Status to adjudicate all claims involving Iraqis, whether Muslim or not. This court had jurisdiction over marriage, divorce, legitimacy, custody, inheritance, succession and religious endowments (*Awqaf*). As a unified code applicable to all Iraqis, the 1959 Code of Personal Status established a standardized code of conduct based on citizenship, not religious affiliation. It replaced the practice of child brides with a minimum age requirement for marriage set at 18 years for both men and women. The new law required judicial permission for under-age marriages, which could only be granted at 15 years with the establishment of

178 *People in the quagmire*

fitness, physical capacity and guardian consent (unless the guardian's intention was judged unreasonable). No third party had the power of compulsion, and a marriage contract concluded by coercion was void if the union had not been consummated. No third party could prevent a person having legal capacity from marrying. Court registration without charge was obligatory and required documentation of age, identity, stipulation of the amount of dower, medical reports, etc. Polygamy was permitted only by judicial permission, mindful of the financial capacity of the man and whether there were fair circumstances to justify the case of polygamy (barrenness of the first wife, or physical disability that interfered with the demands of marital life). In this setting, a husband was obligated to maintain his wives, and a woman's right to divorce where the spouse did not fulfill the legal conditions stipulated by the marriage contract was confirmed. Furthermore, a divorced mother was entitled to custody of boys or girls until the age of 10, extendable to 15 years if it was deemed to be in the minor's best interest. Upon attaining 15 years, the minor could choose which parent to live with, or choose any other relative if such a choice appeared reasonable to the court (Qanun al-Ahwal al-Shakhsiyya wa Ta Dilatuhu [The Personal Status Law and its Amendments], 1978, pp. 3–22).

The 1959 Code of Personal Status propelled Iraqi women into the twentieth century. Before its passage, Iraq was the only part of the former Ottoman Empire which had remained "virtually untouched by legislative enactments in the sphere of the law of personal status which appeared in almost every other country in the Middle East" (Anderson, 1960, p. 543). In effect, with the promulgation of the 1959 code, Iraqi women leapfrogged from the back of the pack into the forefront in terms of the legal recognition of women's rights in the Arab world. Significantly, the new code not only reduced the yoke of tribalism, but also modified two major pillars of patriarchy in the regressive social structural framework of repression—sectarianism and feudalism:

> The radical features in the code [...] consist in the severe limitation, but not complete prohibition, of polygamy; the elimination of child marriage; the grant to a wife of the right to a judicial dissolution of marriage in a variety of different circumstances; the limitation, to some degree, of the appallingly wide scope previously accorded to pronouncements of unilateral repudiation of their wives by Muslim husbands; the insistence on documentary evidence for bequests [...]; [...] and the truly astonishing innovation that the provisions in the Civil Code application to the inheritance of land held on a form of leave from the Government [...] are now made applicable to intestate succession to property of every description.
>
> (Anderson, 1960, p. 546)

The passage of the Personal Status Code initiated the dismantling of the legal framework underpinning the feudal structure of the countryside enshrined within the 1933 Law of Rights and Duties of the Cultivators and the Tribal Disputes Code. The passage of the Agrarian Reform Law in September 1958 initiated land redistribution, placing limits on the size of land holdings and ground rents. Qâsim (1959, p. 394) proposed: "Agrarian reform by itself [...] is a revolution against injustice, tyranny and feudalism." However, according to historian Phebe Marr (1985, p. 170), "the reform law was ambitious in conception, but relatively conservative in the amount of land it left to the landlords. It left middle-level landowners in possession of their land, and although it raised the peasants' share, it did not alter their position substantially." Nevertheless, the framework of feudalism in Iraq was effectively undermined.

Women under the Ba'th regime

The Qâsim regime was overthrown by a Ba'thist-led and CIA-orchestrated coup in February 1963 that initiated a nine-month reign of terror against all progressive forces and killed an estimated 10,000 (al-'Assâf & Jawâd, 2013, pp. 27–29). "At the top of the list were leaders, cadres, and activists of the trade unions and the mass democratic organizations, including the Iraqi Women's League and the General Union of Students of the Iraqi Republic" (Zaher, 1986, p. 32). A military coup removed the Ba'th Party from power in November 1963, and for the next four years Iraq was governed by a pragmatist military regime that attempted to pander to both pan-Arab and tribal affinities. A second military coup returned the Ba'th Party to power in 1968. The party ruled Iraq for the next 35 years, largely under the dictatorship of Saddam Hussein. The Ba'th regime was characterized by its authoritarianism and its repression of all political opposition under the banner of Ba'thist ideology, which proclaimed a mission of building a national identity, a unity of purpose, and fulfillment of the Arab nation. Coupled with its incorporation of all institutions and associations into the state, the Ba'th Party's ruling clique used the state as a vehicle for their "penetration and control of all public institutions and functions, working closely with the multiple security forces" (Zubaida, 2003). While Ba'th machinations eviscerated all potential political opposition, it nonetheless maintained the status of women enshrined in the 1958 Revolution, with minor revisions to appease religious and conservative elements. Partly as a façade for progressive political credentials, partly as a recognition of the advance of women's standing within Iraqi society, and partly as a measure by which to disrupt traditional authority, the Ba'th maintained *de jure* and practical supports for women prior to the militarization, war and externally imposed sanctions era. Women affiliated with politically active partners and families, and women who themselves attempted to oppose the growing Ba'th tyranny, all suffered.

During the 1970s and through the 1980s, social policy under the Ba'th regime served to further replace tribal regulation of family functions with state regulation (J. S. Ismael, 1980, p. 243). The women's struggle for social inclusion became a primary channel for this expansion of state authority. One of the regime's first tasks was the co-option of the women's movement into the state apparatus with the creation of the General Federation of Iraqi Women (GFIW) in 1968. The GFIW absorbed all women's associations within the state apparatus and brought them under effective state control (J. S. Ismael, 1980). The regime's first decade

180   *People in the quagmire*

witnessed the aggressive expansion of female education at all levels. Female enrollment in primary education increased from 29.4 percent of total enrollment to 37.4 percent; in secondary education from 24.7 percent to 29.6 percent; and in universities, colleges and technical institutes, from 22.6 percent to 31 percent (Iraq Ministry of Planning, Central Statistical Organization, 1978, p. 206). In 1976, primary education was made compulsory for all Iraqi children ages 6 to 10 (UN CEDAW, 1998, pp. 11–12); and in 1979, the regime undertook a major campaign against illiteracy, requiring all illiterate persons between the ages of 15 and 45 to attend classes at local literacy centers. As a result, over the next decade, the literacy gap between males and females narrowed considerably (Human Rights Watch, 2003).

Couched as a matter of national development, Saddam Hussein declared, "There is no genuine revolution without genuine liberation of Women, and development of their financial and educational status" (al-'Assâf & Jawâd, 2013, p. 90). He had declared as early as 1963 that there was no popular democracy without women's public participation and that liberating women was both a democratic and human necessity, and therefore a priority, for the Iraqi national socialist revolution. In 1975, then Vice President, Saddam Hussein gave a public speech outlining the Ba'th strategic outlook, arguing:

> Human development is our revolutionary strategic objective, and women's full emancipation is not only a politico-economic necessity for achieving the objective, but also central, and integral, for Iraq's future [...] The backwardness of women, whether socio-economic or cultural, [therefore] poses a formidable obstacle to Iraq's overall development. Women's active role is both noble and paramount in Iraq's struggle against imperial forces and reactionary regimes in order to achieve unity, freedom and socialism.
>
> (al-'Assâf & Jawâd, 2013, pp. 88–90)

Similarly, there was an aggressive effort to increase the female labor force across all economic sectors. The number of females working in industry increased from 7,000 in 1968 to 20,000 in 1976. Between 1972 and 1977, the number of female personnel in government increased from 12.4 percent to 15.4 percent (Iraq Ministry of Planning, Central Statistical Organization, 1978, p. 248). According to a Human Rights Watch (2003) brief on the status of Iraqi women before the US occupation of Iraq:

> The Iraqi government also passed labor and employment laws to ensure that women were granted equal opportunities in the civil service sector, maternity benefits, and freedom from harassment in the workplace. Such laws had a direct impact on the number of women in the workforce. The fact that the government (as opposed to the private sector) was hiring women contributed to the breakdown of the traditional reluctance to allow women to work outside the home.

The Iran–Iraq War saw the expansion of women into ever-larger economic roles. Due to the enormous numbers of male casualties and the loss of men from the economy, women were encouraged to take on new roles. By necessity women became the principal food providers in addition to traditional roles overseeing child care. To encourage the participation of women in the labor force, the regime observed and enacted Labor Law 71 in 1987, which was meant to protect the status of women. The Iraqi Revolutionary Council went further with decrees taking protective responsibility of the widows of dead soldiers, providing the widow with a free plot of land, free housing, as well as social security. One decree provided financial incentives to men willing to marry widows. These decrees were intended to be included in Article 25 of the 1991 Draft Constitution (al-'Assâf & Jawâd, 2013, pp. 88–90).

While female education and labor-force participation were greatly accelerated under the Ba'th regime, state patriarchy was, in spirit, no more benign to women's emancipation than tribal patriarchy. State patriarchy under the Ba'th regime had two interrelated gender dimensions: the transition of women to the service of the state (as opposed to the family) as a prerequisite to the militarization of men in service to the state's aggrandizement. Women, while afforded opportunities outside the home, were still the subject of exploitation as a tool in maintaining the status quo. As explained in a United Nations Development Fund for Women (UNIFEM) (2006) gender profile on Iraq, "many of the [regime's] progressive reforms were instituted [...] because women were needed to maintain civil society while the men were at war." The nature of the state's patriarchy was revealed in October 1982 when the Minister of Defense ordered the arrest and detention of the wives and children of deserters (Omar, 1994, p. 66). Recurrent accounts of incidents reported to the UN Commission on Human Rights (1992) shed further light on the malevolent nature of state patriarchy under the Ba'th regime, maintaining:

> Security personnel would sometimes rape a young woman in order to later use her as an informant under the threat that her non-compliance would result in the revelation of her rape [...] Other women were reportedly raped simply as an act of insult or vengeance directed against families.
>
> (pp. 24–25)

The growth of workforce participation and female involvement in social and economic life outside the home, while robust, did not mirror the experience of other societies. Iraqi sociologist Lâhây Abdul-Ḥussain (2006), in her examination of the statistical record, measured the impact of the Iran–Iraq War on women in education and their work outside the home between 1980 and 1988. She found that, while Ba'thist development did help expand women's opportunities in terms of education, work and occupations, the Iran–Iraq War pushed women heavily toward more segregated work opportunities. Therefore, gender segregation became a concrete reality in the formal workplace. For example, the feminization of elementary school teacher and secretarial jobs compared with the other

182 *People in the quagmire*

occupations became apparent. This was in contrast to the experience of women in many countries experiencing total war, where the opportunity to advance was more meritocratic—even if such opportunities were diminished as gender norms returned following the conflict (Abdul-Hussain, 2006, pp. 135–164).

Under the sanctions regime

With the conclusion of the Iran–Iraq War in 1988, followed by Iraq's invasion of Kuwait in 1990, the imposition of a rigorous regime of international sanctions was imposed against Iraq and its people. Initiated on August 6, 1990, four days after Iraq's invasion of Kuwait, they were maintained on imports and exports by the UN Security Council until May 22, 2003, following the US occupation of Iraq in March 2003. Those sanctions, which governed petroleum revenues and state assets frozen abroad in 1990, were not lifted until December 2010. The severe deprivations suffered by the Iraqi population under the sanctions regime, particularly the vulnerable—women, children, the elderly and infirm—are well documented (al-'Assâf & Jawâd, 2013, pp. 38–57). The sanctions regime, following on the devastation of Iraq's infrastructure during the US-led bombardment of 1991, saw the rapid devastation of Iraqi social life. In short order, the deprivations forced 55 percent of women to sell their property, 40 percent to incur onerous debts, and for many to turn to begging in the street. From 1990 through 1994, miscarriages and anemia in women increased by 265 percent, largely due to medical supplies being quarantined under sanctions. Alarmingly, over the course of the sanctions decade, female illiteracy rose to 45 percent (al-'Assâf & Jawâd, 2013, pp. 95–96). To situate this dramatic deterioration and place it in the context of just how far Iraqi women had come compared to their sisters across the region, Iraqi women constituted 22 percent of the workforce in 1994, while it was 7 percent in Saudi Arabia and Qatar, 9 percent in the UAE, 11 percent in Jordan and 18 percent in Syria. Under the grim impact of the sanctions, the Iraqi regime improvised a policy of funding small business enterprises for women. The 2002 UN Human Development Report underscored female participation at elite levels, as women held 20 percent of the seats in the Iraqi parliament, compared to a total of 3.5 percent in all Arab countries combined (al-'Assâf & Jawâd, 2013, pp. 92–108).

What needs emphasis, however, is the fact that the imposition of sanctions following the Iraqi invasion of Kuwait severely reduced state oil revenue. As virtually the entire economy and society were rendered directly dependent on state oil revenue as a result of the regime's transformation of Iraq into a consumer society dependent on foreign imports, the population's standard of living declined precipitously under sanctions. The consumer market and public services infrastructure systematically built up by the Ba'th regime over the 1970s and 1980s deteriorated rapidly, and gender disparities re-emerged in education and health. In addition, in its efforts to maintain social control by aligning itself with tribal sheikhs, the regime rehabilitated tribal tradition (Baram, 1997), greatly undermining women's position in society (UNIFEM, 2006).[9]

In education, a United Nations Educational, Scientific and Cultural Organization (UNESCO) (2003) report noted that, "before 1990, the educational system in Iraq was one of the best in the region, both from the point of view of access to education and quality." However, with the imposition of sanctions, "the educational system in the Centre/South deteriorated to a great extent" (UNESCO, 2003, p. 27). While female enrollment in primary education was virtually universal before 1990, the report noted that, by the time of the occupation, 31 percent of female children (compared to 17 percent of male children) did not attend school (UNESCO, 2003, p. 57). Before the imposition of sanctions, over 80 percent of Iraqi women were literate as a result of the national literacy campaign initiated in the late 1970s. However, between 1985 and 1995, the female illiteracy rate went from 8 percent to 45 percent,[10] and the UNIFEM (2006) gender profile on Iraq noted that "the UNDP rated Iraq 126/174 on the 2002 Gender Development Index, and its Human Development Report 2002 found Iraq 'far behind' in the targets to eliminate gender disparity at all levels of education."

Before sanctions, Iraq had one of the best health care systems in the Middle East, both in terms of access and quality of care. The population enjoyed health conditions that were high by the standards of middle-income countries, and accordingly the incidence of malnutrition was uncommon. However, health and health care rapidly deteriorated under the impact of sanctions, and by 1997 "general malnutrition (underweight for age) occurred in 24.7 percent of children under five years" (WHO, 2003) and the mortality rate for children under 5 years went from 56 deaths per 1,000 live births before sanctions to 131 deaths per 1,000 live births in the 1994–1999 period (UNICEF, 1999).[11] The impact on women's health was reflected in a tripling of the number of women's deaths during pregnancy and childbirth and in the rise of miscarriages. The impact of poor nutrition on women was reflected in the rise of anemia among women and low birthweight babies (UNFPA, 2003). The overall toll of the sanctions on women's health is reflected in changes in women's life expectancy at birth. Between 1950 and 1990, the life expectancy of Iraqi women steadily increased from 47.9 to 65.2 years; in the 1990–2000 period, it declined to 60.8 years (Suzuki, 2005).

A direct impact of the Ba'th regime's rehabilitation of tribal traditions on women was the passage of the Iraqi Penal Code in 1990 (IRIN, 2003). In Article 111, men were exempted from prosecution and punishment for "honor killing" a female relative, and an estimated 4,000 women were murdered under the guise of "honor killing" between 1990 and 2003.[12] Article 41 of the 1990 penal code legalized wife abuse, "providing for a woman to be punished with 80 lashes of the whip by her husband if she asks for too much" (IRIN, 2003). Prostitution was made punishable with beheading by decree of the Revolutionary Command Council. The total number beheaded is unknown, but in the period from June 2000 to April 2001, Human Rights Alliance, France, estimated that 130 women were beheaded based on "the various figures that have been [provided] and from the numerous pieces of evidence we have been able to gather directly" (Human Rights Alliance, France, 2002).

184 *People in the quagmire*

US occupation and neo-feudal bondage

After 13 years of debilitating international sanctions that pauperized Iraq's population and destroyed its socio-economic infrastructure, the US invaded and occupied Iraq in April 2003 (Ismael & Ismael, 2004). The ostensible basis for American aggression against a sovereign state was tied to fallacious if not overtly falsified assertions. In the words of Jeremy Salt (2008):

> The invasion of Iraq in 2003 was preceded by a propaganda campaign monumental in its deceit and dishonesty [...] an agglomeration of assertions and suppositions buttressed by forged documents and wild claims that had no basis in intelligence or fact. Over the past two centuries, on occasions and in places, too numerous to count, civilisation, western values and democracy have been the mask and brute force the true face.
>
> (pp. 317, 357)

Like the British occupation of Iraq in 1917, in October 2003 the international community legitimated the invasion and occupation after the fact with UNSC Resolution 1511. It essentially gave the US mandatory powers over Iraq by legitimating the role and authority of the Governing Council of Iraq (established by the US occupation). The US-led invasion was an exercise of embodied "creative destruction."[13] Large-scale destruction of infrastructure, mass murder and the comprehensive dismantling of state institutions that left only chaos allowed occupation forces to orient the new political order towards its own interests while leaving ordinary Iraqis helpless in facing daily suffering, lawlessness and insecurity (al-'Assâf & Jawâd, 2013, pp. 122–189). Like Britain a century prior, the US aligned itself with indigenous and regional reactionary forces. In the context of Britain's occupation in the first quarter of the twentieth century, these were tribal and feudal forces advocating maintenance of the status quo social relations. In the twenty-first-century context of US occupation, these were neo-tribal (reinvigorated tribal forces) and neo-feudal forces (military–corporate forces). To examine the nature of the occupation's impact on Iraqi women, the concepts of neo-tribal and neo-feudal forces will be explored.

Amatzia Baram (1997) provided an analysis of Saddam Hussein's tribal policies, arising during and in response to the sanctions. The totalizing impact sanctions generated forced the regime to revisit commitments to gender norms and the benefits accrued to their rule emerging from broader societal acceptance of the regime. Simply, sanctions afforded the clique around Saddam Hussein the opportunity to deepen their control over the population. Thus, traditional authority—long a challenge to the Iraqi state—was not supported, but rather a new class of political actor trussed up with a veneer of tribal authority. Baram (1997) distinguishes neo-tribalism from tribalism because

> the context of many tribal phenomena promoted by the Ba'th was a far cry from the traditional context of tribal behavior and norms. When a highly

centralized regime makes use of tribal values to reimpose its full control over its population, what emerges is something new and very different from the traditional set of values.

(p. 4)

Neo-feudalism should also be understood as a "far cry" from traditional European understandings of feudalism. It has been used as a heuristic concept to describe the form of socio-economic organization emerging in the globalized world order. According to Graham and Luke (2005), following the reorientation of society under sanctions, the post-2003 US occupation of Iraq provides a case illustration of "neo-feudal corporatism"—an emerging global system ruled by a superpower/corporate military complex. Using the global system construct of neo-feudal corporatism, the structure of neo-feudalism in Iraq may be inferred by analogy with historical feudalism (Graham & Luke, 2005, pp. 11–39). In granting the US administrative and legal authority over Iraq, the UN played a role equivalent to the church in the feudal structure, with Iraq as the fiefdom and the US the presumed vassal to the normative power of international law and the international community's civilizing mission. Like the feudal system of the Middle Ages, the neo-feudal corporate model is based on "the social logic of a permanent arms economy" (Graham & Luke, 2005). While the formal legal–military obligations between lord, vassal and fief formed the basis of feudalism, and by analogy the basis of neo-feudalism, the difference between tenth- and twenty-first-century contexts would reasonably suggest that their formal character is significantly different in the contemporary global system. The formal character is not the issue here, however. The issue here is the role and status of women in a neo-feudal Iraq created by such a polity.

To examine the occupation's impact on Iraqi women, the neo-feudal metaphor may be utilized to focus on the intersection of gender with actors, institutions and culture in the neo-feudal order, a global system that is international in its nature and scope. The superpower/corporate military complex sits at the apex of the order, with the UN functioning as a clearing house for the administration and legitimation of the global power politics engaged in by the former. The intersection of gender with the actors and institutions in the global system is manifested in the implicit valorization of the occupation, inherent in the UN's legalization of the Anglo-American exercise of power in Iraq (UNSC, 2003). In effect, it gave international legitimacy to the culture of war blatantly promoted in the Bush Administration's Project for the New American Century (T. Y. Ismael, 2007). Moreover, the Security Council resolution gave cultural legitimacy not only to the business of war; it also gave international administrative and legal legitimacy to the makers of war in Iraq—the US military and foreign contractors on the ground in Iraq.[14] The use of foreign contractors, with the legal imprimatur of the UN, is particularly problematic as "NGOs and the media have shown how PMSCs [private military and security companies] have committed serious human rights abuses, killed or injured innocent civilians, engaged in financial malfeasance and committed many other breaches of the law," while operating within an ill-defined set of legal norms and customs (Pingeot,

186 *People in the quagmire*

2012). Beginning with the TAL, issued by US-appointed viceroy Paul Bremer, and the operationalization of change through the CPA, externally driven social engineering with the adoption of "democracy" and a new constitutional regime were imposed on Iraq. It is at this level that the intersection of gender with institutions, actors and culture is manifest in the everyday life of Iraqi women in terms of the social construction of sex roles.

Like the feudal order, the culture of neo-feudalism is based on the valorization of war,[15] and the social construction of masculinity around the warrior role model—encompassing attributes of virility, aggressiveness and bravery (Braudy, 2003). Femininity is constructed in counterpoint to the masculine warrior role model and encompasses attributes of both *femme fatale* (Dijkstra, 1988) and victim.[16] In either case, the feminine role is objectified against the warrior role model's attributes of virility and aggressiveness and, in the context of war, represents an object for either sexual exploitation or victimization. The social construction of masculinity and femininity in this context presents a script for sexual violence, and this is what has in fact happened to Iraqi women under the occupation. In the first year of the occupation, Human Rights Watch (2003) reported:

> The insecurity and fear of sexual violence or abduction is keeping them [girls and women] in their homes, out of schools, and away from work and looking for employment. The failure of the occupying power to protect women and girls from violence, and redress it when it occurs, has both immediate and long-term negative implications for the safety of women and girls and for their participation in post-war life in Iraq.

In June 2005, Hana Ibrahim (2006), an Iraqi journalist, reported at a global forum organized by the World Tribunal on Iraq, and held in Istanbul, that sexual violence against Iraqi women has been endemic since the occupation: "From the day that the occupation started in Iraq they [women] were kidnapped, raped and even taken to other countries in order to have them work in [global sex trade] networks." A number of reports substantiate these observations, including the so-called Taguba Report, an official US Department of Defense report of 2004, which confirmed that guards at Abu Ghraib had videotaped and photographed naked female detainees (800th Military Police Brigade, 2004, p. 16); the US Department of State's June 2005 report on the trafficking of persons detailed that

> Iraq is a country of origin for women and girls trafficked to Yemen, Syria, Jordan and Gulf countries for the purposes of sexual and labor exploitation […] there are thousands of Iraqi women working in prostitution [in Syria and Yemen] […] under conditions that constitute severe forms of trafficking in persons.
>
> (p. 232)

In a brief presented to the United Nations Commission on Human Rights in March 2005, the Association of Humanitarian Lawyers reported on the documented cases of the illegal detention, rape and sexual violation of Iraqi female detainees, concluding that "these and other incidents are being covered up" and that "the cover-up by the Bush Administration appears to include the silencing of victims" (McNutt, 2005). Amal Kadham Swadi, an Iraqi attorney representing women detainees, reported that "sexualized violence and abuse committed by US troops goes far beyond a few isolated cases" (Harding, 2004). Examining the record of sexual terrorism in Iraq, historian and journalist Ruth Rosen concluded: "Amid the daily explosions and gunfire that make the papers is a wave of sexual terrorism, whose exact dimensions we have no way of knowing, and that no one here notices, unleashed by the Bush administration" (Engelhardt, 2006).

The climate of sexual terrorism that was unleashed by the invasion and occupation of Iraq was institutionalized in the process of political reconstruction that the US initiated in Iraq (T. Y. Ismael, 2007, pp. 43–53). From the beginning, the process was founded on the political empowerment of sectarian religious forces. The rationale for this was laid out in 1999 in a book by David Wurmser, an affiliate of key proponents of the Iraq invasion in the Bush Administration and Vice President Dick Cheney's Middle East adviser after the invasion. In *Tyranny's Ally: America's failure to defeat Saddam Hussein*, Wurmser argued that Iraqi Shi'ites could be used to control Iraq by offering them the opportunity to enhance their power through control of the state. However sanctimonious the plan, as noted by investigative journalist Gareth Porter (2007), the planners had not anticipated

> the Sunnis mounting an effective resistance instead of rolling over. Nor had they anticipated that Shi'ite clerics of Iraq would demand national elections and throw their support behind the militant Shi'ite parties, SCIRI and Da'wa, which had returned from exile in Iran in the wake of the US overthrow of Hussein.

Thus, in the process of its efforts to politically reconstruct Iraq, the US fragmented Iraq into ethnic zones (Arab and Kurdish) and delivered the façade of governance of the Arab area into the hands of sectarian fundamentalist religious elements, while in the Kurdish area, into the hands of chauvinistic Kurdish tribal elements (Hersh, 2007; Longley, 2006). Assessing the results of the 2005 elections in Iraq, the International Crisis Group (2006) report on Iraq noted that

> 2005 will be remembered as the year Iraq's latent sectarianism took wings, permeating the political discourse and precipitating incidents of appalling violence and sectarian "cleansing." The elections that bracketed the year, in January and December, underscored the newly acquired prominence of religion, perhaps the most significant development since the regime's ouster. With mosques turned into party headquarters and clerics outfitting themselves as politicians, Iraqis searching for leadership and stability in profoundly uncertain times essentially turned the elections into confessional exercises.

188 *People in the quagmire*

In this context, the destruction of women's socio-economic existence was hidden behind the façade of electoral representation provided in the new constitutional order. The election installed a National Assembly charged with drafting a new constitution, and in October 2005, under intense pressure from the US, a referendum was held and the constitution adopted in spite of bitter sectarian disagreements within the National Assembly and denunciation outside it from human rights advocates and secularists. The constitution, in effect, delivered women into the hands of sectarian religious fundamentalism. Section 1 invoked the primacy of religious law, establishing Islam as "the official religion of the state" in Article 2, and specifying that "no law may be passed that contradicts the undisputed rules of Islam." Article 39 institutionalized a sectarian personal-status law in providing that Iraqis are "free in their commitment to their personal status according to their religions, sects, beliefs, or choices." Further establishing sectarianism and its economic foundations in the law of the land, Article 41 guaranteed that "the sects are free in the [...] management of the endowments [*Awqaf*], its affairs and its religious institutions" (Iraqi Constitution, 2005; see Appendix 3). These articles necessarily undermine Article 14 of the constitution, which states that "Iraqis are equal before the law without discrimination based on gender" by setting the legal grounds for inequality (NGO Coalition of CEDAW Shadow Report, 2014, p. 3).

Thus, tribal chauvinism and religious sectarianism returned to Iraq, catapulting Iraqi women back to the nineteenth century in terms of rights and freedoms, and into the Middle Ages in terms of security and welfare. The constitution effectively institutionalized sectarianism as the basis of governance in Iraq, and gave sectarian clergy a free hand in restoring the repressive cultural conditions of women discussed above. According to Ta'mim al-'Azawi, an Iraqi lawyer and activist, with the implementation of Article 41 of the constitution:

> We will certainly face [...] (1) the loss of Law 188 of 1959 [the Personal Status Code] and its amendments, and all that the code contained of Iraqi women's rights and privileges, as well as the legal precedents established by it; and (2) the state's relinquishment of [its] role in the determination of personal rights to the religious, sectarian and tribal authorities.
>
> (Al-Mada, 2007)

Al-'Azawi maintained that the provision of primacy given to religious law in Article 2 and to sectarian traditions and practices in the determination of personal status provided in Article 39 of the constitution constitutes an inherent contradiction with Article 16 of the constitution which guarantees equality for all citizens before the law. To illustrate her argument, she pointed to Article 44 of the constitution, which guarantees Iraqis the right to freedom of travel, as already contradicting the legal restrictions of the travel of women under 50 who require the accompaniment of an adult male relative for internal travel, and the permission of an adult male guardian (father or husband) to obtain a passport (Al-Mada, 2007). As expressed by an Iraqi woman at a conference on supporting democracy held in Erbil between April 10 and 12, 2007: "We have no other choice but to confront the religious sectarians [...] They carry weapons and we only have our words. True religion is with us and not with them. If we do not face up to them, they will turn us into concubines" (al-Khaiyyun, 2007). She is an activist from the Middle Euphrates region and received numerous death threats from sectarian groups in control of her area because she dared to go to the villages and talk to women on the dangers encompassed in the abolition of the 1959 personal status law and the enactment of Article 41 in the new constitution. She argued: "If we submit, we sacrifice both our world and our religion" (al-Khaiyyun, 2007).

Article 39 of the constitution introduced the fragmentation of personal status by religious sect. In an effort to resolve this, a new bill was introduced in 2013, the Ja'afri Personal Status Law, and was approved by the cabinet on February 25, 2014 and forwarded to parliament for ratification (Shafaaq News, 2014). Human Rights Watch (2014b) has called the bill "a disastrous and discriminatory step backward for Iraq's women and girls. This personal status law would only entrench Iraq's divisions while the government claims to support equal rights for all." According to Article 16, a boy's puberty occurs at 15 years of age, and a girl's at 9, making her legally fit for marriage (Mamouri, 2014).[17] Article 53 of the Ja'afri bill requires a father's consent to the marriage of his daughter. Article 62 allows a man to have up to four wives. Article 63 prevents a Muslim woman from marrying a non-Muslim man, and also allows for a Muslim man to easily annul a marriage with a non-Muslim woman. Article 74 can deprive grandchildren of their parents' inheritance—allowing uncles to receive it for themselves; the Ja'afri bill leaves the divorced woman without shelter/residence, contrary to the protections of a woman's basic needs guaranteed in the existing personal status laws. Article 101-1 deprives a woman of her right to travel without a male relative's consent. Article 117 favors the male partner's reception of child custody in cases of divorce or separation. Article 124 prohibits the adoption of an orphan, thus undermining Juvenile Law 76 (1983). Physical abandonment by the husband does not constitute a reason for divorce so long as the man is alive, according to Article 162. And according to Article 108, a woman will forfeit any right to alimony if she declines the sexual demands of her husband.

According to a survey of Iraqi notables (412 journalists, educators, civil society leaders and members of parliament) by the Iraqi Research Center for Information and Development, 76 percent of respondents believe the Ja'afri laws would negatively affect Iraqi society, while 79 percent believed they were unconstitutional. In addition, 84 percent believed it would intensify sectarian tensions within Iraq, undermining the national identity (Kitabat, 2014). Even the UN's representative to Iraq, Nickolay Mladenov, condemned the legislation, saying that it "risks constitutionally protected rights for women and international commitment" (al-Salhy, 2014).

The Ministry of Women's Affairs, headed by Ibtehal Qasid al-Zaidi in 2013, like many in the Iraqi parliament, believes that "men must be the guardians of women, and there is no equality of sexes" (al-Shaykhaili, 2012). Likewise, Iraq's *National Strategy to Combat Violence Against Women* was ratified in 2013 but was never allocated a budget or the necessary resources to perform its mandate.

190 *People in the quagmire*

In light of this, it is not surprising that political attitudes towards women's rights have declined to the point that the proposed Ja'afri personal status law was introduced to begin with, while the *Draft Law on Protection from Domestic Violence* (completed in October 2012) has been indefinitely delayed by the executive (NGO Coalition of CEDAW Shadow Report, 2014, p. 5). Even the Iraqi Women's Foundation, one of the only locally organized NGOs for women's rights in Iraq, was forced to cease operations in 2011 "due to a lack of finances and a complete lack of interest in its legal and social output by the concerned governmental agencies" (Mamouri, 2014).[18]

Since the Anglo-American invasion, thousands of Iraqi women have been detained illegally by Iraqi authorities who "have exploited vague provisions in the Anti-Terrorism Law of 2005 to settle personal or political scores—detaining, charging, and trying women based on their association to a particular individual, tribe, or sect" (Human Rights Watch, 2014a). Contrary to Bremer's assertion that women no longer need to worry about "being taken to rape rooms," and Bush affirming "women are no longer carried to torture chambers and rape rooms" (Saletan, 2004), nothing can be further from the truth. From the appalling rape and murder of 14-year-old Abeer Qassim al-Janabi by US forces in 2006 (NGO Coalition of CEDAW Shadow Report, 2014, p. 9), to the "Iraqi security forces and officials," who have now taken the reins, they all "act as if brutally abusing women will make the country safer," according to Joe Stork, a director at Human Rights Watch (Human Rights Watch, 2014a). These victims are most often women targeted only by association to male relatives who have caught the state's anger. In January 2013 al-Mâlikî promised to finally release women who had judicial orders of release as a sign of good will accompanying a promise to reform the criminal justice system; both promises remained unfulfilled as of 2014, fueling the protest movement that preceded the Fallujah crisis of 2014. Women are still arrested *en masse* or at random in areas that are vocal in their disapproval of al-Mâlikî's regime. According to Human Rights Watch (2014a), not even a single judge has opened an inquiry into abuse, despite some women being left visibly and permanently disabled from the torture to which they have been subjected.

Conclusion

Over the course of the twentieth century, Iraqi women struggled for emancipation from the cruel exercise of power that the forces of tribalism, feudalism and sectarianism exercised over their security and welfare. Their story teaches us important lessons about the nature of women's struggle globally. The history of Iraqi women's struggle in the first quarter of the twentieth century revealed the nature of the accord struck by tribal and feudal forces with imperialism as Iraq passed from political suzerainty under Ottoman imperial tutelage to a dependency occupied by British imperial power. This demonstrated the interconnection between women's oppression, national liberation and human rights. In the second half of the twentieth century, the emancipation of women leapt forward as a process integral to the political and economic restructuring initiated by the Qâsim regime, breaking with the colonial heritage imposed by the British mandate and weakening the control of tribal and feudal power over the people's security and welfare. The experience of Iraqi women under the dictatorial Ba'th regime revealed that women's struggle for emancipation is a matter of human rights, not just gender rights. While the Ba'th regime fostered a dramatic rise in women's education and workforce participation, the regime also instituted a tyrannical dictatorship that perpetrated major human rights abuses against men and women. The sanctions regime imposed on Iraq in the final decade of the century revealed the unspoken alliance between international and national tyranny. The impact of sanctions on Iraqi women was part and parcel of the cruel exercise of power at the national and international levels, robbing the Iraqi population of security.

The neo-feudal metaphor was introduced to describe the impact of the occupation on Iraqi women. It revealed the pattern beneath the litany of terror that has disfigured everyday life in Iraq under occupation by examining the intersection of gender across different levels of interaction and the actors, institutions and cultures they encompass. The metaphor revealed, on the one hand, the juxtaposition of the occupation with militarism and sectarianism; and on the other, the culture of sexual terrorism that the juxtaposition sustains. Now, more than a decade after the Anglo-American invasion and occupation, it is without question that women have been disproportionately affected by the violence that befell almost all Iraqis. Thousands of women have been left widowed and vulnerable to predation, while domestic abuse and prostitution have escalated. Polls have indicated that Iraqi women see little difference in the political leaders that came to power with American support. The increasing neo-tribalism associated with the latter period of Saddam Hussein's regime is dwarfed by the suffocating social conservatism that now prevents female participation in public life.[19] Iraqi women are on the front line of women's struggle against the global forces of oppression and sexual terrorism and, as the rights of women are inseparable from human rights, their struggle is a universal struggle.

Notes

1 *Sdah*: males accepted as descendants of the Islamic Prophet Muhammad through his grandsons, Hassan and Husayn, who were the sons of his daughter Fatima Zahra and his cousin and son-in-law Ali ibn Abi Talib.
2 On October 14, 1911, an institute for Jewish girls was opened; on January 25, 1913, the Committee on Union and Progress established the third institute for Muslim girls.
3 Reflecting this, between 1905 and 1930, the Bedouin population of Iraq decreased from 17 percent to 7 percent, while the rural population increased from 59 percent to 68 percent—although the urban population only increased from 24 percent to 25 percent.
4 In February 1916 the British occupying forces applied the "Tribal Criminal and Civil Disputes Regulations of India" to Iraq. On July 27, 1918, a tribal penal code was enacted under the name of *Qanun Da awi al- Asha'ir* (Tribal Civil and Penal Code).
5 These customs, while illegal, have become more frequently practiced since 2003 (Hussain, 2014).

192 *People in the quagmire*

6 According to Daud (1958), the journal was called *Laila* in commemoration of a line from a poem by Jamil Sidqi al-Zahawi: "I am in love with Laila, and Laila is my homeland. And I shall devote all my life to her love till I die."

7 In examining the issue of veiling in the international feminist movement, Charlotte Weber's (2003) dissertation documents that it was a more significant issue to men than women in the struggle for liberation.

8 This constitution would remain in effect through the 1958 Iraqi revolution.

9 The 1990 penal code exempted men from punishment for honor killings and other abuses of women with tribal origins, for example.

10 The year 1985 is the benchmark because of the lack of a record for literacy levels immediately preceding the Persian Gulf War. Suffice to say that, prior to the Gulf War, Iraq was at the forefront of education in the region (UNESCO, 2005, p. iii).

11 See Chapter 6 for more on malnutrition; Table 6.2 shows mortality rates based on the 1998 UNICEF report.

12 There have been 49 honor killings reported in the first months of 2014; however, these crimes are underreported (Quraishi, 2014).

13 See Wikipedia's page on creative destruction (http://en.wikipedia.org/wiki/Creative_destruction) for a concise explanation of Joseph Schumpeter's concept.

14 For more on the role of mercenaries/private security contractors in Iraq see Chandrasekaran (2006), Pingeot (2012), Silverstein & Burton-Rose (2001) and Singer (2003).

15 See Barkawi (2004, pp. 115–147) and Holsinger (1999) for more on the cultural valorization of war.

16 The woman as a victim has been addressed in one way or another in feminist theories. See Butler (1999), Friedan (1963) and Hooks (1999).

17 According to the Minister of Planning, Ali Shukri, 11 percent of marriages performed in Iraq are to underage girls. In March 2014 alone, six of these girls had died as a result of abuse or complications during pregnancy, while 200 have been divorced (making them social pariahs) because of their "poor culinary and sexual skill." Conditions for young brides in the KRG are no better; the most recent (May 22, 2014) atrocity involved the "brutal murder" of a 15-year-old girl at the hands of her 45-year-old husband after she asked for a divorce (Al-Mada, 2014).

18 With the declining conditions they face, many women in Iraq, and in particular Kurdistan, have turned to suicide by self-immolation, a culturally significant form of protest. Despite the many laws that now exist to protect women and promote their rights, support and implementation of these laws remain virtually non-existent across the country. Like honor killings, the number of women who self-immolate is underreported, yet the reported incidences have surpassed 1,000 in the decade since the fall of Saddam Hussein (Stoter, 2013).

19 Once at the vanguard of women's rights in the region, Iraq now ranks 21st out of 22 Arab states in a poll of 336 gender experts published by the Thomson Reuters Foundation (2013).

References

800th Military Police Brigade. (2004). *Article 15-6 Investigation.* Retrieved January 12, 2014, from National Public Radio: www.npr.org/iraq/2004/prison_abuse_report.pdf

Abdul-Ḥussain, L. (2006). *Athar Al-Tanmiyah wa Al-Ḥarb ʿAlâ Al-Nisâʾ fî Al-ʿIrâq: 1968–1988.* Baghdad: Dâr Al-Shuʾûn Al-Thaqâfiyyah Al-ʿÂmmah.

al-Ani, S. M. (1972). Al-Marʾa fi al-Gissa al-Iraqiyya [Women in the Iraqi Story]. In *Silsilat Al-Kutub Al-Haditha.* Baghdad: Iraqi Ministry of Public Information.

al-'Assâf, S. I., & Jawâd, S. N. (2013). *Al-Mar'ah Al-'Irâqiyyah bayna Al-Iḥtilâl Al-Amrîkî wa Mabda' Al-Tadakhkhul Al-Insânî*. Amman: Jinân Al-Jinân.

al-Azzawi, A. (1937). *Asha'ir al-Iraq [Iraq's Tribes]*. Baghdad: Baghdad Press.

al-Bayati, A. G. (2007, March 1). *Al-Haraka al-Nisawiyya al-Iraqiyya [The Iraqi Feminist Movement]*. Retrieved March 2, 2007, from Elaph: www.elaph.com

al-Juburi, A. G. (1977). *Al-Ahzab wa al-Jam Iyyat al-Siyasiyya fi Alqutr al-Iraqi, 1908–1985 [Political Parties and Groups in Iraq, 1908–1985]*. Baghdad: author.

al-Khaiyyun, R. (2007, April 20). Al-Iraq: Al-Intihariyyun Sinfan [Iraq: Two Types of Suicides]. *Al-Sharq al-Awsat*.

Al-Mada. (2007, April 20). Al-Waqi al-Qanun lil Mar'a al-Iraqiyya [The Legal Status of the Iraqi Woman]. *Al-Mada Newspaper*.

Al-Mada. (2014, June 3). [*Cleric Arrested for Marriage of Underage Girl Following Her Murder*]. Retrieved June 4, 2014, from *Al-Mada Newspaper*: www.almadapaper.net/ar/ news/465545/اعتقال-رجل-الدين-الذي-عرى-عقد-جواز-الفت

al-Salhy, S. (2014, March 8). *Iraqi Women Protest Against Proposed Islamic Law in Iraq*. Retrieved March 8, 2014, from Reuters: www.reuters.com/article/2014/03/08/ us-iraq-women-islam-idUSBREA270NR20140308

al-Shaykhaili, S. (2012, January 26). [*To the Issue of Arab Women and Legislation*]. Retrieved March 24, 2014, from Gender Clearinghouse: www.genderclearinghouse. org/upload/Assets/Documents/pdf/ibtihel.pdf

al-'Umari, K. (1969). *Hikayat Siyasiyya min Tarikh al-Iraq al-Hadith [Political Stories from the Modern History of Iraq]*. Egypt: Dar al-Hilal.

al-Zahir, A. R. (1946). *Al-Iqta wa al-Diwan fi al-Iraq [Feudalism and Bureaucracy in Iraq]*. Cairo: Al-Saada Press.

Anderson, J. N. (1960). A Law of Personal Status for Iraq. *The International and Comparative Law Quarterly, 9*(4), 542–563.

Ashby, R., & Ohrn, D. G. (1995). *Herstory: Women who changed the world*. New York: Viking.

Baram, A. (1997). Neo-Tribalism in Iraq: Saddam Hussein's tribal policies, 1991–1996. *International Journal of Middle East Studies, 29*(1), 1–31.

Barkawi, T. (2004). Globalization, Culture, and War: On the popular mediation of small wars. *Cultural Critique, 58*(58), 115–147.

Batatu, H. (1978). *The Old Social Classes and the Revolutionary Movements in Iraq*. Princeton: Princeton University Press.

Bell, G. (1927). *The Letters of Gertrude Bell* (Vol. II). London: Ernest Benn Ltd.

Braudy, L. (2003). *From Chivalry to Terrorism: War and the changing nature of masculinity*. New York: Alfred A. Knopf.

Butler, J. (1999). *Gender Trouble: Feminism and the subversion of identity*. London: Routledge.

Chandrasekaran, R. (2006). *Imperial Life in the Emerald City: Inside Iraq's Green Zone*. New York: Alfred A. Knopf.

Daud, S. a.-S. (1958). *Awwal al-Tariq lil Nahda al-Nisa'iyya fi al-Iraq [The Beginning of the Feminist Renaissance in Iraq]*. Baghdad: Matba at al-Rabitah.

Dijkstra, B. (1988). *Evil Sisters: The threat of female sexuality in twentieth-century culture*. New York: Henry Holt and Company, Inc.

Efrati, N. (2004). The Other "Awakening" in Iraq: The women's movement in the first half of the twentieth century. *British Journal of Middle Eastern Studies, 31*(2), 153–173.

Efrati, N. (2012). *Women in Iraq*. Sussex: Columbia University Press.

194 *People in the quagmire*

Engelhardt, T. (2006, July 13). *Tomgram: Ruth Rosen on sexual terrorism and Iraqi women*. Retrieved April 15, 2007, from TomDispatch: www.tomdispatch.com/index. mhtml?pid=101034

Friedan, B. (1963). *The Feminist Mystique*. New York: Norton.

Goodman, L. (ed.). (1996). *Literature and Gender*. New York: Routledge.

Graham, P., & Luke, A. (2005). The Language of Neofeudal Corporatism and the War on Iraq. *Journal of Language and Politics, 4*(1), 11–39.

Harding, L. (2004, May 20). The Other Prisoners. *The Guardian (UK)*.

Hasan, M. S. (1966). *Dirasat fi al-Igtis ad al-Iraqi* [*Studies in the Iraqi Economy*]. Beirut: Dar al-Tali a.

Hasanayn, M. M. (1967). *Nidham al-Mas'ouliya 'ind al-Asha'ir al-Iraqiya al-Arabiya al-mu Asiria* [*The Accountability Conventions of Contemporary Iraqi Tribes*]. Cairo: Al-Istiqlal al-Kubra Press.

Hersh, S. M. (2007, April 16). Get Out the Vote: Did Washington try to manipulate Iraq's election? *The New Yorker*.

Holsinger, P. M. (1999). *War and American Popular Culture: A historical encyclopaedia*. Westport: Greenwood Press.

Hooks, B. (1999). *Feminist Theory: From margin to center*. Cambridge: South End Press.

Human Rights Alliance, France. (2002). *Iraq: An intolerable, forgotten and unpunished repression*. Retrieved March 4, 2007, from International Federation for Human Rights (FIDH): https://www.fidh.org/en/north-africa-middle-east/iraq/ Iraq-an-intolerable-forgotten-and

Human Rights Watch. (2003, November). *Background on Women's Status in Iraq prior to the Fall of the Saddam Hussein Government*. Retrieved January 11, 2014, from Human Rights Watch: www.hrw.org/legacy/backgrounder/wrd/iraq-women.htm

Human Rights Watch. (2014a, February 6). *Iraq: Secruity forces abusing women in detention*. Retrieved February 6, 2014, from Human Rights Watch: www.hrw.org/ news/2014/02/06/iraq-security-forces-abusing-women-detention

Human Rights Watch. (2014b, March 12). *Iraq: Don't legalize marriage for 9-year-olds*. Retrieved April 9, 2014, from Human Rights Watch: www.hrw.org/news/2014/03/11/ iraq-don-t-legalize-marriage-9-year-olds

Hussain, I. (2014, April 21). [*Premeditated Crimes*]. Retrieved April 21, 2014, from *Al-Mada Newspaper*: http://almadapaper.net/ar/news/463294/ الجنة-جريمة-ينفذها-ابن-العم-مع-سابق-الإصال

Ibrahim, H. (2006). Gender Based Violence. In M. G. Sökmen (ed.), *World Tribunal on Iraq: Istanbul Culminating Session, 23–27 June 2005*. Istanbul: Metis.

Imarah, M. (1972). Al-a mal al-Kamilah lil Imam Muhammad Abduh [Complete Works of Iman Muhammad Abdouh] (Vol. 1). Beirut, Lebanon: al-Mu'assasah al'Arabiyya lil Disârât wa al-Nashr.

International Crisis Group. (2006, February 27). *The Next Iraqi War? Sectarianism and Civil Conflict*. Retrieved January 12, 2014, from International Crisis Group: www. crisisgroup.org/en/regions/middle-east-north-africa/iraq-iran-gulf/iraq/052-the-next-iraqi-war-sectarianism-and-civil-conflict.aspx

Iraq Ministry of Planning, Central Statistical Organization. (1978). *Annual Abstract of Statistics, 1977*. Baghdad: Ministry of Planning.

Iraqi Constitution (2005). Retrieved March 22, 2007, from UNESCO: http:// portal.unesco.org/ci/en/files/20704/11332732689iraqi_constitution_ar.pdf/ iraqi_constitution_ar.pdf

Ireland, P. W. (1937/2005). *Iraq: A study in political development.* London: Routledge.

IRIN. (2003, October 14). *Focus on Increasing Domestic Violence.* Retrieved January 18, 2014, from IRIN, a service of the UN Office for the Coordination of Humanitarian Affairs: www.irinnews.org/report/22380/iraq-focus-on-increasing-domestic-violence

Ismael, J. S. (1980). Social Policy and Social Change: The case of Iraq. *Arab Studies Quarterly, 2*(3), 235–248.

Ismael, J. S., & Ismael, S. T. (2000). Gender and State in Iraq. In J. Saud (ed.), *Gender and Citizenship in the Middle East.* Syracuse: Syracuse University Press.

Ismael, T. Y. (2007). Democratization by Occupation: The Iraqi Quandary. In J. Ismael & W. Haddad (eds), *Barriers to Reconciliation: Case studies on Iraq and the Palestine–Israel conflict.* Toronto: University Press of America.

Ismael, T. Y., & Ismael, J. S. (2004). *The Iraqi Predicament: People in the quagmire of power politics.* London: Pluto Press.

Izz-il-Din, Y. (1960). *Al-Shi al-Iraqi al-Hadith wa Athar al-Taiyyarat al-Syasiyya wa al-Ijtima'iyya fih* [*Iraqi Modern Poems and the Impact of Political and Social Trends*]. Baghdad: Matba at As ad.

Khairi, Z., & Khairi, S. (1984). *Dirasat fi Tarikh al-Hizb al-Shiyu i al-Iraqi* [*Studies in the History of the Iraqi Communist Party*] (Vol. 1). Prague: Iraqi Communist Party.

Kitabat. (2014, April 8). [*Iraqi Elites on the Legal Conditions of the Ja'afri Laws*]. Retrieved April 9, 2014, from Kitabat: www.kitabat.com/ar/page/08/04/2014/25928/ال‌عمتجملا-انامذرشي-ني‌يريفعجلا-لاوحالاو-ءاضقلا-انوناق--ةي‌قارع-بخن.html

Longley, J. (Director). (2006). *Iraq in Fragments* [Motion Picture]. Retrieved April 16, 2007, from Iraq in Fragments.com: www.iraqinfragments.com/background/index.html

Mamouri, A. (2014, March 18). *Women's Movement in Iraq Faces Setbacks.* Retrieved March 24, 2014, from Al-Monitor: www.al-monitor.com/pulse/originals/2014/03/iraq-women-rights-challenges-setbacks.html

Marr, P. (1985). *The Modern History of Iraq.* Boulder: Westview Press.

McNutt, K. (2005). *Sexualized Violence Against Iraqi Women by US Occupying Forces.* Retrieved January 11, 2014, from Psychoanalysts for Peace and Justice: http://psychoanalystsopposewar.org/resources_files/SVIW-1.doc

NGO Coalition of CEDAW Shadow Report. (2014, February). *Iraqi Women in Armed Conflict and Post Conflict Situation.* Retrieved June 9, 2014, from OHCHR: http://tbinternet.ohchr.org/Treaties/CEDAW/Shared%20Documents/IRQ/INT_CEDAW_NGO_IRQ_16192_E.pdf

Omar, S. (1994). Women: Honour, shame and dictatorship. In F. Hazelton (ed.), *Iraq Since the Gulf War: Prospects for democracy.* London: Zed Books.

Pingeot, L. (2012, June). *Dangerous Partnership: Private military & security companies and the UN.* Retrieved February 8, 2014, from Academia.edu: https://www.academia.edu/4519425/Dangerous_Partnership_Private_Military_and_Security_Companies_and_the_UN

Porter, G. (2007, February 7). *How Neocon Shi'ite Strategy Led to Sectarian War.* Retrieved January 11, 2014, from Antiwar.com: www.antiwar.com/orig/porter.php?articleid=10481

Qanun al-Ahwal al-Shakhsiyya wa Ta Dilatuhu [The Personal Status Law and its Amendments]. (1978). Baghdad: Dar al-Hurriyya Print Shop.

Qâsim, A.-u.-K. (1959). *Mabadi' thawrat 14 Tammuz fi khutab Abd-ul-Karim Qasim* [*The Principles of 14 Tammuz Revolution in Abdul-Karim Qasim's Speeches*]. Baghdad: Iraqi Government Press.

196   *People in the quagmire*

Quraishi, Q. (2014, April 17). [*The Killing of Women in Iraq*]. Retrieved April 21, 2014, from *Al-Mada Newspaper*: http://almadapaper.net/ar/news/463062/ قرابني-الجحود-إلى-عالم-المكلكت-قق-لن-السنا

Saletan, W. (2004, May 5). *Rape Rooms: A chronology*. Retrieved February 6, 2014, from Slate: www.slate.com/articles/news_and_politics/ballot_box/2004/05/rape_rooms_a_chronology.html

Salt, J. (2008). *The Unmaking of the Middle East*. Berkeley: University of California Press.

Shafaaq News. (2014, February 25). *Cabinet Approves Passing al-Jaafari Judiciary Law to Parliament*. Retrieved March 6, 2014, from Shafaaq News: http://shafaaq.com/en/index.php?option=com_content&view=article&id=9041:cabinet-approves-passing-al-jaafari-judiciary-law-to-parliament&catid=39:politics&Itemid=53

Silverstein, K., & Burton-Rose, D. (2001). *Private Warriors*. London: Verso.

Singer, P. W. (2003). *Corporate Warriors: The rise of the privatized military industry*. New York: Cornell University Press.

Stoter, B. (2013, June 12). *Self-Immolation Continues Among Iraqi Kurdish Women*. Retrieved April 21, 2014, from Al-Monitor: www.al-monitor.com/pulse/originals/2013/06/self-immolation-kurdish-iraqi-women.html

Suzuki, K. (2005). *Economic and Social Data Ranking*. Retrieved March 30, 2007, from Global Japanese Data Ranking: www.dataranking.com/index.cgi?LG=e&CO=Iraq&GE=ne&RG=0

Thomson Reuters Foundation. (2013, November 12). *Poll: Women's rights in the Arab World*. Retrieved November 17, 2013, from Thomson Reuters Foundation: www.trust.org/spotlight/poll-womens-rights-in-the-arab-world/

UN CEDAW. (1998, October 19). *Second and Third Periodic Reports of States Parties, CEDAW/C/IRQ/2–3*. Retrieved January 11, 2014, from UN: http://www.un.org/womenwatch/daw/cedaw/cedaw23/Iraq%20as%20adopted.html

UN Commission on Human Rights. (1992). *Report on the Situation of Human Rights in Iraq, E/CN.4/1992/31*. Retrieved January 11, 2014, from the University of Minnesota: http://www1.umn.edu/humanrts/commission/country51/56.htm

UNESCO. (2003). *Situation Analysis of Education in Iraq*. Retrieved March 30, 2007, from United Nations Educational, Scientific and Cultural Organization (UNESCO): http://unesdoc.unesco.org/images/0013/001308/130838e.pdf

UNESCO. (2005, January 13). *Iraq Education in Transition: Needs and challenges—2004*. Retrieved February 8, 2014, from United Nations Education, Scientific and Cultural Organization (UNESCO): www.unesco.org/education/iraq/na_13jan2005.pdf

UNFPA. (2003). *Iraq: Reproductive health assessment*. Retrieved March 30, 2007, from United Nations Population Fund (UNFPA): www.unfpa.org/rh/docs/iraq-rept04-08-03.doc

UNICEF. (1999, July). *Results of the 1999 Iraq Child and Maternal Mortality Surveys*. Retrieved January 11, 2014, from Federation of American Scientists: www.fas.org/news/iraq/1999/08/irqscont.pdf

UNIFEM. (2006). *Gender Profile of the Conflict in Iraq*. Retrieved January 11, 2014, from PeaceWomen: www.peacewomen.org/assets/file/iraq_pfv-women_profile.pdf

UNSC. (2003, October 16). *Resolution 1511, S/RES/1511*. Retrieved January 11, 2014, from Refworld: www.refworld.org/cgi-bin/texis/vtx/rwmain?docid=3fa524dd4

US Department of State. (2005, June). *Trafficking in Persons Report*. Retrieved January 12, 2014, from US Department of State: www.state.gov/documents/organization/47255.pdf

Warriner, D. (1975). *Land Reform and Development in the Middle East: A study of Egypt, Syria, and Iraq.* London: Royal Institute of International Affairs.

Weber, C. E. (2003). *Making Common Cause? Western and Middle Eastern feminists in the international women's movement, 1911–1948.* Dissertation, Ohio State University. Retrieved January 11, 2014, from https://etd.ohiolink.edu/

WHO. (2003, March). *Potential Impact of Conflict on Health in Iraq.* Retrieved January 11, 2014, from World Health Organization (WHO): www.who.int/features/2003/iraq/briefings/iraq_briefing_note/en/index.html

Zaher, U. (1986). Political Developments in Iraq, 1963–1980. In CARDRI (ed.), *Saddam's Iraq: Revolution or reaction?* London: Zed Books.

Zubaida, S. (2003, February 5). *The Rise and Fall of Civil Society in Iraq.* Retrieved March 30, 2007, from Open Security: www.opendemocracy.net/conflict-iraqwarquestions/article_953.jsp

8 Iraq in the twenty-first century
Retrospect and prospect

A retrospective appraising Iraq could begin with the dawn of civilization, for indeed Mesopotamia (circa 3100 BCE), with its settled populations and urban civilization(s), was roughly coterminous with the modern state of Iraq. Considered to be the very cradle of civilization, its legacy has long played a role in conceptions of the state projects which followed as well as in the social construction of the societies of the riparian plain between the Tigris and Euphrates rivers. In lieu of this long view, however, focusing the lens on the modern, post-independent Iraqi state emerging from World War I and after the dissolution of the Ottoman Empire, the story of Iraq is a microcosm of the story of the birth, growth and decline of the modern nation-state in the non-European world. It is the relatively short story of the development, evolution and finally the systematic destruction of the state and the fabric of society that underpinned it, and presages a bleak picture of the globalized civilization unfolding in the twenty-first century.

Part I of this book examined the international, regional and national political dimensions of deconstruction and reconstruction as experienced in Iraq. In this framework, deconstruction referred to the process of obliterating the institutions of state in Iraq; and reconstruction to the process of remodeling Iraqi society along the pattern of sectarianism with the institutionalization of the sectarian, ethnic and tribal dynamics of Iraqi society into the formal political structure. The disbanding of the national army and the de-Ba'thization of the civil service demonstrate the deconstruction thesis, while the integration of sectarian militias into the national military reflects the reconstruction thesis. The roles of international and national actors in these processes of deconstruction and reconstruction were examined, largely in terms of the policies promoted by the US occupation forces, attendant international organizations and their construction of a new class of ruling elites through the importation of Iraqi "carpetbaggers" into occupied Iraq.

Part II shifted the analysis from formal politics and examined the impact of the deconstruction–reconstruction theme on two vulnerable groups in Iraqi society—children and women. Children are vulnerable in terms of their health and well-being. Morbidity and mortality rates among them are indicative of the social fabric within a society (insofar as the social fabric is a metaphor for a society's health and robustness). It follows that the deteriorating social, economic and political conditions in Iraq were reflected in increasing morbidity and mortality among Iraqi children. Women are vulnerable in terms of the policies and processes found across patriarchal societies that discriminate against women. It follows that changes in the role and status of women represent the result of deliberate policy choices. Deterioration of the role and status of Iraqi women in post-Saddam Iraq has been reflected in the policy choices made to enhance sectarianism, within which is embedded an extreme form of patriarchy and misogyny.

In American discourse on the Anglo-American invasion of Iraq, critique is often dismissed with the language of liberation: that the Anglo-American invasion removed the Saddam Hussein dictatorship and—in official discourse—brought "democracy" to Iraq. The crimes of the Saddam Hussein regime were legion and well documented, and yet, as bad as life had become under Saddam Hussein's brutal dictatorship, opinion polls indicate that most Iraqis today would say that life under Saddam was better (BBC News, 2007a). Moreover, the official discourse of liberation and democratization is at odds with past US policy, as it supported the Ba'thist regime during its conflict with neighboring Iran, as well as its leading role in enforcing the draconian UN economic sanctions regime imposed from 1990 to 2003. Given the nature of Saddam Hussein's dictatorial regime and the number and severity of its crimes, it is a damning indictment of Anglo-American occupation policy for the preceding era to compare favorably. Weighing the consequences of the Anglo-American invasion and occupation, and assessing responsibility, it is worth recounting the war justifications of its chief proponent and prosecutor, then-President George W. Bush. In a 2005 speech at Fort Bragg, North Carolina, Bush defended the war effort, claiming:

> Our mission in Iraq is clear. We're hunting down the terrorists. We're helping Iraqis build a free nation that is an ally in the war on terror. We're advancing freedom in the broader Middle East. We are removing a source of violence and instability, and laying the foundation of peace for our children and our grandchildren.
>
> (Bush, 2005)

Framing the Iraq war as a campaign to eliminate terrorism, to build democracy in Iraq and beyond, and to remove violence and instability, looks farcical in view of what has developed over the ensuing years. Moreover, it is unlikely that—in the corridors of power and amongst the punditry classes that formulated the invasion and occupation—any effort will be made to reconcile the claims that informed the Iraq war and the actual conditions on the ground that resulted.

In a broader sense, the Anglo-American invasion and occupation of Iraq established a dubious international norm for the post-Cold War era, further undermining normative claims of sovereignty and international law as established by the UN Charter. As discussed at the outset of the book (see Chapter 1), states have violated, indirectly, the sovereignty of other states, in what Richard Cottam (1967) calls "competitive interference," in which one state seeks to subvert the internal environment of another state for foreign policy reasons. And while this Cold War norm would indeed be violated, pressures existed within the international system

200 *Iraq in the twenty-first century*

that limited the frequency of outright violations of sovereignty in the absence of an international legal imprimatur. The 2003 Anglo-American invasion, in contrast, represented a violation of sovereignty that not only lacked UN sanction, but was in outright violation of international law and international norms. The UN Secretary General bemoaned that "the council did not vote for it, but we failed to stop the war and we are still living with the consequences" (Jones, 2014). Moreover, the flimsy (and ultimately disproven) justifications for the invasion of Iraq (WMDs, support for al-Qaeda) lowered the threshold for future adventurism of great powers and, conversely, the ability of those who participated in the Iraq war to morally object to such great power interventions. In 2014, following Russia's "annexation" of Crimea, US Secretary of State John Kerry criticized Russia on the basis: "You just don't invade another country on phony pretexts in order to assert your interests" (Lerman & Giroux, 2014). This ironic statement was treated with the regard one would expect, and was roundly mocked not only on *Russia Today*—Russia's English-language state television (Russia Today, 2014)—but also on *CNN*, which quipped: "It's difficult to say what is more astonishing: the double standards exhibited by the White House, or the apparent total lack of self-awareness of US officials" (Kohn, 2014).

As examined throughout this book, the nature of Iraq's post-war "sovereignty" is highly dubious, with the political–sectarian environment and legal/constitutional apparatus imposed on Iraq by occupation authorities only validated by a patina of indigenous political tokenism through regular elections and a "carpetbagger" political class dependent on external powers for their political status. Moreover, as was made plain, this dubious sovereignty is further complicated through the rule of corruption and violent sectarianism that now dominates Iraq's political and social life. Ultimately, the Anglo-American invasion and occupation of Iraq represented a deconstruction of the post-colonial state-building project in Iraq—commenced as early as the monarchical period—that sought to institutionalize an Iraqi identity that would take precedence over sect, tribe and parochial interest. As a result of invasion and occupation, this post-colonial project was razed, and the very existence of a "sovereign" Iraq as a coherent nation-state was left in question.

The story of Iraq in the twenty-first century has been the repeated and often drastic refashioning of the Iraqi state and the resilience of Iraqi society and culture. As introduced at the beginning of this book, the Anglo-American invasion reversed the trajectory of Iraqi development with the obliteration of the original post-colonial indigenous state in the face of which Iraqi society and culture has been disassembled. This book has been an accounting of this destruction and its various aspects, and based on the argument that such outcomes were deliberative and therefore foreseeable. The most recent reportage and statistics only reinforce the magnitude of this calamity. For instance, on October 7, 2009, *Annahar* (Qasifi, 2009) published an account by journalist Joseph Qasifi on the findings of several statistical reports leaked from important Iraqi government ministries, which reveal the transformation that had swept across Iraq and its people under the tutelage of the US and the regime it imposed. Reports of the Ministry of Women's Affairs and the Ministry of Health portrayed an Iraq ravaged by America's "Shock and Awe" campaign and the sectarian violence that filled the vacuum left by the diminished policing powers of the new Iraqi state. As of December 2008 1 million widows and 4 million orphans were left behind by the 2.5 million who died following the invasion and occupation in March 2003. This, according to the Ministry of the Interior and the Ministry of Migration and Immigration, is in addition to the 800,000 Iraqis who remained unaccounted for, the 4.5 million who fled Iraq, and the 2.5 million who were internally displaced by the chaos and still had no place to call home. To "secure" Iraq, more than 34,000 people had been held in detention centers across the country, as reported by human rights monitors. Beyond the nearly 15.5 million Iraqi lives that had been irreparably shattered by the invasion and occupation, the Ministry of Human Rights reported that 40 percent of Iraqis were experiencing financial struggles, while the number of those living in poverty had increased by 12.5 percent during the period 2006–2013, despite the fact that the Iraqi national budget had increased by 71 percent over that time (GAO, 2008, p. 6; JAPU, 2013, p. 1; Lee, 2013; Qasifi, 2009).

In the environmental/humanitarian domain, disturbing details have emerged related to the American military's use of DU and white phosphorous munitions across Iraq (see discussion in Chapter 6). Dahr Jamail, who has acted as an non-embedded[1] journalist independently and then for *Al Jazeera* throughout the Anglo-American campaign in Iraq, relayed discussions with Dr. Samina Alani, a doctor in the Iraqi city of Fallujah:

> She said it's common now in Fallujah for newborns to come out with massive multiple systemic defects, immune problems, massive central nervous system problems, massive heart problems, skeletal disorders, babies being born with two heads, babies being born with half of their internal organs outside of their bodies, cyclops babies literally with one eye—really, really, really horrific nightmarish types of birth defects.

This account of human catastrophe owing to environmental factors has been confirmed by multiple other sources, including the November 2012 issue of *Environmental Contamination and Toxicology* (Gordts, 2013) as well as a 2010 paper published by the *International Journal of Environmental Research and Public Health* (Kenner, 2012). These preliminary studies suggest long-lasting consequences for affected areas, in terms of congenital defects and cancers, of disturbing magnitude, the depth of which is not yet fully understood.

Finally, Iraq—its cultural mosaic boasting some of the oldest religious communities in the world—has endured the destruction of its multicultural patrimony. Iraq's Chaldo-Assyrian Christian communities, once more than a million, have dwindled to 150,000 following the invasion and occupation, with the number of churches declining from 300 (pre-invasion) to only 57 (Dougherty, 2014). The Iraqi Yazidis, members of a syncretic monotheistic religion, have similarly suffered in the chaos of post-invasion Iraq. In 2007, violence targeting Yazidis peaked with a massacre-bombing of a Yazidi enclave in Mosul, killing 200 (BBC News,

202 *Iraq in the twenty-first century*

2007b). Iraq's Sabian Mandeans, a gnostic sect venerating John the Baptist, have been decimated within Iraq: "In the 1990s about 70,000 Mandaeans lived in Iraq. Today, only around 3,000 or so remain" (Contrera, 2009). The targeting of these vulnerable religious minorities, and the exodus of these ancient communities, represents the destruction of Iraq's cultural patrimony. This violence represents an extension of the phenomenon of political sectarianism (outlined in Chapters 2 and 3), where the destruction of the Iraqi state and the emergence of sectarian militia-parties as a central facet of post-invasion Iraq eroded the conception of Iraq as a multi-ethnic/multi-religious national project.

Anglo-American occupation policy in Iraq proceeded on the assumption that sectarianism was an *intrinsic* component of the Iraqi national character: that Iraq through its state-building process had been dominated and patterned on religious division. Following from this assumption, the Iraqi political system under occupation was quite consciously patterned on sectarian organizing principles, which emergent sectarian political factions were quick to capitalize upon. Such parties were particularly strong in view of the fact that "religious parties established themselves with the support of the regional forces [i.e. Iran, Saudi Arabia] that had hosted and sponsored them for decades, or at least gained such support by aligning themselves with the sectarian strife between the regional parties" (Mamouri, 2013). The secular-nationalist opposition within Iraq was, in any case, rather weak, owing to, among other factors, the association of secular nationalism (however unfairly) to the preceding Ba'thist regime. In any event, the institution of a sectarian logic in post-invasion Iraq saw, at best, the emergence of a Lebanese-style confessional quota system, *Muhasah*, with the Presidency generally assigned to a Kurd, the Head of Parliament to a Sunni, and the Prime Ministership to a Shi'ite. Given this confluence of factors, the domination of sectarian parties within post-invasion Iraq was used as a confirmation of the pre-existing prejudices of occupation authorities.

This view of Iraq was and remains, of course, a vast oversimplification. First, social and folkloric forms of sectarianism have certainly been present in Iraq and sectarian chauvinisms have factored in Iraqi governance, but the modern Iraqi state—through its iterations—was marked by its explicit project of establishing an Iraqi national identity transcending ethno-religious affiliations, with policies designed to integrate Iraq's ethno-sectarian factions into the national project through education, the national army and the bureaucracy (Bashkin, 2009; Davis, 2005). This project, which began to crumble during the 1990s as the erosion of state infrastructure under the sanctions regime forced the re-emergence of primordial social formations (religion, tribe and ethnicity), collapsed under the chaos initiated by Anglo-American invasion and occupation (Jabar, 2000). Second, the re-constitution of the Iraqi state along sectarian lines has—whether this was the explicit goal of occupation planners or not—had the consequence of preventing the emergence of a strong national front in Iraq that could: (a) protect the country's national interests in regards to its oil sector from foreign predation; and (b) resist occupation on a unified basis, unfettered by parochial concerns. Finally, from the vantage point of the cliques that form the power base in new Iraq, sectarian division has served as a cover for various forms of patronage and corruption, the division of spoils among competing factions, while nominally acting on behalf of their respective ethno-sectarian constituencies. The sectarian violence in Iraq, which has dominated the lives of ordinary Iraqis, has—for the powerful within and without Iraq—served certain useful functions.

Adding to this dark view of post-invasion Iraq is the overwhelming stench of corruption that permeates the public and private sectors (as discussed in Chapter 5). According to the government's Iraq Integrity Commission, many of the military and business leaders of the new Iraq have falsified their qualifications, resulting in tens of thousands of falsified post-secondary degrees. According to the Interior Ministry and the Iraqi Syndicate of Journalists, foreign intelligence agencies fund 126 private security groups, 220 newspapers and journals, and 45 television stations operating in Iraq, while, according to the Iraqi Information Commission, a further 67 radio stations are funded by Iraqi intelligence agencies and four major telecommunications companies (KORK, ASIA, ZAIN and ATHIER) are under the ownership of political party leaders; the synergy of these influences introduces significant concerns about the objectivity of Iraqi media. At the level of executive and of national governance, a corrupt system of political spoils is the order of the day under Prime Minister al-Mâlikî, the operation of which the Iraqi paper *Al-Mada* described as

> a sort of underground exchange that trades in a unique product; it has no equivalent in the world. It is an exchange offering ministries "according to their value" in the language of prevalent corruption [...] [On this exchange] an MP will change lists for "one million dollars and an armoured car." If you can buy the allegiance of ten to twenty MPs, you can even become a major member of the cabinet. As for the Kurdish and Sunni speakership and presidency, these are also for sale for the same price as a major cabinet position. The more people you bring from across the major parties, and the more [disruption] you cause, the greater influence you have.
>
> (Karim, 2014)

Ordinary Iraqis are now left at the mercy of a pilfered civil society and security apparatus designed for patronage and run to the benefit of incumbents, leaving citizens beholden to an elite cadre of corrupt Iraqi officials themselves beholden to foreign interests. In this environment, the wealth of Iraq is auctioned off to foreign investors under the guise of a non-existent "state investment law," while privately held offices are at times seized by any of the 43 armed militias loyal to a selection of Iraq's 550 political parties (Qasifi, 2009). These are the outcomes of regime change and are the features of a failed state. The history of modern state building in Iraq followed the framework of the post-colonial project in the developing world. Beginning within the framework of British imperialism in the early twentieth century, and through the historical process of decolonization and Cold War politics, Iraq progressed to a republic in 1958 before morphing into a dictatorship in 1963. This historical process, uneven and marked by periods of war, dictatorship

204 *Iraq in the twenty-first century*

and deprivation, nevertheless had the continuity of a national project, whose social infrastructure was financed by a public oil sector. With the Anglo-American invasion of 2003, this historical state-building project, the consolidation of "Iraqi-ness," was abruptly halted. Under Anglo-American occupation, Iraq was marked by the deconstruction of national identity itself, giving way to the resurgence of reactionary and atavistic social formations as the basis of the "new" Iraqi state.

This "new" power structure in post-invasion Iraq is sectarian in composition, divisive in intent and thoroughly corrupt in its practice. The political class that has risen to power in post-war Iraq, Iraqi "carpetbaggers,"[2] as outlined in Chapter 4, represent an imported political class who, having in most instances lived outside of Iraq for decades as expatriates, have little natural constituency within Iraq, and thus are heavily reliant on external patrons for their support. In the Iraqi case, this support has mainly come from the US or neighboring Iran and, to a lesser but still significant degree, Saudi Arabia, Turkey and some Gulf states. Consequently, such an imported political class tends to be highly pliable, their constituency being, not the Iraqi people, but their external sponsors. In a broader sense, the US has executed its objectives in Iraq through the use of NGOs who—while nominally Iraqi-based and internationalist in character—depend on the US for funding and support and, in the words of former US Secretary of State Colin Powell, serve as "a force multiplier for us, such an important part of our combat team" (Foley, 2009). This strategy, the use of nominally indigenous individuals and organizations as an augmentation of US foreign policy, extends beyond Iraq, most recently represented in US support for groups within Ukraine (Ames, 2014). Ultimately, using these tools of modern imperialism, the Iraqi state that was nurtured under occupation represents, *in toto*, a failed state, whose failure is demonstrated not only in its political leadership but also in its inability to generate a viable political vision for the future of Iraqi society. Based on this grim picture, one is hard pressed to sketch a positive prospect for Iraq. In a failed state such as Iraq, civil society and human capital are unlikely to be afforded an opportunity to develop, given that day-to-day life for most Iraqis has become a matter of basic survival, cast against a backdrop of incinerating violence and sectarian division. At the formal political level, Iraq is reduced to a state of official gangsterism, where political leaders and their cohorts struggle against each other for power and privilege, in many instances acting on behalf of powerful patrons whose concern for Iraqi nationhood is slim to nil. According to *Fund for Peace*'s 2013 "Failed State Index," Iraq is ranked the 11th-most "failed state" in the world, in the company of such tragic cases as Haiti, Somalia, Afghanistan and South Sudan (Fund for Peace, 2013). Likewise, in *Transparency International*'s 2013 Corruption Perception Index, Iraq is considered the 7th-most corrupt country in the world (Transparency International, 2013).

If the withdrawal of American troops in 2011 was to signify that "its work had been done" and that post-invasion Iraq now represented a self-governing and stable political entity, subsequent developments should dispel that illusion. According to the UN, 2013 proved to be the most violent year in Iraq since 2008, with nearly 9,000 Iraqis killed (Harding, 2014). The Iraqi province of Anbar, the epicenter of violence during the worst years of the Anglo-American occupation, has relapsed into its previous state of utter chaos, with the surrounding Sunni-majority provinces faring little better:

> To the north, Nineveh province is seen as a stronghold of al-Qaeda fighters, while to the east of Baghdad, Diyala province has witnessed fighting between Sunni and Shiite armed groups, causing an uptick in internal displacement. The conflict in Sunni regions is creating an atmosphere of perpetual crisis that could tip the country into civil war or be used by Maliki as a justification to stay in power after what is expected to be a closely fought election.
>
> (Parker, 2014)

Indeed, according to official reports from the Iraqi government, in early 2014, Fallujah and Ramadi—two Iraqi cities that had become synonymous with violence under occupation—were captured by al-Qaeda-linked fighters (Associated Press, 2014). In more skeptical coverage, the fighters that captured Fallujah and Ramadi were described as Sunni Arab tribesmen, who had taken to arms in response to, proximately, the arrest of Sunni Arab Member of Parliament Ahmed al-'Alwani on terrorism charges by the government, which resulted in the killing of six of his supporters (Deutsche Welle, 2013). More generally, Sunni Arab militancy in these provinces has been attributed to its distrust of the al-Mâlikî-led government, a sense of political disenfranchisement, and the legacy of clashes between Sunni tribesmen—sometimes affiliated with the previous regime—and Iraqi security forces which are largely recruited from Shi'ite political factions (e.g. ISCI). This conflict, frequently associated with major human rights abuses, severed these predominantly Sunni areas from any affinity with federal authorities. Emblematic of Shi'i particularism was the "Wolf Brigade," an Iraqi security force under the authority of the Iraqi Ministry of the Interior. Trained by US Colonel James Steele and headed by General Mohammed Qureshi (*nom de guerre* Abû Walîd), this commando force was almost exclusively Shi'ite in membership and especially active in the Sunni provinces, where it was accused of human rights abuses, including torture (Chulov, 2010).

The violence and disorder that has dominated post-invasion Iraq has become part and parcel of the surrounding regional violence that threatens the stability and coherence of the broader Middle East. With neighboring Syria having descended into civil war, "Iraq's northwest, Syria's northeast, and portions of some Syrian cities are essentially inter-connected operation[al] areas for Iraq's al-Qaeda groups," while continuing violence could result in "areas in Iraq and Syria where different jihadist groups can act without any form of control. Neither the Iraqi, nor the Syrian, governments will be able to control these areas effectively and long-term" (Deutsche Welle, 2014).

Resisting an untenable future

The prospects for Iraq look grim indeed. However, people not only react to conditions they encounter, but they are also agents who act and interact to overcome

206 *Iraq in the twenty-first century*

hostile conditions. Based on self-organization theory, it can be hypothesized that, in a dystopia, communities of people will spontaneously organize patterns of cooperation to satisfy their basic physiological and security needs (Ismael, 2010; Leydesdorff, 1993). The prospects for Iraq's future lie in the patterns of everyday life emergent in the dystopian chaos sustained by the failed Anglo-American state project. In Iraq, 16.6 million Iraqis, or over 50 percent of the population, are under the age of 18. This means that over half the population of Iraq have lived their entire lives in the shadow of crushing economic sanctions, followed by military invasion and occupation, and the attendant chaos of sectarian violence. The Arab Spring uprisings of 2010 onward signify, if nothing else, the growing impatience of Arab youth with the current poor social and economic prospects, the region's leadership, and attendant tyranny and hypocrisy. It is likely that Iraqi youth are similarly impatient with the leadership and sectarian violence that tyrannize their lives. Not only are instances of organized popular protest increasing but also discourses of discontent with the widespread corruption and the self-serving political establishment are reverberating through the airwaves and especially with the rapid embrace of social media. These patterns of protest have merged, and new patterns of leadership are emerging.

Opportunities for youth engagement, formal education and especially public expression have been stifled through enormous levels of violence. US military operations in 2003 led to the first bloodshed between US forces and civilians when students were denied instruction in Fallujah with their school occupied. Protests organized by the students and their families were met with lethal force, prompting an escalating cycle of violence that sparked the insurgency that followed. Rather than being driven by sectarian, nationalist or Islamist ideological commitment, opposition began with demands to access public services. Anglo-American occupation practices, especially in the predominantly Sunni Anbar Governorate in western Iraq, saw attempts to go about normal life politicized, and Fallujah became a center of armed resistance. Fallujah, in resisting outside control, found itself the target for the US campaign to crush resistance. Ross Caputi (2014), a former soldier who fought in the US siege of Fallujah, recalls:

> The vast majority of the men we fought against in Falluja were locals, unaffiliated with al-Qaida, who were trying to expel the foreign occupiers from their country. There was a presence of al-Qaida in the city, but they played a minimal and marginal role in the fighting. The stories about Abu Musab al-Zarqawi, the alleged leader of al-Qaida in Iraq who was said to be recruiting an army in Falluja, were wildly exaggerated. There is no evidence that Zarqawi ever even set foot in Falluja.

Fallujah's role as an epicenter of resistance against the imposition of rule continued beyond the withdrawal of US forces and it again became the focus of a narrative labeling resistance as terrorism to justify the military siege of an urban population in 2014. In 2013, a peaceful protest movement arose with supporters within both the Sunni and Shia communities across Anbar against the al-Mâlikî government, calling for an end to corruption and repression of dissident voices. Al-Mâlikî, who habitually labeled any opposition group as "terrorists," used the opportunity of a large demonstration in Hawija to crack down on the peaceful protesters by ordering Iraqi security forces to open fire on the demonstrators; at least 50 were killed in this assault (Caputi, 2014). Peaceful demonstrations that had been taking place throughout 2013 in Ramadi, Anbar's major city, were also crushed severely. The need for self-defense created by such crackdowns became the impetus for the arming of what had hitherto been peaceful demonstrators. Al-Mâlikî linked these armed demonstrators to al-Qaeda/the Islamic State of Iraq and the Levant (ISIS) to justify further targeting of those who questioned his rule. In reality, while there was an ISIS presence in Fallujah, given that Anbar borders Syria, it was "not playing a significant role in the fighting in Falluja [...] The [ISIS] flag was removed within five minutes when ordered by tribal leaders. This shows that the tribes control Falluja [and not ISIS]" (Caputi, 2014).

What was being witnessed in Anbar was not the advance of al-Qaeda, as the al-Mâlikî narrative maintained, but rather popular opposition from Iraqis fed-up with al-Mâlikî, corruption and foreign influence (Caputi, 2013). In the early months of 2014, lines were drawn between a heterogeneous collection of domestic armed opposition groups and the Iraqi state, which sent military units to surround Fallujah, thereby increasing the frequency of random artillery shelling across the city in preparation for a ground assault (Ditz, 2014).[3] This assault by government forces came in spite of the mediation efforts of the television news program *Studio 9*, which, on January 30, 2014, invited Anbar's tribal leaders onto its broadcast. Put on the spot by tribal chiefs agreeing to the call, al-Mâlikî appointed his deputy chief of staff to negotiate with them. Later that same day, a number of tribal sheikhs, notables and religious leaders from all over the country expressed their support for Fallujah, culminating in what became known as the "Initiative of the Wisemen to Abort the Confrontation." Tribal sheikhs from the Middle Euphrates and Southern Iraq met in Karbala on February 4, 2014 and called for al-Mâlikî to negotiate in good faith with the Anbari tribal sheikhs to resolve the confrontation peacefully. Moreover, they nominated the religious leaders al-Ṣadr and al-Hakim to mediate the negotiations; and, finally, they invited KRG President Mas'ûd Barzânî to facilitate the negotiations (Studio 9, February 4, 2014). Awareness of the crisis widened, leading to increased public support for those in Fallujah. Thus, the Fallujah crisis was no longer limited to the city itself or even to Anbar, but rather became a national issue, galvanizing popular action against the massacre of civilians regardless of religious and sectarian affiliation. Under public pressure and facing the 2014 Parliamentary elections, on February 5 al-Mâlikî endorsed a peaceful resolution to the crisis (Studio 9, February 5, 2014).

In the 2014 Anbar conflict, a confluence of forces emerged in opposition to the al-Mâlikî government. While some component of this opposition belonged to ISIS and similar armed jihadist groups, the movement expressed the concerns of ordinary citizens, and the majority of political actors adopting leadership roles were comprised of tribal sheikhs, former military officers and others who had used their status to mobilize against al-Qaeda in Iraq (AQI) during the worst days

208 *Iraq in the twenty-first century*

of sectarian violence. The Anbar opposition subsequently became an emblem of the inability of the Iraqi government to address the central political questions of post-occupation Iraqi life: rampant corruption, a lack of opportunity, a sense of foreign domination, and a lack of consensus on the development of the state and national unity. Baghdad seemed unconcerned at the splintering of the territorial contiguity and the spiraling violence, choosing to deal with legitimate concerns and radicalized foreign-sponsored actors alike as a security challenge. Iraqi youth, who, as noted above, comprise over half of Iraq's population, were at the center of this opposition and the struggle for a viable Iraqi national project. On February 6, *Studio 9* reported that al-Mâlikî dispatched directly from his office a special military force to evict everyone from the gathering hall where the sheikhs' meeting took place. In the final analysis, the uptick in violence that marked early 2014 was an emblem of the failure of reconstruction and nation building in post-war Iraq (Fund for Peace, 2013). While a shrewd al-Mâlikî was able to capitalize on the Anbar uprising in winning a plurality in the 2014 parliamentary elections, his stratagems and insider intrigues marked a relinquishing of any pretense to the formal electoral process being representative of a process to bring about national leadership. In March and April 2014, al-Mâlikî gave dozens of television speeches, condemning the uprising as "terrorism," highlighting only the security aspects posed by a small minority in opposition, and leaving unaddressed the legitimate concerns of large swaths of Iraqi citizens. Under the electoral theme of "together to eliminate terrorism," al-Mâlikî would implicitly (or sometimes explicitly) highlight the majority Sunni composition of the Anbar resistance and, conversely, the majority Shi'ite composition of Iraqi armed forces battling the Anbaris, at all times casting the conflict in crude sectarian terms. Although unregistered in the electoral outcome, Ammar al-Hakim of the ISCI, Muqtadâ al-Sadr and the Sunni political factions would all criticize al-Mâlikî for his handling of the crisis. Al-Mâlikî appeared to have been successful in solidifying his authority within the bulk of his political coalition while making naked sectarian appeals, thereby denying any voice to the opposition and leaving unanswered the calls for development and representative governance from across Iraq (Abbas, 2014).

The experience of occupied Iraq, the focus of this book, brought to the fore crucial lessons on the relationship between regime change and the emergence of a failed state. Regime change in Iraq, as carried out through the exercise of Anglo-American force-of-arms, as with the examples of Afghanistan and Libya, entails external powers imposing their political will on weak and vulnerable societies. Where the strong dictate political conditions to the weak, the weak become dependent on the support of the dictating power(s). In the case of Iraq, a society that had been impoverished by a decade of economic sanctions, pummeled by military assault and hollowed out through the deconstruction of the state, its newly empowered political class relied on external support over indigenous legitimacy. Much like the dictatorship they replaced, they had only minority support from amongst the Iraqi populace. Beyond their own narrow base within Iraq in the first instance they looked predominantly, if not solely, to the support of the

Anglo-American occupation apparatus, as the levers of state power afforded considerable opportunity. Nevertheless, having spent much of their political careers outside Iraq, they increasingly came to rely on neighboring states and regional non-state actors. Not wishing to see their opponents profit in Iraq, these state and transnational movement actors were increasingly compelled to support their Iraqi clients. The Islamic Republic of Iran, Turkey and the states of the Gulf Cooperation Council, as well as jihadist and other non-state political movements, all came to engage Iraq and the state-building project initiated by the occupation. This tendency, the dependence of both political authorities and opposition actors on external powers, was reinforced by the nature of the political class that was empowered in post-invasion Iraq. In the process of deconstructing the Iraqi state (most prominently in de-Ba'thification and the disbanding of the national army), occupation authorities created a political vacuum. Aside from Kurdish parties in the north, this void of legitimacy was filled, not by indigenous anti-Saddam forces, but by repatriated diaspora Iraqis or "carpetbaggers." In the chaos of post-invasion Iraq, this new political class served as a chimera of sovereign authority, while centrifugal forces of political sectarianism, corruption and general chaos went unchecked and threatened the viability of Iraq as a coherent nation-state. The "carpetbagger" class, in any case, were quite often implicated in the promotion of the political sectarianism that dominated post-invasion Iraq, seeking to shore up their legitimacy through appeals to subnational factionalism of dubious coherence. In such disarray, political office in Iraq (as discussed in Chapter 5) often became little more than a vehicle for corruption and personal enrichment.

This combination of factors—military assault on a weaker state, the deconstruction/reconstruction of a post-colonial nationalist regime into a weak decentralized state, and the empowerment of an expatriate political class—created an environment in Iraq (and subsequently in Libya following the NATO "intervention" in that country) that led not to comity and political development, but ruination. The reconstructed state was unable to assert credible political/military authority, allowing for the emergence of political-sectarian militias and tribal affiliations—dependent on external support—as the dominant features of the new (dis)order. This political reality, engineered by occupation authorities, as described throughout the text, has led to a humanitarian disaster for Iraqis, threatened regional order, and proved a challenge to the survival of Iraq as a nation. This is a clear abrogation of self-determination. Against this accumulation of social wreckage, very little in the realm of moral accounting has taken place in the congressional and parliamentary halls of power that planned and executed the Iraq war. Iraqis have been left to deal with the consequences of great power politics, while those who delivered such trauma remain impervious. Nonetheless, the Iraqi people have increasingly organized, often against an unresponsive and corrupt government, and their attempts to overcome such ruinous forces deserve our attention.

In conclusion, three primary lessons are to be learned from this study. The first concerns the relationship between regime change and the emergence of the failed state. Regime change was a deliberate coercive policy pursued by external powers, and not the result of internal dynamics or forces. Similarly, the post-2003

210   *Iraq in the twenty-first century*

state, created through foreign interference, remained dependent on foreign interference in order to function as a repository for corruption. In other words, the state lacked internal legitimacy and viability, and was therefore non-self-sustaining. This is directly related to the second lesson learned—that is, the role of the carpetbagger class of political elites that is both a symptom of and means of the policy of regime change in the toolkit of foreign powers. Carpetbaggers, as repatriated expatriates who returned to the state targeted for regime change, owe their role and influence to external allegiance(s). They have no internal power base or constituency and their role and status are non-self-sustaining. Their primary purpose is to grab all they can, while they can, and sending it outside the target country. This directly relates to the culture of corruption that proliferates in the aftermath of regime change. The third lesson learned relates to the reasons for the failure of the state constructed out of regime change. Regime change sets in motion a chain of events that leads to increasing internal violence and corruption, until the state itself dissolves into an isolated enclave of carpetbaggers (i.e. Iraq's "Green Zone") under siege from warring factions blossoming amongst the indigenous population (i.e. Iraq's "Red Zone"). The basic notion that the US brought the "gift of democracy" to Iraq, leaving Iraq "to its people and [as] a fully sovereign Iraqi state that could make decisions about its own future" (Obama, 2014), is therefore simply unfounded. The system of government that has been imposed upon the people of Iraq is anything but a democracy. Rather, at the outset of the occupation, the US dismantled the institutions of the established political order and in their place gave Iraq a series of laws—Bremer's *dictats* through the CPA—designed to open Iraq's borders to foreign money and influence,[4] excise the extant bureaucracy and military,[5] place the agents of the Anglo-American coalition above the law,[6] and enshrine tribal fiefdoms and sectarian divisions that would become the undoing of the Iraqi nation.[7] Although the CPA was dissolved in June 2004, many of its orders served as the foundation for Iraq's new constitution, which was itself drafted through a contentious selection of the new political class of carpetbaggers[8] imported by the coalition.[9]

Within Iraq's newly formulated constitution lies an assortment of pitfalls to the establishment of a democratic system. These include the lack of limits to government power and the lack of an effective division and separation of executive, legislative and judicial powers allowing for the power of each branch of government to be subject to checks and balances by the other branches. The vagueness and omissions of the constitution on these important principles of democratic structure afforded al-Mâlikî the ability to act without democratic oversight or accountability and to overtly concentrate power in his hands. In his first term in office (2006–2010), he successfully assumed control of the judiciary by appointing a chief justice and dozens of judges loyal to his person. In effect, then, rather than an independent judiciary, this established the judiciary as an arm of the executive. While government commissions are supposed to be apolitical, the lack of democratic oversight or accountability allowed al-Mâlikî to fill many of the important commissions, including the Election Commission, with representatives loyal to the Prime Minister's Office (PMO). Reflecting the concentration of power in the executive branch, al-Mâlikî also pushed through the federal supreme court an interpretation of the constitution that leaves parliament unable to discuss or present any legislation that has not been drafted by the PMO.[10] Effectively, al-Mâlikî controls the judicial and legislative institutions of the Iraqi state, allowing the vagaries of the constitution to leave the executive branch unaccountable to parliament. With such a lack of oversight, Ministers refuse to appear before parliament at all.[11]

This political subversion of the country's administrative and bureaucratic institutions alongside the centralization of power within al-Mâlikî's PMO has highly distorted Iraqi "democracy." In May 2014, a video was released of State of Law MP Mahmoud al-Hassan before a group of farmers in Diwaniyah province. In the video, "[al-Hassan] is holding a stack of real estate title deeds and telling the farmers that Prime Minister Nouri al-Maliki has sent him to give them plots of land in exchange for their votes in favor of his coalition in the elections" (Hasan, 2014). This episode of corruption, bad as it was, was relatively small-stakes (and, as it turned out, the deeds were fraudulent) compared to the broader machinations of the al-Mâlikî regime, whose tendencies have been towards centralizing state power within the office of the executive or, more specifically, within the executive office of the personage of al-Mâlikî and his loyalists. One noted example is the politically motivated staffing of the (nominally) nonpartisan Electoral Commission, a process that naturally raises questions about the legitimacy of Iraqi elections. Hoshyar Malo, the coordinator of Shams Network, an NGO that monitored the Iraqi parliamentary elections in 2014, emphasized that there was clear evidence that the election had been tampered with, an opinion echoed by all political parties apart from al-Mâlikî's State of Law Coalition. The Electoral Commission stood accused of "organized electoral fraud perpetrated by the official employees of the commission" under the guidance of the major administrators of the Commission, all of whom were from the Da'wa Party and a number of whom were relatives. The Commission also exceeded its mandate by "instituting regulations related to campaign financing in 2013, which [was] the prerogative of the parliament and not the commission" (Studio 9, January 30, 2014). General suspicion of the 2014 election results were voiced across the political factions and, with the rising political acrimony, it became clear that it would take months of negotiation to form a government (Mustafa, 2014). Ayatollah al-Sistânî, the most prominent Shi'i religious leader in Iraq, adopted a quietist position towards the election, neither praising nor condemning it, but instead exhorted Iraqis to vote for the "honest and righteous" while eschewing the "bad and corrupt" (Kadhimi, 2014). In view of the current state of Iraqi politics, seemingly corrupt at every level, this religious/moral principle did not offer many choices for Iraqi voters.

Another major pitfall to democratization on the constitutional pathway to political development established by the new constitution was the lack of popular sovereignty. The political order that emerged in post-war Iraq was not a happenstance or merely the natural product of a sectarian cultural environment, but had the clear markings of design. The CPA orders at the outset of the Anglo-American occupation, the Iraqi constitution that was midwifed by the occupation authorities

212 *Iraq in the twenty-first century*

and the expatriate "carpetbaggers" supported by external power, and the general political sectarian tone of post-invasion politics were the result of policy, not some inherent Iraqi national character. Rather, the primacy of religious sectarianism was embedded within the Iraqi system through Article 2 of the Iraqi constitution, which established religion as the foundation of the Iraqi state. Political power in Iraq was thereafter exercised by elite sectarian, and highly corrupt, political blocs that have effectively shut out popular input into government policy, charting instead a blatantly sectarian course that "replays similar deficiencies [as those seen] during the previous decades of Baathist and monarchist rule" (Khouri, 2014).

The consequences of the failed Iraqi state are the foreseeable results of the project of regime change, deliberately and illegally initiated by US and UK leaders. These powers cannot excuse themselves with the alibi that "stuff happens." It is untenable that in the twenty-first century people like the Iraqis, Libyans, Afghanis, Somalis, Syrians or Congolese are forced to live by Thucydides' maxim that "the strong do what they can and the weak suffer what they must" (Thucydides, 1996, 5.89).

Notes

1 In contrast to "embedded journalists," as in journalists attached to US military units. Given the camaraderie that would naturally develop in such a situation, it raises serious questions related to journalistic ethics and objectivity.
2 The term "carpetbaggers" originally refers to the Republican political appointees who administered the defeated Confederate States following the US Civil War, and were imported from the north. In the colloquial sense, and as used here, the term refers to opportunistic politicians who change their place of residency for self-serving reasons.
3 This strategy of indiscriminate shelling would be joined by the use of "barrel bombs," generally oil or water tanks filled with high explosives and scrap metal, in May 2014. These unguided munitions have been dropped from Iraqi Army helicopters over neighborhoods, causing incredible damage to the city. One security official described the policy of using barrel bombs: "My government [...] decided to destroy the city instead of trying to invade it." This destruction has also included the deliberate targeting of Fallujah General Hospital, which has been subject to shelling and rocket attacks dozens of times since January 2014 (Human Rights Watch, 2014).
4 See Chapter 3.
5 See Chapter 3.
6 See Chapter 5.
7 See Chapter 4.
8 See Niqash (2005) for a full list of the drafting committee.
9 See Chapter 4.
10 See Chapter 5.
11 See Chapter 5.

References

Abbas, M. (2014, May 19). *Maliki Got Election Assist from Anbar Crisis*. Retrieved June 7, 2014, from Al-Monitor: http://www.al-monitor.com/pulse/originals/2014/05/iraq-maliki-elections-anbar-benefit.html

Iraq in the twenty-first century   213

Ames, M. (2014, February 28). *Pierre Omidyar Co-Funded Ukraine Revolution Groups with US Government, Documents Show*. Retrieved March 9, 2014, from Pando Daily: http://pando.com/2014/02/28/pierre-omidyar-co-funded-ukraine-revolution-groups-with-us-government-documents-show/

Associated Press. (2014, January 5). *Top Iraqi Commander Vows to Re-Capture Fallujah and Ramadi After al-Qa'ida-Linked Fighters Take Control of Key Cities*. Retrieved January 31, 2014, from *The Independent*: www.independent.co.uk/news/world/middle-east/topiraqi-commander-vows-to-recapture-fallujah-and-ramadi-after-alqaidalinked-fighters-take-control-of-key-cities-9039681.html

Bashkin, O. (2009). *The Other Iraq: Pluralism, intellectuals and culture in Hashemite Iraq, 1921–1958*. California: Stanford University Press.

BBC News. (2007a, March 19). *Iraq Poll March 2007: In graphics*. Retrieved February 3, 2014, from BBC News: http://news.bbc.co.uk/2/hi/middle_east/6451841.stm

BBC News. (2007b, August 15). *Deadly Iraq Sect Attacks Kill 200*. Retrieved January 31, 2014, from BBC News: http://news.bbc.co.uk/2/hi/middle_east/6946028.stm

Bush, G. W. (2005, June 28). *Iraq and the Global War on Terror*. Speech given in Fort Bragg, North Carolina. Retrieved March 12, 2014, from US Department of State Archive: http://2001-2009.state.gov/p/nea/rls/rm/48716.htm

Caputi, R. (2013, January 17). *Iraqi Protests Defy the Maliki Regime and Inspire Hope*. Retrieved February 6, 2014, from *The Guardian*: www.theguardian.com/commentisfree/2013/jan/17/iraq-protest-defy-maliki-regime

Caputi, R. (2014, January 10). *I Helped Destroy Falluja in 2004. I won't be complicit again*. Retrieved February 6, 2014, from *The Guardian*: www.theguardian.com/commentisfree/2014/jan/10/iraq-fallujah-destruction-alqaida-maliki

Chulov, M. (2010, October 28). *Iraq War Logs: The US was part of the Wolf Brigade operation against us*. Retrieved January 31, 2014, from *The Guardian*: www.theguardian.com/world/2010/oct/28/iraq-war-logs-iraq

Contrera, R. (2009, August 8). *Saving the People, Killing the Faith*. Retrieved January 31, 2014, from Holland Sentinel: www.hollandsentinel.com/x1558731033/Saving-the-people-killing-the-faith

Cottam, R. W. (1967). *Competitive Intereference and Twentieth Century Diplomacy*. Pittsburgh: University of Pittsburgh Press.

Davis, E. (2005). *Memories of State: Politics, history, and collective identity in modern Iraq*. London: University of California Press.

Deutsche Welle. (2013, December 28). *Iraqi Troops Arrest Sunni Lawmaker amid Deadly Gunfight*. Retrieved January 31, 2014, from Deutsche Welle: www.dw.de/iraqi-troops-arrest-sunni-lawmaker-amid-deadly-gunfight/a-17328320

Deutsche Welle. (2014, January 4). *Al Qaeda Growing Stronger in Iraq and Syria*. Retrieved January 31, 2014, from Deutsche Welle: www.dw.de/al-qaeda-growing-stronger-in-iraq-and-syria/a-17340739

Ditz, J. (2014, February 2). *Iraq Escalates Fallujah Shelling, Prepares Ground Invasion*. Retrieved November 15, 2014, from Antiwar.com: http://news.antiwar.com/2014/02/02/iraq-escalates-fallujah-shelling-preparing-ground-invasion/

Dougherty, M. B. (2014, January 23). *The World's Most Ancient Christian Communities are Being Destroyed—And no one cares*. Retrieved January 31, 2014, from The Week: http://theweek.com/article/index/255403/the-worlds-most-ancient-christian-communities-are-being-destroyed-mdash-and-no-one-cares

214 *Iraq in the twenty-first century*

Foley, C. (2009, June 23). *Beware Human Rights Imperialism*. Retrieved March 9, 2014, from *The Guardian*: www.theguardian.com/commentisfree/2009/jun/23/human-rights-imperialism-western-values

Fund for Peace. (2013). *The Failed State Index 2013*. Retrieved January 31, 2014, from Fund for Peace: http://ffp.statesindex.org/

Gordts, E. (2013, March 20). *Iraq War Anniversary: Birth defects and cancer rates at devastating high in Basra and Fallujah*. Retrieved January 31, 2014, from *Huffington Post*: www.huffingtonpost.com/2013/03/20/iraq-war-anniversary-birth-defects-cancer _n_2917701.html

Government Accountability Office (GAO). (2008, January). *Iraq Reconstruction: Better data needed to assess Iraq's budget execution*. Retrieved April 7, 2014, from GAO: www.gao.gov/new.items/d08153.pdf

Harding, L. (2014, January 1). *Iraq Suffers its Deadliest Year since 2008*. Retrieved January 31, 2014, from *The Guardian*: www.theguardian.com/world/2014/jan/01/ iraq-2013-deadliest-year-since-2008

Hasan, H. (2014, May 15). *Iraqi MP Fined for Offering Land for Votes*. Retrieved June 7, 2014, from Al-Monitor: www.al-monitor.com/pulse/originals/2014/05/iraq-rise-political-patronage.html

Human Rights Watch. (2014, May 27). *Iraq: Government attacking Fallujah Hospital*. Retrieved May 28, 2014, from Human Rights Watch: www.hrw.org/node/125880

Ismael, J. (2010). Self-Organization and Self-Governance. *Philosophy of the Social Sciences, 41*(3), 327–351.

Jabar, F. A. (2000). Shaykhs and Ideologues: Detribalization and retribalization in Iraq, 1968–1998. *Middle East Report, 215*, 28–48.

Joint Analysis Policy Unit (JAPU). (2013, January). *Iraq Budget 2013: Background paper*. Retrieved April 7, 2014, from ReliefWeb: http://reliefweb.int/sites/reliefweb.int/files/ resources/Iraq%20Budget%202013%20Background%20Paper.pdf

Jones, S. (2014, May 23). *Kofi Annan: Syrians pay with their lives while regional powers wage proxy wars*. Retrieved May 25, 2014, from *The Guardian*: www.theguardian. com/global-development/2014/may/23/kofi-annan-syrians-regional-proxy-wars

Kadhimi, M. (2014, May 20). Sistani keeps distance from Iraqi election politics. Retrieved June 7, 2014, from Al-Monitor: www.al-monitor.com/pulse/originals/2014/05/iraq-sistani-distance-political-disputes.html

Karim, F. (2014, June 4). [*The Marketplace for Deputies' Votes and Cabinet Positions*]. Retrieved June 6, 2014, from Al-Mada: www.almadapaper.net/ar/news/465671/ روبةةفلاتلا-ةعاضبلا-ةميق-ةلودلا-ليمحت-بيع

Kenner, D. (2012, October 29). *Iraq's Youngest Casualties of War*. Retrieved January 31, 2014, from Foreign Policy: http://blog.foreignpolicy.com/posts/2012/10/29/ iraqs_youngest_casualties_of_war

Khouri, R. G. (2014, May 28). *Reading a Painful Guide to Iraqi Decay*. Retrieved November 15, 2014, from *The Daily Star Lebanon*: http://www.dailystar.com.lb/ Opinion/Columnist/2014/May-28/257925-reading-a-painful-guide-to-iraqi-decay.ashx

Kohn, S. (2014, March 6). *GOP's Hypocrisy on Ukraine Hurts America*. Retrieved March 10, 2014, from CNN: www.cnn.com/2014/03/06/opinion/kohn-ukraine-politics/

Lee, J. (2013, August 28). *18.9% Live Below Poverty Line*. Retrieved April 7, 2014, from Iraq Business News: www.iraq-businessnews.com/2013/08/28/18-9-live-below-poverty-line/

Lerman, D., & Giroux, G. (2014, March 2). *Obama Weighs Sanctions on Russia as Kerry Travels to Kiev*. Retrieved March 12, 2014, from Bloomberg: www.bloomberg.com/ news/2014-03-02/kerry-says-u-s-weighing-sanctions-on-russia-over-ukraine.html

Iraq in the twenty-first century 215

Leydesdorff, L. (1993). Is Society a Self-Organizing System? *Journal for Social and Evolutionary Systems, 16*, 331–349.

Mamouri, A. (2013, September 18). *Iraqi Secularists Struggle to Establish Political Presence*. Retrieved June 7, 2014, from Al-Monitor: www.al-monitor.com/pulse/originals/2013/09/iraq-secular-absent-protests.html

Mustafa, H. (2014, May 20). *Tension Mounts in Baghdad after Initial Election Results Announced*. Retrieved May 20, 2014, from Asharq Al-Awsat: www.aawsat.net/2014/05/article55332452

Niqash. (2005, March 6). *Members of the Constitution Drafting Committee*. Retrieved June 7, 2014, from Niqash: www.niqash.org/articles/?id=672&lang=en

Obama, Barack. (2014, March 26). *Remarks by the President in Address to European Youth*. Speech in Brussels, Belgium. Retrieved April 2, 2014, from The White House: www.whitehouse.gov/the-press-office/2014/03/26/remarks-president-address-european-youth

Parker, N. (2014, January 4). *Why Iraq's Most Violent Province Is a War Zone Again*. Retrieved January 31, 2014, from *Time Magazine*: http://world.time.com/2014/01/04/why-iraqs-most-violent-province-is-a-war-zone-again/

Qasifi, J. (2009, October 7). *Annahar* (Beirut), Volume 77, No. 2387.

Russia Today. (2014, March 3). *Seriously, What?! Kerry tells Russia "you don't invade a country on a completely phony pretext."* Retrieved March 8, 2014, from *Russia Today*: http://rt.com/news/kerry-russia-us-pretext-494/

Studio 9. (2014, January 30). *Al-Baghdadia*.

Studio 9. (2014, February 4). *Al-Baghdadia*.

Studio 9. (2014, February 5.) *Al-Baghdadia*.

Thucydides. (1996). *The Landmark Thucydides: A comprehensive guide to the Peloponnesian War* (R. B. Strassler, trans.). New York: Free Press.

Transparency International. (2013). *Corruption Perceptions Index*. Retrieved January 31, 2014, from Transparency International: http://cpi.transparency.org/cpi2013/results/

Epilogue
Blowback from regime change

The collapse of Iraqi state authority across north-western Iraq, dramatically punctuated by the retreat of the Iraqi Army from the city of Mosul on June 10, 2014, concentrated global attention on the hollow state apparatus implanted through Anglo-American occupation. While the retreat of the Nuri al-Mâlikî regime's military and security forces laid bare both their lack of capacity as well as the dereliction of state officials to provide for the safety of Iraq's citizenry, attentive observers had long been identifying the deficiencies of the post-2003 order. International media, as well as scholarly and policy circles, had become less interested following the nominal US military withdrawal of December 2011. However, this withdrawal was only a veneer placed over the still-raging conflict that was unleashed over a decade prior. As with the May 1, 2003 "Mission Accomplished" speech by US President George W. Bush and the June 28, 2004 unceremonious retreat of US administrator Paul Bremer with the shuttering of the CPA, the conflict in Iraq was not at an end. As with the previous declarations choreographed from Washington DC, based on American timeframes and reflecting American desires to leave evident failure in an unremarked past, such manufactured resolution was without reality. While the narrative of "the surge" had convinced its proponents and many in the West of a fantastical success, the reality facing Iraqis was altogether different. The devastation of the physical and ecological terrain, plundering of the economy, evisceration of the comity between Iraqis, ruination of the Iraqi state and the attendant humanitarian misery could not be resolved by any "surge." Nor was it addressed sufficiently by an unrepresentative and illegitimate regime put in place through Anglo-American machination. While the Al-Mâlikî regime came to reflect an ever-narrowing portion of the Iraqi polity, the legitimacy of the desires expressed by a wide array of Iraq's diverse peoples to live in security, access the resources of the state for socio-economic development, and to feel included in any aspirational future was ignored. Portrayed with a newly crafted sectarian pastiche, which had informed the institutions imposed from above, Iraqi communities found outlet for such legitimate grievances through sectarian logics and violent exposition.

As detailed in this volume, the state-building project initiated in 2003 was destined for failure. It was an alien fabrication meant to mimic a modern state. Rather than structured so as to be responsive to its citizens, it instead failed to

Epilogue   217

incorporate indigenous expressions of self-determination, provide for the day-to-day material or security needs of Iraqis, nor reflect shared Iraqi desires for the future. Unlike the monarchical and republican projects of Iraqi state building, the post-2003 order enshrined ethno-sectarian identity as the central component of citizenship rather than communal state institutions and shared aspirational futures. This "Lebanonization" may well have reflected outsiders' notions of Iraq's varied communities, but in valorizing ethnic and sectarian communities in preference to the national project, it empowered entrepreneurial politicians beholden to homogenized and narrow groups as well as foreign patrons, while at the same time according clerical establishments free license to enter the political domain. Thus, the so-called "Islamic State"[1] emerged to terrify the populace, challenge regional and global order, and presage the rendering of Iraqi territorial continuity not as a causal factor of the 2014 deterioration, but as a consequence, of the failures of the post-2003 Iraqi state.

To be plain, the Iraqi state project which had emerged over eight decades (1921–2003) was eviscerated and rendered institutionally inoperative from 2003. Anglo-American power, which empowered the carpetbaggers and rootless front men of the Iraqi diaspora as described previously, failed in its responsibility, granted as a *post hoc* imprimatur through the UN (UNSC Resolution 1483), following the illegal 2003 invasion. The challenge faced by occupation administrators and Iraqis was to craft a polity purposed to Iraqi society and the aspirations of its diverse peoples. Iraqi expressions of self-determination had been subverted through the authoritarianism of the Ba'th Party and Saddam Hussein's dictatorship, and exacerbated by the wars and attendant international economic sanctions imposed following the 1990 invasion of Kuwait. However, as we have demonstrated, the ability of Iraqis to freely express their desires for a future state and society were also subverted through the occupation and imposition of the new Iraqi state established by Anglo-American *dictat* and embodied by the CPA and successor's such as the al-Mâlikî regime.

The eruption of political violence and enormous humanitarian calamity accompanying Anglo-American occupation saw ceaseless efforts to rhetorically identify all challenges to the new state project as foreign in origin and "anti-Iraqi." This effort denied the realities of popular opposition within Iraq to the Anglo-American occupation and its aftermath, and was only bolstered by the outbursts of transnational Islamist factions, including an emergent al-Qaeda franchise under Abu Musab al-Zarqawi. Moreover, the occupation and attendant disenfranchisement of Iraqis encouraged the self-interested efforts of regional states to intervene. Such meddling by regional states and transnational actors, ostensibly in the name of Iraqis opposed to the occupation's imposition of a new state, nonetheless afforded enough confusion for the occupation to successfully avoid the need to directly address the multivariate popular indigenous oppositions to the Anglo-American project.

Rather than a design flaw, or the personal failure of any individual, the post-2003 state was structured in a manner making it incapable of responding to the day-to-day needs and popular aspirations of the Iraqi people. *Mohassasa* (ethnic

218   *Epilogue*

and sectarian quotas) were both institutionalized and perhaps more consequentially entrenched in popular consciousness. While not entirely new to Iraqi social relations, its institutionalization emerged only with the state founded in 2003. This was especially imposed through a labyrinthine process of "de-Ba'thification." A politicized process, de-Ba'thification fell preponderantly upon the Sunni members of the former state apparatus and not its constituents from other Iraqi communities. Moreover, it reached far beyond the elite that had held power and therefore responsibility for the crimes of the regime. The institutionalization of mohassasa brought about the "Lebanonization" of Iraq. It was set in place, as both space and identity were rendered through a violent process at the same time both intimate and indiscriminate. Prodigious bloodletting and the terror of indiscriminate bombings corralled the population through security checkpoints and blast walls to denote supposedly homogenized ethno-sectarian zones. This (re) territorialization of wholly new political boundaries divided communities and reorganized their social and economic ties. Moreover, the deterritorialization marked by the withdrawal of an autonomous Iraqi Kurdistan under the Kurdistan Regional Government (KRG), largely outside central state authority since 1991, altered notions of national cartography. Altogether, these processes, set in motion by the occupation and institutionalization in the post-2003 state, denied Iraq's manifest diversity a shared history, as well as the patrimony afforded by bountiful natural resources. Finally, the lack of indigenous political leadership and the evident orientation of the new Iraqi political class to Iranian and American patronage undermined the successful operationalization of procedural democratic expression. Successive Parliamentary elections (2005, 2010 and 2014), local and provincial elections and Constitutional referendums all evidenced a manifest national desire for participatory democratic practice and support for the institutionalization of representative democracy. However, inclusive institutions allowing for free expression and inclusive debate over the future polity failed to materialize. Civil society and alternative political actors were denied expression, functionally as well as legally. Having their cartographic sense of self erased, erstwhile efforts for indigenous expression or input into redesigned state institutions denied to them, and their national patrimony of natural resources handed to actors unknown and not responsible to the citizenry, Iraqis were denied the option of a shared future.

In the morass of security failure and social dislocation, evidenced by millions of internally displaced persons (IDPs) and refugees, the centrifugal forces of Iraq, similar to those found in any state, privileged regional divergence within the territorial confines often operationalized as well as the empowerment of local actors over those advocating a national response. Kurdish nationalism, embodied in the KRG in the north, and a variety of Shi'ite political actors in the south who had grown from the transnational opposition formed against the Ba'th regime, successfully entrenched themselves in the new polity. Within the contested environs of Baghdad and Kirkuk, as well as across the predominantly Sunni-majority central and western Iraq, local authority was denied such opportunities. Indigenous local authority, rather than being incorporated into the reformulated

Epilogue 219

polity, found itself denied legitimacy and targeted by the new regime's security apparatus. Thus, legitimate actors were denied the opportunity to represent local communities, especially to express grievances against the new political order, based entirely on their potential vestiges of the former Ba'th regime or ties to transnational terrorism. This distinctly privileged some regions over others within the new order—regardless of their predispositions or orientations. The weight of counterinsurgency operations from the Anglo-American occupation was followed by the neglect and military responses of the al-Mâlikî regime to any expression of local demands. The communal devastation wrought through oppressive security measures, the corrupt practices of both state representatives and non-state actors and the denial of local actors to have a voice in national governance alienated large swaths of a diverse population in the affected regions. The denial of local agency to manage local affairs, as well as rebuffing access to the institutional and financial resources of the central government, was effectively uninterrupted from the onset of the post-2003 occupation through the al-Mâlikî era.[2]

With the 2011 US military withdrawal, much of the exorbitant largesse related to the enterprise of occupation—and its attendant opportunity for corruption— was also ended. However, the rent-seeking behavior of the new Iraqi political class, institutionalized under Anglo-American occupation, was unabated under al-Mâlikî. With Iraqi pre-war reserves depleted and the dispensation of funds from the US government staunched, Iraqi carpetbaggers were left to compete over the spoils provided by the state institutions as well as what could be levied from amongst the impoverished Iraqi population. Without political representation, or basic security, this left northern and western Iraq outside the writ of the KRG particularly vulnerable. Composed of a majority of Sunni Arabs, as well as an enormously diverse array of ethnic and religious minorities, these regions had borne the brunt of heavy fighting in opposition to occupation and the new political order implanted by Anglo-American military power. Those trumpeting the success of the surge were silent on the impacts of no longer having American forces and the financial largesse they distributed across central and northwest Iraq. Now safe at bases in Kuwait, or returned to the US, they were no longer targets for insurgent attack. The wherewithal of local security forces, no longer coordinated with or funded by the Iraqi state, was left unattended. Nor was a replacement for the means of support provided to these communities through US military bribes and targeted development funds. American surge tactics, such as the Commanders' Emergency Response Fund, dispensed enormous sums of unrecorded black pools of cash to local proxies so as to blunt their activities against the undetectable central government, dissuade them from attacking US forces, and to withdraw their support for al-Qaeda and other radicals. While successfully blunting attacks against US forces and removing an immediate threat to central state authority, the initiative merely postponed the resolution of issues of governance for an equivocal future. In effect, the tactic acted as large-scale extortion scheme rather than a sustainable governance model. With the withdrawal of US forces, the flows of cash and the provision of weapons and training, as well as the forced coordination with the central government, evaporated. Moreover, the patina of

220   *Epilogue*

state authority provided to the levies raised from amongst the population and their implied incorporation into the new Iraqi state was shown to be a lie.

Across the 24 months following the US withdrawal, this untenable disconnect between the new state and large swaths of its territory and population went largely unremarked in mainstream conversation. While the Kurdistan region continued to develop and untether itself from the broader Iraqi federal project and the al-Mâlikî government concentrated on Baghdad and the internecine competition between the predominantly Shi'ite south, Anbar and Nineveh provinces were left to wither. Thus, it should be no surprise that Iraqi state authority in these regions faced increasing discontent and organized opposition. While global attention focused on the "Arab Spring" and the descent of Syria into a charnel house of cruel bloodletting, these regions of Iraq were also ignored in global media coverage and policy circles. In 2010 the region's voice was denied legitimate access to the decision-making apparatus of the new state, in spite of electoral participation in the anti-al-Mâlikî coalition led by Ayad Állawi. Further, federal security and military forces were increasingly hollowed out and their activities informed by the corruption of the officers nominated for command by the al-Mâlikî government instead of their mission to protect Iraqis. As locals were pushed to pay petty bribes, to see family members arrested without charge and to suffer the indignities of petty graft at security checkpoints, the federal government was increasingly seen as an occupying force. No longer believed to act in the name of the federal whole, central government forces were seen to represent Baghdad and an avowedly sectarian Shi'ite-oriented regime unconcerned with the legitimate grievances and future prospects of a largely Sunni population.

Under such conditions, direct opposition emerged through popular non-violent protest, triggered by the December 2012 raid on the home of Finance Minister Rafi al-Íssawi, a Sunni politician from Anbar. Protests grew across Anbar, informed by opposition to the undemocratic al-Mâlikî regime and the regional uprisings against tyranny. Centered on the city of Hawija, west of Kirkuk, the protesters established a camp that stood as a monument against the new order. Smaller camps and localized protests spread across Anbar and Nineveh, as well as in the Sunni-majority portions of Samarra, Diyala and Kirkuk. While focused on redressing nominally Sunni grievances, the protests received support from cross-sectarian leaders such as Muqtadâ al-Ṣadr as well as Kurdish lawmakers. Many outside the increasingly small circle around al-Mâlikî recognized the concentration of power he was marshaling and desired amelioration through non-violent constitutional means. Unwilling to accede to the protesters' demands, to incorporate local elected leaders within the decision-making process federally, nor to legitimize their grievances, the al-Mâlikî regime targeted the protests with state security. On April 23, 2013, a military raid against the protest encampment led to dozens of civilian deaths and cemented the sectarian divide. Fears of a return to the wide-scale sectarian civil war period were not enough to staunch the re-emergence of several insurgent groups opposed to the al-Mâlikî government and the state apparatus loyal to his person. It is worth noting that the general lack of acknowledgment of the enormous levels of violence that pre-dated the US surge

Epilogue 221

have colored international analysis and understandings. Both the magnitude as well as the barbarity of the 2006–2008 period has escaped English-language scrutiny. While driven by US efforts to portray all such violence as driven by "terrorism" as well as to obscure the failed state-building project, by not acknowledging the suffering of Iraqis across sectarian and ethnic divides, the tinder for future conflict was left to accumulate.

This return to violent conflict, infused by sectarian identity and demonstrative of the rejection of the new state project by many Iraqis, failed to register outside the country. The commitment to portraying the surge as a success, polls as the realization of democratic practice and the legitimation of the al-Mâlikî regime based solely on their victory in those polls overcame a sober acknowledgment that the new institutions were not meeting with necessary public support. The corruption, expansive institutionalization of sectarianism and incapacity to marshal state resources to meet the needs of all Iraqis were evident throughout Iraq. Southern-based calls for greater autonomy as a region, the pace of the Kurdistan Regional Government's ever-advancing autonomy from Baghdad's writ and any shared future with the rest of Iraq also demonstrated the fraying of the Iraqi state.

Thus, the prefabricated institutional arrangements hastily erected in the guise of a new Iraqi state from 2003 buckled, largely as that new state reflected assumptions out of touch with the realities of Iraqi history. Without the ballast provided by such sensibilities exhibited within Iraqi society over the longue durée, the state project was left solely with oppression as a means to rule. Such sensibilities had been both opposed and coopted by the Ba'thist regime, leading to general opposition to its rule across Iraqi society. However, they were ignored entirely by the Anglo-American project, eviscerated with physical violence when they rose through public expression, and therefore amplified the impact of regional interventions within Iraqi politics. Taking as given the cliquish authoritarianism of Saddam Hussein's late-Ba'th regime, along with the sectarian formulations promoted regionally by those opposed to modern nationalism, the new state project failed to reflect Iraqi social custom and expectations of comity. The imposed "new order" privileged narrow identifications easily manipulated by political entrepreneurs and carpetbaggers rather than the lived realities of Iraqis. The Iraq envisioned by Anglo-American design, fronted by diaspora Iraqis, and tempered by the interests of regional powers, denied the historical Iraqi experience as much as it did Iraqi self-determination. The social fabric knit over centuries evidenced comity, with ethno-sectarian violence arising as rare and noted deviations, usually in conjunction with the arrival or departure of foreign invaders. The post-2003 implantation of a sectarian-infused state structure ignored this history, pulling from it the rare instances of inter-communal strife, thereby assuming the exceptional over that of the norm. To do so required taking advantage of the legacy of authoritarianism, the chaos attendant with the Anglo-American occupation, and the presumption of analysts and observers that "Iraq" had seemingly begun in 2003.

It should come as no surprise therefore that the state's exclusion of those refusing to identify with a homogenized and narrow ethno-sectarian identity, established as a constitutional prerequisite to political inclusion, faced resistance.

222　*Epilogue*

Within the context of this popular enmity, to the new state the organizational capacity of ISIS assumed itself as a further challenge to both the pre-2003 state as well as the new order. The 2014 challenge to public order and the adverse prospects for Iraq's future did not emerge from the rise of the radicals of ISIS alone, nor from the other transnational actors so prevalent following the Anglo-American fragmentation of the Iraqi polity. In fact, such transnational actors failed in repeated attempts to impress themselves on the Iraqi political landscape prior to 2003, being routinely rejected by the polity and smashed by the Iraqi state. Rather, the success of particularistic ethno-sectarian radicals is a response to the occupation and the state it bequeathed Iraqis. Therefore, much analysis of ISIS confuses cause and effect.

The emergence of ISIS

The Islamic State emerged from the cataclysm coincident with the erasure of state authority in both Iraq and Syria.[3] In large measure the retreat of state authority in both countries can be attributed to US policy in the region. All analysis of their rise that absents this connection between cause and effect, that instead portrays ISIS as representative of legitimate popular sovereignty, having descended from the sky, or as some actor stalking the globe from late antiquity lavishly committed to a pure heroic form of Islamic exegesis, mistakes propaganda for reality. As we have seen, the failed invasion and occupation of Iraq and the heir to Anglo-American state building, the al-Mâlikî regime, alienated the population and lost both legitimacy and authority across western and northern Iraq. In Syria, a desire to support the overthrow of the Assad dynasty saw uncritical Western and Arab state support for a wide range of indigenous and foreign actors. They had little in common aside from their willingness to supplant the Ba'thist regime. While initiated by Syrians as a peaceful attempt to reform the state long commandeered by the regime of Hafez al-Assad, the violent response from the regime devastated any hopes for a non-violent Syrian uprising. Evincing conviction to remove the Assad regime, the Syrian opposition increasingly responded with arms to the flagrant abuses against the population by Syrian state security and militias aligned with the regime. Western and Arab Gulf states began supporting and even arming the opposition, including foreign fighters who increasingly flocked to Syria bringing their capacity for violence and varied political designs to a population simply looking to get out from under the yoke of authoritarianism.

This anarchic landscape allowed for the intervention of foreign jihadists who, without indigenous foundation, transplanted both organizational capacity as well as ideological paradigms to the Jazira plains, a large outwash plain that spans Northwestern Iraq, Northeastern Syria and Southeastern Turkey. With the Syria conflict descending into internecine bloodletting and a humanitarian crisis of global import, the more radical fighters increasingly established hegemony, as local populations became objects rather than the source of political legitimacy to all factions engaged in the conflict. Along with the regionalization of the war in Syria and the intervention of international radicals, the conflict spoke intimately to that ongoing in Iraq. Trans-border linkages of both historical and more recent vintage allude to sincere affinities and affiliations and therefore drew the two conflicts together. The cauldron of the Syrian civil war invited Iraqi fighters to support both kin and ideological allies. While Shi'ite militias buttressed the Assad regime, and the KRG was compelled to support their Syrian-based allies in the emergent Kurdish polity of *Rojava* in a primarily inter-Kurdish competition with the Marxist PKK, a bevy of Arab Sunni Iraqis with tribal, familial and ideological affinities also joined the conflict. Within this later trend were the remnants of al-Qaeda in Iraq, a wide range of tribal and Islamist movements, and criminal organizations that had long profited from cross-border illicit trade. The grouping identified as al-Qaeda in Iraq (AQI) had been a franchise of the global network initiated by Osama bin Laden. It had evolved from the foundations established under Abu Musáb al-Zarqawi's *Jama'at al-Tawhid wal-Jihad* (Group of Monotheism and Jihad). A Jordanian national, born Ahmad Fadhil al-Nazal al-Khalayleh, al-Zarqawi had fought in Afghanistan and established his organization as a rival to that of bin Laden's. Transiting to Iraq in late 2002, al-Zarqawi had planned to develop a fighting force to challenge the post-Ba'thist order through terrorism while acting as a vanguard against the Anglo-American occupation. To do so he surrounded himself with fellow "Afghan-Arabs," jihadists who had fought in Afghanistan against the Soviet occupation of that country, or more broadly the international volunteers who had trained at camps maintained during the era following that war when the Taliban ruled Afghanistan. Al-Zarqawi successfully recruited Iraqi Arabs and Kurds as well as other internationals to his organization, was ruthless in the use of extreme violence, and succeeded in escalating the sectarian rationalization for the enormous bloodshed that followed the Anglo-American invasion and occupation of Iraq. While US forces killed al-Zarqawi in June 2006, his zealous organization would survive the surge, carrying forward under Abu Omar al-Baghdadi.

The 2005 populist "National Council for the Salvation of Iraq," a coalition of Sunni tribal forces that rose up in opposition to both the brutality of Abu Omar al-Baghdadi's faction of al-Qaeda as well as Iraqi state security's heavy-handed efforts to control the terrain of Anbar and Nineveh, saw AQI greatly diminished. US efforts to support these "Sons of Iraq" in their "awakening" joined local Iraqi efforts with their own "surge." Following the Iraqis' ousting of jihadists from amongst Iraq's predominantly Sunni regions, US commentators declared victory and abandoned their nominal Iraqi allies to their fates. However, as we have seen, such US machinations failed to anticipate the sectarian antipathies unleashed by the invasion and subsequent civil war as well as the resilience of jihadist radicals generally and al-Qaeda in particular. In not institutionalizing the "Sons of Iraq," volunteers into the Iraq state apparatus's future conflict within Iraq was virtually ensured. Such a lack of foresight demonstrated a genuine misunderstanding of the underlying forces unleashed by the invasion and overestimated the role played by US forces and tactics in bringing about the short period of stability allowing for the US withdrawal.

224   *Epilogue*

Representing a new generation of radical jihadist, affronted by what they could only feel as a deep betrayal by those whom they had sought to avenge against the "crusader" Americans and "Persian" Shi'ite forces now governing in Baghdad, Omar al-Baghdadi's successor, Abu Bakr al-Baghdadi, refashioned the AQI organization, eventually declaring the Islamic State in June 2014. Al-Baghdadi maintained al-Zarqawi's fusion of the transnational membership, modernized the organization's fighting and organizational capabilities, and deepened a commitment to fomenting an Islamic State. The "betrayal" by Iraqis was seen as evidence of the perfidy of local leaders and an acknowledgment that his organization would be required to rule the local population rather than simply engage in war fighting with occupation forces, whether they were Christian crusaders or Shia interlopers. Crucially, the provision of state services would not be in an effort to engineer popular support or consent, for legitimate sovereignty lay with God and not the people; rather, such services were a means to fashion life and allow for population controls as well as an alternative to regional states in an effort to make plain their lack of Islamic authenticity as defined by ISIS's exegesis in opposition to traditional Islamic foundations and understandings.

Thus, ISIS's challenge is unique, for while it is not the sole militant political actor challenging state authority across the *Mashriq* (the Arab states east of Egypt), it has successfully assembled an ideological challenge to the regional order. The diversity and never-ending reformulations of the Syrian opposition parties has been well acknowledged, especially as the radical international jihadist factions became ascendant throughout the course of the fighting against the Assad regime. However, much like the secular nationalists opposing the Ba'th regime in Damascus, the al-Qaeda-affiliated *al-Nusra Front* and *Ahrar al-Sham* have focused their actions on supplanting Bashar al-Assad's rule—not abandoning the Syrian state project, but capturing it. As al-Baghdadi established his authority over al-Zarqawi's organization, shifting much of its focus to the war in Syria, it also reformulated its methods, objectives and goals. While never entirely vacating the Iraqi terrain, ISIS maintained cadres inside Iraq and increasingly dominated the illicit trade across the border into suburban Mosul, and the organization nonetheless reconstituted itself, asserting its will through devastating military prowess and the use of draconian violence. It justified barbarous cruelty through idiosyncratic and largely unprecedented interpretations of Shari'a, whereby captured populations were exposed to acts of immense violence. The sexualized nature of the violence and the assault against the physical body saw the group step outside all norms established by both international law and Islamic praxis. While demonstrably exceeding the levels previously exhibited, the experience of any Iraqi of Baghdadi's age, as well as that of many of his fighters, has to include the legacy of the authoritarian Ba'thist regimes found in Iraq as well as Syria, the actions of Anglo-American death squads and enhanced interrogation programs which permeated the "War on Terror" as it informed their occupation Iraq, as well as the predations of the al-Mâlikî regime's security forces where corruption had devalued human life even further. None of this behavior is justifiable, though it needs to be foregrounded as a reminder of the environment in which Iraqis and now Syrians

Epilogue 225

find themselves. Moreover, as a political orientation which sees legitimation for its rule arise from unorthodox readings of scripture rather than the consent of the governed, ISIS should be acknowledged as a direct challenge to human dignity.

Such barbarity, military prowess, control of territory and captured populations, as well as the economic rents accrued from illicit trade saw ISIS grow to envelop much of the Syrian opposition. It did so while avoiding battles of attrition against the Ba'thist regime, thereby demonstrating its desire to control territory and captured populations in domains left ungoverned in the chaos of civil war, rather than challenging established authorities. Its adversaries, especially those who found themselves denuded and overtaken while suffering under the regime's counteroffensives, often misinterpreted this distinction. Losing territories to the revanchist Assad regime, while being co-opted if not usurped by ISIS, they failed to acknowledge that their shared objectives with ISIS only went as far as their opposition to Assad's rule. Syrians failed to comprehend the global aspirations al-Baghdadi had implanted within ISIS. His new ideology, a political Islam formulated to challenge Arab nationalism and its legacy, itself tainted by authoritarian regimes wed in their later periods to neoliberal economic designs, rejected the state system incorporated into the region by European imperial power a century before. By dismissing the staid state system and its regional order for their failure to adhere to al-Baghdadi's neo-Islamic exegesis, ISIS poses a challenge to both outside designs as well as existing indigenous traditional authority. The fragmentation of social relations and erasure of borders—not only that between Syria and Iraq, but the entire skeletal outline of regional state actors—presents the potential for new boundaries, as well as alliances between transnational groups, actors and identities. Even if defeated on the battlefield, the ideological challenge posed will find resonance across a region challenged from both within and without by generational change, demographic transformation, developmental failure, ecological modification and entanglement in an ever-more connected global society.

We would be mistaken in overstating the potential growth of ISIS, as regional and international powers will not cede their privileges without contestation and the organization is lacking considerable tangible resources and political allies, as well as the resources required to achieve their maximalist goals. It has succeeded not through the superiority of its project, nor the power of its ideology to best express the legitimate grievances of indigenous populations, but rather as an actor best suited to parasitically take advantage of the retreat of state apparatus and the devastation of legitimate political representatives. Its offensive military capacity is based on a nefarious proficiency to undermine the stability associated with a functioning state as well as the short-lived bounty provided by the capture of heavy weaponry following the retreat of Iraqi forces. The heavy weaponry will be degraded through conflict with neighboring actors over time and cannot be replaced without further blunders by more powerful actors. However, the ISIS's ideological proposition and ability to enact tradecraft capable of challenging state functions will endure. What is pivotal is recognition that their potential need not be dismissed as being simply that of a "terrorist" organization. The multifaceted conflict between political identities, states' ideologies and the orientation

226   *Epilogue*

of social and economic life will attract adherents and more broadly lead many to see the possibilities of regional transformation. While such challenges to order in a globalized world could well bring the conflict to western states, this mode has more predominantly been that of ISIS's competitor, al-Qaeda. Moreover, ISIS's success has been without acknowledgment that it has not acted alone, nor outside terrain predominantly Arab and Sunni in orientation, where it has been able to portray itself as an ally against outside actors decried by local populations. Within Iraq the "Islamic State" or ISIS is allied with actors who have similar political projects to the Syrian opposition, focused on the seizure of—or devolution of—power in Baghdad—tribal formations, neo-Ba'thist militias melded with and bolstered by disgruntled former "Awakening" members, and the Army of the Men of the Naqshbandi Order, ostensibly inspired by the leadership of Izzat Ibrahim al-Douri, a former lieutenant to Saddam Hussein. This unwieldy coalition, not to mention the tacit compliance of the broader population over which they have come to rule, reflect the traditional and grounded society bequeathed to modern Iraqis. ISIS, for all its innovation, barbarism, and efficiency, represents a challenge to the Iraqi and Syrian social fabric as much as American neoliberalism or the Islamic Republic of Iran. With the region awash in IDPs and refugees, the demographic transformation of a new generation, the ungoverned spaces rendered by Anglo-American aggression and the Assad regime's violent opposition to any sharing of power, the *Mashriq* was left open to new challengers. The reflexive relationship between such neo-Islamist movements and the global order in which they craft themselves undermines their claim of being the reincarnated first-companions (*Sahabah*) of the Prophet Mohammed.

The failure of the violent opposition to Anglo-American occupation to congeal around an agreed Iraqi nationalist idiom and command structure should also cause us to question the breathless formulations of ISIS found in the Western media. Limited to ethno-sectarian environs akin to its own membership, Western media reportage tended to portray the group as conquering Mosul and sweeping across the region, materializing out of the desert as marauders from the seventh century. This telling both fails to recognize the sophisticated operations conducted as well as the tenuous hold such a small force would have amongst a large population and even wider territory should the local population resist. Put simply, the city of Mosul "fell" to ISIS, as Mosulis decidedly rejected Iraqi state authority, more than it was conquered. Likewise, the group's material resources are undetermined. Its wealth and economic resources are certainly overstated, for while functional they are based on the bounty of conquest as well as economic rents collected through taxation, extortion, illicit trade and kidnappings, all of which are not productive behaviors, nor immune from diminution from state or alternative actors. With the expanding reach and commitment to ISIS's nascent state apparatus, expenditures will necessarily expand as well. Moreover, while the organization has maintained strict hierarchical control during its successful expansion, a split between its international and indigenous members may emerge moving forward. The challenge posed by al-Baghdadi's ideological innovations will force a decision as to whether the expansive revolutionary effort should be pursued, or if holding what

Epilogue 227

they've achieved to date will satiate the organization's members and its allies. As with all such radical challenges, a period of *thermidor* will ensue, allowing regional opponents to adjust and counter ISIS.

With its apparent advanced administrative capacity, organizational rigor, self-financing through illicit activities and advanced fighting skills, all embellished from sophisticated branding and propaganda across a wide spectrum of media platforms, ISIS now poses a challenge to the regional order. Its adherence to a coherent ideological view with a global following and the singular criminality of its killings raise concern as attested by the global community's recognition of such crimes in Iraq and Syria. While rightly focusing on the treatment of Christian and Yazidi minorities in the summer of 2014, such recognition was not afforded to ISIS's earlier predominantly Muslim victims, nor couched within the reality that such minorities had suffered similar losses and displacements across the period of Anglo-American occupation. This selective recognition of Iraqi suffering and its employment to engender opposition to a global pariah nonetheless evinces power in its ability to determine who is to be grieved.

Tri-partition of Iraq and the expansion of chaos

From the onset of military operations in 2003, Anglo-American policies have undermined the Iraqi state—both as a functional institution as well as an ideal. While strongly arguing that they favored a unitary state based on liberal democratic norms, all state-building exercises have countered such an eventuality. The suffering of the Iraqi people has been decidedly minimized and even been left unrecognized, spoken of only in broad terms when noted at all, and its causation not attributed to the policies of Western governments. This is why ISIS, a phenomenon forged in the warfare of the post-2003 invasion of Iraq and the post-2011 internecine bloodletting in Syria, has been able to pose a challenge to the regional order established following World War I. Much as the radical neoliberal project foisted on Iraqis by the George W. Bush Administration, ISIS also proposes a radical project uninformed by historical precedence in the region, nor accounting for popular sovereignty and the desires of its people. ISIS incorporates Zarqawi's radicalism amongst a globally attuned transnational membership, directing it towards a grounded state-building project at odds with al-Qaeda's global network model of challenging Western hegemony. Embracing escalating brutality to enforce its designs, ISIS abrogates the dignity and human rights of all who fall under its rule. The breaking up of the Iraqi state—an institution that has since 1920 become the focus of a robust nationalist identity for the vast majority of ordinary Iraqis—raises questions as to even the minimal claims that the 2003 invasion and disastrous occupation was "worth it" as it led to the end of the dictatorship of Saddam Hussein. Due to the removal of the state apparatus from 2003, the state Saddam's clique had captured and considerably emptied through parasitic rent-seeking behaviors, the population of Iraq was not afforded an opportunity to renovate their state based on a shared aspirational future. Rather—as we have seen—they were left naked, without the superstructure of the state apparatus and

228   *Epilogue*

pilloried by outside actors. In this train of oppressive rulers taking up residence in Iraq, ISIS is only the latest exemplar.

The artificiality of regional states and the propaganda of ending Sykes-Picot (signed by the UK and France on May 16, 1916) afforded to ISIS across the summer of 2014 failed to denote the aspects of success the Iraqi state embodied in the minds of its citizens. Moreover, such claims of artificiality do not reflect the empirical reality of the historical record. Sykes-Picot was about establishing "spheres of influence" rather than borders, in the process denying indigenous popular sovereignty. The ongoing Anglo-American marshaling of the international community's adherence to the artifacts of statehood, rather than a project providing for a legitimate expression of Iraqi popular sovereignty, threatens the widespread abandonment of the state project for alternatives. Facing decades of war, authoritarian and incompetent rule, international approbation and the theft of its natural resources and historical patrimony, in addition to widespread human rights abuses and massive levels of displacement and death, Iraqis' desire to achieve a peaceable state of affairs must be heard. Giving voice to their desires and aspirations should take precedence over the continued effort to discuss Iraq as an object. Denied a clear institutional framework within which to express national self-determination, Iraq's reformulation as an "Islamic state" preceded the rise of ISIS. The empowerment of clergy and especially the role afforded to Shiʻite marjá in constitutional affairs as well as the direction of government formation, first by US administrators and then by the al-Mâlikî regime, institutionalized sectarianism. This "Lebanization" in practice entwined sectarianism with constitutional and political practices into the sinews of the post-2003 state in spite of its not having been a feature of the modern state era.

Moreover, the corrupt foundations of the new state crafted authoritarian pathways to state power. Established under the occupation, they were then maneuvered by Prime Minister al-Mâlikî. This cemented their praxis, and making them inescapable without substantial alteration to the state—a prospect not likely to be entertained by the carpetbaggers and unrepresentative apparatchiks who came to power through Anglo-American force-of-arms. Through their invasion and occupation, US policymakers redrew the socio-political and cognitive map of Iraq with the hopes of impacting the broader Middle East to their favor. The rendering of the Iraqi state, carried out by means of massive dislocation and human suffering, was not in support of liberal democracy, but rather the sectarianization of Iraqi institutions and the promulgation of a failed state. While US administrators mimicked their British imperial predecessors, this supposedly failed implementation has been blamed on the cultural affinities of Iraqis and the elites hand-selected by US decision-makers to lead the project. Occupation administrators' assumptions were consolidated into policy, and policy into institutional reality, leading to the neo-Ottoman partition of Iraq. Ignoring the diversity of many individual Iraqis and most tribal affinities, as well as urban landscapes, the occupation and bloodletting following the invasion has fashioned a Sunni region aligned with Turkey and transnational affinities to the Gulf states, a Kurdish region aligned with Turkey, and a Shiʻi region aligned with Iran. This formulation promotes

Epilogue 229

not only continued regional conflict, directly challenging GCC minorities along sectarian lines, and those of Turkey and Iran along ethnic lines for instance, but also fails to stabilize notions of citizenship necessary for democratic governance. The corruption encouraged and institutionalized across the new Iraqi state, as evidenced in this volume, eviscerated the accountability required for democratic governance and attracted those unmoored to the social fabric of Iraq to positions of authority for their willingness to afford US and then regional interests primacy over those of Iraqi citizens.

Facing the collapse of state authority across the western and northern provinces as well as the growing distance between the federal regime in Baghdad and the KRG's desire for autonomy and the capacity to develop its state and economy, the al-Mâlikî regime failed to respond. State security forces fled at the approach of ISIS and its local allies, accommodation was not found to allow for comity within the federal structure between Baghdad and Erbil, and clerical authority was deemed necessary to defend the state itself. That the fall of Mosul may well have been ordered by Al-Mâlikî himself will require thorough investigation so as to determine culpability and command accountability, a prerequisite for any future Iraqi military command and constitutionally mandated civilian oversight. Allegations that Al-Mâlikî attempted a coup against the newly elected government also require further explication and redress should extra-constitutional actions have been taken against the state. The abrogation of secular authority, inability to bring together a diverse array of forces to defend the state or to explain the dire failure of the security apparatus calls for radical redress. That his deputy, Haider al-Abadi, replaced Al-Mâlikî as Prime Minster, with al-Mâlikî shifting to a Vice Presidency, with the new government then composed of figures who had adorned previous cabinets, undermined both confidence in the capacity they brought to face the ISIS challenge as well as in any democratic principles this opportunity for change afforded. The failure to have established a political party law, a status that maintains an opaqueness over elected representatives and the process by which they are selected, needs to be a high priority to put the concerns associated with Al-Mâlikî's rule in the past. During the interregnum of al-Mâlikî's agreed departure and al-Ábadi's new government taking office, the outgoing Prime Minister continued to abuse the authority afforded his office. Shi'ite militias outside the framework of the Iraqi security forces were deputized and afforded authority over the defense of Baghdad and in leading the counteroffensive against ISIS. Ballooning in size, estimates had them numbering in excess of 2.5 million men, the legitimacy of such groups was provided primarily by clerical establishments and their funding and training represented an abrogation of state oversight or control with open involvement in their operations by irregulars and supposed state security officials from the Islamic Republic of Iran. In so doing the authority, capacity and development of the constitutionally formulated security and military apparatus was further denuded. Documented human rights violations and abuses by these forces, predominantly of communities identified as being in ethnic and sectarian opposition to the regime in Baghdad, spoke to a broader institutionalization of sectarianism as not being merely the orientation of a single regime or

230 *Epilogue*

leader.[4] This empowerment of extra-constitutional authority, solely sectarian in orientation, further undermines the state and its potential to represent the aspirations of all Iraqis.

The September 2014 announcement of al-Ábadi's new government, buttressed with a grandiose platform restating a commitment to the aspirations of the previous al-Mâlikî regime, underlines the continuity attending the prospect of his rule. This was evidenced by the delay in the appointment of the primary state security ministerial posts as well as their orientation once identified. Muhammad Salim al-Ghabban, who was Hadi Al-'Amari's (the head of the Badr organization) chief of staff, would assume duties atop the Ministry of the Interior in a gambit to provide Al-'Amari with proxy control of the Ministry, emerging from an organization anathema to many Iraqis for its associations with Iran during the 1980s Iraq–Iran war as well as the extrajudicial killings of the 2005–2008 civil war period. Similarly, Khaled al-Obeidi running under the Muttahidoon list, a Sunni long-associated with Asama Al-Najafi (the former Speaker of Parliament and head of the Muttahidoon list in the 2014 federal election), was appointed to reform and develop the Iraqi military as Minister of Defence. This critical task will bear close scrutiny to see if the institution can be marshaled to both defeat ISIS as well as see it return to its historical role as a nation-building institution constituted from all of Iraq's varied communities. The legislative program attached to al-Abadi's first months in office also suggested continuity as the proposed 'Law on the Freedom of Expression of Opinion, Assembly, and Peaceful Demonstration' was brought forward from the Al-Mâlikî regime. It raised broad and profound concerns from Iraqi civil society and suggested a renewed effort to entrench and even expand state authority over expression and assembly at a time when such freedoms were required to staunch the ideological challenge posed by ISIS.

In considered fashion, the return of US military forces to the country to combat ISIS, both accentuated the incapacity of the Iraqi state established under the occupation, while also conflating a rise in violence with a denial of the need for political resolutions required for a peaceable future. Ascribed with the task of reforming the same security forces they had prepared for the failure in Mosul, the focus on ISIS as primarily a security challenge confirms the lack of recognition of the challenges posed by rampant corruption and competing state-building projects across the Mashriq. Once again, Iraqis, denied accountable representatives committed to their welfare, appear about to endure a catastrophe unleashed by their former occupiers, as they face the prospect of being strafed and bombed by Western air forces. This catastrophe, like those suffered by Iraqis over the previous decade, is yet another instance of "blowback," the foreseeable consequence of American actions.

Notes

1 Within Iraq and Syria, the movement is more often referred to by its Arabic acronym *Da'ish* for *al-Dawla al-Islamiya fi Iraq wa al-Sham*, although they themselves have opposed this usage and even persecuted those found using it within domains under ISIS

Epilogue 231

control. With the U.S. government referring to them as ISIL (Islamic State in Iraq and the Levant), the French government adopting the more common Arabic usage *Da'ish* as a decidedly oppositional response, and the international media and many others using the more ubiquitous ISIS (Islamic State in Iraq and Syria), the nomenclature has taken on a political nature. See: The Economist Explains. "The many names of ISIS (also known as IS, ISIL, SIC and Da'ish)." *The Economist*, September 28, 2014. http://www.economist.com/blogs/economist-explains/2014/09/economist-explains-19

2 This continuity was nominally broken by the "surge" in 2007, as evidenced by the numerous refrains by US officials that locals were being listened to, incorporated into the Iraqi state security apparatus and supplied with locally focused development funds. That this came over four years into the Anglo-American occupation and that it was not institutionalized is seemingly not questioned in the triumphal embrace of the "surge."

3 See: Yossi Alpher, "The U.S.-led campaign against the Islamic State: many questions, few answers," NOREF (Norwegian Peacebuilding Resource Centre) (October 14, 2014). http://www.peacebuilding.no/Regions/Middle-East-and-North-Africa/Syria/Publications/The-U.S.-led-campaign-against-the-Islamic-State-many-questions-few-answers; and Richard Barrett, Patrick Skinner, Robert McFadden, and Lila Ghosh, "The Islamic State," The Soufan Group (October 28, 2014). http://soufangroup.com/the-islamic-state

4 See: Human Rights Watch, "For Iraq's Sunnis, Sectarian Militias Pose an Extra Threat," (October 23, 2014) [http://www.hrw.org/news/2014/10/24/iraq-s-sunnis-sectarian-militias-pose-extra-threat] as well as, "Iraq: Survivors Describe Mosque Massacre," (November 1, 2014). http://www.hrw.org/news/2014/11/01/iraq-survivors-describe-mosque-massacre

Appendix 1
Declaration of the Shia of Iraq (2002)

Introduction

A series of meetings were held in London during 2001 and 2002 to discuss the sectarian problem in Iraq and its effects on Iraq's present conditions and future. A broad range of personalities were involved in these meetings ranging from intellectuals, politicians, military personnel, writers, tribal chiefs, academics, to businessmen and professionals, drawn from a wide political spectrum, including Islamists, nationalists, socialists and liberals. These meetings were not constrained by any particular ideological or organizational considerations, with the participants being motivated primarily by a concern for the national interests of Iraq. The ideas expressed at these meetings were strictly those of the participants in their individual capacities, even though a number of them were attached to specific political groups or ideational currents.

The meetings had the important effect of facilitating the formulation of commonly accepted parameters regarding the sectarian problem in Iraq, and the methods that should be employed to tackle this issue in any future restructuring of the political order in the country. This document—*Declaration of the Shia of Iraq*—is the result of these discussions and deliberations.

1. The genesis of the problem

Following the establishment of the constitutional entity that became modern Iraq in 1923, and the organization of its administrative and political affairs, the sectarian paradigm became a key organizing principle of the governing powers. It then quickly evolved into a set of fixed political rules of power and control that has continued into present times.

A number of Iraq's leading political figures were acutely aware of the dangers of pursuing a deliberate sectarian policy on the part of the state and its deleterious effects on the country. They introduced a number of political initiatives and programs that were designed to highlight and reverse the sectarian framework of governmental policies, and to counter the hardening of official sectarian discrimination against the Shia. The most important of these initiatives would include:

Appendix 1   233

- The detailed letter that King Faysal I addressed to his ministers in 1932, and in which he highlighted the injustice that has been afflicted on the Shia and the critical importance of addressing their concerns and sense of betrayal by the state.
- The letter that was addressed to the Iraqi Government by Sheikh Muhammed Hussein Kashif al-Ghita in which he drew attention to the discrimination that has been meted out to the Shia and the necessity of removing its causes and manifestations.
- The initiative of the Shia religious authorities under the guidance of the Imam Sayyid Muhsin al-Hakim in the 1960s that encompassed representations to the authorities on the sectarian issue.
- The 1964 letter of Sheikh Muhammed Ridha al-Shibibi that was addressed to the then Prime Minister of Iraq, Abdul Rahman Al Bazzaz, and which detailed the condition of the Shia and their grievances.

All of these initiatives shared a common concern that rejected the sectarian bases of political power and authority in Iraq, and its decidedly anti-Shia bias. These initiatives called for the abandonment of these sectarian policies, the granting of full political and civil rights to the Shia, and called for their treatment within the framework of sound constitutional principles based on a notion of citizenship that was inherently inclusive and fair.

These initiatives also provided the catalyst for subsequent activities in the fight against sectarianism that was joined by writers, intellectuals and the *ulema*, all of whom called for the dissolution of the sectarian structures of policy-making and the confirmation of the Shia's civil and political rights in line with those of other groups in society.

However, none of these initiatives and activities met with anything but total rejection by the state, which continued in its sectarian biases irrespective of the damage that this caused, and would continue to cause, to the fabric of society and its integrity. The authorities simply ignored the catastrophic consequences of these policies, which were to influence all Iraqis regardless of their sectarian, ethnic or religious affiliations.

The Iraqi Shia problem is now a globally recognized fault line and is no longer restricted to the confines of Iraq's territory. It has ceased to be a local issue, for the international community and its organizations (such as Amnesty International, Human Rights Watch, the UN's Special Rapporteur on Iraq) have now acknowledged openly the existence of a serious sectarian problem in Iraq, and have expressed their sympathy and solidarity with the plight of the Shia of Iraq and the sectarian biases that they daily encounter from the authorities.

The sectarian issue has now emerged into the light of day in spite of the Iraqi authorities' attempts, through their political and media apparatuses, to cover up its reality. The rights of the Shia are now an issue that is central to the present and future conditions of Iraq, and must now be included in any plan or program that tries to tackle the reconstruction of the Iraqi state. It is for the very reason of its criticality that a calm and reasoned debate is now called for to discuss the rights and demands of the Shia.

234   *Appendix 1*

This declaration draws on the long line of similar efforts made in the past by the leaders of the Shia in Iraq. It follows closely on their path of calling, responsibly and persistently, for the legitimate rights that are due the Shia, and in a manner that reflects properly the views of the Iraqi Shia as a whole. This is especially relevant today where the Shia in Iraq do not have an authoritative leadership that can tackle the issues and problems that concern them, not least their political, cultural and civil rights.

2. Who are the Shia?

A dictionary definition of the Shia would be those who claim a historic loyalty to the Household of the Prophet and their school of Islam. In the context of Iraq, however, the Shii is any person who belongs to the Jaafari sect of Islam either by birth or choice. The Shia in Iraq are not an ethnic group nor a race nor nation, but rather, can comprise any social combination that believes that its Shia fealty has led it to suffer from persistent sectarian disadvantage over the centuries.

The policies of discrimination against the Shia of Iraq have caused every Shii to believe that he or she is targeted because of their Shiism and for no other reason. The Shii is treated as a second-class citizen almost from birth, and is deliberately distanced from any major position of authority or responsibility. He or she suffers from an in-built preference given to others even though others are less skilled or qualified.

This sectarian pattern has been employed in Iraq over the centuries. The Shia were frequently the objects of the retribution and oppression of the authorities simply because of sectarian considerations, even though the intensity and frequency of the anti-Shia activities of the authorities might have ebbed and flowed. However, the oppression has been ratcheted up drastically over the past 20 years.

The determination of the authorities to implement these policies and their insistence on the continuing isolation of the Shia from any meaningful exercise of power has contributed, in the modern period, to the transformation of the Iraqi Shia into a recognizable social entity with its own peculiarities, far from any specific ideological and religious considerations. In other words the crystallization of the Shia as a distinct group owes far more to the policies of discrimination and retribution than to any specifically sectarian or religious considerations. This condition now defines the status of the Shia in Iraq irrespective of the individual Shii's doctrinal, religious or political orientations.

3. The Shia and the modern Iraqi state

The Shia's disillusioning experience with the circumstances that underpinned the formation of the first Iraqi government in 1920 was the defining historical factor in their political evolution. This statement can be amply justified by any number of impartial historical studies. The Iraqi state was designed within clear sectarian boundaries, with the intention of distancing the Shia and their leadership from the

Appendix 1   235

decision-making structures of the nascent state. And even though the sectarian principles of power and authority were not explicitly set out in the original basic law of the country, they became the unwritten code for generations of politicians in both monarchical and republican Iraq.

This is painfully ironic in as much as the Shia played a pivotal role in establishing the conditions for an independent Iraq, being the main actors in the Iraqi Uprising of 1920. The subsequent gross diminution of the position of the Shia in the Iraqi state cannot be reconciled in any way therefore with the importance that their leaders had in the struggle against foreign rule. The connivance of the foreign controlling power in the establishment of sectarian bases of political power set the stage for the evolution of the sectarian system that has continued to the present day.

4. The authorities' objectives in pursuing sectarianism

The British occupation of Iraq was met by rejection from a united front between the Shia and Sunni populations of Iraq. Both groups were unanimous in refusing the occupation and insistent on the formation of a national government free of foreign control. This unity was further strengthened by the rejection of the two communities of all the projects and programs advanced by the occupying administration to reconcile them to their condition, culminating in the common positions adopted by them in their support for the 1920 Uprising. However, Britain succeeded in dividing the two communities when it proposed the formation of an Iraqi government that was based on sectarian principles and advantage, and this became the model, which was followed scrupulously by subsequent governments.

The powers that controlled the Iraqi state strove to convince the Sunnis of Iraq that all the emblems and trappings of power, both civil and military, were the lot of their community by right, and that any serious Shia involvement in the government would be at the expense of their controlling share of power. The authorities, both in monarchical and republican Iraq, succeeded therefore in both the weakening of any potential or real inter-sectarian solidarity as well as in marginalizing the role of the Shia. The raising of any specifically Shia demand for redress became the subject of vitriolic accusations of "sectarianism" by the authorities, even though the Shia were the prime victims of the state's sectarianism. Patriotism and national unity became appropriated by the state as a cover for this sectarian reality.

The famous dictum of Iraq's first prime minister, Abd el-Rahman an-Naqib, addressed to the Shia leadership who were advocating the rejection of the Mandate terms:

> *"I am the owner [governor] of this land, so what do you [the Shia] have to do with it?"*

is an accurate gauge of the political direction that Iraq was to take. The principle of rejecting serious Shia participation in the state became the dominant recurring

236   *Appendix 1*

theme of the governing authorities. Sunnis were to rule by their vigilant control over the main sources of civil, military and social power, while the Shia majority were to be marginalized and isolated. In this way, the Shia's numerical majority in Iraq would be overridden by the deliberate policies of sectarian preference and discrimination, and if need be, oppression.

This has been the basis of Iraq's political life, with the state actively waging war against the Shia's sense of identity, self-confidence and purpose. Violent propaganda campaigns were waged against the Shia and their beliefs, while the state never ceased to remind the Sunnis of the Shia menace and the threat that the Shia posed to their rights and privileges and to their superior social and political status.

The authorities never relented in their discriminatory policies against the Shia. Each new ruler in Iraq found himself confronted with the inchoate anger of the Shia, to which the classic response was to deflect and defuse that threat by a further reduction of the Shia's presence and role. This constant increase in the level and extent of discrimination and state violence against the Shia has made an explosion inevitable.

This relentless increase of sectarian discrimination against the Shia has culminated in the present ruling powers aggressively working towards the elimination of any aspect of Shii public life, within a calculated plan to destroy the institutions of the Shia and thereby weaken and eliminate their communal underpinnings. Shia schools and institutions of higher learning, such as the *Fiqh* (Jurisprudence) College in Najaf and the College of Religious Sciences in Baghdad, were closed as was the cancellation of the Shia-inspired and backed but broadly non-religious University of Kufa. Shia merchants and businessmen were deported in droves, mainly to destroy the economic and commercial vitality of the Shia. The violence perpetrated against the Shia *ulema* and study circles has been unprecedented, driving the Shia specifically, and the country generally, into an extremely dangerous crisis situation.

5. The nature of the Shia opposition

In spite of the fact that the Shia in Iraq subscribe to numerous political and intellectual groupings, it is the Islamist movement that has acted as the main political drive for the Shia at the present moment. The Islamist current has been broadly connected, by political commentators and analysts in the region and internationally, with the aspirations of the Shia as a whole. As such, the Islamist movement has been seen as reflective of the Shia's views and aims, and in certain respects its proxy. To some extent this is an inappropriate attribution as the Islamist parties in Iraq have an explicitly Islamic, rather than sectarian, orientation. Moreover, the condition of the Shia in Iraq is such that they can owe allegiances to a variety of political and cultural currents that are not necessarily Islamic in direction.

The Shia's opposition to the state in Iraq is based on political rather than sectarian considerations and has evolved as a consequence of a prolonged process of continuing sectarian discrimination and cruel oppression by the state.

6. The politics of sectarianism

In spite of the long-standing nature of the policies of sectarian discrimination, Iraq has not witnessed social discrimination in terms of one community, the Sunnis, consciously oppressing another, the Shia. The discrimination with which the Shia have been afflicted is entirely the work of the state. This is a vital point to ponder, as the crises with which Iraq had to contend are a consequence of official rather than communal discrimination. Any program that hopes to reconstruct the terms of power in Iraq has to start from the point of officially inspired discrimination and not mutual communal hostility.

It is crucial to differentiate between legitimate sectarian differences due to doctrinal and other factors, and a policy of officially sanctioned sectarian advantage and discrimination. Iraq suffers from a sectarian system and not from communal sectarianism per se. There is no overt problem between Iraq's sectarian communities, but rather the opposite is the case, as Iraq has managed to accommodate, at the social level, the differences between its ethnic and sectarian groups. A relatively high degree of harmony has prevailed between the Sunnis and the Shia, in many ways superior to the conditions prevailing in most multi-ethnic and multi-sectarian countries. The struggle for national sovereignty and independence was joined equally by both the Sunnis and the Shia, at the level of their respective leaderships and right down to the community rank and file. Most of the national parties had a broad base of sectarian representation, and sectarian considerations did not dominate the response to key issues and moments that affected the destiny of the country.

The Shia's main driving forces in their struggle for national independence and the building of the modern Iraqi state were the rejection of foreign hegemony over Iraq and the insistence on sovereign independence. By acceding to the granting of the crown of Iraq to one of Sharif Hussain's sons, Faysal, the Shia clearly indicated their willingness to transcend purely sectarian considerations when dealing with vital national issues, even though it could have been possible for them to demand a Shia king, given their relative weight in Iraq's social and political landscape at that time. It is quite possible that the kingship of Faysal would not have materialized if the Shia religious and political leadership had been vigorously opposed to it.

Iraq's political crisis has nothing to do with either social discrimination or a latent Shia sense of inferiority towards the Sunnis, or vice versa. It is entirely due to the conduct of an overtly sectarian authority determined to pursue a policy of discrimination solely for its own interests of control, a policy that has ultimately led to the total absence of political and cultural liberties and the worse forms of dictatorship. It is not possible for Iraq to emerge out of this cul-de-sac without the complete banishment of official sectarianism from any future political construct, and its replacement by a contract premised on a broad and patriotic definition of citizenship that is far removed from sectarian calculations and divisions.

Any policy that calls for the official adoption of the division of powers on the basis of overt sectarian percentages—such as the situation in Lebanon—cannot

238   *Appendix 1*

be workable in the context of Iraq, given its social and historical experience, and will not resolve the current impasse. It is quite probable that such a solution may well result in further problems, dilemmas and crises being laid in store for the country. The only way out of this conundrum is the total rejection of the anti-Shia practices of the state, and the adoption of an inclusive and equitable system of rule that would define the political direction of the future Iraq. This is what the Shia want and not some bogus solution based on the division of the spoils according to demographic formulae, a condition that would very probably result in communal sectarianism becoming a social and political reality rather than a manifestation of an unscrupulous state authority.

The airing in public of the sectarian issues facing Iraq does not subject Iraq's unity to any serious threat. It is intended to confront the problem directly, in order to correctly define its nature and to proffer solutions that would lead to its elimination. Ignoring the problem, or sweeping it under the carpet because of some ill-defined "threat" to national unity, only compounds the issue and is an affront to the memory of the untold multitudes that have perished or suffered hardships and indignities because of their sectarian identity and allegiances.

There is the unavoidable reality that there are two sects in Iraq, a fact which it would be foolish to deny or ignore. The imposition of an enforced and artificial homogeneity on this reality only serves to compound the problem and pushes it to the point where an explosion becomes inevitable. The recognition and even celebration of Iraq's sectarian diversity is an important platform in reconstructing the terms of dialogue between the state and the people, and by confirming the civil and religious rights of all the sects and groups in Iraq, the ground is strengthened for enhancing the sense of unity and patriotism in the country.

The sectarian issue in Iraq will not be solved by the imposition of a vengeful Shia sectarianism on the state and society. It can only be tackled by defining its nature and boundaries and formulating a complete national program for its resolution. At the same time, the imperative of national unity should not be used as a pretext to avoid the necessity of dismantling the sectarian state and its harmful policies.

7. Sectarian differences and sectarian discrimination

The distinction between the existence of sectarian differences and sectarian discrimination, as such, must be established clearly. The state has masked its exploitation of the existence of sectarian differences in order to pursue its policy of sectarian discrimination.

The sectarian differences within Islam can be traced to the dawn of the Islamic era. Iraq's Muslim population is divided between Sunnis and Shia and there should be no harm or fear about acknowledging this fact. The sects have co-existed by and large for generations with no serious sectarian crises resulting in consequence. Sectarian differences do not constitute a social, intellectual or political issue in the Iraqi context, and sectarian affiliations should be a matter of course.

Appendix 1 239

The real issue is official sectarianism rather than sectarian differences. Or in other words, the exploitation of the differences between the sects for the purpose of discriminating between them in order to promote a specific policy of power and control. It is this deliberate policy of enshrining sectarian differences to promote discriminatory and retrograde policies that has been used to strip the Shia of their political and civil rights and to reduce them to the status of second-class citizens. The label of "Shia" has been sufficient cause to remove the ordinary Shii from any consideration of positions of power and authority irrespective of his qualities and competences, and in spite of his political affiliations. To be a Shia in Iraq is to be condemned to a lifetime of powerlessness, fear, anxiety and discrimination.

The absence of any noticeable Shia representation in the upper reaches of state and power is clearly evident and incontrovertible, as is the manifest discrimination employed against them. The reconstruction of Iraq's state and society requires therefore a deep understanding of what the Shia actually want from their state, starting from the abolition of official discrimination and the return to them of their civil and constitutional rights from which they have been deprived for decades.

Civil and political rights must be guaranteed through the development of a body of laws and institutions that guard against sectarian discrimination. These should also aim to remove all traces of sectarian practices in Iraq and would be empowered with the authority to enforce these new policies. Sectarian loyalties that unite peoples who share a common heritage and history are a natural occurrence and each person should be free to declare his sectarian affinities without fear or anxiety. But this should not result in the enshrining of sectarianism as a policy or as a basis for political action.

8. The Shia of Iraq and national unity

The lessons drawn from Iraq's history are clear—the Shia have at no point sought to establish their own state or unique political entity. Rather, whenever the opportunity was afforded to them, they participated enthusiastically in nation-wide political movements and organizations, ever conscious of the need to maintain national unity and probably more so than other groups inside Iraq. This can be abundantly established by examining the Shia's involvement in the struggle to establish the independent Iraqi state within its current recognized borders. The Shia, both in their Islamist and non-Islamist manifestations, have avoided being dragged into separatist schemes, and have been steadfast in their commitment to the unitary Iraqi state. The vital support that they gave to the claims of the Sharifian candidate to the Iraqi throne, in addition to the general sympathy that was exhibited to the cause of the Sharifs of Mecca after the Great War, was symptomatic of their patriotism.

This historic position of the Shia in favor of the unitary constitutional Iraqi state was not given its due measure, unfortunately, by successive Iraqi governments. In fact, the Shia role in safeguarding the unity of Iraq was constantly belittled and frequently ignored. The earliest political parties and movements in

240   *Appendix 1*

which the Shia were involved were clear in their platforms and programs of an absolute commitment to an independent and constitutional state stretching from the Province of Mosul in the north to the Province of Basra in the south. The slogan, "An Arab Islamic Government," that was demanded by the Shia leadership in the referendum of 1919 is the incontrovertible evidence of the commitment of the Shia to an Arab/Muslim form of rule for Iraq, and the rejection of any status not commensurate with full political independence for the country.

This position of the Shia remained firm in spite of their oppression and discrimination at the hands of successive governments. The expulsion of Sheikh Mahdi al-Khalisi to Iran by the government of Muhsin as-Saadoun, in blithe disregard of the role that he played in securing popular approval for the demand for national sovereignty and independence, was one of the first manifestations of the policy of official anti-Shiism in action. But the constant harassments and threats that the Shia leadership were subjected to in the early days of independence did not deflect them from their commitment to the Iraqi state.

Even as we are in the midst of the present explosive situation, where state anti-Shiism has reached unprecedented levels of violence, the Shia have not raised the banner of withdrawal from the body politic of Iraq. The insistence on national unity as a clear starting principle has been the common denominator for all the active Iraqi Shia oppositionists, as has been the recognition that the problems arising from the atrocious misgovernment of the multi-ethnic and multi-sectarian state that is Iraq could best be resolved in the context of a single Iraqi state.

The Shia of Iraq, in spite of being constantly and maliciously tested as to the depth of their national loyalty, have proven, time and again, their commitment to Iraq even at the expense of their own sectarian interests. Their call for the restitution of their civil and political rights can in no way be seen as a threat to national unity, when they have indisputably proven that they have been its principal protectors in word and in deed.

9. What do the Shia want?

The demands of the Shia can be succinctly summarized as follows:

1   The abolition of dictatorship and its replacement with democracy.
2   The abolition of ethnic discrimination and its replacement with a federal structure for Kurdistan.
3   The abolition of the policy of discrimination against the Shia.

The *Declaration of the Shia of Iraq* aims to elaborate on a Shia perspective on the political future of Iraq. Its principal points are as follows:

1   Abolition of ethnic and sectarian discrimination, and the elimination of the effects of these erroneous policies.
2   The establishment of a democratic parliamentary constitutional order, that carefully avoids the hegemony of one sect or ethnic group over the others.

Appendix 1   241

3   The consolidation of the principles of a single citizenship for all Iraqis, a common citizenship being the basic guarantor of national unity.
4   Full respect for the national, ethnic, religious and sectarian identities of all Iraqis, and the inculcation of the ideals of true citizenship amongst all of Iraq's communities.
5   Confirmation of the unitary nature of the Iraqi state and people, within the parameters of diversity and pluralism in Iraq's ethnic, religious and sectarian identities.
6   Reconstruction of, and support for, the main elements of a civil society and its community bases.
7   Adoption of the structures of a federal state that would include a high degree of decentralization and devolution of powers to elected provincial authorities and assemblies.
8   Full respect for the principles of universal human rights.
9   Protection of the Islamic identity of Iraqi society.

First: democracy

Dictatorship has been one of the main factors that have buttressed the structures of official sectarian and ethnic discrimination, and constitutional democracy, operating through vital and effective institutions, is the necessary cure for this virulent ailment. The Shia do not want to solve their sectarian problems by creating an analogous one for other groups. Rather, they are seeking redress through a system that would guard the rights of all the constituent elements of Iraq's society, whereby all will be treated on an equal footing.

Second: federalism

One of the key elements of the Iraqi conundrum is the near exclusive concentration of powers in the capital, Baghdad, in a manner that has robbed the outlying regions of any opportunity to address their local concerns, needs and special conditions and particularities. The solution has to be in the devolution of powers and authorities to these areas within a framework of broad administrative decentralization.

Federalism as a system would be designed to negotiate between the need to have a central authority with effective but not hegemonic powers, and regions that enjoy a high order of decentralized powers, all within a framework of careful delineation of rights and responsibilities as between the center and the regions. Ideally, a federal system would also legislate for the maintenance of Iraq's unitary nature, but recognizes the need to fully accommodate Iraq's diversity.

Iraq's federal structure would not be based on a sectarian division but rather on administrative and demographic criteria. This would avoid the formation of sectarian-based entities that could be the prelude for partition or separation.

The proposed federal system would grant considerable powers to the regions, including legislative, fiscal, judicial and executive powers, thereby removing

242   *Appendix 1*

the possibility of the center falling under the control of a dominant group which would extend its hegemony over the entire country. Iraq's federalist structures would benefit greatly from the experience of countries that have adopted this system of government successfully.

Third: abolition of the policies of sectarianism

The *Declaration of the Shia of Iraq* envisages the elimination of official sectarianism through the adoption of specific political and civil rights that would eliminate the disadvantage of the Shia.

A: political rights

In order to eliminate the accumulation of sectarian policies and codes of conduct employed by the authorities over decades, it would be necessary to examine the administrative structures of the Iraqi state and its civil and military institutions. In particular, the employment and promotion policies that have been pursued in the past must be remedied by policies that stress merit, effectiveness and competence as the basis for all employment. A federal authority with a remit to combat sectarianism would be established, which would examine closely the principles employed for filling all senior governmental posts, and which would be charged also with adjudicating all complaints and cases of sectarianism. The federal authority's mandate could be extended to include the combat of all forms of sectarianism in official and private institutions.

A fund would be established to compensate all those who have been harmed as a result of sectarian and ethnic discrimination and policies. Such a fund would be administered by a council that would establish the norms and procedures for evaluating the extent of damages and the restitution due.

A set of laws would be introduced to abolish sectarianism and that would criminalize sectarian conduct.

A new nationality law would be introduced that would be based on a notion of citizenship that would emphasize loyalty to Iraq rather than to any sectarian, national or religious affiliation.

B: civil rights

The key civil rights that have a special resonance for the Shia would include:

1 Their right to practice their own religious rites and rituals and to autonomously administer their own religious shrines and institutions, through legitimate Shia religious authorities.
2 Full freedom to conduct their religious affairs in their own mosques, meeting halls and other institutions.
3 Freedom to teach in their religious universities and institutions with no interference by the central or provincial authorities.

Appendix 1 243

4 Freedom of movement and travel and assembly on the part of the higher Shia religious authorities, *ulema* and speakers, and guarantees afforded to the teaching circles—the hawzas—to conduct their affairs in a manner that they see fit.
5 Ensuring that the Shia's religious shrines and cities are entered into UNESCO's World Heritage Sites and are thus protected from arbitrary acts of change and destruction.
6 Full freedoms to publish Shia tracts and books and to establish Shia religious institutions and assemblies.
7 The right to establish independent schools, universities and other teaching establishments and academies, within the framework of a broad and consensual national education policy.
8 Introduction of the elements of the Jafari creed and rites into the national educational curriculum, in a manner similar to the way in which other schools of Islamic jurisprudence are taught.
9 Revising the elements of the history curriculum to remove all disparagement of the Shia, and the writing of an authentic history that would remove any anti-Shia biases.
10 Freedom to establish Shia mosques, meeting halls and libraries.
11 Respect for the burial grounds of the Shia.
12 Official recognition by the state of the key dates of the Shia calendar.
13 Repatriation of all Iraqis who were forcibly expelled from Iraq, or who felt obliged to leave under duress, and the full restitution of their constitutional and civil rights.

Conclusion

It is essential that all the elements of Iraq's political spectrum, as well as the representatives of Iraq's varied communities, become involved in the process of finding a way out of the terrible situation that Iraq finds itself in now and which threatens its very survival. All these groups must participate in the process of change and the design of a new Iraqi state so that all have a stake in the outcome and could feel themselves true and equal partners in the country.

The Iraqi crisis has to be tackled at all its levels: political, through the elimination of dictatorship; sectarian, through the abolition of sectarian discrimination; and ethnic, through the elimination of ethnic and national preference. Furthermore, it would be necessary to consider policies and programs that would provide redress to the many aggrieved groups in the country, and to establish a vision of Iraq's future in which all would share. Any shortfall from this objective by adopting one perspective over another, on the grounds of a gradualism that postpones the tackling of these issues to some indeterminate date in the future, is a recipe for further suffering and possibly disaster.

Constitutional guarantees and rights must be afforded to all of Iraq's groups and communities, as well as the means to defend or enforce them. This must be the minimum requirement for rebuilding the Iraqi state on a new basis. The order

244   *Appendix 1*

of priorities in this declaration have been ranked in a methodical manner, and the sequential adoption of the policies that underpin needed change are based on the principle of their voluntary adoption through information dissemination and persuasion rather than their imposition by force or fiat.

The adoption of the constituent components of Iraq's society of the elements of this declaration is important, not least for the reason that each should feel that they have accepted the main sources of grievance and redress of the other groups, and that they have all participated equally in the fashioning of a new Iraqi order.

Annex

The following are the main studies and works that have tackled the Iraqi Shia problem:

1   The speech given by Sayyid Baqir al-Hakim in Tehran under the title: *Shia Consciousness in Iraq*, dated 1402 AH.
2   The book *The Crisis of Power in Iraq*, by Abd el-Karim al-Uzri.
3   The book *The Shia and the Nationalist State*, by Hassan al-Alawi.
4   The booklet *What Do the Shia of Iraq Want?*, by Sayyid Muhammed Bahr al-Uloom.
5   The seminar on *Facets of the Shia Crisis in Iraq* that was held under the auspices of Sayyid Abd el-Majid al-Khoe'i in the Khoe'i Foundation, London, 2000.
6   The book *The Shia Issue in Iraq and the Husseini Rites*, by Ibrahim Hamoudi.
7   The book *The Present Circumstances of the Shia of Iraq*, by Sayyid Muhammed al-Hayderi.
8   The book *The New World Order and the Shia of Iraq*, by Adel Abd el-Mahdi.
9   The book *An Assessment of the Fighting Capabilities of the Shia of Iraq*, by Mahdi Abd el-Mahdi.
10 The booklet *The Shia Pronouncement*, by Ghalib Shabandar.

Source

Adapted from the *Declaration of the Shia of Iraq*. (2002, July). Translated by Al-Bab. Retrieved January 22, 2014, from Al-Bab: www.al-bab.com/arab/docs/iraq/shia02a. htm

Appendix 2

Law of Administration for the State of Iraq for the Transitional Period [TAL]

March 8, 2004

Preamble

The people of Iraq, striving to reclaim their freedom, which was usurped by the previous tyrannical regime, rejecting violence and coercion in all their forms, and particularly when used as instruments of governance, have determined that they shall hereafter remain a free people governed under the rule of law.

These people, affirming today their respect for international law, especially having been amongst the founders of the United Nations, working to reclaim their legitimate place among nations, have endeavored at the same time to preserve the unity of their homeland in a spirit of fraternity and solidarity in order to draw the features of the future new Iraq, and to establish the mechanisms aiming, amongst other aims, to erase the effects of racist and sectarian policies and practices.

This Law is now established to govern the affairs of Iraq during the transitional period until a duly elected government, operating under a permanent and legitimate constitution achieving full democracy, shall come into being.

Chapter 1: fundamental principles

Article 1

(A) This Law shall be called the "Law of Administration for the State of Iraq for the Transitional Period," and the phrase "this Law" wherever it appears in this legislation shall mean the "Law of Administration for the State of Iraq for the Transitional Period."

(B) Gender-specific language shall apply equally to male and female.

(C) The Preamble to this Law is an integral part of this Law.

Article 2

(A) The term "transitional period" shall refer to the period beginning on June 30, 2004 and lasting until the formation of an elected Iraqi government pursuant to a permanent constitution as set forth in this Law, which in any case shall be no later than December 31, 2005, unless the provisions of Article 61 are applied.

(B) The transitional period shall consist of two phases:

246   *Appendix 2*

(1)   The first phase shall begin with the formation of a fully sovereign Iraqi Interim Government that takes power on June 30, 2004. This government shall be constituted in accordance with a process of extensive deliberations and consultations with cross-sections of the Iraqi people conducted by the Governing Council and the Coalition Provisional Authority and possibly in consultation with the United Nations. This government shall exercise authority in accordance with this Law, including the fundamental principles and rights specified herein, and with an annex that shall be agreed upon and issued before the beginning of the transitional period and that shall be an integral part of this Law.

(2)   The second phase shall begin after the formation of the Iraqi Transitional Government, which will take place after elections for the National Assembly have been held as stipulated in this Law, provided that, if possible, these elections are not delayed beyond December 31, 2004, and, in any event, beyond January 31, 2005. This second phase shall end upon the formation of an Iraqi government pursuant to a permanent constitution.

Article 3

(A)   This Law is the Supreme Law of the land and shall be binding in all parts of Iraq without exception. No amendment to this Law may be made except by a three-fourths majority of the members of the National Assembly and the unanimous approval of the Presidency Council. Likewise, no amendment may be made that could abridge in any way the rights of the Iraqi people cited in Chapter 2; extend the transitional period beyond the timeframe cited in this Law; delay the holding of elections to a new assembly; reduce the powers of the regions or governorates; or affect Islam, or any other religions or sects and their rites.

(B)   Any legal provision that conflicts with this Law is null and void.

(C)   This Law shall cease to have effect upon the formation of an elected government pursuant to a permanent constitution.

Article 4

The system of government in Iraq shall be republican, federal, democratic and pluralistic, and powers shall be shared between the federal government and the regional governments, governorates, municipalities and local administrations. The federal system shall be based upon geographic and historical realities and the separation of powers, and not upon origin, race, ethnicity, nationality or confession.

Article 5

The Iraqi Armed Forces shall be subject to the civilian control of the Iraqi Transitional Government, in accordance with the contents of Chapters 3 and 5 of this Law.

Article 6

The Iraqi Transitional Government shall take effective steps to end the vestiges of the oppressive acts of the previous regime arising from forced displacement, deprivation of citizenship, expropriation of financial assets and property, and dismissal from government employment for political, racial or sectarian reasons.

Article 7

(A) Islam is the official religion of the State and is to be considered a source of legislation. No law that contradicts the universally agreed tenets of Islam, the principles of democracy or the rights cited in Chapter 2 of this Law may be enacted during the transitional period. This Law respects the Islamic identity of the majority of the Iraqi people and guarantees the full religious rights of all individuals to freedom of religious belief and practice.
(B) Iraq is a country of many nationalities, and the Arab people in Iraq are an inseparable part of the Arab nation.

Article 8

The flag, anthem and emblem of the State shall be fixed by law.

Article 9

The Arabic language and the Kurdish language are the two official languages of Iraq. The right of Iraqis to educate their children in their mother tongue, such as Turcoman, Syriac or Armenian, in government educational institutions in accordance with educational guidelines, or in any other language in private educational institutions, shall be guaranteed. The scope of the term "official language" and the means of applying the provisions of this Article shall be defined by law and shall include:

(1) Publication of the official gazette, in the two languages;
(2) Speech and expression in official settings, such as the National Assembly, the Council of Ministers, courts and official conferences, in either of the two languages;
(3) Recognition and publication of official documents and correspondence in the two languages;
(4) Opening schools that teach in the two languages, in accordance with educational guidelines;
(5) Use of both languages in any other settings enjoined by the principle of equality (such as bank notes, passports and stamps);
(6) Use of both languages in the federal institutions and agencies in the Kurdistan region.

Chapter 2: fundamental rights

Article 10

As an expression of the free will and sovereignty of the Iraqi people, their representatives shall form the governmental structures of the State of Iraq. The Iraqi Transitional Government and the governments of the regions, governorates,

248   *Appendix 2*

municipalities and local administrations shall respect the rights of the Iraqi people, including those rights cited in this Chapter.

Article 11

(A) Anyone who carries Iraqi nationality shall be deemed an Iraqi citizen. His citizenship shall grant him all the rights and duties stipulated in this Law and shall be the basis of his relation to the homeland and the State.
(B) No Iraqi may have his Iraqi citizenship withdrawn or be exiled unless he is a naturalized citizen who, in his application for citizenship, as established in a court of law, made material falsifications on the basis of which citizenship was granted.
(C) Each Iraqi shall have the right to carry more than one citizenship. Any Iraqi whose citizenship was withdrawn because he acquired another citizenship shall be deemed an Iraqi.
(D) Any Iraqi whose Iraqi citizenship was withdrawn for political, religious, racial or sectarian reasons has the right to reclaim his Iraqi citizenship.
(E) Decision Number 666 (1980) of the dissolved Revolutionary Command Council is annuled, and anyone whose citizenship was withdrawn on the basis of this decree shall be deemed an Iraqi.
(F) The National Assembly must issue laws pertaining to citizenship and naturalization consistent with the provisions of this Law.
(G) The Courts shall examine all disputes airising from the application of the provisions relating to citizenship.

Article 12

All Iraqis are equal in their rights without regard to gender, sect, opinion, belief, nationality, religion or origin, and they are equal before the law. Discrimination against an Iraqi citizen on the basis of his gender, nationality, religion or origin is prohibited. Everyone has the right to life, liberty and the security of his person. No one may be deprived of his life or liberty, except in accordance with legal procedures. All are equal before the courts.

Article 13

(A) Public and private freedoms shall be protected.
(B) The right of free expression shall be protected.
(C) The right of free peaceable assembly and the right to join associations freely, as well as the right to form and join unions and political parties freely, in accordance with the law, shall be guaranteed.
(D) Each Iraqi has the right of free movement in all parts of Iraq and the right to travel abroad and return freely.
(E) Each Iraqi has the right to demonstrate and strike peaceably in accordance with the law.
(F) Each Iraqi has the right to freedom of thought, conscience and religious belief and practice. Coercion in such matters shall be prohibited.

Appendix 2   249

(G) Slavery, the slave trade, forced labor and involuntary servitude with or without pay shall be forbidden.
(H) Each Iraqi has the right to privacy.

Article 14

The individual has the right to security, education, health care and social security. The Iraqi State and its governmental units, including the federal government, the regions, governorates, municipalities and local administrations, within the limits of their resources and with due regard to other vital needs, shall strive to provide prosperity and employment opportunities to the people.

Article 15

(A) No civil law shall have retroactive effect unless the law so stipulates. There shall be neither a crime, nor punishment, except by law in effect at the time the crime is committed.
(B) Police, investigators or other governmental authorities may not violate the sanctity of private residences, whether these authorities belong to the federal or regional governments, governorates, municipalities or local administrations, unless a judge or investigating magistrate has issued a search warrant in accordance with applicable law on the basis of information provided by a sworn individual who knew that bearing false witness would render him liable to punishment. Extreme exigent circumstances, as determined by a court of competent jurisdiction, may justify a warrantless search, but such exigencies shall be narrowly construed. In the event that a warrantless search is carried out in the absence of an extreme exigent circumstance, the evidence so seized, and any other evidence found derivatively from such search, shall be inadmissible in connection with a criminal charge, unless the court determines that the person who carried out the warrantless search believed reasonably and in good faith that the search was in accordance with the law.
(C) No one may be unlawfully arrested or detained, and no one may be detained by reason of political or religious beliefs.
(D) All persons shall be guaranteed the right to a fair and public hearing by an independent and impartial tribunal, regardless of whether the proceeding is civil or criminal. Notice of the proceeding and its legal basis must be provided to the accused without delay.
(E) The accused is innocent until proven guilty pursuant to law, and he likewise has the right to engage independent and competent counsel, to remain silent in response to questions addressed to him with no compulsion to testify for any reason, to participate in preparing his defense, and to summon and examine witnesses or to ask the judge to do so. At the time a person is arrested, he must be notified of these rights.
(F) The right to a fair, speedy and open trial shall be guaranteed.
(G) Every person deprived of his liberty by arrest or detention shall have the right of recourse to a court to determine the legality of his arrest or detention without delay and to order his release if this occurred in an illegal manner.

250 *Appendix 2*

(H) After being found innocent of a charge, an accused may not be tried once again on the same charge.
(I) Civilians may not be tried before a military tribunal. Special or exceptional courts may not be established.
(J) Torture in all its forms, physical or mental, shall be prohibited under all circumstances, as shall be cruel, inhuman or degrading treatment. No confession made under compulsion, torture or threat thereof shall be relied upon or admitted into evidence for any reason in any proceeding, whether criminal or otherwise.

Article 16

(A) Public property is sacrosanct, and its protection is the duty of every citizen.
(B) The right to private property shall be protected, and no one may be prevented from disposing of his property except within the limits of law. No one shall be deprived of his property except by eminent domain, in circumstances and in the manner set forth in law, and on condition that he is paid just and timely compensation.
(C) Each Iraqi citizen shall have the full and unfettered right to own real property in all parts of Iraq without restriction.

Article 17

It shall not be permitted to possess, bear, buy or sell arms except on licensure issued in accordance with the law.

Article 18

There shall be no taxation or fee except by law.

Article 19

No political refugee who has been granted asylum pursuant to applicable law may be surrendered or returned forcibly to the country from which he fled.

Article 20

(A) Every Iraqi who fulfills the conditions stipulated in the electoral law has the right to stand for election and cast his ballot secretly in free, open, fair, competitive and periodic elections.
(B) No Iraqi may be discriminated against for purposes of voting in elections on the basis of gender, religion, sect, race, belief, ethnic origin, language, wealth or literacy.

Article 21

Neither the Iraqi Transitional Government nor the governments and administrations of the regions, governorates and municipalities, nor local administrations, may interfere with the right of the Iraqi people to develop the institutions of civil society, whether in cooperation with international civil society organizations or otherwise.

Appendix 2 251

Article 22

If, in the course of his work, an official of any government office, whether in the federal government, the regional governments, the governorate and municipal administrations or the local administrations, deprives an individual or a group of the rights guaranteed by this Law or any other Iraqi laws in force, this individual or group shall have the right to maintain a cause of action against that employee to seek compensation for the damages caused by such deprivation, to vindicate his rights, and to seek any other legal measure. If the court decides that the official had acted with a sufficient degree of good faith and in the belief that his actions were consistent with the law, then he is not required to pay compensation.

Article 23

The enumeration of the foregoing rights must not be interpreted to mean that they are the only rights enjoyed by the Iraqi people. They enjoy all the rights that befit a free people possessed of their human dignity, including the rights stipulated in international treaties and agreements, other instruments of international law that Iraq has signed and to which it has acceded, and others that are deemed binding upon it, and in the law of nations. Non-Iraqis within Iraq shall enjoy all human rights not inconsistent with their status as non-citizens.

Chapter 3: the Iraqi Transitional Government

Article 24

(A) The Iraqi Transitional Government, which is also referred to in this Law as the federal government, shall consist of the National Assembly; the Presidency Council; the Council of Ministers, including the Prime Minister; and the judicial authority.
(B) The three authorities, legislative, executive and judicial, shall be separate and independent of one another.
(C) No official or employee of the Iraqi Transitional Government shall enjoy immunity for criminal acts committed while in office.

Article 25

The Iraqi Transitional Government shall have exclusive competence in the following matters:

(A) Formulating foreign policy and diplomatic representation; negotiating, signing and ratifying international treaties and agreements; and formulating foreign economic and trade policy and sovereign debt policies;
(B) Formulating and executing national security policy, including creating and maintaining armed forces to secure, protect and guarantee the security of the country's borders and to defend Iraq;
(C) Formulating fiscal policy, issuing currency, regulating customs, regulating commercial policy across regional and governorate boundaries in Iraq,

250 *Appendix 2*

drawing up the national budget of the State, formulating monetary policy, and establishing and administering a central bank;

(D) Regulating weights and measures and formulating a general policy on wages;

(E) Managing the natural resources of Iraq, which belongs to all the people of all the regions and governorates of Iraq, in consultation with the governments of the regions and the administrations of the governorates, and distributing the revenues resulting from their sale through the national budget in an equitable manner proportional to the distribution of population throughout the country, and with due regard for areas that were unjustly deprived of these revenues by the previous regime, for dealing with their situations in a positive way, for their needs, and for the degree of development of the different areas of the country;

(F) Regulating Iraqi citizenship, immigration and asylum; and

(G) Regulating telecommunications policy.

Article 26

(A) Except as otherwise provided in this Law, the laws in force in Iraq on June 30, 2004 shall remain in effect unless and until rescinded or amended by the Iraqi Transitional Government in accordance with this Law.

(B) Legislation issued by the federal legislative authority shall supersede any other legislation issued by any other legislative authority in the event that they contradict each other, except as provided in Article 54(B).

(C) The laws, regulations, orders and directives issued by the Coalition Provisional Authority pursuant to its authority under international law shall remain in force until rescinded or amended by legislation duly enacted and having the force of law.

Article 27

(A) The Iraqi Armed Forces shall consist of the active and reserve units, and elements thereof. The purpose of these forces is the defense of Iraq.

(B) Armed forces and militias not under the command structure of the Iraqi Transitional Government are prohibited, except as provided by federal law.

(C) The Iraqi Armed Forces and its personnel, including military personnel working in the Ministry of Defense or any offices or organizations subordinate to it, may not stand for election to political office, campaign for candidates or participate in other activities forbidden by Ministry of Defense regulations. This ban encompasses the activities of the personnel mentioned above acting in their personal or official capacities. Nothing in this Article shall infringe upon the right of these personnel to vote in elections.

(D) The Iraqi Intelligence Service shall collect information, assess threats to national security, and advise the Iraqi government. This Service shall be under civilian control, shall be subject to legislative oversight and shall operate pursuant to law and in accordance with recognized principles of human rights.

(E) The Iraqi Transitional Government shall respect and implement Iraq's international obligations regarding the non-proliferation, non-development,

Appendix 2 253

non-production and non-use of nuclear, chemical and biological weapons, and associated equipment, materiel, technologies and delivery systems for use in the development, manufacture, production and use of such weapons.

Article 28

(A) Members of the National Assembly; the Presidency Council; the Council of Ministers, including the Prime Minister; and judges and justices of the courts may not be appointed to any other position in or out of government. Any member of the National Assembly who becomes a member of the Presidency Council or Council of Ministers shall be deemed to have resigned his membership in the National Assembly.

(B) In no event may a member of the armed forces be a member of the National Assembly, minister, Prime Minister or member of the Presidency Council unless the individual has resigned his commission or rank, or retired from duty at least 18 months prior to serving.

Article 29

Upon the assumption of full authority by the Iraqi Interim Government in accordance with Article 2(B)(1) above, the Coalition Provisional Authority shall be dissolved and the work of the Governing Council shall come to an end.

Chapter 4: the transitional legislative authority

Article 30

(A) During the transitional period, the State of Iraq shall have a legislative authority known as the National Assembly. Its principal mission shall be to legislate and exercise oversight over the work of the executive authority.

(B) Laws shall be issued in the name of the people of Iraq. Laws, regulations and directives related to them shall be published in the official gazette and shall take effect as of the date of their publication, unless they stipulate otherwise.

(C) The National Assembly shall be elected in accordance with an electoral law and a political parties law. The electoral law shall aim to achieve the goal of having women constitute no less than one-quarter of the members of the National Assembly and of having fair representation for all communities in Iraq, including the Turcomans, Chaldo-Assyrians and others.

(D) Elections for the National Assembly shall take place by December 31, 2004 if possible, and in any case no later than by January 31, 2005.

Article 31

(A) The National Assembly shall consist of 275 members. It shall enact a law dealing with the replacement of its members in the event of resignation, removal or death.

(B) A nominee to the National Assembly must fulfill the following conditions:

254   *Appendix 2*

(1) He shall be an Iraqi no less than 30 years of age.
(2) He shall not have been a member of the dissolved Ba'th Party with the rank of Division Member or higher, unless exempted pursuant to the applicable legal rules.
(3) If he was once a member of the dissolved Ba'th Party with the rank of Full Member, he shall be required to sign a document renouncing the Ba'th Party and disavowing all of his past links with it before becoming eligible to be a candidate, as well as to swear that he no longer has any dealings or connection with Ba'th Party organizations. If it is established in court that he lied or fabricated on this score, he shall lose his seat in the National Assembly.
(4) He shall not have been a member of the former agencies of repression and shall not have contributed to or participated in the persecution of citizens.
(5) He shall not have enriched himself in an illegitimate manner at the expense of the homeland and public finance.
(6) He shall not have been convicted of a crime involving moral turpitude and shall have a good reputation.
(7) He shall have at least a secondary school diploma, or equivalent.
(8) He shall not be a member of the armed forces at the time of his nomination.

Article 32

(A) The National Assembly shall draw up its own internal procedures, and it shall sit in public session unless circumstances require otherwise, consistent with its internal procedures. The first session of the Assembly shall be chaired by its oldest member.
(B) The National Assembly shall elect, from its own members, a president and two deputy presidents of the National Assembly. The president of the National Assembly shall be the individual who receives the greatest number of votes for that office; the first deputy president the next highest; and the second deputy president the next. The president of the National Assembly may vote on an issue, but may not participate in the debates, unless he temporarily steps out of the chair immediately prior to addressing the issue.
(C) A bill shall not be voted upon by the National Assembly unless it has been read twice at a regular session of the Assembly, on condition that at least two days intervene between the two readings, and after the bill has been placed on the agenda of the session at least four days prior to the vote.

Article 33

(A) Meetings of the National Assembly shall be public, and transcripts of its meetings shall be recorded and published. The vote of every member of the National Assembly shall be recorded and made public. Decisions in the National Assembly shall be taken by simple majority unless this Law stipulates otherwise.

Appendix 2　255

(B) The National Assembly must examine bills proposed by the Council of Ministers, including budget bills.

(C) Only the Council of Ministers shall have the right to present a proposed national budget. The National Assembly has the right to reallocate proposed spending and to reduce the total amounts in the general budget. It also has the right to propose an increase in the overall amount of expenditures to the Council of Ministers if necessary.

(D) Members of the National Assembly shall have the right to propose bills, consistent with the internal procedures that are drawn up by the Assembly.

(E) The Iraqi Armed Forces may not be dispatched outside Iraq even for the purpose of defending against foreign aggression except with the approval of the National Assembly and upon the request of the Presidency Council.

(F) Only the National Assembly shall have the power to ratify international treaties and agreements.

(G) The oversight function performed by the National Assembly and its committees shall include the right of interpellation of executive officials, including members of the Presidency Council, the Council of Ministers, including the Prime Minister, and any less senior official of the executive authority. This shall encompass the right to investigate, request information and issue subpoenas for persons to appear before them.

Article 34

Each member of the National Assembly shall enjoy immunity for statements made while the Assembly is in session, and the member may not be sued before the courts for such. A member may not be placed under arrest during a session of the National Assembly, unless the member is accused of a crime and the National Assembly agrees to lift his immunity or if he is caught *in flagrante delicto* in the commission of a felony.

Chapter 5: the transitional executive authority

Article 35

The executive authority during the transitional period shall consist of the Presidency Council, the Council of Ministers and its presiding Prime Minister.

Article 36

(A) The National Assembly shall elect a President of the State and two Deputies. They shall form the Presidency Council, the function of which will be to represent the sovereignty of Iraq and oversee the higher affairs of the country. The election of the Presidency Council shall take place on the basis of a single list and by a two-thirds majority of the members' votes. The National Assembly has the power to remove any member of the Presidency Council of the State for incompetence or lack of integrity by a three-fourths majority of its members' votes. In the event of a vacancy in the Presidency Council,

256 *Appendix 2*

the National Assembly shall, by a vote of two-thirds of its members, elect a replacement to fill the vacancy.

(B) It is a prerequisite for a member of the Presidency Council to fulfill the same conditions as the members of the National Assembly, with the following observations:

(1) He must be at least 40 years of age.

(2) He must possess a good reputation, integrity and rectitude.

(3) If he was a member of the dissolved Ba'th Party, he must have left the dissolved Party at least ten years before its fall.

(4) He must not have participated in repressing the *intifada* of 1991 or the Anfal campaign and must not have committed a crime against the Iraqi people.

(C) The Presidency Council shall take its decisions unanimously, and its members may not deputize others as proxies.

Article 37

The Presidency Council may veto any legislation passed by the National Assembly, on condition that this be done within 15 days after the Presidency Council is notified by the president of the National Assembly of the passage of such legislation. In the event of a veto, the legislation shall be returned to the National Assembly, which has the right to pass the legislation again by a two-thirds majority not subject to veto within a period not to exceed 30 days.

Article 38

(A) The Presidency Council shall name a Prime Minister unanimously, as well as the members of the Council of Ministers upon the recommendation of the Prime Minister. The Prime Minister and Council of Ministers shall then seek to obtain a vote of confidence by simple majority from the National Assembly prior to commencing their work as a government. The Presidency Council must agree on a candidate for the post of Prime Minister within two weeks. In the event that it fails to do so, the responsibility of naming the Prime Minister reverts to the National Assembly. In that event, the National Assembly must confirm the nomination by a two-thirds majority. If the Prime Minister is unable to nominate his Council of Ministers within one month, the Presidency Council shall name another Prime Minister.

(B) The qualifications for Prime Minister must be the same as for the members of the Presidency Council except that his age must not be less than 35 years upon his taking office.

Article 39

(A) The Council of Ministers shall, with the approval of the Presidency Council, appoint representatives to negotiate the conclusion of international treaties and agreements. The Presidency Council shall recommend passage of a law by the National Assembly to ratify such treaties and agreements.

Appendix 2 257

(B) The Presidency Council shall carry out the function of commander-in-chief of the Iraqi Armed Forces only for ceremonial and protocol purposes. It shall have no command authority. It shall have the right to be briefed, to inquire and to advise. Operationally, national command authority on military matters shall flow from the Prime Minister to the Minister of Defense to the military chain of command of the Iraqi Armed Forces.

(C) The Presidency Council shall, as more fully set forth in Chapter 6, below, appoint, upon recommendation of the Higher Juridical Council, the Presiding Judge and members of the Federal Supreme Court.

(D) The Council of Ministers shall appoint the Director-General of the Iraqi National Intelligence Service, as well as officers of the Iraqi Armed Forces at the rank of general or above. Such appointments shall be subject to confirmation by the National Assembly by simple majority of those of its members present.

Article 40

(A) The Prime Minister and the ministers shall be responsible before the National Assembly, and this Assembly shall have the right to withdraw its confidence either in the Prime Minister or in the ministers collectively or individually. In the event that confidence in the Prime Minister is withdrawn, the entire Council of Ministers shall be dissolved, and Article 40(B), below, shall become operative.

(B) In the event of a vote of no confidence with respect to the entire Council of Ministers, the Prime Minister and Council of Ministers shall remain in office to carry out their functions for a period not to exceed 30 days, until the formation of a new Council of Ministers, consistent with Article 38 above.

Article 41

The Prime Minister shall have day-to-day responsibility for the management of the government, and he may dismiss ministers with the approval of a simple majority of the National Assembly. The Presidency Council may, upon the recommendation of the Commission on Public Integrity after the exercise of due process, dismiss the Prime Minister or the ministers.

Article 42

The Council of Ministers shall draw up rules of procedure for its work and issue the regulations and directives necessary to enforce the laws. It also has the right to propose bills to the National Assembly. Each ministry has the right, within its competence, to nominate deputy ministers, ambassadors and other employees of special grade. After the Council of Ministers approves these nominations, they shall be submitted to the Presidency Council for ratification. All decisions of the Council of Ministers shall be taken by simple majority of those of its members present.

258   *Appendix 2*

Chapter 6: the federal judicial authority

Article 43

(A) The judiciary is independent, and it shall in no way be administered by the executive authority, including the Ministry of Justice. The judiciary shall enjoy exclusive competence to determine the innocence or guilt of the accused pursuant to law, without interference from the legislative or executive authorities.

(B) All judges sitting in their respective courts as of July 1, 2004 will continue in office thereafter, unless removed from office pursuant to this Law.

(C) The National Assembly shall establish an independent and adequate budget for the judiciary.

(D) Federal courts shall adjudicate matters that arise from the application of federal laws. The establishment of these courts shall be within the exclusive competence of the federal government. The establishment of these courts in the regions shall be in consultation with the presidents of the judicial councils in the regions, and priority in appointing or transferring judges to these courts shall be given to judges resident in the region.

Article 44

(A) A court called the Federal Supreme Court shall be constituted by law in Iraq.

(B) The jurisdiction of the Federal Supreme Court shall be as follows:

  (1) Original and exclusive jurisdiction in legal proceedings between the Iraqi Transitional Government and the regional governments, governorate and municipal administrations, and local administrations.

  (2) Original and exclusive jurisdiction, on the basis of a complaint from a claimant or a referral from another court, to review claims that a law, regulation or directive issued by the federal or regional governments, the governorate or municipal administrations, or local administrations is inconsistent with this Law.

  (3) Ordinary appellate jurisdiction of the Federal Supreme Court shall be defined by federal law.

(C) Should the Federal Supreme Court rule that a challenged law, regulation, directive or measure is inconsistent with this Law, it shall be deemed null and void.

(D) The Federal Supreme Court shall create and publish regulations regarding the procedures required to bring claims and to permit attorneys to practice before it. It shall take its decisions by simple majority, except decisions with regard to the proceedings stipulated in Article 44(B)(1), which must be by a two-thirds majority. Decisions shall be binding. The Court shall have full powers to enforce its decisions, including the power to issue citations for contempt of court and the measures that flow from this.

Appendix 2   259

(E) The Federal Supreme Court shall consist of nine members. The Higher Juridical Council shall, in consultation with the regional judicial councils, initially nominate no less than 18 and up to 27 individuals to fill the initial vacancies in the aforementioned Court. It will follow the same procedure thereafter, nominating three members for each subsequent vacancy that occurs by reason of death, resignation or removal. The Presidency Council shall appoint the members of this Court and name one of them as its Presiding Judge. In the event an appointment is rejected, the Higher Juridical Council shall nominate a new group of three candidates.

Article 45

A Higher Juridical Council shall be established and assume the role of the Council of Judges. The Higher Juridical Council shall supervise the federal judiciary and shall administer its budget. This Council shall be composed of the Presiding Judge of the Federal Supreme Court, the presiding judge and deputy presiding judges of the federal Court of Cassation, the presiding judges of the federal Courts of Appeal, and the presiding judge and two deputy presiding judges of each regional court of cassation. The Presiding Judge of the Federal Supreme Court shall preside over the Higher Juridical Council. In his absence, the presiding judge of the federal Court of Cassation shall preside over the Council.

Article 46

(A) The federal judicial branch shall include existing courts outside the Kurdistan region, including courts of first instance; the Central Criminal Court of Iraq; Courts of Appeal; and the Court of Cassation, which shall be the court of last resort except as provided in Article 44 of this Law. Additional federal courts may be established by law. The appointment of judges for these courts shall be made by the Higher Juridical Council. This Law preserves the qualifications necessary for the appointment of judges, as defined by law.
(B) The decisions of regional and local courts, including the courts of the Kurdistan region, shall be final, but shall be subject to review by the federal judiciary if they conflict with this Law or any federal law. Procedures for such review shall be defined by law.

Article 47

No judge or member of the Higher Juridical Council may be removed unless he is convicted of a crime involving moral turpitude or corruption or suffers permanent incapacity. Removal shall be on the recommendation of the Higher Juridical Council, by a decision of the Council of Ministers, and with the approval of the Presidency Council. Removal shall be executed immediately after issuance of this approval. A judge who has been accused of such a crime as cited above shall be suspended from his work in the judiciary until such time as the case arising from

260   *Appendix 2*

what is cited in this Article is adjudicated. No judge may have his salary reduced or suspended for any reason during his period of service.

Chapter 7: the Special Tribunal and national commissions

Article 48

(A) The statute establishing the Iraqi Special Tribunal issued on December 10, 2003 is confirmed. That statute exclusively defines its jurisdiction and procedures, notwithstanding the provisions of this Law.
(B) No other court shall have jurisdiction to examine cases within the competence of the Iraqi Special Tribunal, except to the extent provided by its founding statute.
(C) The judges of the Iraqi Special Tribunal shall be appointed in accordance with the provisions of its founding statute.

Article 49

(A) The establishment of national commissions such as the Commission on Public Integrity, the Iraqi Property Claims Commission and the Higher National De-Ba'thification Commission is confirmed, as is the establishment of commissions formed after this Law has gone into effect. The members of these national commissions shall continue to serve after this Law has gone into effect, taking into account the contents of Article 51 below.
(B) The method of appointment to the national commissions shall be in accordance with law.

Article 50

The Iraqi Transitional Government shall establish a National Commission for Human Rights for the purpose of executing the commitments relative to the rights set forth in this Law and to examine complaints pertaining to violations of human rights. The Commission shall be established in accordance with the Paris Principles issued by the United Nations on the responsibilities of national institutions. This Commission shall include an Office of the Ombudsman to inquire into complaints. This office shall have the power to investigate, on its own initiative or on the basis of a complaint submitted to it, any allegation that the conduct of the governmental authorities is arbitrary or contrary to law.

Article 51

No member of the Iraqi Special Tribunal or of any commission established by the federal government may be employed in any other capacity in or out of government. This prohibition is valid without limitation, whether it be within the executive, legislative or judicial authority of the Iraqi Transitional Government. Members of the Special Tribunal may, however, suspend their employment in other agencies while they serve on the aforementioned Tribunal.

Appendix 2 261

Chapter 8: regions, governorates and municipalities

Article 52

The design of the federal system in Iraq shall be established in such a way as to prevent the concentration of power in the federal government that allowed the continuation of decades of tyranny and oppression under the previous regime. This system shall encourage the exercise of local authority by local officials in every region and governorate, thereby creating a united Iraq in which every citizen actively participates in governmental affairs, secure in his rights and free of domination.

Article 53

(A) The Kurdistan Regional Government is recognized as the official government of the territories that were administered by that government on March 19, 2003 in the governorates of Dohuk, Arbil, Sulaimaniya, Kirkuk, Diyala and Neneveh. The term "Kurdistan Regional Government" shall refer to the Kurdistan National Assembly, the Kurdistan Council of Ministers and the regional judicial authority in the Kurdistan region.

(B) The boundaries of the 18 governorates shall remain without change during the transitional period.

(C) Any group of no more than three governorates outside the Kurdistan region, with the exception of Baghdad and Kirkuk, shall have the right to form regions from amongst themselves. The mechanisms for forming such regions may be proposed by the Iraqi Interim Government, and shall be presented and considered by the elected National Assembly for enactment into law. In addition to being approved by the National Assembly, any legislation proposing the formation of a particular region must be approved in a referendum of the people of the relevant governorates.

(D) This Law shall guarantee the administrative, cultural and political rights of the Turcomans, Chaldo-Assyrians and all other citizens.

Article 54

(A) The Kurdistan Regional Government shall continue to perform its current functions throughout the transitional period, except with regard to those issues which fall within the exclusive competence of the federal government as specified in this Law. Financing for these functions shall come from the federal government, consistent with current practice and in accordance with Article 25(E) of this Law. The Kurdistan Regional Government shall retain regional control over police forces and internal security, and it will have the right to impose taxes and fees within the Kurdistan region.

(B) With regard to the application of federal laws in the Kurdistan region, the Kurdistan National Assembly shall be permitted to amend the application of any such law within the Kurdistan region, but only to the extent that this relates to matters that are not within the provisions of Articles 25 and 43(D) of this Law and that fall within the exclusive competence of the federal government.

Article 55

(A) Each governorate shall have the right to form a Governorate Council, name a Governor, and form municipal and local councils. No member of any regional government, Governor or member of any governorate, municipal or local council may be dismissed by the federal government or any official thereof, except upon conviction of a crime by a court of competent jurisdiction as provided by law. No regional government may dismiss a Governor or member or members of any governorate, municipal or local council. No Governor or member of any governorate, municipal or local council shall be subject to the control of the federal government except to the extent that the matter relates to the competences set forth in Articles 25 and 43(D) above.

(B) Each Governor and member of each Governorate Council who holds office as of July 1, 2004, in accordance with the law on local government that shall be issued, shall remain in place until such time as free, direct and full elections, conducted pursuant to law, are held, or, unless, prior to that time, he voluntarily gives up his position, is removed upon his conviction for a crime involving moral turpitude or related to corruption, or upon being stricken with permanent incapacity, or is dismissed in accordance with the law cited above. When a governor, mayor or member of a council is dismissed, the relevant council may receive applications from any eligible resident of the governorate to fill the position. Eligibility requirements shall be the same as those set forth in Article 31 for membership in the National Assembly. The new candidate must receive a majority vote of the council to assume the vacant seat.

Article 56

(A) The Governorate Councils shall assist the federal government in the coordination of federal ministry operations within the governorate, including the review of annual ministry plans and budgets with regard to activities in the governorate. Governorate Councils shall be funded from the general budget of the State, and these Councils shall also have the authority to increase their revenues independently by imposing taxes and fees; to organize the operations of the Governorate administration; to initiate and implement province-level projects alone or in partnership with international and non-governmental organizations; and to conduct other activities insofar as is consistent with federal laws.

(B) The *Qada'* and *Nahiya* councils and other relevant councils shall assist in the performance of federal responsibilities and the delivery of public services by reviewing local ministry plans in the afore-mentioned places; ensuring that they respond properly to local needs and interests; identifying local budgetary requirements through the national budgeting procedures; collecting and retaining local revenues, taxes and fees; organizing the operations of the local administration; initiating and implementing local projects alone or in conjunction with international and non-governmental organizations; and conducting other activities consistent with applicable law.

Appendix 2 263

(C) Where practicable, the federal government shall take measures to devolve additional functions to local, governorate and regional administrations, in a methodical way. Regional units and governorate administrations, including the Kurdistan Regional Government, shall be organized on the basis of the principle of de-centralization and the devolution of authorities to municipal and local governments.

Article 57

(A) All authorities not exclusively reserved to the Iraqi Transitional Government may be exercised by the regional governments and governorates as soon as possible following the establishment of appropriate governmental institutions.
(B) Elections for governorate councils throughout Iraq and for the Kurdistan National Assembly shall be held at the same time as the elections for the National Assembly, no later than January 31, 2005.

Article 58

(A) The Iraqi Transitional Government, and especially the Iraqi Property Claims Commission and other relevant bodies, shall act expeditiously to take measures to remedy the injustice caused by the previous regime's practices in altering the demographic character of certain regions, including Kirkuk, by deporting and expelling individuals from their places of residence, forcing migration in and out of the region, settling individuals alien to the region, depriving the inhabitants of work, and correcting nationality. To remedy this injustice, the Iraqi Transitional Government shall take the following steps:

   (1) With regard to residents who were deported, expelled or who emigrated, it shall, in accordance with the statute of the Iraqi Property Claims Commission and other measures within the law, within a reasonable period of time, restore the residents to their homes and property, or, where this is unfeasible, shall provide just compensation.

   (2) With regard to the individuals newly introduced to specific regions and territories, it shall act in accordance with Article 10 of the Iraqi Property Claims Commission statute to ensure that such individuals may be resettled, may receive compensation from the state, may receive new land from the state near their residence in the governorate from which they came, or may receive compensation for the cost of moving to such areas.

   (3) With regard to persons deprived of employment or other means of support in order to force migration out of their regions and territories, it shall promote new employment opportunities in the regions and territories.

   (4) With regard to nationality correction, it shall repeal all relevant decrees and shall permit affected persons the right to determine their own national identity and ethnic affiliation free from coercion and duress.

(B) The previous regime also manipulated and changed administrative boundaries for political ends. The Presidency Council of the Iraqi Transitional

264   *Appendix 2*

Government shall make recommendations to the National Assembly on remedying these unjust changes in the permanent constitution. In the event the Presidency Council is unable to agree unanimously on a set of recommendations, it shall unanimously appoint a neutral arbitrator to examine the issue and make recommendations. In the event the Presidency Council is unable to agree on an arbitrator, it shall request the Secretary General of the United Nations to appoint a distinguished international person to be the arbitrator.

(C) The permanent resolution of disputed territories, including Kirkuk, shall be deferred until after these measures are completed, a fair and transparent census has been conducted and the permanent constitution has been ratified. This resolution shall be consistent with the principle of justice, taking into account the will of the people of those territories.

Chapter 9: the transitional period

Article 59

(A) The permanent constitution shall contain guarantees to ensure that the Iraqi Armed Forces are never again used to terrorize or oppress the people of Iraq.

(B) Consistent with Iraq's status as a sovereign state, and with its desire to join other nations in helping to maintain peace and security and fight terrorism during the transitional period, the Iraqi Armed Forces will be a principal partner in the multi-national force operating in Iraq under unified command pursuant to the provisions of United Nations Security Council Resolution 1511 (2003) and any subsequent relevant resolutions. This arrangement shall last until the ratification of a permanent constitution and the election of a new government pursuant to that new constitution.

(C) Upon its assumption of authority, and consistent with Iraq's status as a sovereign state, the elected Iraqi Transitional Government shall have the authority to conclude binding international agreements regarding the activities of the multi-national force operating in Iraq under unified command pursuant to the terms of United Nations Security Council Resolution 1511 (2003), and any subsequent relevant United Nations Security Council resolutions. Nothing in this Law shall affect rights and obligations under these agreements, or under United Nations Security Council Resolution 1511 (2003), and any subsequent relevant United Nations Security Council resolutions, which will govern the multi-national force's activities pending the entry into force of these agreements.

Article 60

The National Assembly shall write a draft of the permanent constitution of Iraq. This Assembly shall carry out this responsibility in part by encouraging debate on the constitution through regular general public meetings in all parts of Iraq and through the media, and receiving proposals from the citizens of Iraq as it writes the constitution.

Appendix 2 265

Article 61

(A) The National Assembly shall write the draft of the permanent constitution by no later than August 15, 2005.

(B) The draft permanent constitution shall be presented to the Iraqi people for approval in a general referendum to be held no later than October 15, 2005. In the period leading up to the referendum, the draft constitution shall be published and widely distributed to encourage a public debate about it among the people.

(C) The general referendum will be successful and the draft constitution ratified if a majority of the voters in Iraq approve and if two-thirds of the voters in three or more governorates do not reject it.

(D) If the permanent constitution is approved in the referendum, elections for a permanent government shall be held no later than December 15, 2005 and the new government shall assume office no later than December 31, 2005.

(E) If the referendum rejects the draft permanent constitution, the National Assembly shall be dissolved. Elections for a new National Assembly shall be held no later than December 15, 2005. The new National Assembly and new Iraqi Transitional Government shall then assume office no later than December 31, 2005, and shall continue to operate under this Law, except that the final deadlines for preparing a new draft may be changed to make it possible to draft a permanent constitution within a period not to exceed one year. The new National Assembly shall be entrusted with writing another draft permanent constitution.

(F) If necessary, the president of the National Assembly, with the agreement of a majority of the members' votes, may certify to the Presidency Council no later than August 1, 2005 that there is a need for additional time to complete the writing of the draft constitution. The Presidency Council shall then extend the deadline for writing the draft constitution for only six months. This deadline may not be extended again.

(G) If the National Assembly does not complete writing the draft permanent constitution by August 15, 2005 and does not request extension of the deadline in Article 61(F) above, the provisions of Article 61(E), above, shall be applied.

Article 62

This Law shall remain in effect until the permanent constitution is issued and the new Iraqi government is formed in accordance with it.

Source

Adapted from the Coalition Provisional Authority. (2004, March 8). Law of Administration for the State of Iraq for the Transitional Period [TAL]. Retrieved March 3, 2014, from The Internet Archive: http://web.archive.org/web/20090423064920/http://www.cpa-iraq.org/government/TAL.html

Appendix 3
Iraqi Constitution (2005)

The preamble

In the name of God, the Most merciful, the Most compassionate
(We have honored the sons of Adam)

We, the people of Mesopotamia, the homeland of the apostles and prophets, resting place of the virtuous imams, cradle of civilization, crafters of writing, and home of numeration. Upon our land the first law made by man was passed, and the oldest pact of just governance was inscribed, and upon our soil the saints and companions of the Prophet prayed, philosophers and scientists theorized, and writers and poets excelled.

Acknowledging God's right over us, and in fulfillment of the call of our homeland and citizens, and in a response to the call of our religious and national leaderships and the determination of our great authorities and of our leaders and politicians, and in the midst of international support from our friends and those who love us, marched for the first time in our history towards the ballot boxes by the millions, men and women, young and old, on the thirtieth of January 2005, invoking the pains of sectarian oppression inflicted by the autocratic clique and inspired by the tragedies of Iraq's martyrs, Shi'ite and Sunni, Arabs and Kurds and Turkmen and from all other components of the people, and recollecting the darkness of the ravage of the holy cities and the South in the Sha'abaniyya uprising and burnt by the flames of grief of the mass graves, the marshes, Al-Dujail and others and articulating the sufferings of racial oppression in the massacres of Halabcha, Barzan, Anfal and the Fayli Kurds and inspired by the ordeals of the Turkmen in Bashir and the sufferings of the people of the western region, as is the case in the remaining areas of Iraq where the people suffered from the liquidation of their leaders, symbols and Sheiks and from the displacement of their skilled individuals and from drying out of its cultural and intellectual wells, so we sought hand in hand and shoulder to shoulder to create our new Iraq, the Iraq of the future, free from sectarianism, racism, complex of regional attachment, discrimination and exclusion.

Accusations of being infidels, and terrorism, did not stop us from marching forward to build a nation of law. Sectarianism and racism have not stopped us

Appendix 3   267

from marching together to strengthen our national unity, following the path of peaceful transfer of power, adopting the course of just distribution of resources, and providing equal opportunity for all.

We, the people of Iraq, who have just risen from our stumble, and who are looking with confidence to the future through a republican, federal, democratic, pluralistic system, have resolved with the determination of our men, women, elderly and youth to respect the rule of law, to establish justice and equality, to cast aside the politics of aggression, to pay attention to women and their rights, the elderly and their concerns, and children and their affairs, to spread the culture of diversity, and to defuse terrorism.

We, the people of Iraq, of all components and across the spectrum, have taken upon ourselves to decide freely and by choice to unite our future, to take lessons from yesterday for tomorrow, and to enact this permanent Constitution, through the values and ideals of the heavenly messages and the findings of science and man's civilization. The adherence to this Constitution preserves for Iraq its free union of people, of land and of sovereignty.

Section One

Fundamental principles

Article 1

The Republic of Iraq is a single federal, independent and fully sovereign state in which the system of government is republican, representative, parliamentary and democratic, and this Constitution is a guarantor of the unity of Iraq.

Article 2

First: Islam is the official religion of the State and is a foundation source of legislation:

A   No law may be enacted that contradicts the established provisions of Islam.
B   No law may be enacted that contradicts the principles of democracy.
C   No law may be enacted that contradicts the rights and basic freedoms stipulated in this Constitution.

Second: This Constitution guarantees the Islamic identity of the majority of the Iraqi people and guarantees the full religious rights to freedom of religious belief and practice of all individuals such as Christians, Yazidis and Mandean Sabeans.

Article 3

Iraq is a country of multiple nationalities, religions and sects. It is a founding and active member in the Arab League and is committed to its charter, and it is part of the Islamic world.

268 *Appendix 3*

Article 4

First: The Arabic language and the Kurdish language are the two official languages of Iraq. The right of Iraqis to educate their children in their mother tongue, such as Turkmen, Syriac and Armenian, shall be guaranteed in government educational institutions in accordance with educational guidelines, or in any other language in private educational institutions.

Second: The scope of the term "official language" and the means of applying the provisions of this article shall be defined by a law and shall include:

A   Publication of the Official Gazette, in the two languages;
B   Speech, conversation and expression in official domains, such as the Council of Representatives, the Council of Ministers, courts and official conferences, in either of the two languages;
C   Recognition and publication of official documents and correspondence in the two languages;
D   Opening schools that teach the two languages, in accordance with the educational guidelines;
E   Use of both languages in any matter enjoined by the principle of equality such as bank notes, passports and stamps.

Third: The federal and official institutions and agencies in the Kurdistan region shall use both languages.

Fourth: The Turkomen language and the Syriac language are two other official languages in the administrative units in which they constitute density of population.

Fifth: Each region or governorate may adopt any other local language as an additional official language if the majority of its population so decides in a general referendum.

Article 5

The law is sovereign. The people are the source of authority and legitimacy, which they shall exercise in a direct, general, secret ballot and through their constitutional institutions.

Article 6

Transfer of authority shall be made peacefully through democratic means as stipulated in this Constitution.

Article 7

First: Any entity or program that adopts, incites, facilitates, glorifies, promotes or justifies racism or terrorism or accusations of being an infidel (takfir) or ethnic cleansing, especially the Saddamist Ba'th in Iraq and its symbols, under any name whatsoever, shall be prohibited. Such entities may not be part of political pluralism in Iraq. This shall be regulated by law.

Appendix 3 269

Second: The State shall undertake to combat terrorism in all its forms, and shall work to protect its territories from being a base, pathway or field for terrorist activities.

Article 8

Iraq shall observe the principles of good neighborliness, adhere to the principle of noninterference in the internal affairs of other states, seek to settle disputes by peaceful means, establish relations on the basis of mutual interests and reciprocity, and respect its international obligations.

Article 9

First:

A   The Iraqi armed forces and security services will be composed of the components of the Iraqi people with due consideration given to their balance and representation without discrimination or exclusion. They shall be subject to the control of the civilian authority, shall defend Iraq, shall not be used as an instrument to oppress the Iraqi people, shall not interfere in the political affairs, and shall have no role in the transfer of authority.

B   The formation of military militias outside the framework of the armed forces is prohibited.

C   The Iraqi armed forces and their personnel, including military personnel working in the Ministry of Defense or any subordinate departments or organizations, may not stand for election to political office, campaign for candidates, or participate in other activities prohibited by Ministry of Defense regulations. This ban includes the activities of the personnel mentioned above acting in their personal or professional capacities, but shall not infringe upon the right of these personnel to cast their vote in the elections.

D   The Iraqi National Intelligence Service shall collect information, assess threats to national security, and advise the Iraqi government. This Service shall be under civilian control, shall be subject to legislative oversight, and shall operate in accordance with the law and pursuant to the recognized principles of human rights.

E   The Iraqi government shall respect and implement Iraq's international obligations regarding the non-proliferation, non-development, non-production and non-use of nuclear, chemical and biological weapons, and shall prohibit associated equipment, materiel, technologies and delivery systems for use in the development, manufacture, production and use of such weapons.

Second: Military service shall be regulated by law.

Article 10

The holy shrines and religious sites in Iraq are religious and civilizational entities. The State is committed to assuring and maintaining their sanctity, and to guaranteeing the free practice of rituals in them.

270   *Appendix 3*

Article 11

Baghdad is the capital of the Republic of Iraq.

Article 12

First: The flag, national anthem and emblem of Iraq shall be regulated by law in a way that symbolizes the components of the Iraqi people.

Second: A law shall regulate honors, official holidays, religious and national occasions and the Hijri and Gregorian calendar.

Article 13

First: This Constitution is the preeminent and supreme law in Iraq and shall be binding in all parts of Iraq without exception.

Second: No law that contradicts this Constitution shall be enacted. Any text in any regional constitutions or any other legal text that contradicts this Constitution shall be considered void.

Section Two

Rights and liberties

Chapter One [Rights]
First: civil and political rights

Article 14

Iraqis are equal before the law without discrimination based on gender, race, ethnicity, nationality, origin, color, religion, sect, belief or opinion, or economic or social status.

Article 15

Every individual has the right to enjoy life, security and liberty. Deprivation or restriction of these rights is prohibited except in accordance with the law and based on a decision issued by a competent judicial authority.

Article 16

Equal opportunities shall be guaranteed to all Iraqis, and the State shall ensure that the necessary measures to achieve this are taken.

Article 17

First: Every individual shall have the right to personal privacy so long as it does not contradict the rights of others and public morals.

Second: The sanctity of the homes shall be protected. Homes may not be entered, searched or violated, except by a judicial decision in accordance with the law.

Appendix 3   271

Article 18

First: Iraqi citizenship is a right for every Iraqi and is the basis of his nationality.

Second: Anyone who is born to an Iraqi father or to an Iraqi mother shall be considered an Iraqi. This shall be regulated by law.

Third:

A   An Iraqi citizen by birth may not have his citizenship withdrawn for any reason. Any person who had his citizenship withdrawn shall have the right to demand its reinstatement. This shall be regulated by a law.
B   Iraqi citizenship shall be withdrawn from naturalized citizens in cases regulated by law.

Fourth: An Iraqi may have multiple citizenships. Everyone who assumes a senior, security or sovereign position must abandon any other acquired citizenship. This shall be regulated by law.

Fifth: Iraqi citizenship shall not be granted for the purposes of the policy of population settlement that disrupts the demographic composition of Iraq.

Sixth: Citizenship provisions shall be regulated by law. The competent courts shall consider the suits arising from those provisions.

Article 19

First: The judiciary is independent and no power is above the judiciary except the law.

Second: There is no crime or punishment except by law. The punishment shall only be for an act that the law considers a crime when perpetrated. A harsher punishment than the applicable punishment at the time of the offense may not be imposed.

Third: Litigation shall be a protected and guaranteed right for all.

Fourth: The right to a defense shall be sacred and guaranteed in all phases of investigation and the trial.

Fifth: The accused is innocent until proven guilty in a fair legal trial. The accused may not be tried for the same crime for a second time after acquittal unless new evidence is produced.

Sixth: Every person shall have the right to be treated with justice in judicial and administrative proceedings.

Seventh: The proceedings of a trial are public unless the court decides to make it secret.

Eighth: Punishment shall be personal.

272   *Appendix 3*

Ninth: Laws shall not have retroactive effect unless stipulated otherwise. This exclusion shall not include laws on taxes and fees.

Tenth: Criminal laws shall not have retroactive effect, unless it is to the benefit of the accused.

Eleventh: The court shall appoint a lawyer at the expense of the State for an accused of a felony or misdemeanor who does not have a defense lawyer.

Twelfth:

    A   Unlawful detention shall be prohibited.
    B   Imprisonment or detention shall be prohibited in places not designed for these purposes, pursuant to prison laws covering health and social care, and subject to the authorities of the State.

Thirteenth: The preliminary investigative documents shall be submitted to the competent judge in a period not to exceed 24 hours from the time of the arrest of the accused, which may be extended only once and for the same period.

Article 20

Iraqi citizens, men and women, shall have the right to participate in public affairs and to enjoy political rights including the right to vote, elect and run for office.

Article 21

First: No Iraqi shall be surrendered to foreign entities and authorities.

Second: A law shall regulate the right of political asylum in Iraq. No political refugee shall be surrendered to a foreign entity or returned forcibly to the country from which he fled.

Third: Political asylum shall not be granted to a person accused of committing international or terrorist crimes or to any person who inflicted damage on Iraq.

Second: economic, social and cultural liberties

Article 22

First: Work is a right for all Iraqis in a way that guarantees a dignified life for them.

Second: The law shall regulate the relationship between employees and employers on economic bases and while observing the rules of social justice.

Third: The State shall guarantee the right to form and join unions and professional associations, and this shall be regulated by law.

Article 23

First: Private property is protected. The owner shall have the right to benefit, exploit and dispose of private property within the limits of the law.

Appendix 3 273

Second: Expropriation is not permissible except for the purposes of public benefit in return for just compensation, and this shall be regulated by law.

Third:

- A Every Iraqi shall have the right to own property anywhere in Iraq. No others may possess immovable assets, except as exempted by law.
- B Ownership of property for the purposes of demographic change is prohibited.

Article 24

The State shall guarantee freedom of movement of Iraqi manpower, goods and capital between regions and governorates, and this shall be regulated by law.

Article 25

The State shall guarantee the reform of the Iraqi economy in accordance with modern economic principles to ensure the full investment of its resources, diversification of its sources, and the encouragement and development of the private sector.

Article 26

The State shall guarantee the encouragement of investment in the various sectors, and this shall be regulated by law.

Article 27

First: Public assets are sacrosanct, and their protection is the duty of each citizen.

Second: The provisions related to the preservation of State properties, their management, the conditions for their disposal and the limits for these assets not to be relinquished shall all be regulated by law.

Article 28

First: No taxes or fees shall be levied, amended, collected or exempted, except by law.

Second: Low-income earners shall be exempted from taxes in a way that guarantees the preservation of the minimum income required for living. This shall be regulated by law.

Article 29

First:

- A The family is the foundation of society; the State shall preserve it and its religious, moral and national values.
- B The State shall guarantee the protection of motherhood, childhood and old age, shall care for children and youth, and shall provide them with the appropriate conditions to develop their talents and abilities.

274   *Appendix 3*

Second: Children have the right to upbringing, care and education from their parents. Parents have the right to respect and care from their children, especially in times of need, disability and old age.

Third: Economic exploitation of children in all of its forms shall be prohibited, and the State shall take the necessary measures for their protection.

Fourth: All forms of violence and abuse in the family, school and society shall be prohibited.

Article 30

First: The State shall guarantee to the individual and the family—especially children and women—social and health security, the basic requirements for living a free and decent life, and shall secure for them suitable income and appropriate housing.

Second: The State shall guarantee social and health security to Iraqis in cases of old age, sickness, employment disability, homelessness, orphanhood or unemployment, shall work to protect them from ignorance, fear and poverty, and shall provide them housing and special programs of care and rehabilitation, and this shall be regulated by law.

Article 31

First: Every citizen has the right to health care. The State shall maintain public health and provide the means of prevention and treatment by building different types of hospitals and health institutions.

Second: Individuals and entities have the right to build hospitals, clinics or private health care centers under the supervision of the State, and this shall be regulated by law.

Article 32

The State shall care for the handicapped and those with special needs, and shall ensure their rehabilitation in order to reintegrate them into society, and this shall be regulated by law.

Article 33

First: Every individual has the right to live in safe environmental conditions.

Second: The State shall undertake the protection and preservation of the environment and its biological diversity.

Article 34

First: Education is a fundamental factor for the progress of society and is a right guaranteed by the state. Primary education is mandatory and the state guarantees that it shall combat illiteracy.

Appendix 3 275

Second: Free education in all its stages is a right for all Iraqis.

Third: The State shall encourage scientific research for peaceful purposes that serve humanity and shall support excellence, creativity, invention and different aspects of ingenuity.

Fourth: Private and public education shall be guaranteed, and this shall be regulated by law.

Article 35

The State shall promote cultural activities and institutions in a manner that befits the civilizational and cultural history of Iraq, and it shall seek to support indigenous Iraqi cultural orientations.

Article 36

Practicing sports is a right of every Iraqi and the State shall encourage and care for such activities and shall provide for their requirements.

Chapter Two [Liberties]

Article 37

First:

A   The liberty and dignity of man shall be protected.
B   No person may be kept in custody or investigated except according to a judicial decision.
C   All forms of psychological and physical torture and inhumane treatment are prohibited. Any confession made under force, threat or torture shall not be relied on, and the victim shall have the right to seek compensation for material and moral damages incurred in accordance with the law.

Second: The State shall guarantee protection of the individual from intellectual, political and religious coercion.

Third: Forced labor, slavery, slave trade, trafficking in women or children and sex trade shall be prohibited.

Article 38

The State shall guarantee in a way that does not violate public order and morality:

A   Freedom of expression using all means.

B   Freedom of press, printing, advertisement, media and publication.

C   Freedom of assembly and peaceful demonstration, and this shall be regulated by law.

276 *Appendix 3*

Article 39

First: The freedom to form and join associations and political parties shall be guaranteed, and this shall be regulated by law.

Second: It is not permissible to force any person to join any party, society or political entity, or force him to continue his membership in it.

Article 40

The freedom of communication and correspondence, postal, telegraphic, electronic and telephonic, shall be guaranteed and may not be monitored, wiretapped or disclosed except for legal and security necessity and by a judicial decision.

Article 41

Iraqis are free in their commitment to their personal status according to their religions, sects, beliefs or choices, and this shall be regulated by law.

Article 42

Each individual shall have the freedom of thought, conscience and belief.

Article 43

First: The followers of all religions and sects are free in the: A—Practice of religious rites, including the Husseini rituals. B—Management of religious endowments (waqf), their affairs and their religious institutions, and this shall be regulated by law.

Second: The State shall guarantee freedom of worship and the protection of places of worship.

Article 44

First: Each Iraqi has freedom of movement, travel and residence inside and outside Iraq.

Second: No Iraqi may be exiled, displaced or deprived from returning to the homeland.

Article 45

First: The State shall seek to strengthen the role of civil society institutions, and to support, develop and preserve their independence in a way that is consistent with peaceful means to achieve their legitimate goals, and this shall be regulated by law.

Second: The State shall seek the advancement of the Iraqi clans and tribes, shall attend to their affairs in a manner that is consistent with religion and the law, and shall uphold their noble human values in a way that contributes to the development of society. The State shall prohibit the tribal traditions that are in contradiction with human rights.

Appendix 3   277

Article 46

Restricting or limiting the practice of any of the rights or liberties stipulated in this Constitution is prohibited, except by a law or on the basis of a law, and insofar as that limitation or restriction does not violate the essence of the right or freedom.

Section Three

Federal powers

Article 47

The federal powers shall consist of the legislative, executive and judicial powers, and they shall exercise their competencies and tasks on the basis of the principle of separation of powers.

Chapter One [The Legislative Power]

Article 48

The federal legislative power shall consist of the Council of Representatives and the Federation Council.

First: The Council of Representatives

Article 49

First: The Council of Representatives shall consist of a number of members, at a ratio of one seat per 100,000 Iraqi persons representing the entire Iraqi people. They shall be elected through a direct secret general ballot. The representation of all components of the people shall be upheld in it.

Second: A candidate to the Council of Representatives must be a fully qualified Iraqi.

Third: A law shall regulate the requirements for the candidate, the voter and all that is related to the elections.

Fourth: The elections law shall aim to achieve a percentage of representation for women of not less than one-quarter of the members of the Council of Representatives.

Fifth: The Council of Representatives shall promulgate a law dealing with the replacement of its members on resignation, dismissal or death.

Sixth: It is not permissible to combine membership in the Council of Representatives with any work or other official position.

Article 50

Each member of the Council of Representatives shall take the following constitutional oath before the Council prior to assuming his duties:

Appendix 3

"I swear by God Almighty to carry out my legal duties and responsibilities with devotion and integrity and preserve the independence and sovereignty of Iraq, and safeguard the interests of its people, and ensure the safety of its land, sky, water, wealth and federal democratic system, and I shall endeavor to protect public and private liberties, the independence of the judiciary, and pledge to implement legislation faithfully and neutrally. God is my witness."

Article 51

The Council of Representatives shall establish its bylaws to regulate its work.

Article 52

First: The Council of Representatives shall decide, by a two-thirds majority, the authenticity of membership of its members within 30 days from the date of filing an objection.

Second: The decision of the Council of Representatives may be appealed before the Federal Supreme Court within 30 days from the date of its issuance.

Article 53

First: Sessions of the Council of Representatives shall be public unless, for reasons of necessity, the Council decides otherwise.

Second: Minutes of the sessions shall be published by means considered appropriate by the Council.

Article 54

The President of the Republic shall call upon the Council of Representatives to convene by a presidential decree within 15 days from the date of the ratification of the general election results. Its eldest member shall chair the first session to elect the speaker of the Council and his two deputies. This period may not be extended by more than the aforementioned period.

Article 55

The Council of Representatives shall elect in its first session its speaker, then his first deputy and second deputy, by an absolute majority of the total number of the Council members by direct secret ballot.

Article 56

First: The electoral term of the Council of Representatives shall be four calendar years, starting with its first session and ending with the conclusion of the fourth year.

Second: The new Council of Representatives shall be elected 45 days before the conclusion of the preceding electoral term.

Appendix 3   279

Article 57

The Council of Representatives shall have one annual term, with two legislative sessions, lasting eight months. The bylaws shall define the method to convene the sessions. The session in which the general budget is being presented shall not end until approval of the budget.

Article 58

First: The President of the Republic, the Prime Minister, the Speaker of the Council of Representatives or 50 members of the Council of Representatives may call the Council to an extraordinary session. The session shall be restricted to the topics that necessitated the call for the session.

Second: The legislative session of the Council of Representatives may be extended for no more than 30 days to complete the tasks that require the extension, based on a request from the President of the Republic, the Prime Minister, the Speaker of the Council or 50 members of the Council of Representatives.

Article 59

First: The Council of Representatives' quorum shall be achieved by an absolute majority of its members.

Second: Decisions in the sessions of the Council of Representatives shall be made by a simple majority after the quorum is achieved, unless otherwise stipulated.

Article 60

First: Draft laws shall be presented by the President of the Republic and the Council of Ministers.

Second: Proposed laws shall be presented by ten members of the Council of Representatives or by one of its specialized committees.

Article 61

The Council of Representatives shall be competent in the following:

First: Enacting federal laws.

Second: Monitoring the performance of the executive authority.

Third: Electing the President of the Republic.

Fourth: Regulating the ratification process of international treaties and agreements by a law, to be enacted by a two-thirds majority of the members of the Council of Representatives.

Fifth: Approving the appointment of the following:

280   *Appendix 3*

A   The President and members of the Federal Court of Cassation, the Chief Public Prosecutor and the President of the Judicial Oversight Commission by an absolute majority, based on a proposal from the Higher Juridical Council.

B   Ambassadors and those with special grades, based on a proposal from the Council of Ministers.

C   The Iraqi Army Chief of Staff, his assistants, those of the rank of division commander and above, and the director of the intelligence service, based on a proposal from the Council of Ministers.

Sixth:

A   Questioning the President of the Republic, based on a petition with cause, by an absolute majority of the members of the Council of Representatives.

B   Relieving the President of the Republic by an absolute majority of the Council of Representatives after being convicted by the Federal Supreme Court in one of the following cases: 1—Perjury of the constitutional oath. 2—Violating the Constitution. 3—High treason.

Seventh:

A   A member of the Council of Representatives may direct questions to the Prime Minister and the Ministers on any subject within their specialty and each of them shall answer the members' questions. Only the member who has asked the question shall have the right to comment on the answer.

B   At least 25 members of the Council of Representatives may raise a general issue for discussion in order to inquire about a policy and the performance of the Council of Ministers or one of the Ministries and it shall be submitted to the Speaker of the Council of Representatives, and the Prime Minister or the Ministers shall specify a date to come before the Council of Representatives to discuss it.

C   A member of the Council of Representatives, with the agreement of 25 members, may direct an inquiry to the Prime Minister or the Ministers to call them to account on the issues within their authority. The debate shall not be held on the inquiry except after at least seven days from the date of submission of the inquiry.

Eighth:

A   The Council of Representatives may withdraw confidence from one of the Ministers by an absolute majority and he shall be considered resigned from the date of the decision of withdrawal of confidence. A vote of no confidence in a Minister may not be held except upon his request or on the basis of a request signed by 50 members after

Appendix 3   281

the Minister has appeared for questioning before the Council. The Council shall not issue its decision regarding the request except after at least seven days from the date of its submission.

B   1—The President of the Republic may submit a request to the Council of Representatives to withdraw confidence from the Prime Minister. 2—The Council of Representatives may withdraw confidence from the Prime Minister based on the request of one-fifth of its members. This request shall not be submitted except after an inquiry directed at the Prime Minister and after at least seven days from the date of submitting the request. 3—The Council of Representatives may decide to withdraw confidence from the Prime Minister by an absolute majority of the number of its members.

C   The Government is deemed resigned in case of withdrawal of confidence from the Prime Minister.

D   In case of a vote of withdrawal of confidence in the Council of Ministers as a whole, the Prime Minister and the Ministers continue in their positions to run everyday business for a period not to exceed 30 days until a new Council of Ministers is formed in accordance with the provisions of Article 76 of this Constitution.

E   The Council of Representatives may question independent commission heads in accordance with the same procedures related to the Ministers. The Council shall have the right to relieve them by absolute majority.

Ninth:

A   To consent to the declaration of war and the state of emergency by a two-thirds majority based on a joint request from the President of the Republic and the Prime Minister.

B   The state of emergency shall be declared for a period of 30 days, which can be extended after approval each time.

C   The Prime Minister shall be delegated the necessary powers which enable him to manage the affairs of the country during the period of the declaration of war and the state of emergency. These powers shall be regulated by a law in a way that does not contradict the Constitution.

D   The Prime Minister shall present to the Council of Representatives the measures taken and the results during the period of the declaration of war and the state of emergency within 15 days from the date of its end.

Article 62

First: The Council of Ministers shall submit the draft general budget bill and the closing account to the Council of Representatives for approval.

Second: The Council of Representatives may conduct transfers between the sections and chapters of the general budget and reduce the total of its sums,

282   *Appendix 3*

and it may suggest to the Council of Ministers that they increase the total expenses, when necessary.

Article 63

First: A law shall regulate the rights and privileges of the speaker of the Council of Representatives, his two deputies and the members of the Council of Representatives.

Second:

A   A member of the Council of Representatives shall enjoy immunity for statements made while the Council is in session, and the member may not be prosecuted before the courts for such.

B   A Council of Representatives member may not be placed under arrest during the legislative term of the Council of Representatives, unless the member is accused of a felony and the Council of Representatives members consent by an absolute majority to lift his immunity or if he is caught in *flagrante delicto* in the commission of a felony.

C   A Council of Representatives member may not be arrested after the legislative term of the Council of Representatives, unless the member is accused of a felony and with the consent of the speaker of the Council of Representatives to lift his immunity or if he is caught in *flagrante delicto* in the commission of a felony.

Article 64

First: The Council of Representatives may be dissolved by an absolute majority of the number of its members, or upon the request of one-third of its members by the Prime Minister with the consent of the President of the Republic. The Council shall not be dissolved during the period in which the Prime Minister is being questioned.

Second: Upon the dissolution of the Council of Representatives, the President of the Republic shall call for general elections in the country within a period not to exceed 60 days from the date of its dissolution. The Council of Ministers in this case is deemed resigned and continues to run everyday business.

Second: The Federation Council

Article 65

A legislative council shall be established named the "Federation Council," to include representatives from the regions and the governorates that are not organized in a region. A law, enacted by a two-thirds majority of the members of the Council of Representatives, shall regulate the formation of the Federation Council, its membership conditions, its competencies, and all that is connected with it.

Appendix 3   283

Chapter Two [The Executive Power]

Article 66

The federal executive power shall consist of the President of the Republic and the Council of Ministers and shall exercise its powers in accordance with the Constitution and the law.

First: The President of the Republic

Article 67

The President of the Republic is the Head of the State and a symbol of the unity of the country and represents the sovereignty of the country. He shall guarantee the commitment to the Constitution and the preservation of Iraq's independence, sovereignty, unity and the safety of its territories, in accordance with the provisions of the Constitution.

Article 68

A nominee to the Presidency of the Republic must be:

First: An Iraqi by birth, born to Iraqi parents.

Second: Fully qualified and must be over 40 years of age.

Third: Of good reputation and political experience, known for his integrity, uprightness, fairness and loyalty to the homeland.

Fourth: Free of any conviction of a crime involving moral turpitude.

Article 69

First: The provisions for nomination to the office of the President of the Republic shall be regulated by law.

Second: The provisions for nomination to the office of one or more Vice Presidents of the Republic shall be regulated by law.

Article 70

First: The Council of Representatives shall elect a President of the Republic from among the candidates by a two-thirds majority of the number of its members.

Second: If none of the candidates receive the required majority vote then the two candidates who received the highest number of votes shall compete and the one who receives the majority of votes in the second election shall be declared President.

Article 71

The President shall take the constitutional oath before the Council of Representatives according to the language stipulated in Article 50 of the Constitution.

284   *Appendix 3*

Article 72

First: The President of the Republic's term in office shall be limited to four years. He may be re-elected for a second time only.

Second:

A   The President of the Republic's term in office shall end with the end of the term of the Council of Representatives.

B   The President of the Republic shall continue to exercise his duties until after the end of the election and the meeting of the new Council of Representatives, provided that a new President of the Republic is elected within 30 days from the date of its first convening.

C   In case the position of the President of the Republic becomes vacant for any reason, a new President shall be elected to complete the remaining period of the President's term.

Article 73

The President of the Republic shall assume the following powers:

First: To issue a special pardon on the recommendation of the Prime Minister, except for anything concerning a private claim and for those who have been convicted of committing international crimes, terrorism or financial and administrative corruption.

Second: To ratify international treaties and agreements after the approval by the Council of Representatives. Such international treaties and agreements are considered ratified after 15 days from the date of receipt by the President.

Third: To ratify and issue the laws enacted by the Council of Representatives. Such laws are considered ratified after 15 days from the date of receipt by the President.

Fourth: To call the elected Council of Representatives to convene during a period not to exceed 15 days from the date of approval of the election results and in the other cases stipulated in the Constitution.

Fifth: To award medals and decorations on the recommendation of the Prime Minister in accordance with the law.

Sixth: To accredit ambassadors.

Seventh: To issue Presidential decrees.

Eighth: To ratify death sentences issued by the competent courts.

Ninth: To perform the duty of the High Command of the armed forces for ceremonial and honorary purposes.

Appendix 3 285

Tenth: To exercise any other presidential powers stipulated in this Constitution.

Article 74

A law shall fix the salary and the allowances of the President of the Republic.

Article 75

First: The President of the Republic shall have the right to submit his resignation in writing to the Speaker of the Council of Representatives, and it shall be considered effective after seven days from the date of its submission to the Council of Representatives.

Second: The Vice President shall replace the President in case of his absence.

Third: The Vice President shall replace the President of the Republic in the event that the post of the President becomes vacant for any reason whatsoever. The Council of Representatives must elect a new President within a period not to exceed 30 days from the date of the vacancy.

Fourth: In case the post of the President of the Republic becomes vacant, the Speaker of the Council of Representatives shall replace the President of the Republic in case he does not have a Vice President, on the condition that a new President is elected during a period not to exceed 30 days from the date of the vacancy and in accordance with the provisions of this Constitution.

Second: Council of Ministers

Article 76

First: The President of the Republic shall charge the nominee of the largest Council of Representatives bloc with the formation of the Council of Ministers within 15 days from the date of the election of the President of the Republic.

Second: The Prime Minister-designate shall undertake the naming of the members of his Council of Ministers within a period not to exceed 30 days from the date of his designation.

Third: If the Prime Minister-designate fails to form the Council of Ministers during the period specified in clause "Second," the President of the Republic shall charge a new nominee for the post of Prime Minister within 15 days.

Fourth: The Prime Minister-designate shall present the names of his members of the Council of Ministers and the ministerial program to the Council of Representatives. He is deemed to have gained its confidence upon the approval, by an absolute majority of the Council of Representatives, of the individual Ministers and the ministerial program.

286   *Appendix 3*

Fifth: The President of the Republic shall charge another nominee to form the Council of Ministers within 15 days in case the Council of Ministers did not win the vote of confidence.

Article 77

First: The conditions for assuming the post of the Prime Minister shall be the same as those for the President of the Republic, provided that he has a college degree or its equivalent and is over 35 years of age.

Second: The conditions for assuming the post of Minister shall be the same as those for members of the Council of Representatives, provided that he holds a college degree or its equivalent.

Article 78

The Prime Minister is the direct executive authority responsible for the general policy of the State and the commander-in-chief of the armed forces. He directs the Council of Ministers, presides over its meetings, and has the right to dismiss the Ministers, with the consent of the Council of Representatives.

Article 79

The Prime Minister and members of the Council of Ministers shall take the constitutional oath before the Council of Representatives according to the language stipulated in Article 50 of the Constitution.

Article 80

The Council of Ministers shall exercise the following powers:

First: To plan and execute the general policy and general plans of the State and oversee the work of the ministries and departments not associated with a ministry.

Second: To propose bills.

Third: To issue rules, instructions and decisions for the purpose of implementing the law.

Fourth: To prepare the draft of the general budget, the closing account and the development plans.

Fifth: To recommend to the Council of Representatives that it approve the appointment of undersecretaries, ambassadors, state senior officials, the Chief of Staff of the Armed Forces and his deputies, division commanders or higher, the Director of the National Intelligence Service and heads of security institutions.

Sixth: To negotiate and sign international agreements and treaties, or designate any person to do so.

Appendix 3   287

Article 81

First: The President of the Republic shall take up the office of the Prime Minister in the event the post becomes vacant for any reason whatsoever.

Second: If the event mentioned in "First" of this Article occurs, the President shall charge another nominee to form the Council of Ministers within a period not to exceed 15 days in accordance with the provisions of Article 76 of this Constitution.

Article 82

A law shall regulate the salaries and allowances of the Prime Minister and Ministers, and anyone of their grade.

Article 83

The responsibility of the Prime Minister and the Ministers before the Council of Representatives is of a joint and personal nature.

Article 84

First: A law shall regulate the work and define the duties and authorities of the security institutions and the National Intelligence Service, which shall operate in accordance with the principles of human rights and shall be subject to the oversight of the Council of Representatives.

Second: The National Intelligence Service shall be attached to the Council of Ministers.

Article 85

The Council of Ministers shall establish internal bylaws to organize the work therein.

Article 86

A law shall regulate the formation of ministries, their functions and their specializations, and the authorities of the minister.

Chapter Three [The Judicial Power]

Article 87

The judicial power is independent. The courts, in their various types and levels, shall assume this power and issue decisions in accordance with the law.

Article 88

Judges are independent, and there is no authority over them except that of the law. No power shall have the right to interfere in the judiciary and the affairs of justice.

Article 89

The federal judicial power is comprised of the Higher Juridical Council, the Federal Supreme Court, the Federal Court of Cassation, the Public Prosecution

288   *Appendix 3*

Department, the Judiciary Oversight Commission and other federal courts that are regulated in accordance with the law.

First: Higher Juridical Council

Article 90

The Higher Juridical Council shall oversee the affairs of the judicial committees. The law shall specify the method of its establishment, its authorities and the rules of its operation.

Article 91

The Higher Juridical Council shall exercise the following authorities:

First: To manage the affairs of the judiciary and supervise the federal judiciary.

Second: To nominate the Chief Justice and members of the Federal Court of Cassation, the Chief Public Prosecutor and the Chief Justice of the Judiciary Oversight Commission, and to present those nominations to the Council of Representatives to approve their appointment.

Third: To propose the draft of the annual budget of the federal judicial authority, and to present it to the Council of Representatives for approval.

Second: Federal Supreme Court

Article 92

First: The Federal Supreme Court is an independent judicial body, financially and administratively.

Second: The Federal Supreme Court shall be made up of a number of judges, experts in Islamic jurisprudence and legal scholars, whose number, the method of their selection and the work of the Court shall be determined by a law enacted by a two-thirds majority of the members of the Council of Representatives.

Article 93

The Federal Supreme Court shall have jurisdiction over the following:

First: Overseeing the constitutionality of laws and regulations in effect.

Second: Interpreting the provisions of the Constitution.

Third: Settling matters that arise from the application of the federal laws, decisions, regulations, instructions and procedures issued by the federal authority. The law shall guarantee the right of direct appeal to the Court to the Council of Ministers, those concerned individuals and others.

Fourth: Settling disputes that arise between the federal government and the governments of the regions and governorates, municipalities and local administrations.

Fifth: Settling disputes that arise between the governments of the regions and governments of the governorates.

Sixth: Settling accusations directed against the President, the Prime Minister and the Ministers, and this shall be regulated by law.

Seventh: Ratifying the final results of the general elections for membership in the Council of Representatives.

Eighth:

A   Settling competency disputes between the federal judiciary and the judicial institutions of the regions and governorates that are not organized in a region.

B   Settling competency disputes between judicial institutions of the regions or governorates that are not organized in a region.

Article 94

Decisions of the Federal Supreme Court are final and binding for all authorities.

Third: general provisions

Article 95

The establishment of special or extraordinary courts is prohibited.

Article 96

The law shall regulate the establishment of courts, their types, levels and jurisdiction, and the method of appointing and the terms of service of judges and public prosecutors, their discipline and their retirement.

Article 97

Judges may not be removed except in cases specified by law. Such law will determine the particular provisions related to them and shall regulate their disciplinary measures.

Article 98

A judge or public prosecutor is prohibited from the following:

First: Combining a judicial position with legislative and executive positions and any other employment.

Second: Joining any party or political organization or performing any political activity.

Article 99

A law shall regulate the military judiciary and shall specify the jurisdiction of military courts, which are limited to crimes of a military nature committed by members of the armed forces and security forces, and within the limits established by law.

290   *Appendix 3*

Article 100

It is prohibited to stipulate in the law the immunity from appeal for any administrative action or decision.

Article 101

A State Council may be established, specialized in functions of the administrative judiciary, issuing opinions, drafting and representing the State and various public commissions before the courts except those exempted by law.

Chapter Four [Independent Commissions]

Article 102

The High Commission for Human Rights, the Independent Electoral Commission and the Commission on Public Integrity are considered independent commissions subject to monitoring by the Council of Representatives, and their functions shall be regulated by law.

Article 103

> First: The Central Bank of Iraq, the Board of Supreme Audit, the Communication and Media Commission and the Endowment Commissions are financially and administratively independent institutions, and the work of each of these institutions shall be regulated by law.
>
> Second: The Central Bank of Iraq is responsible before the Council of Representatives. The Board of Supreme Audit and the Communication and Media Commission shall be attached to the Council of Representatives.
>
> Third: The Endowment Commissions shall be attached to the Council of Ministers.

Article 104

A commission named The Martyrs' Foundation shall be established and attached to the Council of Ministers, and its functions and competencies shall be regulated by law.

Article 105

A public commission shall be established to guarantee the rights of the regions and governorates that are not organized in a region to ensure their fair participation in managing the various state federal institutions, missions, fellowships, delegations and regional and international conferences. The commission shall be comprised of representatives of the federal government and representatives of the regions and governorates that are not organized in a region, and shall be regulated by a law.

Article 106

A public commission shall be established by a law to audit and appropriate federal revenues. The commission shall be comprised of experts from the federal

Appendix 3 291

government, the regions, the governorates and its representatives, and shall assume the following responsibilities:

First: To verify the fair distribution of grants, aid and international loans pursuant to the entitlement of the regions and governorates that are not organized in a region.

Second: To verify the ideal use and division of the federal financial resources.

Third: To guarantee transparency and justice in appropriating funds to the governments of the regions and governorates that are not organized in a region in accordance with the established percentages.

Article 107

A council named the Federal Public Service Council shall be established and shall regulate the affairs of the federal public service, including appointments and promotions, and its formation and competencies shall be regulated by law.

Article 108

Other independent commissions may be established by law, according to need and necessity.

Section Four

Powers of the federal government

Article 109

The federal authorities shall preserve the unity, integrity, independence and sovereignty of Iraq and its federal democratic system.

Article 110

The federal government shall have exclusive authorities in the following matters:

First: Formulating foreign policy and diplomatic representation; negotiating, signing and ratifying international treaties and agreements; negotiating, signing and ratifying debt policies; and formulating foreign sovereign economic and trade policy.

Second: Formulating and executing national security policy, including establishing and managing armed forces to secure the protection and guarantee the security of Iraq's borders and to defend Iraq.

Third: Formulating fiscal and customs policy; issuing currency; regulating commercial policy across regional and governorate boundaries in Iraq; drawing up the national budget of the State; formulating monetary policy; and establishing and administering a central bank.

Fourth: Regulating standards, weights and measures.

292 *Appendix 3*

Fifth: Regulating issues of citizenship, naturalization, residency and the right to apply for political asylum.

Sixth: Regulating the policies of broadcast frequencies and mail.

Seventh: Drawing up the general and investment budget bill.

Eighth: Planning policies relating to water sources from outside Iraq and guaranteeing the rate of water flow to Iraq and its just distribution inside Iraq in accordance with international laws and conventions.

Ninth: General population statistics and census.

Article 111

Oil and gas are owned by all the people of Iraq in all the regions and governorates.

Article 112

First: The federal government, with the producing governorates and regional governments, shall undertake the management of oil and gas extracted from present fields, provided that it distributes its revenues in a fair manner in proportion to the population distribution in all parts of the country, specifying an allotment for a specified period for the damaged regions which were unjustly deprived of them by the former regime, and the regions that were damaged afterwards in a way that ensures balanced development in different areas of the country, and this shall be regulated by a law.

Second: The federal government, with the producing regional and governorate governments, shall together formulate the necessary strategic policies to develop the oil and gas wealth in a way that achieves the highest benefit to the Iraqi people using the most advanced techniques of the market principles and encouraging investment.

Article 113

Antiquities, archeological sites, cultural buildings, manuscripts and coins shall be considered national treasures under the jurisdiction of the federal authorities, and shall be managed in cooperation with the regions and governorates, and this shall be regulated by law.

Article 114

The following competencies shall be shared between the federal authorities and regional authorities:

First: To manage customs, in coordination with the governments of the regions and governorates that are not organized in a region, and this shall be regulated by a law.

Second: To regulate the main sources of electric energy and its distribution.

Appendix 3 293

Third: To formulate environmental policy to ensure the protection of the environment from pollution and to preserve its cleanliness, in cooperation with the regions and governorates that are not organized in a region.

Fourth: To formulate development and general planning policies.

Fifth: To formulate public health policy, in cooperation with the regions and governorates that are not organized in a region.

Sixth: To formulate the public educational and instructional policy, in consultation with the regions and governorates that are not organized in a region.

Seventh: To formulate and regulate the internal water resources policy in a way that guarantees their just distribution, and this shall be regulated by a law.

Article 115

All powers not stipulated in the exclusive powers of the federal government belong to the authorities of the regions and governorates that are not organized in a region. With regard to other powers shared between the federal government and the regional government, priority shall be given to the law of the regions and governorates not organized in a region in case of dispute.

Section Five

Powers of the regions

Chapter One [Regions]

Article 116

The federal system in the Republic of Iraq is made up of a decentralized capital, regions and governorates, as well as local administrations.

Article 117

First: This Constitution, upon coming into force, shall recognize the region of Kurdistan, along with its existing authorities, as a federal region.

Second: This Constitution shall affirm new regions established in accordance with its provisions.

Article 118

The Council of Representatives shall enact, in a period not to exceed six months from the date of its first session, a law that defines the executive procedures to form regions, by a simple majority of the members present.

Article 119

One or more governorates shall have the right to organize into a region based on a request to be voted on in a referendum submitted in one of the following two methods:

294   *Appendix 3*

First: A request by one-third of the council members of each governorate intending to form a region.

Second: A request by one-tenth of the voters in each of the governorates intending to form a region.

Article 120

Each region shall adopt a constitution of its own that defines the structure of powers of the region, its authorities and the mechanisms for exercising such authorities, provided that it does not contradict this Constitution.

Article 121

First: The regional powers shall have the right to exercise executive, legislative and judicial powers in accordance with this Constitution, except for those authorities stipulated in the exclusive authorities of the federal government.

Second: In case of a contradiction between regional and national legislation in respect to a matter outside the exclusive authorities of the federal government, the regional power shall have the right to amend the application of the national legislation within that region.

Third: Regions and governorates shall be allocated an equitable share of the national revenues sufficient to discharge their responsibilities and duties, but having regard to their resources, needs and the percentage of their population.

Fourth: Offices for the regions and governorates shall be established in embassies and diplomatic missions, in order to follow cultural, social and developmental affairs.

Fifth: The regional government shall be responsible for all the administrative requirements of the region, particularly the establishment and organization of the internal security forces for the region such as police, security forces and guards of the region.

Chapter Two [Governorates that are not Incorporated in a Region]

Article 122

First: The governorates shall be made up of a number of districts, sub-districts and villages.

Second: Governorates that are not incorporated in a region shall be granted broad administrative and financial authorities to enable them to manage their affairs in accordance with the principle of decentralized administration, and this shall be regulated by law.

Third: The governor, who is elected by the Governorate Council, is deemed the highest executive official in the governorate to practice his powers authorized by the Council.

Fourth: A law shall regulate the election of the Governorate Council, the governor and their powers.

Fifth: The Governorate Council shall not be subject to the control or supervision of any ministry or any institution not linked to a ministry. The Governorate Council shall have independent finances.

Article 123

Powers exercised by the federal government can be delegated to the governorates or vice versa, with the consent of both governments, and this shall be regulated by law.

Chapter Three [The Capital]

Article 124

First: Baghdad in its municipal borders is the capital of the Republic of Iraq and shall constitute, in its administrative borders, the governorate of Baghdad.

Second: This shall be regulated by a law.

Third: The capital may not merge with a region.

Chapter Four [The Local Administrations]

Article 125

This Constitution shall guarantee the administrative, political, cultural and educational rights of the various nationalities, such as Turkomen, Chaldeans, Assyrians and all other constituents, and this shall be regulated by law.

Section Six

Final and transitional provisions

Chapter One [Final Provisions]

Article 126

First: The President of the Republic and the Council of the Ministers collectively, or one-fifth of the Council of Representatives members, may propose to amend the Constitution.

Second: The fundamental principles mentioned in Section One and the rights and liberties mentioned in Section Two of the Constitution may not be amended except after two successive electoral terms, with the approval of two-thirds of the members of the Council of Representatives, the approval of the people in a general referendum, and the ratification by the President of the Republic within seven days.

296 *Appendix 3*

Third: Other articles not stipulated in clause "Second" of this Article may not be amended, except with the approval of two-thirds of the members of the Council of Representatives, the approval of the people in a general referendum, and the ratification by the President of the Republic within seven days.

Fourth: Articles of the Constitution may not be amended if such amendment takes away from the powers of the regions that are not within the exclusive powers of the federal authorities, except by the approval of the legislative authority of the concerned region and the approval of the majority of its citizens in a general referendum.

Fifth:

    A   An amendment is considered ratified by the President of the Republic after the expiration of the period stipulated in clauses "Second" and "Third" of this Article, in case he does not ratify it.

    B   An amendment shall enter into force on the date of its publication in the Official Gazette.

Article 127

The President of the Republic, the Prime Minister, members of the Council of Ministers, the Speaker of the Council of Representatives, his two Deputies, members of the Council of Representatives, members of the Judicial Authority and people of special grades may not use their influence to buy or rent any state properties, to rent or sell any of their assets to the state, to sue the state for these assets or to conclude a contract with the state under the pretense of being building contractors, suppliers or concessionaires.

Article 128

The laws and judicial judgments shall be issued in the name of the people.

Article 129

Laws shall be published in the Official Gazette and shall take effect on the date of their publication, unless stipulated otherwise.

Article 130

Existing laws shall remain in force, unless annulled or amended in accordance with the provisions of this Constitution.

Article 131

Every referendum mentioned in this Constitution is deemed successful with the approval of the majority of the voters unless otherwise stipulated.

Appendix 3 297

Chapter Two [Transitional Provisions]

Article 132

First: The State shall guarantee care for the families of the martyrs, political prisoners and victims of the oppressive practices of the defunct dictatorial regime.

Second: The State shall guarantee compensation to the families of the martyrs and the injured as a result of terrorist acts.

Third: A law shall regulate matters mentioned in clauses "First" and "Second" of this Article.

Article 133

The Council of Representatives shall adopt in its first session the bylaws of the Transitional National Assembly until it adopts its own bylaws.

Article 134

The Iraqi High Tribunal shall continue its duties as an independent judicial body, in examining the crimes of the defunct dictatorial regime and its symbols. The Council of Representatives shall have the right to dissolve it by law after the completion of its work.

Article 135

First: The High Commission for De-Ba'thification shall continue its functions as an independent commission, in coordination with the judicial authority and the executive institutions within the framework of the laws regulating its functions. The Commission shall be attached to the Council of Representatives.

Second: The Council of Representatives shall have the right to dissolve this Commission by an absolute majority after the completion of its function.

Third: A nominee to the positions of the President of the Republic, the Prime Minister, the members of the Council of Ministers, the Speaker, the members of the Council of Representatives, the President, members of the Federation Council, their counterparts in the regions or members of the judicial commissions and other positions covered by de-Ba'thification statutes pursuant to the law may not be subject to the provisions of de-Ba'thification.

Fourth: The conditions stated in clause "Third" of this Article shall remain in force unless the Commission stated in item "First" of this Article is dissolved.

Fifth: Mere membership in the dissolved Ba'th Party shall not be considered a sufficient basis for referral to court, and a member shall enjoy equality before the law and protection unless covered by the provisions of De-Ba'thification and the directives issued according to it.

298 *Appendix 3*

Sixth: The Council of Representatives shall form a parliamentary committee from among its members to monitor and review the executive procedures of the Higher Commission for De-Ba'thification and state institutions to guarantee justice, objectivity and transparency and to examine their consistency with the laws. The committee's decisions shall be subject to the approval of the Council of Representatives.

Article 136

First: The Property Claims Commission shall continue its functions as an independent commission in coordination with the judicial authority and the executive institutions in accordance with the law. The Property Claims Commission shall be attached to the Council of Representatives.

Second: The Council of Representatives shall have the right to dissolve the Commission by a two-thirds majority vote of its members.

Article 137

Application of the provisions of the articles related to the Federation Council, wherever it may be cited in this Constitution, shall be postponed until the Council of Representatives issues a decision by a two-thirds majority vote in its second electoral term that is held after this Constitution comes into force.

Article 138

First: The expression "the Presidency Council" shall replace the expression "the President of the Republic" wherever the latter is mentioned in this Constitution. The provisions related to the President of the Republic shall be reactivated one successive term after this Constitution comes into force.

Second:

    A The Council of Representatives shall elect the President of the State and two Vice Presidents who shall form a Council called the "Presidency Council," which shall be elected by one list and with a two-thirds majority.

    B The provisions to remove the President of the Republic present in this Constitution shall apply to the President and members of the Presidency Council.

    C The Council of Representatives may remove a member of the Presidency Council with a three-fourths majority of the number of its members for reasons of incompetence and dishonesty.

    D In the event of a vacant seat in the Presidency Council, the Council of Representatives shall elect a replacement by a two-thirds majority vote of its members.

Third: Members of the Presidency Council shall be subject to the same conditions as a member of the Council of Representatives and must:

Appendix 3   299

A   Be over 40 years of age.
B   Enjoy good reputation, integrity and uprightness.
C   Have quit the dissolved (Ba'th) Party ten years prior to its fall, in case he was a member of it.
D   Have not participated in suppressing the 1991 and Al-Anfal uprisings. He must not have committed a crime against the Iraqi people.

Fourth: The Presidency Council shall issue its decisions unanimously and any member may delegate to one of the two other members to take his place.

Fifth:

A   Legislation and decisions enacted by the Council of Representatives shall be forwarded to the Presidency Council for their unanimous approval and for its issuance within ten days from the date of delivery to the Presidency Council, except the stipulations of Articles 118 and 119 that pertain to the formation of regions.
B   In the event the Presidency Council does not approve, legislation and decisions shall be sent back to the Council of Representatives to reexamine the disputed issues and to vote on them by the majority of its members and then shall be sent for the second time to the Presidency Council for approval.
C   In the event the Presidency Council does not approve the legislation and decisions for the second time within ten days of receipt, the legislation and decisions are sent back to the Council of Representatives, which has the right to adopt it by three-fifths majority of its members, which may not be challenged, and the legislation or decision shall be considered ratified.

Sixth: The Presidency Council shall exercise the powers of the President of the Republic stipulated in this Constitution.

Article 139

The Prime Minister shall have two deputies in the first electoral term.

Article 140

First: The executive authority shall undertake the necessary steps to complete the implementation of the requirements of all subparagraphs of Article 58 of the Transitional Administrative Law.

Second: The responsibility placed upon the executive branch of the Iraqi Transitional Government stipulated in Article 58 of the Transitional Administrative Law shall extend and continue to the executive authority elected in accordance with this Constitution, provided that it accomplishes completely (normalization and census and concludes with a referendum in Kirkuk and other disputed territories to determine the will of their citizens), by a date not to exceed December 31, 2007.

300 *Appendix 3*

Article 141

Legislation enacted in the region of Kurdistan since 1992 shall remain in force, and decisions issued by the government of the region of Kurdistan, including court decisions and contracts, shall be considered valid unless they are amended or annulled pursuant to the laws of the region of Kurdistan by the competent entity in the region, provided that they do not contradict with the Constitution.

Article 142

First: The Council of Representatives shall form at the beginning of its work a committee from its members representing the principal components of the Iraqi society with the mission of presenting to the Council of Representatives, within a period not to exceed four months, a report that contains recommendations of the necessary amendments that could be made to the Constitution, and the committee shall be dissolved after a decision is made regarding its proposals.

Second: The proposed amendments shall be presented to the Council of Representatives all at once for a vote upon them, and shall be deemed approved with the agreement of the absolute majority of the members of the Council.

Third: The Articles amended by the Council of Representatives pursuant to item "Second" of this Article shall be presented to the people for voting on them in a referendum within a period not exceeding two months from the date of their approval by the Council of Representatives.

Fourth: The referendum on the amended Articles shall be successful if approved by the majority of the voters, and if not rejected by two-thirds of the voters in three or more governorates.

Fifth: Article 126 of the Constitution (concerning amending the Constitution) shall be suspended, and shall return into force after the amendments stipulated in this Article have been decided upon.

Article 143

The Transitional Administrative Law and its Annex shall be annulled on the seating of the new government, except for the stipulations of Article 53(A) and Article 58 of the Transitional Administrative Law.

Article 144

This Constitution shall come into force after the approval of the people thereon in a general referendum, its publication in the Official Gazette, and the seating of the government that is formed pursuant to this Constitution.

Source

Adapted from the Iraqi Constitution. (September 18, 2005). Retrieved March 11, 2014, from World Intellectual Property Organization: www.wipo.int/wipolex/en/text.jsp?file_id=230000

Index

Page numbers in *italics* denotes a figure/
table

al-Abadi, Haidar 81, 103, 229, 230
Abbasid Dynasty 13, 80, 83–4
Abduh, Muhammad 171
Abdul-Hussain, Lâhây 181
Abdullah, King of Jordan 40
Abu Ghraib 160
Agrarian Reform Law (1958) 178–9
Agresto, John 23
agriculture 18, 172
Ahtisaari, Martti 152
Aiyyûb, Târiq 56
Al Jazeera 56; bombing of Baghdad
  bureau by US aircraft 56
Al-Iraqiyya 115
al-Istiqlal Party 176
Al-Jazeera 100
al-Qaeda 40, 41, 48; links to Iraq issue 51,
  58, 60
al-Qaeda in Iraq *see* AQI
Al-Sharq Al-Awsat 100
'al-Tawafuq' principle 86
Albright, Madeleine 162
Alexander, Justin 66
Alfalh, Ali 103
Algiers Agreement 29
'Ali, Faiq al-Shaikh 41, 86, 87
'Alî Ibn Abi-Tâlib 80
al-A'li, Mushtaq Hussain 136
Al-Ali, Zaid 22, 26, 63, 66, 111
'Allâwî, Ayad 22, 31–2, 65–6, 69, 85, 86,
  87, 88–9, 95, 101, 113, 123
'Allâwî, Sabâh 85–6
al-'Alwani, Ahmed 205
Al-'Amari, Hadi 128–9, 230
al-Amin, Ali 90
Amin, Qasim 171

Anbar conflict (2014) 120, 206–8
Anbar province 5, 102, 204–5, 207
Anderson, J. 177
Anfal campaign 29
al-Ani, Shuja Muslim 170–1
Annan, General Kofi 7, 33
AQI (al-Qaeda in Iraq) 160, 161, 207–8,
  223–4
Arab American Institute 33
Arab Spring 40, 120, 206
Arab Women's Congress 174–5
Arab world: anti-American sentiment 33
al-A'rajî, Bahâ 116
Arbour, Louise 33
army, Iraqi: and corruption 123–4; dis-
  banding of 2, 60, 61, 62–3, 93, 198;
  integration of militias into 61–2, 123,
  128
Army of the Men of the Naqshbandi Order
  226
al-Asadi, Adnan 128
al-Askarî, Sâmi 99
Axelrod, Jim 55
Ayyar, Farid 68
al-'Azawi, Ta'mim 188

Ba'ath regime/party 20, 26–7, 84, 199;
  banning and purging of by US 2, 60–1,
  93–4, 97, 109, 123, 135, 209, 218;
  characteristics of 179; comes to power
  15; coup (1963) 6, 15; relationship with
  the United States 5; social policy 179;
  totalitarian rule of 15–16; women under
  179–82, 191
Badr Brigade 84, 94, 128
Badr Corps 94, 99
Baghdad 13
Baghdad census incident (1904) 171
al-Baghdadi, Abu Bakr 116, 224, 225

Index   303

al-Baghdadi, Abu Omar 223, 224
Baram, Amatzia 184–5
Barzânî, Mas'ud 29, 30, 134
Barzânî, Mulla Mustafa 28–9
Barzânî Rebellion (1931-32) 28
Batatu, Hanna 173
Bearing Point 97
Bedouins 81–2, 83, 172
Beirut conference (1991) 87
Bell, Gertrude 171–2, 174
Bellamy, Carol 19
Ben Ali 40
Biden, Joe 61
Birds of Paradise 161
Blair, Tony 4, 56
Blix, Dr. Hans 52, 53, 54
Blunkett, David 56
bomb detection devices contracts 120
Bowen, Stuart 117
Bremer, Paul 4, 22, 30, 49, 59, 60, 63, 64, 89–90, 186
Britain: occupation of Iraq 14–15, 26, 27, 82–3, 114, 172–3
Bureau of the General Commander of the Armed Forces 134
Burton, Michael 55
Bush, President George H.W. 17
Bush, President George W. 21, 42, 199; 'Axis of Evil' speech (2002) 50; Iraq and the politics of hegemony in the administration of 46–50

cancer: in children and link with DU munitions 154, 158–9, 201
Caputi, Ross 206
Carnegie Endowment for International Peace (CEIP), report (2004) 59–60
Carothers, Thomas 22
carpetbaggers 85, 89, 102, 113, 144, 198, 200, 204, 209, 210, 212, 217, 219, 228
Casey, General George W. 95, 100
CENTCOM 43, 49
Central Bank of Iraq (CBI) 112, 131
Central Committee of the Iraqi Patriotic Alliance 25
Chalabi, Ahmad 33, 51, 57–8, 67, 87, 88, 100
Chaldo-Assyrian Christian communities 201
Cheney, Dick 47, 52
Chilcot Inquiry 7
children 149–65, 198–9; acceptance of child suffering as legitimate cost of war

discourse 162; cancer and link with use of DU munitions 154–7, 158–9; detaining of 160; disabled 161; during US occupation 159–62; impact of Gulf War on 153–5; impact of sanctions on 151–7, 162–3; invasion context 157–9; and malnutrition 154, 157, *157*; mental health of 154, 158, 161–2; mortality rates 18, 151, *151*, 154, 157, *157*, 161, 162–3, *163*, 165, 183; orphaned 161, 201; population figures 164–5; post-invasion military occupation context 159–62; post-traumatic stress in 161; present situation 165; profiled as security threat 160–1; as refugees/internally displaced persons 160, 161; UN and civil society discourse on 149, *150*
Chomsky, Noam 6–7
Christopher, Warren 17
Churchill, Winston 14
CIA 51, 58, 87; funding of INC 87; support of Ba'athist coup (1963) 15
Cirincione, Joseph 60
civil servants/service 61, 99; dismissal of Iraq's 93–4, 198
Clarke, Richard 48
Clarke, Victoria 55
Clinton, Hilary 3
Clinton, President Bill 17, 43, 44
Coalition Provisional Authority *see* CPA
Code of Personal Status (1959) 177–8
Cole, Juan 65
collateral damage 162
Commanders' Emergency Response Fund 219
Commission on Public Integrity *see* CPI
competitive interference 6, 199
constitution: (1958) 176, 177; (2005) 66–9, 89, 98, 188–9, 211–12, 266–300
Constitutional Monarchy Movement (CMM) 88
contracting process: and corruption 118–20, 122
corruption 65, 93, 98, 103, 110–37, 200, 203, 210, 211; bomb detection devices contracts 120; and Central Bank of Iraq 131; and contracting process 118–20, 122; definition 111; and economic and financial matters 117–18; and electoral process 135–6, 211; and exiled Iraqis 113–14; forms of Iraqi 118–19; impact of 111–12; ineffectiveness of annual financial disclosure 129; initiation of by CPA 114–15; judicial 132–3; lack

304 Index

of action from Commission of Integrity 116, 121–2; and al-Mâlikî government 110, 121, 122, 124, 126–7, 128; media efforts against 115–16; and Ministries of Education and Higher Education 125–6; and Ministry of Defense 122–4; and Ministry of Health 127–8; and Ministry of Industry and Minerals 124–5; and money laundering 112–13, 127; nepotism 128–9; and oil industry 119; Pincus Report (2007) 112; and political parties 122; post-invasion 120, 203–4, 211, 219; proliferation of 112–13; public servants and petty 120–2; ranking of Iraq by Transparency International 116, 204; salaries for parliamentarians 129–30; and 'school biscuit scandal' 126; and sectarian violence 113; and al-Shahristânî case 124–5; and al-Sûdânî case 124; types of 111; and US construction funds 117–19; view of by Iraqi citizens 136

Cottam, Richard 6, 199
Council of Representatives (COR) 135–6
Council for Strategic Policy 69
Court of Personal Status 177
Court of Publishing and Media 133
CPA (Coalition Provisional Authority) 31, 63, 89–90, 114, 117, 186, 210, 211–12
CPI (Commission on Public Integrity) 112, 116, 120–1
Crocker, Ryan 100

Dabbas, Fadel 120
Dahler, Don 55
Damascus 85
Damazer, Mark 55
Da'wa party 30, 84–5, 94, 101
de-Ba'thification 2, 60–1, 93–4, 97, 109, 123, 135, 209, 218
Declaration of the Shia of Iraq (2002) 88–9, 232–44
decolonization 25, 203
Defence Intelligence Agency (DIA) 51
democracy 110, 199, 210; pitfalls to establishment of 210–12
depleted uranium (DU) munitions: impact of on health 154–7, 158–9, 201
detentions 160, 201
Diamantides, Dr. Marinos 66
Diamond, Larry 22
disabled children 161
displacement 4, 160 *see also* internally displaced persons

Dodge, Toby 62
al-Dulaimî, 'Ali Sulaimân 83
Dulaimi, Naziha 176
al-Dulaimi, Raghad 126
Durakovic, Dr. Asaf 156

economic policy: initiated by Bremer in US-occupied Iraq 63–4, 67
economy: and corruption 117–18; impact of power outage crisis 119; impact of sanctions on 17–18; impact of war with Iran on 16–17; prior to Gulf War 151
Edelman, Eric 47
edicts 93
education 126, 165; impact of sanctions on 183; and women 171, 174, 180, 183
Education Ministry: and corruption 125–6
Efrati, Noga 175
Egypt 40–1; overthrow of Mubarak 40–1
elections 91, 218; (2005) 29, 32, 65–6, 67, 94, 135, 187–8; (2010) 100, 136; (2014) 101, 211; post-2003 91
Electoral Commission 133, 211
electoral system 91–2, 92–3, 135; and corruption 135–6, 211
electricity 119; access to 65
embedded journalists 55
ethnosectarian politics 88
exiles, political *see* carpetbaggers

Faisal I, King 14, 26, 62, 82
Fallujah 205, 206; as epicenter of resistance against Mâlikî regime 206–7; sieges of (2004) 23–4, 32, 33, 61, 206
al-Fatalâwî, Hanân 94
Feith, Douglas 48, 50
Fisk, Robert 154
folkloric sectarianism 78, 202
Franks, General Tommy 19, 41
Fukuyama, Francis 45

Gaddafi, M. 40
Gaffney, Frank 56
Galbraith, Peter 31, 68
Garner, General Jay 58–9
General Federation of Iraqi Women (GFIW) 179
al-Ghabban, Muhammad 230
Goldsmith, Lord 56
Goodno, Barbara 155
Gordon, Joy 19, 34
Gouré, Daniel 49
Graham, Patrick 63–4, 185

Greenspan, Alan 97
Guardino, Matt 54–5
Gulf War (1991) 5, 6, 17, 77, 85, 135, 151, 152–3, 182; impact of on children 153–4

Haass, Richard 5, 41
Haddad, Judge Munir 133
Hadley, Stephen J. 47–8
Hajzin, Dr. Ra'd 126
al-Hakîm, Bâqir 88
Halliday, Denis 17, 163
Hammûd, Farîd Jâsim 116–17
Haquona (Our Rights) 116
Hardân, Dr. Ahmad 158
al-Hashimi, Tariq 132–3
al-Hassan, Mahmoud 211
Hawza 24, 32
Hayes, Danny 54–5
health/health care: impact of sanctions on 183
Hedges, Chris 43–4
Hersh, S.M. 51
Hewar Iraqi 121
honor killing 183
Hoon, Geoff 55
Human Rights Watch 186, 190
al-Husain 80
al-Husain Solace 80, 81

Ibrahim, Hana 186
IGC (Iraq Governing Council) 2–3, 64, 67, 90, 114; composition 90
INA (Iraq National Alliance) 86, 88
INC (Iraqi National Congress) 57–9, 87, 88
infant mortality 135, 151, *151*, 154, 157, 165
Initiative of the Wisemen to Abort the Confrontation 207
Integrity Commission 123, 124, 126, 127, 129, 133, 203
Interim Constitution *see* TAL
internally displaced persons (IDPs) 64, 96, 160, 161, 201
International Republican Institute 68
Iran 40, 46–7, 89, 101; growth of influence 41; and Iraq 98–100, 101–2; support of Shia militias in Iraq 99–100
Iran-Iraq war (1980-88) 16–17, 29, 151, 181
Iraq: British occupation 14–15, 26, 27, 82–3, 114, 172–3; emergence of as a

republic 15; as failed state 204; history 13–15; impact of Saddam Hussein's dictatorship 15–17; linking of to 'war on terror' 50; modern politics and the development of political diaspora 84–9; and the politics of hegemony in the Bush Administration 46–50; resistance to British occupation 82–3; social setting of pre-invasion 78–84; withdrawal of US soldiers (2011) 2, 40, 96, 204, 216
Iraq Body Count (IBC) 158, 161
Iraq Governing Council *see* IGC
Iraq Liberation Act (1998) 46
Iraq (post-occupation) 4–5, 35, 203–12, 216, 219–22; al-Abadi's new government 230; Anbar uprising (2014) 120, 206–8; corruption 120, 203–4, 211, 219; instability of political and social situation in 69; opposition 120; pitfalls to the establishment of democracy 210–11; popular protests and resistance against Mâlîki regime 206–8; prospects 205–6; sectarian violence 21, 35, 40, 62, 69, 203, 209; state of 4–5, 35, 64–5, 204, 216; Sunni Arab militancy 205; tri-partition and expansion of chaos 229–30; violence and disorder 204–5, 220–1
Iraq Sanctions Committee 19
Iraq (US-occupied) 101, 184, 199–200, 200–2, 217–18, 228–9; and children 159–62; constitution (2005) 66–9, 188–9, 211–12, 266–300; de-Ba'thification 2, 60–1, 93–4, 97, 109, 123, 135, 209, 218; death toll 21, 64; destruction of cultural patrimony 201–2; detentions 160, 201; disbanding of Iraqi army and consequences 2, 60, 61, 62–3, 93, 198; dwindling of religious communities 201–2; economic policies under Bremer and impact of 63–4, 67; elections (2005) 29, 32, 65–6, 67, 94, 135, 187–8; exclusion of significant national political forces in nation-building process 32; failure and sources 2–3, 34, 54; formation of IGC 31–4, 64; growing international criticism of 33; impact of occupation on Iraqi population 161–2, 201; Kurdish question 30–1; military pacification strategy 25; neo-tribal and neo-feudal forces 184–6; neoliberalization of 60–5, 67; oil issue 97; patterns of insecurity and instability 159–61;

306 *Index*

privatization policy 67–8; protests and armed resistance against occupation 23–5, 26, 61, 63–4, 217; reconstruction efforts 21–3; role of businessmen in insurgency 63–4; sectarianism/sectarian violence in 89–96, 160, 187, 201; Shock and Awe campaign 14, 50, 118, 157–8, 201; sieges of Fallujah (2004) 23–4, 32, 33, 61, 206; TAL (Interim Constitution) 64, 66, 245–65; use of foreign contractors 185–6; and women 184–90

Iraq War (2003) 6–7, 20–1, 34, 77; 9/11 as trigger for 48–9; Anglo-American orchestration for 50–4; combined roles of the INC and OSP 57–9; impact of on children 157–9; impact on Iraqi people 1, 4, 21; justifications for 40, 110, 184, 199; looting and destruction of cultural symbols 20–1; and neoconservatives 51–2, 56, 58; role of media 54–6; violation of sovereignty 200; WMDs and connection to al-Qaeda issues 50–4, 58, 59–60, 200

Iraqi Communist Party 175
Iraqi Islamic Party 32
Iraqi Kurdistan Front 29
Iraqi Liberation Act (1998) 88
Iraqi National Alliance *see* INA
Iraqi National Congress *see* INC
Iraqi Women's Foundation 190
Iraqi Women's League 179
Iraqi Women's Union 175–6
Iraqi youth 206, 208
ISIS (Islamic State of Iraq and the Levant) 1, 4, 207, 217, 228, 229; emergence of 222–7; takeover of Mosul (2014) 1, 4, 90, 102, 226, 229
Islamic Party 32
Israel 16, 20, 34, 45–6, 57
al-Issawi, Rafi 132
al-Istrabâdî, Faisal 61

al-Jabouri, Mohammad 126
Jabr, Sa'd Sâlih 87
Jabur, Faleh 27
JAC (Joint Action Committee) 85, 87
al-Ja'farî, Ibrâhîm 110
Jamail, Dahr 201
al-Janabi, Abeer Qassim 190
Jenkins, Simon 96
Jewish Institute for National Security Affairs (JINSA) 58

Jihad Movement 82
Joint Action Committee *see* JAC
journalism, Iraqi 115–16
judiciary 131, 210; control of by al-Mâlikî 131–2, 133, 210; and corruption 132–3
Justice and Accountability Commission (JAC) 136

Kagan, Robert 45
al-Karbouli, Ahmed 124
al-Karbouli, Jamal 124
Karim, Fakhari 93
Kay, David 59
KBR (Kellog, Brown and Root) 118, 120
KDP (Kurdistan Democratic Party) 28, 29, 30, 32, 87
Keefer, P. 113
Keegan, John 45
Kennedy, John F. 54
Kerry, John 200
Khalilzad, Zalmay 66, 67, 68
al-Khoe'i Foundation 84–5
al-Khuzai'i, Khidr 110
Klein, Naomi 64, 66–7, 118; *The Shock Doctrine* 158
Knack, S. 113
Knight's Charge Operation 103
KRG (Kurdistan Regional Government) 29–31, 119, 218, 219, 223, 229
Kristol, William 45
Kurdish question 27–31
Kurdistan 27–9, 220; and oil 119; uprising (1991) 87
Kurdistan Alliance 69
Kurdistan Democratic Party *see* KDP
Kurdistan Regional Government *see* KRG
Kurds 27–31, 32, 87; 'Autonomy Accord' with Ba'ath regime 28–9; Barzânî Rebellion (1931-32) 28; and elections (2005) 65; nationalism 28, 218; relations with US 30; Saddam's Anfal campaign against 29
Kuwait: invasion of by Iraq (1990) 17, 20, 85, 151; *see also* Gulf War (1991)

Laila (magazine) 174
Lang, Patrick 51
Law of Land Settlement 83
League for the Defense of Iraqi Women's Rights 175, 176–7
Leeper, Steve 155
Libby, Lewis 47
Libby, Scooter 51

Libya 3
life expectancy: and women 183
Lincoln Group, The 56
London conference (2002) 88
Looney, Robert 113
Luke, A. 185
Luti, William 47

McClellan, Scott 41, 56
McCormick, Jim 120
Mahdi army 99; 'Knights Assault' on (2008) 99
al-Mahmoud, Medhat 131–2
al-Mâlikî, Nuri 3, 4, 69, 91, 93, 96, 97, 99, 100–1, 102–3, 207, 228; and Anbar uprising 208; attempted coup against newly elected government 229; centralization of power within the office of 134–5, 210–11; control of judiciary 131–2, 133, 210; and corruption 110, 121, 122, 124, 126–7; and fall of Mosul 229; nepotism and patronage 128, 129; strategy against detractors 133–4
malnutrition 19, 21, 135, 154, 157, *157*, 183
Maloof, F. Michael 51
Marr, Phebe 179
marriage 177–8, 189
Matthews, Weldon 15
Mearsheimer, John 45–6
media 115; role of in Iraq War 54–6
Mesopotamia 13, 198
militarism: and United States 42–4
militias 94, 103; incorporation into army 61–2, 123, 128
Ministry of Defense: and corruption 122–3
Ministry of Health: and corruption 127–8
Ministry of Higher Education: and corruption 126
Ministry of Industry and Minerals: and corruption 124–5
Ministry of the Interior: and corruption 131
Ministry of Women's Affairs 189
miscarriages 183
Mitchell, Sandra 68
Mladenov, Nickolay 189
money laundering 112–13, 127
Monsoor, Peter 2–3
Morsi, President Mohamed 41
Mosul: ISIS occupation of 1, 4, 90, 102, 226, 229
al-Moussawi, Áli 103

Mubarak, Hosni 40–1
Muhsin, 'Âdil 127
Musharraf, General Pervez 43
Muslim Brotherhood 41
Myers, Richard 50

Nadi al-Nahda al-Nisa'iyya 174
Najaf, siege of (2004) 24
Al-Najafi, Asama 230
al-Najafi, Grand Ayatollah Bashir 101
nation building: versus state building 25–7
National Conference (2013) 110
National Council for the Salvation of Iraq 223
National Democratic Party 176
National Endowment for Democracy (NED) 22
National Iraqi Alliance 94
National Strategy to Combat Violence Against Women 189
nationalism 78
Naughton, Colonel James 159
neo-feudalism 184–5, 191
neo-tribalism 184–5, 191
neoconservatives 44–5, 47–8; and Iraq War 51–2, 56, 58
neoliberalism 44
nepotism 128–9
9/11 (2001) 48–9
al-Nujaifi, Usâmah 99, 110

Obama, Barack 1–2, 3, 44, 96
al-Obeidi, Khaled 230
Office of Special Plans *see* OSP
Oil-for-Food program 18, 19, 30, 162
oil/oil industry 119, 151; exploitaton of oil reserves 65; sectarianism and the patrimony of Iraq's 96–8
Operation Desert Storm 17, 20
orphaned children 161, 201
OSP (Office of Special Plans) 50–1, 57–9
Othman, Mahmoud 99
Ottoman Empire 13–14, 27; dissolution of 78
Ottoman-Safavid wars 82

Pace, Peter 50
Pakistan 43
party lists 92
patriarchy, state 181
Patriotic Union of Kurdistan *see* PUK
patronage 93, 126–7, 128, 137, 203
Penal Code 183

308　*Index*

Pentagon-Hollywood nexus 43
Peri, Smadar 57
Perle, Richard 47, 88
Personal Status Law: (1959) 177; (2014) 189, 190
Petraeus, General David 43
Philip, Mark 111–12
Pillar, Paul 3
Pincus, Walter 112
political diaspora, development of 84–9
political parties 92–3; and corruption 122
Pollack, Kenneth 60
polygamy 178
post-traumatic stress: and children 161
poverty 201
Powell, Colin 54, 59, 204
power outages 119
Project for a New American Century (PNAC): *Rebuilding America's Defences* 46
public expenditure *16*
PUK (Patriotic Union of Kurdistan) 20, 29, 30, 32, 87

Qasifi, Joseph 200
Qasim, General 'Abud-ul-Karîm 15, 28, 176–9
Qattân, Zaid 122–3
quasi-feudal system 172–3
Quds Force 99, 100

al-Râdhî, Hamzah Râdhî 121, 122, 123
Ramadi 205, 207
RAND Corporation 54
Rangwala, Dr. Glen 59
Record, Jeffrey 60
refugees 160, 161
regime change: and emergence of failed state 209–10
regionalism 89
Rendon Company 87
Research Triangle Institute (RTI) 21–2
retirement law 129–30
Revolt (1920) 14, 82, 83, 175
Rice, Condoleezza 49
Richardson, Bill 162
Ricks, Thomas 6
Ritter, Scott 53
Rizer, Colonel Kenneth 153
rogue state status 6–7
Rokke, Doug 155
Romney, Mitt 44
Roosevelt, Theodore 42

Rosen, Ruth 187
Rothschild, Major General Danny 57
RTI (Research Triangle Institute) 21–2
al-Rubai'î, Nadâ 25
al-Rubal'î, Muwaffaq 84, 88, 100
Rumsfeld, Donald 48, 49–50, 51, 54, 56, 95
Russia: annexation of Crimea 200; military intervention in Ukraine 2

Sabian Mandeans 202
Saddam Hussein 26–7, 52, 81, 85, 179, 180, 199; impact of dictatorship 15–17; tribal policies 184
al-Sa'dî, Sheik Sabâh 122, 137
al-Sadr, Muqtada 24, 33, 130
al-Said, Nûrî 176
salaries: for parliamentarians 129–30
Sâlhi, Najib 123
Salih, Barham 113
Samarra incident (2006) 95
al-Samirra'i, Ayham 122
sanctions, UN 17–20, 34, 77, 135, 182; impact of on children 151–7, 162–4; impact of on economy 17–18; impact of on health/health care 183; impact of on Iraqi people 152, 157, 182; objective of 164; tool to achieve political objectives 152; and women 182–3
Saudi Arabia 85, 87
school biscuit scandal 126
schools 126
SCIRI (Supreme Council for Islamic Revolution in Iraq) 84, 87, 88, 94
sectarianism/sectarian violence 8, 77–103, 94, 102, 198, 200, 202, 203, 212; and corruption 93–4, 113; folkloric 78, 202; influence of 77–8; and the patrimony of Iraq's oil 96–8; political 79–80; post-occupation 21, 35, 40, 62, 69, 203, 209; roots of 78–9; social 78–9, 202; US occupation of Iraq and the engineering of political 89–96, 160, 187–8, 202–3
al-Shabîbî, Sinân 131
al-Shahristani, Hussain 124–5
Shams Network 211
Sharon, Ariel 20
Shi'ites/Shia 80–2; commemoration of al-Husain 80–1; and *Declaration of the Shia of Iraq* 88–9, 232–44; differences between Sunnis and 83–4; and elections (2005) 65; and IGC 32, 90; and Jihad Movement 82; origins 80; resistance

to British occupation 82–3; support of
militias by Iran 99
al-Sh'lân, Hâzim 122–3
Shock and Awe campaign 14, 50, 118,
157–8, 201
Shulsky, Abram 50
SIGIR (Special Inspector General for Iraq
Reconstruction) 4, 117, 119
al-Sistânî, Ayatollah 'Ali 24, 65, 90, 101,
103, 211
Soviet Union: collapse of 45
Sponeck, Hans von 5–6, 17, 164
state building: versus nation building 25–7
State of Law coalition 93
Stork, Joe 190
Strategic Studies Institute: *Bounding the
Global War on Terrorism* 60
Studio 9 programme 122, 126, 137, 208
al-Sûdânî, Fâlah 124
Suleimani, Qassem 100, 101
Sunni Arab militancy 205
Sunni Muslim Clerics' Association 32
Sunnis 82; boycott of elections (2005) 65,
135; differences between Shi'ites and
83–4; and draft Constitution 66; and
IGC 32
Supreme Council for Islamic Revolution in
Iraq *see* SCIRI
Swadi, Amal Kadham 187
Sykes-Picot 228
Syrian civil war 3, 27, 40, 205, 222,
222–3, 224, 225

Taguba Report (2004) 186
al-Tai, Sarmad 133
TAL (Traditional Administrative Law) 30,
31, 64, 66, 186, 245–65
Tâlabânî, Jalâl 29, 30, 69
al-Tamîmî, Ali Mohsen 134
al-Tamimi, Hasan Suhail 83
Tenet, George 51
Traditional Administrative Law *see* TAL
trafficking 186
Transparency International 4, 111, 116, 204
tribal migrations 81
tribal sheikhs 172–3
tribes/tribalism 135, 173, 178, 184–5; and
warriorship 81–2
al-Turaihi, 'Aqîl 120
Turkey 41

Ukraine 2, 3
Ullman, Harlan 157, 158

al-'Umari, Khairi 174
Umayyad Dynasty 80
UN Security Council (UNSC): report
(1991) 152; Resolution (1441) 52,
53; Resolution (1483) 60; sanctions
imposed on Iraq (1990) 17–20
UN (United Nations) 185; charter 7; sanc-
tions imposed on Iraq *see* sanctions,
UN
UNESCO report (2003) 183
UNICEF (United Nations Children's
Fund) 149; *Annual Report for Iraq*
(2012) 165; *Iraq Child and Maternal
Mortality Surveys* report (1999) 162
United Iraqi Alliance 65
United Nations Development Programme
(UNDP): Report (1999-2000) 17–18
United Nations Monitoring, Verification
and Inspection Commission
(UNMOVIC) 53
UNSCOM 52
al-'Uqaili, Rahîm 121
USAID (United States Agency for
International Development) 21

Van Buren, Peter 2
veiling 174
Vietnam War 42, 44

Wade, James 157, 158
al-Wakil, Sheik 124
Walker, David 120
Walt, Stephen 46
'war on terror' 33, 45, 50
al-Wardi, 'Ali 77–8, 81
Warrick, Tom 58
warriorship: and tribes 81–2
water shortages 134
water treatment systems: US destruction of
during Gulf War 152–3
Weden, Fritz 22
Westerman, Douglas 156
Westphalian sovereignty 6
Wilson, Woodrow 42
WMDs (weapons of mass destruction) 40,
50, 51–3, 58, 59–60, 200
Wolf Brigade 94–5, 205
Wolfowitz, Paul 47, 48, 50, 51, 57–8
women 170–91, 199; Baghdad census
incident (1904) 171; beheading of 183;
and Code of Personal Status (1959)
177–8; and constitution (2005) 188–9;
and education 171, 174, 180, 183;

310 *Index*

emergence of onto the state of modern Iraqi history 170–6; 'honor killing' of 183; illegal detention of 190; illiteracy rate 182, 183; impact of Iran-Iraq war on 181–2; impact of sanctions on health of 183; invisibility of in historical records 170; and Iraqi Communist Party 175; life expectancy 183; organizations formed 175–6; participation in labor force 180–1; participation in struggle for Iraqi independence 175; and Personal Status Law (2014) 189; representation themes 170–1; sexual violence against 186–7, 190; and state patriarchy 181; struggle for emancipation during British occupation 173–4; and tribal customs 173; under Ba'ath regime 179–82, 191; under Qasim's regime 176–9, 190–1; under sanctions regime 182–3, 191; US occupation and neo-feudal bondage 184–90, 191; and veiling 174

Women's League Against Nazism and Fascism 175
Woodword, Bob 49
World Bank 4
World Food Programme (WFP) 19
Wurmser, David 48, 51, 187; *Tyranny's Ally* 187

Yamukovych, Viktor 3
Yaphe, Judith 58
Yazidis 201–2

al-Zahawi, Asma' 174–5
al-Zamili, Hakim 127–8
Zangana, Sawaiba 122
al-Zarqawi, Abu Musab 217, 223
Zinni, General Anthony 43
Zubaida, Sami 176
al-Zuhairi, Sheik 'Abdul Halim 102